Skalat

Memorial Book

Published by JewishGen

An Affiliate of the Museum of Jewish Heritage—A Living Memorial to the Holocaust
New York

Notes to the Readers

This Skalat Memorial Book is assembled using three different sources:

1. SKALAT
   A Memorial Anthology for a
   Community Destroyed in the Holocaust

2. Death of a Shtetl (Skalat, Ukraine)

3. Skalat Memorial Scroll in the Hall of Names at Yad Vashem (Ukraine)

For detailed information about these components, please refer to the copyright page (page v)

The Skalat Memorial Book is comprised of:

SKALAT
A Memorial Anthology for a Community Destroyed in the Holocaust (Ukraine)
Translation of: *Skalat: Kovets Zikaron LeKehila ShHarva BaShoah*
Edited by: Chaim Bronshtain
Published in Tel Aviv, 1971
Project Coordinator: Janet R. Perlmutter Schwartz
Translator: Neil H. Tannebaum
Editor: Henry Jorisch

DEATH OF A Shtetl (Skalat, Ukraine)
By: Abraham Weissbrod
Translation of: *Es shtarbt a shtetl; megiles Skalat*
Edited by: J. Kaplan
Published (in Yiddish) by the Central Historical Commission of the Central
Committee of Liberated Jews in the American Zone of Germany, Munich, 1948
Project Coordinator: Kathryn M. Wallach
Translations arranged by: Joseph Kofler, Lusia Milch
English Text and Additional Testimonies of Witnesses
Edited by Lusia Milch U.S.A., 1995

Skalat Memorial Scroll in the Hall of Names at Yad Vashem (Ukraine)
Prepared by the Organization of the Former Residents of Skalat and the
Surroundings in Israel and the Diaspora
May 1961 (7 Sivan 5721)
Our sincere appreciation to Yad Vashem for the submission of this material for
placement on the JewishGen web site.

Layout and Name Indexing: Jonatan Wind
Cover Design: Rachel Kolokoff Hopper

Published by JewishGen, Inc.
An Affiliate of the Museum of Jewish Heritage
A Living Memorial to the Holocaust
36 Battery Place, New York, NY 10280

Printed in the United States of America by Lightning Source, Inc.

Library of Congress Control Number (LCCN): 2021930120

ISBN: 978-1-954176-04-1 (hard cover: 458 pages, alk. paper)

Cover Credits:

Backgrounds on the front and back covers:

Floral photograph with original textures and filters by Rachel Kolokoff Hopper blended with an illustration from the original book page 8, "Map of Skalat, with the Towns and Cities around it."

Front cover:

Illustration by Tzipporah Hermoni from the original book page 98, "Water–drawer in Skalat."

Back cover photographs clockwise from top left:

"Girls of the Akiva Movement in Skalat" from the original book page 40;
"In the Belzec Death Camp" from the original book page 85;
 Photo of Skalat from the original book page 12;
"Children of the Hebrew School in Skalat, 1937" from the original book page 17.

Back cover poem:

A Vow by Abraham Shlonsky from the original book page 9.

JewishGen and the Yizkor Books in Print Project

This book has been published by the **Yizkor Books in Print Project**, as part of the **Yizkor Book Project** of JewishGen, Inc.

JewishGen, Inc. is a non-profit organization founded in 1987 as a resource for Jewish genealogy. Its website [www.jewishgen.org] serves as an international clearinghouse and resource center to assist individuals who are researching the history of their Jewish families and the places where they lived. JewishGen provides databases, facilitates discussion groups, and coordinates projects relating to Jewish genealogy and the history of the Jewish people. In 2003, JewishGen became an affiliate of the **Museum of Jewish Heritage—A Living Memorial to the Holocaust** in New York.

The **JewishGen Yizkor Book Project** was organized to make more widely known the existence of Yizkor (Memorial) Books written by survivors and former residents of various Jewish communities throughout the world. Later, volunteers connected to the different destroyed communities began cooperating to have these books translated from the original language—usually Hebrew or Yiddish—into English, thus enabling a wider audience to have access to the valuable information contained within them. As each chapter of these books was translated, it was posted on the JewishGen website and made available to the general public.

The **Yizkor Books in Print Project** began in 2011 as an initiative to print and publish Yizkor Books that had been fully translated, so that hard copies would be available for purchase by the descendants of these communities and also by scholars, universities, synagogues, libraries, and museums.

These Yizkor books have been produced almost entirely through the volunteer effort of researchers from around the world, assisted by donations from private individuals. The books are printed and sold at near cost, so as to make them as affordable as possible. Our goal is to make this important genre of Jewish literature and history available in English in book form, so that people can have the personal histories of their ancestral towns on their bookshelves for themselves and for their children and grandchildren.

A list of all published translated Yizkor Books in the project with prices and ordering information can be found at:
http://www.jewishgen.org/Yizkor/ybip.html

Lance Ackerfeld, Yizkor Book Project Manager
Joel Alpert, Yizkor-Book-in-Print Project Coordinator
Susan Rosin, Yizkor-Book-in-Print Project Associate Coordinator

JewishGen
Yizkor Book Project

This book is presented by the
Yizkor-Books-In-Print Project
Project Coordinator: Joel Alpert

Part of the Yizkor Books Project of JewishGen. Inc.
Project Manager: Lance Ackerfeld

These books have been produced solely through efforts of volunteers
from around the world. The books are printed using the Print-on-Demand technology and sold at
near cost, to make them as affordable as possible.

Our goal is to make this intimate history of the destroyed Jewish shtetls
of Eastern Europe available in book form in English, so that people can
experience the near-personal histories of their ancestral town on their
bookshelves and those of their children and grandchildren.

All donations to the Yizkor Books Project, which translated the books,
are sincerely appreciated.

Please send donations to:

Yizkor Book Project
JewishGen, Inc.
36 Battery Place
New York, NY, 10280

JewishGen, Inc. is an affiliate of the
Museum of Jewish Heritage
A Living Memorial to the Holocaust

Notes to the Reader:

We apologize ahead of time for the poor quality of images in the book. Often these images had been scanned from the original Yizkor books which were of poor quality to begin with, being copies of old photographs. Each transfer results in loss of quality. We have done the best we could, given the original material and the resources and technology at hand. Even though images often appear of higher quality on computer screens, that does not transfer to high quality images in print. A reader can view the original scans on the web sites listed below.

Within the text the reader will note "{34}" standing ahead of a paragraph. This indicates that the material translated below was on page 34 of the original book. However, when a paragraph was split between two pages in the original book, the marker is placed in this book after the end of the paragraph for ease of reading.

Also please note that all references within the text of the book to page numbers, refer to the page numbers of the original Yizkor Book.

In order to obtain a list of all Shoah victims from Skalat, the reader should access the Yad Vashem web site listed below; one can also search for specific family names using family name option. These lists are continually updated by Yad Vashem, so it is worthwhile to periodically search these lists.

There is much valuable information available on this web site, including the Pages of Testimony, etc.
http://yvng.yadvashem.org

A list of this book and all books available in the Yizkor-Book-In-Print Project along with prices is available at:
http://www.jewishgen.org/Yizkor/ybip.html

Geopolitical Information:

Skalat, Ukraine is located at 49°26' N 25°59' E, 213 miles WSW of Kyyiv

Period	Town	District	Province	Country
Before WWI (c. 1900):	Skałat	Skałat	Galicia	Austrian Empire
Between the wars (c. 1930):	Skałat	Skałat	Tarnopol	Poland
After WWII (c. 1950):	Skalat			Soviet Union
Today (c. 2000):	Skalat			Ukraine

Alternate names for the town:
Alternate names: Skalat [Ukr, Yid, Rus], Skałat [Pol], Skałat Stary

Nearby Jewish Communities:

Hrymayliv 7 miles SSE
Kam'yanky 8 miles N
Pidvolochys'k 10 miles NE
Volochysk 11 miles NE
Tarnoruda 11 miles E
Tovste 12 miles SSE
Stryyivka 14 miles NNW
Khorostkiv 14 miles SSW
Terebovlya 15 miles SW
Mikulintsy 17 miles W
Ozhyhivtsi 18 miles NE
Strusiv 18 miles WSW
Sataniv 18 miles SE
Horodnystya 18 miles SSE
Zbarazh 18 miles NNW
Dolyna 19 miles SW
Ternopil 20 miles WNW
Yabloniv 20 miles SSW
Tribukhovtsy 21 miles SSE

Sukhostav 21 miles SSW
Darakhov 22 miles WSW
Budaniv 22 miles SSW
Vyshhorodok 23 miles N
Kopychyntsi 23 miles S
Romanivka 24 miles SW
Vasyl'kivtsi 24 miles S
Belozërka 25 miles NNE
Kupil 27 miles ENE
Kuz'myn 27 miles ESE
Husyatyn 27 miles SSE
Probezhna 28 miles S
Horishnya Vyhnanka 29 miles SSW
Zolotnyky 29 miles WSW
Burkaniv 29 miles WSW
Bazaliya 29 miles NE
Kozliv 30 miles WNW
Chortkiv 30 miles SSW
Lanivtsi 30 miles N

Jewish Population in 1900: About 3,000

MAP OF UKRAINE IN 2014

Map of Ukraine with Skalat, Ukraine

SKALAT

A Memorial Anthology for a
Community Destroyed in the Holocaust
(Ukraine)

49°26' / 25°59'

Translation of
Skalat: Kovets Zikaron LeKehila ShHarva BaShoah

Edited by: Chaim Bronshtain

Published in Tel Aviv, 1971

Acknowledgments:

Translation Project Coordinator: Janet R. Perlmutter Schwartz

Translator: Neil H. Tannebaum

Editor: Henry Jorisch

This is a translation from: *Skalat: Kovets Zikaron LeKehila ShHarva BaShoah*
SKALAT: A Memorial Anthology for a Community Destroyed in the Holocaust, ed.
Chaim Bronshtain.
The Yaakov Krol School of Petach Tikvah, and The Organization of Skalat Jews in
Israel 1971/5731
OT Press, 48 Wolfson Street, Tel Aviv

סקאלאט

קובץ זכרון
לקהילה שחרבה בשואה

העורך: חיים ברונשטיין

SKALAT

A Memorial Anthology for a
Community Destroyed in the Holocaust

The original Hebrew Book can be found at:

https://digitalcollections.nypl.org/items/743ff2c0-3aef-0133-69ba-
00505686a51c

Or:

https://www.yiddishbookcenter.org/collections/yizkor-books/yzk-
nybc313994/bronshtain-hayim-skalat-kovets-zikaron-li-kehilah-she-harvah-ba-shoah

TABLE OF CONTENTS

Preface 2020/5781

I have always had a keen interest in genealogy and in the Holocaust, ever since I was a young child. My father, Arthur Perlmutter (z"l), and his war experience, played a large part in that. In my youth, I would always ask to look at his old black-and-white photo album. The album was filled with photos from Skalat – photos that were duplicated for my father after the war, by his aunt in Israel, since my father had been left without any keepsakes. I had so many questions about the people in the photos. These were people I didn't know. Were they like me, in any way? What did I miss by not growing up around them? What would I have been like, had I grown up in Skalat and not in the United Sates?

Despite the emotional pain I sensed my father carried on a daily basis, I remained unafraid to ask him questions about life during the war. I certainly didn't wish to inflict *more* pain with my questions, but I felt it was important to get answers. I needed those answers to better understand him, as well as to understand the world around me. And my father was willing enough to indulge me. The older I got, the braver my questions became. The more I asked, the more he eventually divulged.

Once my parents were gone from this earth – and perhaps *because* they were gone – my interest in my ancestry continued to grow. I found myself on the Internet, gathering incredible information, and finding cousins I never knew I had. If only my parents were still around to see this, how astounded they'd be. I found that the more I plowed through the information online, the more questions I had. If only my parents were alive to answer them. I found old information that I wanted to verify with them, and I found new information I wanted so badly to share with them. (I *also* wanted to share with them the beauty of Google Maps. They would have *loved* the app.)

In addition to doing genealogical research, I began to help my cousin, Henry Jorisch, build a family tree online. I had some information that he didn't have, and he had some information that I didn't have. So we shared. We were also greatly aided by a family tree that our cousin, Jurek Hirschberg, had worked on for a very long time. Jurek's tree reveals a more than 200 year lineage in Skalat.

One day, Henry was doing some research and emailed me to say that he had discovered a Skalat Yizkor Book, on JewishGen.org, that was unknown to either one of us. We were surprised, as we had grown up with Abraham Weissbrod's Yizkor Book, *Death of a Shtetl*, and hadn't known that any other existed. I immediately emailed Lance Ackerfeld, a volunteer at JewishGen, who assisted me in getting a hard copy of the book.

Skalat: A Memorial Anthology for a Community Destroyed in the Holocaust was compiled and edited by Chaim Bronshtain. It was written in Hebrew, and I felt compelled to find out what was in its pages. Henry felt the same way. Perhaps it contained some new information that our family had never before been privy to. How great that would be! However, I would need one of my Hebrew-speaking acquaintances to translate it for us.

Lance Ackerfeld, in our back-and-forth emails about the book, encouraged me to raise money for the translation through JewishGen. Why not share the work with other descendants of Skalaters, as well? Great idea! What a beautiful way to honor our loved ones -- those who survived the Holocaust, and those who perished.

Finding a translator for the Yizkor Book was not an easy feat, it turns out. I showed the book to some Israelis and to some Americans well-versed in Hebrew, none of whom felt capable of translating it. The book contained poetry, Biblical and Talmudic references, historical information. Not your ordinary, easy-to-read novel. To top things off, the language was high level, floral, and syntactically very different from our everyday English. The task of translation would require a very special person -- someone whose knowledge is vast in the realms of Jewish history, Torah, Talmud, European history, politics, and linguistics. The project became blessed when my brother-in-law, Ephraim Dardashti, introduced me to his friend, Neil Tannebaum. Only Neil was up to the challenge of translating this Yizkor Book. Neil, with his breadth of knowledge in all the aforementioned arenas, and with his patience for that unusual, foreign syntax (think: "Yinglish"), was a Godsend. A brilliant polymath and scholar. A perfect fit. Neil translated the book by hand, verbatim, onto hundreds of yellow-lined sheets of paper. I typed up the pages and went over them with him to make sure I understood his handwriting, as well as to have him explain certain phrases, or certain references that I was unfamiliar with. Then I emailed the typed pages to my cousin Henry – another Godsend.

Henry Jorisch, a retired teacher of both English and Information Technology, graciously offered his time and expertise to edit the Yizkor Book, so it would read smoothly. (He was also incredibly patient with my lack of computer knowledge in our back-and-forth editing process.) It was immediately apparent to Henry that an English-speaking reader from a *non*-European household might have a hard time comfortably reading the translated Yizkor Book. He and I are both used to the "Yinglish" syntax of our Skalater parents, but that might not be the case for every reader. As a result, Henry spent numerous hours correcting prepositions, and putting passive phrases (so typical of Yiddish speakers) into active form. He used current English expressions to clarify older European ones, double-checked many names, words, and facts for accuracy, and made the paragraphs within individual essays much more orderly and comprehensible. I had so many "aha!" moments, while reading his edited version of the work (as in "Ahhh...so this is what the author actually meant to say!"). Henry's editing made a huge impact on the translation.

And for all the time he spent reading aloud the last set of edits, as I compared them to the first set of edits, I must thank my husband, Steve. He helped me to simplify an overwhelming task. This body of work was much too complicated to put into any type of difference-checking online app. I needed a special person willing and able to help me sort everything out. Steve understood my process, and worked many hours reading and comparing the text with me. Thank you, Love.

I am certain readers will benefit from the efforts that both Neil Tannebaum and Henry Jorisch put into this translation. I, myself, cannot thank them enough for all of their hard work. They have enabled me, and other descendants of Skalaters, to read this Yizkor Book in English, and to learn new and different information about our ancestral town and its inhabitants. They have also enabled English speaking Holocaust scholars, who are already familiar with Weissbrod's book, to find out *more* about the Jews of Skalat, their life in the shtetl, and the horrors of their experiences before, during, and after World War II.

I am thankful that we have been able to bring this new 50th Anniversary English Language edition to a new generation of readers. If only my parents, Arthur Perlmutter (z"l) and Esther Farber Perlmutter (z"l), were still alive to see this project come to fruition!

Janet R. Perlmutter Schwartz Philadelphia

Introduction

By Neil H. Tannebaum, Esq.
Natan Tzvi-Hirsch Tannebaum

When I was approached by Mrs. Janet Schwartz to undertake the project of translating the Skalat Memorial book that had been published in Israel, from Hebrew to English, I eagerly agreed for several reasons:

1. I am an inveterate history enthusiast or buff, with an intense interest in Jewish history;

2. I have personally known several individuals who were either natives of Skalat (including my teacher, the late Prof. Ephraim A. Speiser, a distinguished Biblical and Assyriological scholar) or children of surviving Skalaters (e.g., Jonas Weissbrod, then an undergraduate at the University of Pennsylvania);

3. On my father's side of the family, I am a descendant of Hasidic Galician (Galitzianer) Jews, my paternal grandparents (o.b.m.), having been natives of Lemberg, (a.k.a. Lwow, a.k.a. Lviv), the major metropolis not far from Skalat. I have maintained a nostalgic interest in that ancestral region; and,

4. As one steeped in the Hebrew language and literature of all periods, which I once taught on the university level, I felt Iinguistically and culturally qualified for this task; and, lastly, and most importantly,

5. I view the perpetuation of the memory of the historic European Jewish communities, which were so utterly and cruelly extirpated in the Holocaust, as a necessary and indeed sacred obligation.

Once engaged in the work of translation, I found it to be a most rewarding learning experience. I discovered detailed descriptions of the rich Jewish life, which flourished in Skalat in the pre-Holocaust period, including the Great Synagogue and numerous small shtiblach, the educational institutions, Husiatyn Hasidut, economic activities, a range of Zionist youth groups, and more. With tears in my eyes, I read the harrowing and most depressing account of the annihilation of the Skalat Jews and Jews of other Galician communities in the Belzec death factory. I further learned details of the experience of escapees from Skalat in various far-flung locales: the surrounding forests, with various Partisan groups, in Soviet Russia (including Siberia and the Urals), and for some, surreptitious Aliyah in the post-War years to Eretz Yisrael and commencing a new life there.

I wish to thank my collaborators in this project, Mrs. Janet Schwartz, who patiently deciphered my long-hand translation texts and reduced them to printed form, and to Mr. Henry Jorisch, who performed the final editing of the work.

May the memory of the martyred Jews of Skalat and their beautiful community be for a blessing! Y'hi Zichram Barukh!

טנבאום הירש-צבי נתן

Forward

האמת דיין ברוך: I write this forward in honor of my Mother and Father, the Survivors, the Six Million Martyrs, ישראל בית כל, the generations that came before them, from them, and all the future generations to come:

The Jewish part of Skalat was a special place filled with love and kindness. My great grandparents, the same as Janet's, Marcus and Basia Perlmutter, lived there surrounded by family. They were beloved and respected in the community, and the Jewish townsfolk often sought out their wisdom, compassion and counsel. My grandfather, Joseph Wechsler, came to Skalat from Tarnopol, and the moment he met Pepa Perlmutter, he fell in love with her. They married and raised three children, Gusta, Benjamin and Betty. My father, Martin Jorisch, came to Skalat from Podvolochisk and fell in love with my mother, Gusta Wechsler. They were in the first blossom of youth and love, but much more was in store for them. In Skalat, they were embraced by the many relatives who lived there before the *Shoah*. None of them could have known that they would all soon walk through the Valley of the Shadow of Death.

Three weeks after Rosh Hashanah, in October 1942, in a third major roundup called the 'Wild Aktion,' over 3,000 Jews from the town, including our entire family, were taken by the Germans to be murdered at the Belzec extermination camp. My father and grandfather were selected for slave labor instead, and so they lived. My mother had hidden in an attic.

In the middle of 1943, after months in the Skalat and Kamionka labor camps, my parents and grandfather, along with a small group of mostly teenagers, saw that they too would soon become victims and decided to take the chance to escape late at night from Skalat into the Ostra-Mogila forest. They banded together and helped one another stay alive for almost two years, until the war was over. Janet's father and grandfather, Arthur and Jacob Perlmutter, did the same. And of the original thirty-two in this group that fled into the forest together, miraculously, twenty-nine survived. But few from Skalat survived to tell their stories. Janet and I have been working on our joint genealogical records for several years now in order to recover this family history. That is a story in itself.

Of the 160 Jewish Skalat residents who survived through those years, a number of the youngsters were able to reach safety in what was then Palestine. There, they came together to form a hometown *landsmanshaft* organization, and then to personally testify to what they had experienced. They wrote and published this book, *Skalat: A Memorial Anthology for a Community Destroyed in the Holocaust*, and it is where they recorded and preserved the memories of their lives before, during and after the war. They published this volume of memoirs in Hebrew in 1971. Their stories add depth and profound heartache for lost loved ones, a layer of context and history to the stories that I heard from my parents from the time I was very young. Through this anthology, these Skalaters have given us an extraordinary view into the most horrific crime committed against the Jewish People in our history, and this occurred only as recently as the mid-twentieth century.

I read Abraham Weissbrod's 1948 book, *Skalat, the Death of a Shtetl* many years ago. I found that Janet's grandfather, Jacob, and my grandfather, Joseph, had been interviewed by Weissbrod and listed in the book as 'authoritative witnesses' to the events in Skalat. That gave me a deeper appreciation of belonging to the larger community descended from the families of this 'little' town.

When Janet and I began to explore Bronshtain's Skalat book, we knew it was yet an additional treasure that we were determined to get translated into English so it could be shared with a greater English speaking community. Janet asked Neil to translate the book. His masterful translation uncovered so much information of these Skalaters' horror-filled, yet heroic experiences in the harrowing and heart-rending stories told in the following pages.

I am grateful to my wife, Andee, and my two younger sons, Benjamin and Michael, who constantly checked in on me. Their love sustained me during work on this book. As I progressed through the testimonies, Ben also read the text, and we shared new-found details that put into focus the stories that we knew about my parents' experiences during the war. We had ongoing conversations about how the content and language in the book affected us. Michael helped me with technical aspects of the production and sharing of the book, while I made sure to keep him informed about what I found in the manuscript. The passing down of family history and memory is a precious legacy we owe our children.

I am thankful to Janet and Neil for the joint effort that made this new 50th Anniversary English Language edition possible. I want to thank Ruben Perlmutter, Jurek Hirschberg, Magda Sadura and Abraham Weissbrod (the author's grandson) who helped build the foundation that led us to this book.

Many thanks to the David and Sylvia Steiner Yizkor Book Collection and the Steven Spielberg Digital Yiddish Library, the underwriting funders of their Collections, and the New York Public Library - National Yiddish Book Center Yizkor Book Project for making the electronic version of the original Hebrew publication of *Skalat* available online. Thank you to Lance Ackerfeld and Binny Lewis for their encouragement and guidance, and for making sure that this English version of the book takes its righteous place among the JewishGen Yizkor Books of Remembrance.

It is with deepest gratitude toward all the writers in the anthology, האלה הקדושים, for sharing their testimonies of the events that occurred in and around Skalat and other places, that we bring their work forward. And my highest respect to the educators and students of Israel who have made the Holocaust and the adoption of *shtetlach* like Skalat an essential part of their curriculum.

If anyone can be credited with making this edition of *Skalat* come into being, it is Janet. Her love, determination, hard work and inner light is what turned what was just an idea into a reality.

I dedicate this work to my wife, children, and grandchildren, that they may always know where we come from.

As heartbreaking, tragic and painful as the descriptions of the horrors of the Holocaust are in this book, it has been a sacred duty, an honor and a labor of love to be involved with it.

Reader! With all my heart, I hope you will see yourself as if you too were there in Skalat in the pages of these memoirs, which are filled with such profound belief, courage, grief, despair, hope, renewal and redemption.

Henry Jorisch
NYC 5871

[Page 3]

Acknowledgements
Offerings of Thanks

Chaim Bronshtain

It is incumbent upon me to thank all the people of my city who acted and assisted in the preparation of this anthology. I cannot name all of them, but I offer special thanks.

A faithful and devoted partner, who acted indefatigably for the perpetuation of the memory of the town, our shtetl, Skalat, in this anthology was, for me my comrade in work and mindset, Ze'ev Reuveni. A dear man, a native of our city, Chaim Dlugacz, was of great assistance to us with his professional knowledge in the field of printing. He aided greatly in the external layout of this anthology.

Likewise, blessings are due the workers of the OT Press for their devotion and their patience, and for their beautiful work.

[Page 7]

May these Pages be a Memorial Candle

This anthology is modest in its scope and does not at all pretend to serve as an inclusive and comprehensive expression of how the Holocaust affected the Jews of *Skalat*. That would require a massive book.

There exists great doubt whether such a book will ever be written. Those who had the ability to shoulder this difficult task perished in the *Shoah*. The events were cruel, and did not leave any opportunities to create testimonies in writing. Memories were left behind with those who perished. Only pain remains.

And even if many years have passed since then, our pain continues to echo in space. It is eternal pain, and will last until our departure from the face of the earth.

May these pages, in which the cry of our pain is contained, be a memorial candle for all the residents of our town, Skalat: fathers and mothers, brothers and sisters, relatives and friends, who watered the ground of Skalat, Belzec and all the land of Poland with their blood.

Poland, do not cover their blood!

The Editor, **Chaim Bronshtain** 1971

[Page 8]

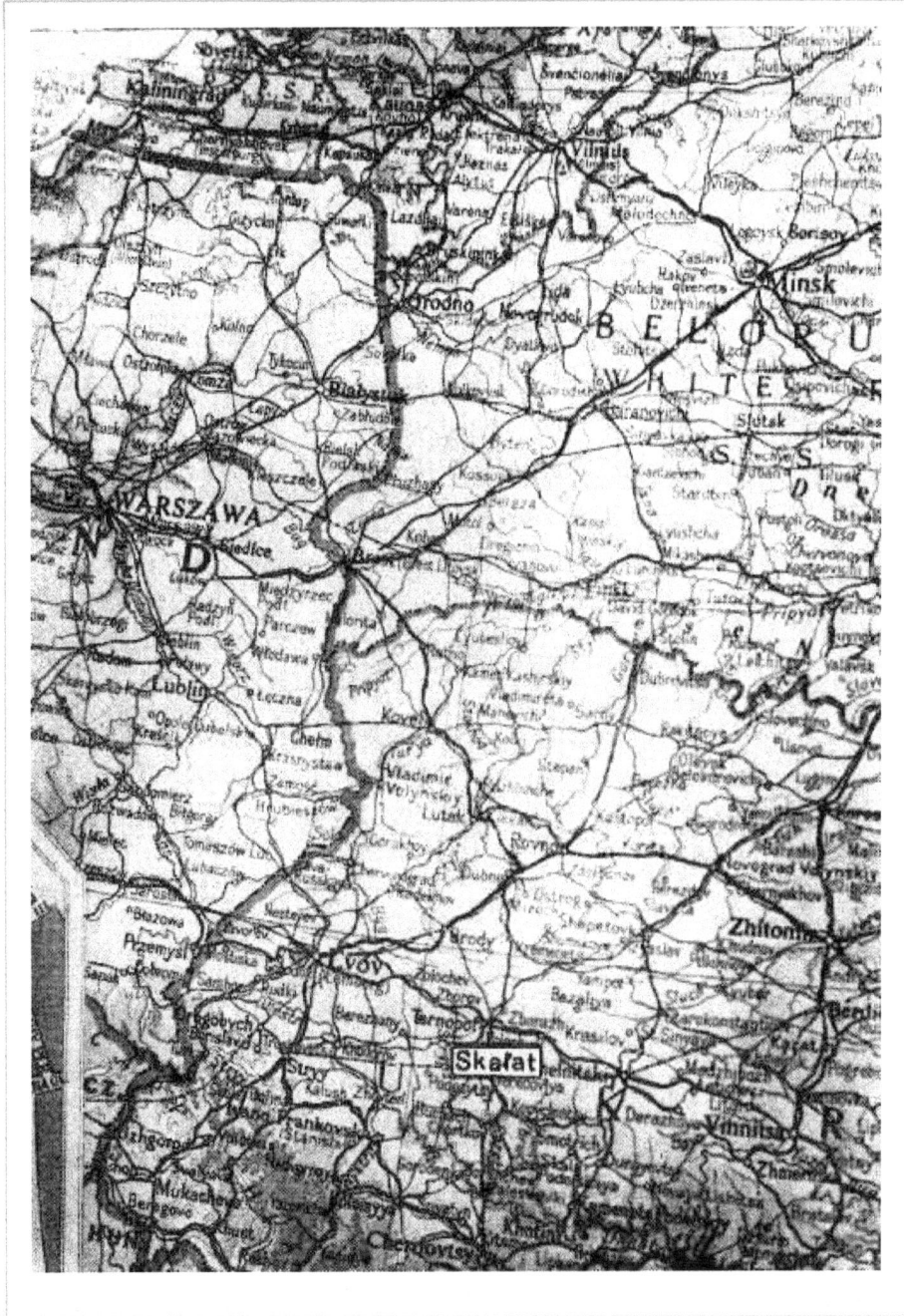

Map of Skalat, with the Towns and Cities around it

[Page 9]

A Vow

Abraham Shlonsky

> With the assent of my eyes
> which behold the bereavement
> and heaped cries
> upon my bowed heart,
> With the blessing of my compassion
> which taught me to forgive
> until days came
> which prohibited me from forgiving,
> I have made the vow
> to remember everything,
> to remember –
> and not to forget a thing.

[Page 10]

20 Teveth 5728 (1-21-68)

In Honor of:

Mr. Ze'ev Reuveni
Principal of the Krol School

Dear Mr. Reuveni,

I am unfortunately unable to be with you at the ceremony memorializing the Skalat community which will take place this coming Tuesday, 22 Teveth, this week. I will therefore suffice with a few words, in writing.

The project of the memorializing of the communities is, in my eyes, one of the important projects that enable the creation of a monument to a Jewry, which was destroyed in the years of the Holocaust. Through the bond with one of the communities that was exterminated, it is possible to recognize a point of original Jewish life. Here is a basis for testifying to an entire center of Jewish life to which Skalat belonged, where there was both a secular life and the milieu of Sabbath and Festivals. Here one can recognize the educational institutions, culture and the life of spiritual creativity. One can understand the worry about existence and livelihood. We discover and learn about the distinguished personalities and the common folk, about the creators and their creations, and about those who drew on inspirational sources and devoted so much of their time to Torah study.

All of these existed and no longer exist. But tomorrow cannot exist without yesterday.

Through memorializing the communities, through the attachment of a school to a specific community, this one or another – all of us can recognize the life that was, and the good and the beautiful which our ancestors bequeathed to us, that we may establish our home in Israel.

It is my trust that all of you who now memorialize the Skalat community, will know how to persist in the study of the life which existed in it, and thus will provide a monument to the preservation of its memory.

Respectfully,

Y. Frischman
General Vice-Director

[Page 11]

The Project of Memorializing the Communities

By Dr. Baruch Ben Yehudah

I will admit it and not be ashamed. When they started to talk about "The Project of Memorializing the Communities" by schoolchildren, I hesitated about the educational power of the idea. Insofar as the thought occurred to me, I am certain that consciousness of the Holocaust needs to become a foundation of first rank in the education of our generations. I cast doubt on this path out of lack of faith in the possibility of converting forms of life and social values, which are only in the memories of the teachers alone, into exciting, moving and interesting educational material.

And then, I had occasion to convene delegations from all the schools in the country in the National Convention Center Auditorium in Jerusalem for summarizing the year of action for the project. Hundreds and hundreds of children filled the great auditorium. Mr. Gideon Hausner spoke to them, and the children read and carried out different performances. I directed my eyes not to the stages but behind me, to the children's benches. What silence, what concern on every face, what cooperation with what was being said and being done on stage! It seemed to me the children heard the rustling of the wings of the Divine Presence hovering between the rows and the weeping of the *Shekhinah...*

And something moved in my heart. And then I was invited by my friend, Mr. Ze'ev Reuveni, principal of the school named for Krol, in Petach-Tikvah, to be present at the ceremony for the adoption of his community, the Skalat community, that was in Galicia, by the children of his school. And, again, that impression returned - a true experience of children, a precious and intensive educational time, a pure-hearted activity on the part of the students, and cooperation arousing a bond between the principal, the teachers and the students.

These two things removed any hesitation from my heart. I had erred in that I had considered the children alone, and had not added to the calculation the part of the educators. But if the latter brings to their students a chapter of Truth, which is recognizable in every movement of their lips, in every movement of their eyes, and in every slight hoarseness in their throats, which comes in lieu of restrained tears – there is nothing greater than the power of truth in education.

Even today, Ze'ev Reuveni feels the pain of his community, which was destroyed. So too did Gideon Hausner, who, in the opening speech in the Eichmann Trial, riveted the entire nation of Israel and the entire world with the feeling that the six million souls were hovering over our world and demanding justice and retribution to the evil-doer. He too converted the truth, which was in his heart, into an education moment.

May your hands be strengthened, my dear friend, Reuveni. And may the hands of all the educators be strengthened – and at the head, Mr. Dov Alloni – for they succeeded with the truth, which was in their hearts, to attach myriads of children to the chain of the life of the nation in its generations.

[Page 12]

The History of the Town

By Chaim Bronshtain

Of the historiography of the Jewish town, the *Shtetl* in Eastern Europe is the weakest link in Holocaust research. Small towns left behind them few traces in books or chronicles, are almost not mentioned, and the little bit remaining leaves behind it many gaps.

One who attempts to uncover the history of a small town is in the category of a person searching in expanses of desert sands for a lost pin. History, as it were, passed by these small neglected towns, and left them at the sides of the road. Despite the fact that the economic, religious and social activity in the small town was suffused with much tension, no mention was left of this daily existence.

The historiographic poverty in the area of the history of the Jewish small town is striking, and this poverty consigns the fate of the small town to be forgotten, to be entirely erased. Towns in which Jews lived for hundreds of years would not be remembered in coming generations.

The Holocaust issued a total verdict against the Jewish town. With the kind help of the people of Yad Vashem in Jerusalem, and particularly that of Mr. Yitzchak Lan, we succeeded in discovering traces of the history of the town Skalat in several sources:

1. *Encyklopedia Powszechna* T. 23. Rok 1866

2. *Slownik Geograficzny Krolewstwa Polskiego* T. 10. Rok 1889

[Page 13]

According to the *Encyklopedia Powszechna*, from 1866, Skalat was located, in ancient generations, in the Russian Kingdom. In the second half of the 19th century, Skalat was found in the territory of Galicia, in the vicinity of the Gnula River. An ancient fortress, which was built in the 16th century for defensive purposes, enhanced the city. In this period, there were three thousand residents in Skalat.

Slownik Geograficzny from 1889 contains more details about the town. At the end of the 19th century, Skalat is the *Miasto Powiatove*, the county town in East Galicia, southeast of Tarnopol. In 1870, there were 4,592 residents, 2,552 of them Jewish.

According to Korftinitski, in *Geography of Galicia* from 1786, it is clear that Skalat was the inheritance of the Tarlov Family of Shaknovitz, from which the land of Skalat passed to the Princes of the House of Poniatowski. They sold it, around 1869, to a Jew named Ziskind Rosenstock.

Rosenstock was a famous Jew in his generation, the holder of the title Baron. One of his descendants, Alexander, converted to Christianity. He sold the land of Skalat, which Joseph Tenenbaum bought, specifically the land of Novosilka in 1920.

The source of the following information is from the population census held in Poland in 1921. According to this census, there were 5,957 residents in Skalat, 2,919 of them Jews.

According to the *Bletter Far Geschichte* for the Jewish Historical Institute in Poland, from 1953, there were 4,600 Jews in Skalat in 1941. In 1942, because of the forced move of Jews from the environs, the Jewish population increased to 8,500.

According to Abraham Weissbrod, in his book, *Death of a Shtetl*, of all the Jews of Skalat, there remained only 160 persons after the war.

[Page 14]

Reflections with a Cry of Pain

By Chaim Bronshtain

The Audience at the Ceremony of the Adoption of Skalat

More than a half jubilee of years has passed since I left the city of my birth, Skalat, for the last time. The city let me drink from its golden cup, but also one from the goblet of poison – in its last days.

A person drinks only once from the days of childhood. It is from Skalat's streets, its alleys, and its landscapes, that this city took form. And even if many years have passed since you boarded the train that carried you far, far from it, and in your heart there is a severe curse against the city and its inhabitants, you are unable to be reminded of it without yearnings and pain. You are unable to free yourself of the feeling that this city is part of your being, and you carry it inside you wherever you turn.

Skalat is a small city. Its streets are few and its alleys are numerous. In my eyes, there is nothing more beautiful than Skalat, in the hot days of summer, in the days of idleness from study. We ran around in its streets and were caught up in the wagons of the farmers and peasants loaded with the sheaves of the field. And even when the whip whistled, the sweetness of the experience did not dissipate.

Between the walls of the cramped *Cheder*, we sat learning around the table, riveted to the square letters, and absorbing the words of the *Melammed*, the Jewish Primary Teacher. And he, the elderly *Melammed*, opened up before us the gates and doorways to hidden worlds, filling all the chambers of our heart, to feel the heavenly Jerusalem and the earthly Jerusalem, the Western Wall and Rachel's Tomb, Hebron and Bethlehem. The entire Land of Israel is here, dwelling among the walls of the *Cheder*, and you stroll in its expanses. The rebukes of the rabbi, our teacher, the sharp pinch of his yellowed thumb, did not have the power to make us forget Rachel's tears, the ultimate Matriarch, who refused to be comforted.

In the dark winter nights, in the fierce snowstorms, with the small city lantern in your hand, you make your way from the *Cheder*. It's cold outside but warm inside. You walk, erect and proud of everything around you, with mercy in your heart toward the vanities of the Gentiles who did not know the Truth of the Torah. You feel no hatred but, rather, sorrow for the Gentiles.

There passing before your eyes are the multitudes of the House of Israel who inhabit both its lofty and its small houses. Here they are, the wealthy of the town, passing by in their splendid coaches, who arouse in you a bit of envy, and the masses running about in its markets and its alleys in order to find a crust of bread. Jews adorned with beards and *kapotes*, kaftans. Jews with cut–off sidelocks wearing hats on their heads, slightly embarrassed for having 'broken down the fence,' that is, having deviated from Orthodox norms, but their trust in God still with them. On Shabbat nights, and on the eve of every festival, you will find them in the synagogues. Their faces shine, serious, gathered into themselves, with their ears attentive to the distant song of the stars.

And suddenly everything was silenced. A great darkness prevailed over the world and covered the eye of the Sun.

In July 1941, the Red Army retreated, day and night, on the main roads leading eastward. Tens of thousands and hundreds of thousands are fleeing in panic, some by vehicle and some on foot. Hungry, torn and wounded, they gallop eastward. The iron skies above keep silent. But the dust of burning rises in the air, its odor sharp and threatening.

Then everything was silenced. The last of the Russian soldiers left the city. At the twilight hour, the silence of a cemetery surrounds you. It is like the day of the creation of the world, and you do not know what to expect.

At midnight, Friday night, at the beginning of the month of July, automobile horns and noise of wheels announced the entry of the German Army to the inhabitants of the city who were enclosed in their homes, inclining their ears with worry and anticipation. And in the morning, after a night of watchfulness, you saw them up close, proud, erect, sitting in their vehicles on their way eastward. Their uniforms pressed. Their boots sparkling, and their weapons polished. Thus the victorious conquerors of the world always appeared, in all generations.

And moreover, on that day, in the afternoon hours, the first Jews were taken out of their houses and executed in gruesome ways. Some by water and some by fire, and yet the heart refused to admit that something awful had occurred, that we were standing at the entrance of a depth whose end we could not foresee.

A new day, Sunday, hundreds of Jews – men, youths and elders – were taken out of their houses, at the sounds of laughter of crowds of Poles and Ukrainians, residents of the city. They did not return again to their homes. In cellars of old fortresses, at the edge of the city, they were all executed, young and old.

And still it seemed that this was an accident, at the hands of malicious people. It was not possible. Until days came which threatened forgetfulness. Famine, forced labor, disgrace and humiliation, taxes which sucked the marrow out of bones, wandering with shadows past the boundaries of the Ghetto – what are all these compared to the days of terrors which came afterward.

The summer of 1942. The *Judenrat* was assigned to supply a quota of men to the Germans to be executed. Even Satan was not capable of inventing a malicious trick more terrifying than that. The day was appointed. The hour was set. And you, O man, arise and select who will live and who will die. The lot fell upon the elders of the city. Grandfathers and grandmothers were separated from their children, their grandchildren, and their great–grandchildren, and were forced out onto the road. They were gathered in the interior of the synagogue. From there they would be taken out in trucks to their last destination. They were naïve, believing that in death they would be saving their offspring and the entire remainder of the community.

But they were mistaken. A few months after the city was emptied of its elders, the axe was waved anew. At dawn, the ghetto was surrounded. This time all of them went, young and old, fathers and mothers, children and infants. The end of the world arrived. Doors were forced open. Windowpanes were shattered. There were roars of human beasts who were bursting in like preying wolves to the apartments of people sunken in sleep, broken vessels wherever you would look, people dressing hurriedly, mute, frozen, shocked to the point of silence. At the distance of a step, you seek a father, a mother, a brother, a sister, pushed and exiting. You want to cry, but you know if you desire to live, you disappear into the midst of the ground and pretend not to notice.

And once the storm has passed, and you have remained alive, you learn that over three thousand Jews have been removed from here in the course of two days, and there was but a step between you and them. One *Aktion* follows another. And always someone remains, and always many, many disappear, until half way into 1943, there is no more ghetto. There are no more Jews. There are no more *Aktions*....

Remnants of the community still struggle for their lives in a camp, which is in the vicinity. Every morning they go out to the stone quarries, which are outside the city. Again, death is upon their faces. They know that their fate is sealed. A few remain. Their families have perished, and even their days are numbered.

Indeed their days were numbered. Speedily, even this small remnant was led to pre–dug, deep pits that were previously prepared.

Life was over!

And when the day came that the city was liberated, and the last remnants were gathered to it – and they were very few – they stood mute, suppressing their grief inside, and were not even able to cry. The sound of tears was dried up.

They still managed to visit the graves of their loved ones in the expanse of the field. Wherever you tread, you hear the cry of the tortured, and you know that you will no longer find rest for your soul.

Not many days have passed, and the entire remnant gathered and then left here, the giant cemetery, whose name is Skalat.

Twenty–five years have passed since I left here. Somewhere in the world, there still dwell loving people in its houses, streets, alleys, living, breathing. Surely, they sleep their sleep at night, and do not shudder when the spirits of the dead knock on their doors with their fists...

And still I think, while awake and in dreams, of the city of my childhood. And I know that the following words were said of me, when the poet wrote:

AND IF THE ANGEL SHOULD ASK:

My son, where is your soul?

Fly in the world, seek, oh my Angel!

There is in the world a peaceful village,

Surrounded by a wall of forests, and the village

Has a sky of blue, a sky without limits.

And the sky of blue has an only daughter

In the middle: a single cloud, white and small

And in the afternoon of a solitary summer day

A boy played there, a boy left to his soul,

Tender and singular and dreaming –

And I am the boy, oh my Angel!

Remarks at the Ceremony of the Perpetuation of the Community of Skalat, at the Jacob Krol School in Petach–Tikvah on 22, Teveth 5728

Children of the Hebrew School in Skalat, 1937

[Page 18]

Skalat in the Days of the First World War

By Shlomo Ansky

This narrative is taken from Shlomo Ansky's book, *The Destruction of Galicia* (translated by Shmuel Zitron). Ansky, also the author of *The Dybbuk*, visited Jewish settlements in the region during the years of the First World War, and organized aid to war victims on the front. His impressions of the desolation, which the war wrought on Eastern European Jewry, are described in his book. Here is a segment, which relates his impressions of his visit to Skalat.

Chaim Bronshtain

At a late night hour, I came to Skalat. At the only inn located in the town, there was one room, but the cold inside was as great as outside.

I awoke from my sleep just when dawn came up. When I withdrew my head from the hairy blankets with which I was covered, I saw that there was an old woman in the room standing by the stove. When she saw that I had awakened, she gestured with her hand as if calming me, and she said, "Sleep, sleep, I'll wait!"

"What's up with you?" I asked her with astonishment. "I have something to tell you," she says. "People will come to you from the entire city and you will not have free time, so I came to wait until you awoke from your sleep. I will sit here in this lodging–place".

It was already known who and what I am, and the woman had come early with her request. Even though she gave me permission to sleep longer, she nevertheless began speaking and narrating. She was one of those who had been exiled from Podvolochisk. She had been a prosperous housewife. Now she and her children were experiencing awful days. The owner of the lodging house was a relative and had allowed her a corner of the house. In return for that, she and her children had to perform every kind of crushing labor. And not only that, but she had to flatter the mistress of the house and offer her ingratiating talk. Far be it for the woman to complain to her about how much she and her children suffered from hunger and cold for the eighteen months she had been living here in Skalat in the house of her relative! Her children, two girls who had reached puberty – were both beautiful and talented. They spent the entire year in the house, lacking shoes. Now, they had received eighteen rubles for shoes from the Committee. But what can one do with eighteen rubles? Besides there was also a need for dresses as well.

The woman already knew that I had brought a bundle of blankets, and now she was asking that I give the blankets to her and her daughters.

While her words were still on her tongue, another woman came in dressed in prosperous clothing, with a gold watch protruding from her pocket. Right away, she says that this watch is the only thing left of her former wealth. A young man, a member of the Local Aid Committee, had entered the room with her. The woman had one request: her only son, a youth of distinguished talents, had completed the school curriculum in five classes at the *gymnasium*. For the two years since, he has been idle. So she has requested that the Committee hire him a teacher to prepare him for the university.

The committeeman interrupts her speech and says, "Your son is able to acquire teaching preparation, and to become a teacher and earn."

"Teaching lessons?" The woman cries from insult. "My son is not from such a family that he could consent to engage in teaching on hourly pay." She wants him to reach for more.

The Rabbi of the town came to greet me. He entered the room with a fervent smile of piety. He opened his remarks with praise and commendation for my good heart. He says he has brought a statement from the Sages of the town. He explains to me, kabbalistically, that the thirty–two rubles, which the Committee pays him monthly, are not enough for him and the six members of his household, so he requests an addition.

Then a short Jew with small, piercing eyes full of anger enters cautiously, closes the door, looks sideways and begins talking with a low emotional voice. He does not request anything from me. He has come to me to open my eyes and let me know that all the aid, which we give the inhabitants, has not helped. Not only that, but it brings harm. The only ones who need aid are widows and orphans. For their needs, a sum of one thousand rubles per month is sufficient, and the remaining fifteen thousand rubles per month, they leave on the deer's horn, meaning, they waste the money away.

"I am not saying, God forbid, that the Committee is misappropriating the money," he said mildly, "but don't you understand that around a fat pot the hands become fat and everyone's hand is in it?"

"And what is there to do?" I asked him. "What?" he cried heatedly, "No money! You have made all of us beggars, especially those with extended hands! It would be better if you would lobby that they should allow us to return to our homes in Podvolochisk. And we would stand there on our own feet, and again be human beings."

After him came a few members of the Local Relief Committee, for the representation of local householders and local exiles. Those who came were only representatives of the exiles. Homalski had already told me that the relations between the two parts of the Committee are not peaceful. According to the first few words, I recognized that the members of the Committee of the exiles were completely contemptuous of the local members. Podvolochisk, whose exiles to Skalat are in the great majority, was always a city of 'Important People' while Skalat was always considered a 'City of Beggars.' Now the wheel was reversed, and the people of Podvolochisk were forced to be at the mercy of the people of Skalat. The people of Skalat are not able to understand why the Committee donates to the exiles, and it allots only a few hundred rubles to the local inhabitants. At the same time, they try with all their might to prevent the exiles from returning to their homes in Podvolochisk, and the matter is not surprising. Every month, they receive more than two thousand rubles in rent from the exiles, aside from other income that they bring in.

The number of Jewish inhabitants of the place amounts, all told, to three thousand souls. Of those, 1,057 are considered poor. Part of them, 534 souls, are war–injured. And they have the right to receive support. They receive aid from the Zemstavot Organization. The exiles, most of them from Podvolochisk, found here, number 1,897 souls. Of those, 1,781 receive aid. The allocation for the month of January amounts to 16,209 rubles – 14,400 for the benefit of the exiles, 900 for the benefit of the needy of Skalat, and 900 rubles for the Jewish residents of the surrounding villages.

I use my free time to visit the residences of the exiles and to consider the city. The single largest building by which the city is distinguished is the synagogue. It is built of bricks. They say that the first stone in the foundation of the synagogue was laid by Rabbi Levi Yitzchak of Berdichev. So too that the "Righteous Convert" visited the synagogue.

When he approached the synagogue, he bent to his knees and entered by crawling into the synagogue. And he approached the Holy Ark upon the benches. When they asked him the reason he walked that way, he answered, "Upon this floor stood people so great and holy, and I am not worthy to stand on the place which their feet trod upon."

Now, the floor of the synagogue has been trampled by the feet of the exiles. They sit crowded and pressed together in the synagogue in every corner. They add their baggage, their bundles and their beds as if they are in a way station at the time of a panicked retreat.

I visited many camps of exiles. One dwelling particularly made an impression on me. It had a large room, one of its walls half inclining, and there were inside it large spaces covered with torn garments. The walls were draped with frost. In this room dwelled a woman in childbirth and several sick people. Afterwards, the husband of the pre–partum woman came to me at my dwelling place. He requested that they should give him double bread, and that they should add to the measure of wood and milk that come with his portion. I fulfilled his request and gave him three rubles cash.

In the evening, Mr. Homalski came to the Committee session. Homalski read the budget listing, according to which the local needy were allotted only nine hundred rubles. The local members of the Committee rose up and announced that they did not find that sufficient.

According to our records, 534 poor who suffered from the war were listed. A third came to us and at least one fourth of the sum of money was allocated, amounting to four thousand rubles.

Concerning this, Homalski said, "The Kiev Committee appropriated aid to the exiles, simple and poor, and even war injured, like those who remain living in their place. We have in Russia numbers in the millions, and the Committee cannot afford to come to their aid. The Local Committee needs to be concerned about their benefits."

"How can you compare the communities in Russia to those of ours?"

Hearing these words, Homalski became angry and cried out:

"To whom do you tell your stories? Don't I know the situation in Skalat? I know that with you there are people who, in the days of war, acquired wealth. The city profited a great deal and there is in its ability, the means to support the local poor. It is possible that even the nine hundred rubles which I allotted were superfluous."

"Who told you that the city became rich? That is only a fake report, which the Podvolochiskers circulated. They are envious of everyone", cried one of the locals heartily! "I decided to add another two thousand rubles for the benefit of the local poor."

[Page 21]

My Town, Skalat

By Hadassah Katz

My desire is to commemorate my childhood home, my father's house, where I drew the strength to live my life. I carry the memory of that home in my heart. Time has the power to heal wounds, but not those that are in my soul. The horrors of that time only deepen the wounds, which I will take with me to my eternal rest.

I want to set down in these few words some of the things that characterized our town. Skalat was not only a city of Jews. It also had a large Christian population that harassed us every day, and made our lives difficult. Both Jewish children and young adults grew up in the midst of a population that was hostile to Jews.

A profound memory that I can see through the distance of time, a great occurrence for all the Jews of Skalat, was the annual visit of the Rebbe to our shtetl. On the eve of the Shavuot Festival, every year, the Rebbe of Husiatyn would visit our town. The Jews rejoiced at his arrival. He was a ray of light in the life of the Jews of Skalat. He brought profound joy mixed with the grayness of our fight for existence. Our hearts yearned for the merit of his blessing, his encouragement and his advice. Hassidic fervor filled our hearts.

The beginning of our young adult lives was spent in the embrace of the activity of Zionist youth groups. We rebelled against the certainties, the routine, and the parents who did not encourage our participation in our Zionist dream. Our ally was the Hebrew Day School, which taught us about youngsters striving to settle in the Land of Israel. We studied Hebrew and Hebrew literature. In the halls of Zionist youth clubs, forbidden by some of our parents, we secretly worked to achieve our Zionist dream. At our gatherings, we expressed our distaste for our secular Polish education, where the Christian students expressed their hatred towards us. That was the beginning of the great human tragedy, which we did not entirely understand. Among the millions who perished, were the Jews of Skalat.

We incorporated these feelings in our daily lives along with the new ideals filling our souls, the dream of *Aliyah*. The charitable giving of Zionist youth in our city constituted an expression of our Zionist fervor – the Keren Kayemet L'Yisrael, the Permanent Fund of Israel, and the Keren HaYesod, the Foundation Fund, and all the Zionist parties – Beitar, the General Zionists, the Mizrachi – these were our contributions to the realization of *Aliyah* in the Land of Israel. The "Unification" gave its portion for this purpose, each one in its own way, for the common goal of building the Land of Israel.

I operated within and devoted most of my energy to Gordonia, the Pioneering Socialist Youth Movement, established in Poland in 1925, and named after A.D.

Gordon, whose writing and teaching on Labor Zionist settlement in Palestine formed the ideological foundation of the movement. Many of the children of Skalat were educated within the movement, and there they found a home for their love of Zion. Many who had a difficult childhood found that Gordonia offered them a source of creative joy.

It was clear to us that without the consciousness created by the movement, we would not realize our ideals. We organized summer settlements. We arranged conferences, to which we would flee at any opportunity. We were in need of much strength for the realization of our dream. The environment in Skalat did not always nurture our spirit or our aspirations. Jewish youths from petit–bourgeois homes went to agricultural *Hachsharah*, preparatory experiences needed to become tillers of the soil in the Land of Israel.

Hadassah Katz in the Midst of the Pupils of the "Gordonia" Movement

In the area surrounding Skalat, we organized a *Hachsharah* farm. For the enhancement of our preparation, we reached out to more distant places. We struggled and we prevailed. We bequeathed this heritage to our children, who stand guard over our freedom in the Motherland, Eretz Yisrael, to this very day.

May my words be a memorial candle for my parents, my brothers and sisters, and all the Jews of Skalat who marched in the paths of affliction and grief, both low and oppressed. I remember with heavy heart and revulsion those who, in order to save their own lives, led our loved ones to death and aided the Nazi murderers in their detestable work.

I will never forget my father's house, or my mother's Shabbat candles, her eyes filled with tears when she poured out her soul in prayer and supplication.

The First Group of Hebrew Speakers in Skalat

[Page 24]

The Pioneers of Agricultural Settlement in Skalat

By Moshe Marder

Only a few of the residents of our city made Aliyah to the Land of Israel as pioneers, with the intention of living there in a Kibbutz framework. Therefore, even in this small note, I will be able to mention almost all of those who lived to do so. Even now, some few survivors continue to arrive.

The Jewish youth in our city were wonderful, vital, alert, and filled with the deep spirit of Zionism. They belonged to parties and youth organizations. Each youth joined a group that matched his or her *weltanschauung*, world outlook.

Each young Zionist Skalater had the training and desire, not only to do physical labor for the sake of the Land of Israel, but also to realize his or her dream. More than once I asked myself why were there so few who had the power to join the pioneer movement, yet remained in Skalat, only to have their lives end in that awful hell?

If only there had been a leader with the authority and charisma who could have convinced those youngsters that the time to go had arrived. Such a person could have organized a mass exodus before it was too late. He might have pressed us to consider the reality of our lives in Skalat, to rise up and make Aliyah to Palestine, and to realize for ourselves all that we advocated. I am certain that many would have joined the pioneer camp, and would have made Aliyah despite the difficulties and barriers.

The initiative of the pioneer movement began to catch fire in our town in 1925. The Unified Groups were organized and began training for agricultural readiness. At the end of the agricultural season, they returned to Skalat to ready themselves for making Aliyah, but discovered all manner of obstacles blocking the path. There was a great financial crisis at the time, severe limits on Aliyah by the British Mandatory Government, and the lack of available travel certificates. Instead, there was a pervasive belief that it might take years until Aliyah would be permitted.

My brother, Israel, was the first person from Skalat to make Aliyah to the Land as a pioneer. After months of wandering through many places, with much suffering along the way, Israel and his companions from other towns in Galicia organized as a pioneer team, and succeeded in arriving and settling in Binyamin. At the time, there was a great crisis in Palestine so they found a temporary place. Later, they were forced to disperse to other locations, and my brother was able to get into the Betzalel Academy of Art and Design for his studies.

Shortly after that, the Greenfeld sisters arrived. The two of them were determined to live an agricultural village life, and joined the Alef Settlement. They found their place in the village of Bilu.

[Page 25]

The older sister, Salka, of blessed memory, lived and worked in the village until her death. The second sister, Branka, still lives there.

After several years, Malka Hecht, one of the graduates of Gordonia and the Unification, arrived. She found a place in the collective Shachariya in Migdal. Later, she went to Kibbutz Mizra in the Jezreel Valley. Currently, she resides in Haifa.

In 1932, Hadassah Katz made Aliyah. Her way was clear to her. She joined the first settlers of Hulda, and her task was to greet those who came after her. Hadassah still lives there along with her daughter, her sons, and many grandchildren.

Moshe Marder among the Graduating Level in the Gordonia Movement

Sarah Shpatziner, of the Gordonia Movement, made Aliyah to Palestine after continuous preparation, anticipation and unlimited patience. She joined Kibbutz Kiryat Anavim, and has been there since.

At about that same time, our friend Yitzchak Teller made Aliyah. He also joined the collective Kiryat Anavim, became a member for a short period, and for different reasons, he left and went to another place.

At the beginning of 1935, Tzilla Branzon arrived, and she and I joined Kibbutz Hulda.

A short time after this, Devorah Landsman of blessed memory and Leah'ka Ratzinshtein arrived in the Land. These two lovely young women entered the Ayanot Agricultural School, under the direction of Adah Maimon. At the conclusion of their studies, Devorah joined Kibbutz Ramat–David, and was active there in many areas. Leah'ka joined Kiryat Anavim. She lived there for many years. Today she is a resident of Jerusalem.

Shmuel Visilberg (Hermoni) and his lady friend, Tzipporah Katzur, made Aliyah and joined Kibbutz Hanita. Shmuel volunteered for the *Haganah* and in the battle on the mountains of Gilboa against the army of Qawukji, fell in defense of the homeland. His wife Tzipporah established a small agricultural farm in Even Yehudah. In recent years, she has devoted herself to the art of drawing. Many art lovers visited and enjoyed her large exhibit two years ago.

Tzvi Hermon, Shmulik's brother, made Aliyah through the Organization of Zionist Youth, though he was the only one of that movement to do so. He became a member of Kibbutz Usha.

The Aliyah was continual. In a short period of time, several more friends came. First, Pinchas Balbat Dagani, then Hannah Neuman and Berta Kleiner. Pinchas Dagani became a member of Kibbutz Ramat–David, active in many fields. In recent years, he has been involved in educational matters. Hannah Neuman joined Kibbutz Degania Alef, but because of the climatic hardships in the Jordan Valley, she was forced to move to the center of Israel. Today she is a resident of Tel–Aviv.

[Page 26]

Berta Kleiner stayed in Hulda for a short while. She worked in Ben–Shemen, and afterwards moved to Moshav Atarot. In the War of Independence, the community was conquered by Jordanian Legionnaires. The members subsequently reorganized and founded Benei–Atarot, where she lives with her family and continues her work.

And so our friends from Skalat, who came at different periods, connected their lives with agricultural and settlement communities.

Yehudah Oren, Leah'ka Yisraeli's brother, reached the Land via Vienna, and since then has been an active member of the farm S'deh–Nachum in the Beth–Shean Valley. Sarah Axelrod, too, is a member of Kibbutz S'deh–Nachum. Dov Engel lives in the settlement of Ain–Shemen. All of these people reached Palestine before the outbreak of the Second World War.

With the conclusions of the war, remnants of the survivors arrived, and a portion of them turned to working settlements. Mordechai Wisman and his sister Yocheved Sarid (Sarid means 'survivor') are both people of tradition and religion, the grandchildren of a *Shochet*, and they built their homes in the collective, Yavneh, and established families of activists in the life of the Kibbutz.

Ya'akov Zharkover, of blessed memory, came to visit me in Hulda, one day. He wanted advice from me. "I want to be a farmer," he said. He had been advised by others to acquire a farm on Moshav Avigdor. I blessed him for his intentions, and encouraged him to accept the suggestion. And that's what he did. He worked his farm side by side with his wife and children. But in recent years, fate was cruel to him. Illness kept him in his bed for a long time. A short time ago, he passed away.

Israel Wallach first immigrated to South America. From there he made Aliyah to Israel, and settled in K'far Argentina. Today he is a resident of Rishon L'Tzion.

Gershon Ratzenshtein Tarshish joined Kibbutz Ma'ale Hachamisha, and from there moved to Moshav Kfar Warburg. Currently, he serves as the coordinator of the farm's physical plant.

All told, a small contribution to the Jewish state, but a wonderful one.

[Page 27]

The Great Synagogue of Skalat

By Eliezer Rosenstock

It is very difficult for me to determine the date of the original founding of the Great Synagogue in Skalat. In the seventeenth century, Skalat Castle and the walls around it were rehabilitated, and so the foundation was laid for the market square by the Lithuanian Princess, Maria Shtzipionova. The Great Synagogue and the Catholic Church are mentioned in the documentation of that period, and they stood close together in that place which is remembered by every one of us. The fact that the Great Synagogue was built a short distance from the church demonstrates the freedoms enjoyed by the Jews of Skalat, because in that early period, Jews were generally not permitted to build synagogues in proximity to Catholic churches. The Synagogue was located within the city walls, protected from the outside, showing the good relations between the Jews and Christians of Skalat in the 1600's. Most of the Jews of the city lived in the area of the Synagogue.

It is difficult for me to say something about the appearance of the old synagogue, for in our days there did not remain a vestige of it. However in the 18th century, the Baal Shem Tov, in his glory and person, had officiated as Prayer Leader in the older synagogue. And so it became a tradition, in the course of many generations, prevalent among elders of the Hassidim in Skalat, that leading prayer in that synagogue was therefore considered a great honor.

A huge conflagration, at the end of the 19th century, destroyed part of the city of Skalat. This tremendous fire destroyed the area of the marketplace, and both the Great Synagogue and the Catholic Church went up in flames. The reconstruction of the Great Synagogue, which was recognizable to all of us, was accomplished shortly after.

The Poles entrusted the rebuilding of the Catholic Church to a renowned architect of the day. And if my memory does not mislead me, his name was Tarnowski. This man became famous because of the beautiful churches he had built. Among others, he planned the church named for Saint Elizabeth in Lvov/Lemberg, and the Parpilanic Church in Tarnopol. And it is interesting that the Jews entrusted this Catholic architect, after the Great Fire, with rebuilding the synagogue as well.

Tarnowski built the synagogue in the Gothic ecclesiastic style, but instead of a cross, he designed the upper portion of the building in the shape of the Latin letter "T." In the lower portion of the building, he added a row of structures, which served as a women's section and a synagogue for the men. In this way, he differentiated the synagogue from the church.

The interior of the synagogue was adorned by the artist Sak. He was from Salonika, but fled from there in his youth. He wandered for many years and finally settled in Podvolochisk. His grandson was the well–known photographer, Bryer, in Skalat. In the later period of the 1930's, when he was already 82 years old, the artist Sak rehabilitated his original adornments in the synagogue, which were distinguished by their attractive appeal. Additional details concerning our Great Synagogue are not known to me.

[Page 28]

If You Wish To Know

By Chaim Nachman Bialik

If you wish to know the fountain
From which your slain brethren drew
In days of evil, such strength, spiritual powers,
Going out joyous to face death, to extend their throats
To any burnished knife, to any impending axe,
To ascend to the pyre, to jump into the fire,
And with the "One" to die the death of martyrs.

And if you desire to know the fountain
From which your oppressed brethren drew

Between the Straits of Sheol and the pressures of the Pit,
Among scorpions – divine consolations,
Trust, power, patience, and the strength of iron
To bear the hand of any hardship,
A shoulder extended to suffer a life of degradation.

To suffer without end, without bound, without future.
O, my afflicted brother!
If you do not know all these,
Turn to the old, ancient Bet Midrash.

[Page 29]

In the streets of Skalat

In the Streets of Skalat

[Page 30]

The Beitar Movement in Skalat

By Monio Chaim Dickstein

The Beitar Movement in Skalat was founded in the year 1930 or 1931, relatively late, since the youth in Skalat was already 'taken' by other movements which preceded Beitar, such as Gordonia, the Zionist Youth and B'nei Akiva.

The founders of Beitar in Skalat were, according to their ranks: The Commander Ya'akov Zharkover, of blessed memory, the Assistant Commander Monio Dickstein, and the Secretary, Hofman. Ezra Samet was a member of the Command and also the librarian. I don't remember all of them, and it is probable that I have not mentioned the names of more central members.

In the first days of the movement, an apartment was rented which served as a club. It was in an alley that led to the house of the local Rabbi. Immediately, with the opening of the club, dozens of teen boys and girls streamed to it. "To me! Are there left yet any unaffiliated youth in Skalat?" (This was an imitation of the Biblical Verse: "*Mi La Shem Elai*!") It is logical that a portion of them came from other organizations, and another portion of them came after they heard 'living words' about the ambitions of Beitar – the establishment of a State of Israel immediately, and not just the slogans: "A *Dunam* and another *Dunam*," referring to a measurement of land, or "A Bi–National Home." The Beitar movement began to develop with giant steps, quickly becoming an important factor in the city.

The activities that were pursued were the study of the History of the People of Israel and of Zionist history. And we also trained with military exercises. Beitar preached the idea of the establishment of a State of Israel in our *own* days.

Joyfully, the idea took shape – "To teach the sons of Judah the Bow," to practice military self–defense and not be passive. It was not in vain, and it is only too bad that the head of Beitar did not live to see the realization of his philosophy.

Trembling and profound sadness afflict me when I think of the youth of Skalat in Beitar, healthy in body and spirit, who were uprooted from our nation in gruesome deaths.

May their memory be blessed!

[Page 31]

The Husiatyn Hassidim in Skalat

By Tunka Pickholz

Even though our town was small, there were many Hassidim in it, divided among the Courts of *Admorim*, which is an acronym for Hassidic Rabbis for *Adoneinu, Moreinu, ve Rabeinu*, namely of Husiatyn Hassidim, Chortkov Hassidim, Vizhnitz Hassidim, and others. The most famous Admor Rebbe in our city was the Husiatyn Rebbe. And indeed, he had many admirers in Skalat.

Thanks to my father, who was one of the Hassidic followers of the Husiatyn Rebbe, I have preserved many memories and impressions of the Hassidic milieu of those days.

A prosperous Jew in Skalat, Joseph Milgrom, owner of the flourmill, and a great admirer of the Rebbe of Husiatyn, was accustomed to hosting the Rebbe in his home. Milgrom lived in a large house at the edge of the town. The house bordered on a garden whose ground was slanted, creating a kind of natural slope. At the edge of the garden, Milgrom set up a wooden hut – a 'schloss,' a stately, little safehouse. Behind the schloss there were pastures, fields and a flowing creek.

An internal partition divided the schloss into two sections. In the small section, the Rebbe of Husiatyn prayed. Generally, the Rebbe stayed there by himself.

The second section included the central hall of the hut, which resembled a prayer room. Tables and benches were arranged around the walls. Similarly, a kind of step, attached to the wall, arose in order to enable the Hassidim to observe the radiance of the Rebbe's face at the time of prayer.

The Rebbe would arrive in Skalat near the holiday of Shavuot, and would spend six to eight weeks. Normally, he resided in Vienna. His fixed visit in Skalat was apparently connected to his pilgrimage to the grave of his father, who was buried in Husiatyn. His visit became an event for all the Jews of the city. They all went out into the streets to greet him. A delegation of chosen Hassidim went out in carriages to greet the Rebbe outside the town. In front of the house where the Rebbe stayed, his followers arranged themselves in two rows, and greeted him with a festive "*Shalom Aleichem!*" Just a glimpse of the Rebbe sufficed in order to enflame the multitudes who believed in the sanctity of the man.

During this period, hundreds of Hassidim, from all corners of Poland, and especially from Galicia, streamed into Skalat. Hotels, lodging places and even private apartments could not contain all the people who arrived. The city seethed with life. In the courtyard of the schloss, multitudes sang and danced, especially on the holiday and on Shabbat.

They revered the Rebbe as holy, and awarded him royal honors. The Rebbe excelled in his great knowledge, whether in medical matters or legal ones. The simple Jews of Skalat had an address and someone to whom to turn to seek advice, particularly at a time of distress. The Rebbe was accustomed to directing sick people who knocked on his door to doctors famous in his generation. It happened also that non–Jewish Poles would turn to the Rebbe and seek advice from him as well.

[Page 32]

The period of the Rebbe's stay in the city temporarily improved the economic situation. More than a few families waited for his visit with anticipation. Lodging the guests in their homes made an important contribution to the improvement of the town's economic health. I remember Hassidim from Zhuslov and Karkov who lodged in our house. In late hours of the night, they would sit together, argue over subjects of faith and religion, and would tell many stories concerning the greatness of the Rebbe. The meeting between every Hassid and the Rebbe would become the central experience in the life of the believing man.

Before leaving Europe, the Rebbe traveled around advising Jews to flee and go to Palestine. He was known to say, "Whoever has some sense should flee while he can – even in his slippers!" He understood what was about to happen and did his best to alert the people. The Rebbe of Husiatyn made Aliyah to the Land of Israel in 1937 at the age of 80. He died at 92. His grave is in the old cemetery in Tiberias among the students of the Baal Shem Tov.

Husiatyn Hassidim in Skalat

[Page 33]

The Russians 'Liberate' Skalat in 1939

By Ben–Zion Benshalom

The following is a chapter taken from Ben–Zion Benshalom's book, <u>In the Storm in the Days of the Whirlwind</u>, by Masada Press. The author, a refugee from Western Poland, fled from the advance of the German army, eastward, at the outbreak of the Second World War, and in the course of his wanderings, passed through Skalat.

SKALAT. I stop a young Jewish man and ask him how the mood is in this place. He tells me that the people of Skalat still live normal lives. Several times, planes appeared in the skies of the town, but there were no bombings. Thousands of refugees have already flooded the town and the surrounding villages. There are new camps of refugees arriving every day. Vanguard German squads are not far away at all, and I hear the thunder of muted artillery, but for the time being, there is complete quiet in the place, and a large army is encamping here. There is no lack of food, because the environment is blessed by God and overflows with everything good. The young man advises me to remain here and wait until the situation is clarified. "You've already reached the border," he adds. "Where will you flee to now?"

The town is beautiful, rich in vegetation and very charming. Its houses are beautiful. Its streets are clean. In its streets, men, women and children move in groups. However, we see that the town is full of refugees, and that there is no room left. I meet many refugees from my own town, and they too advise that I should remain with them in this lovely place. I accept their opinion and go to the office of *Satrusta*, the municipal officer, to seek permission to remain in the town. The *Satrusta* is not there. With difficulty, I manage to get an interview with his assistant. I present him with my request. He looks at me and sees that I am broken and exhausted, and that it is hard for me to continue traveling. He examines my papers and asks all kinds of questions, and then finally informs me that he is unable to permit me to remain in the town. There is no room. All the apartments are full. I tell him that I have found friends who want to give me lodging, and that my wounded legs are in need of medical treatment, but he, for his part, says, "Impossible, there is no room." Polish refugees receive permission to stay in a few minutes, and I exit in disappointment, and boiling with anger. When I leave, I decide I will remain without permission!

The sun is setting and a sweet, delicate, glimmering radiance bathes the town. One by one stars are lit in the sky. Evening comes – a late summer evening, warm and beautiful. I stroll in Skalat's darkening streets and enjoy the respite I had so needed, and that I had not known since the day of the outbreak of the war. The night covers street after street. The town gradually settles into darkness. Afterwards, I sit with my acquaintances at the lodging house, and we take our time in conversation. From the time they arrived in town a few days ago, they dwelled in relative peace. They could hear radio broadcasts, while I struggled, pursued by bombs day and night. They tell me that the situation is gradually improving. The Germans indeed reached as far as Lvov, but they were stopped there. Lvov is being defended courageously. Near Warsaw, the battles are fierce and the casualties are many. The Germans completely control the airspace of Poland, and their planes bomb the entire country, but when battles are actually waged on the ground, the Germans are repulsed. The positions of the Poles are gradually being strengthened and a front is being created. Many Polish divisions are concentrated in the eastern region of the country, and a great conflict is going to erupt there. We sit and speak about events of recent days and about our families, whom we sent away from our hometowns before the war broke out, and we do not know how far they traveled or where they are at the moment. We drink tea. My heart is full of yearning for the days of tranquility which are now gone. Someone mentions the names of acquaintances and friends who were killed or captured, and expresses the hope that we will not suffer in vain, and not shed blood. Our hope is that *Amalek* will be overthrown and evil will pass away entirely.

[Page 34]

The moments pass. The hour is late. People go off to sleep. I receive a bed. A bed? After many nights which have passed for me without normal sleep–a real bed! With the aid of two roommates, also refugees from Western Poland, I remove the torn shoes from my injured feet. After that, I strip off my clothes. It has been about 10 days that I have not removed them. At last, I lay in the bed. My eyes close, and against my will, I fall asleep immediately.

In the dead of night, I awaken. I hear my roommates conversing in whispers. I immediately feel that something has happened. In the room – darkness. Nevertheless, I see that my companions are standing near one of the walls, and I hear them whispering. What are they doing there? I strengthen my eyes. Yes. I am not mistaken. Two of them are standing next to one of the walls of the room, with their ears glued to the wall. They stand silently, listening, whispering from time to time. I call out to them. They approach my bed and tell me in a whisper that something has happened, but they don't know what. A Polish sergeant was staying in the neighboring room with members of his household. A few minutes ago, a military squad knocked on his door to awaken him. My companions were standing near the wall next to the sergeant's room, listening.

We decide we should get dressed. We dress in the darkness. In the adjoining apartment, someone is wailing quietly. We strain our ears to listen. The sergeant says goodbye to his wife and after several minutes, we hear the muted banging of the door, which signifies that the sergeant has left the house. We hear the sound of his footsteps in the garden and in the silent street. And beyond the wall, his wife is wailing softly. What has happened? We must absolutely have information! We knock on the wall. She approaches. The wall is thin and our conversation is carried on without difficulty. We asked what happened? What is she crying about? Where was the sergeant summoned to? For a short time, she is crying and finally we hear, "Poland has fallen. There is no escape – everything is lost – there is nowhere to run. The end has come!" "But what happened?" we shout, excited and panicked. She is silent for several minutes. Afterwards, she whispers, "The Russians have crossed the border."

The Russians have crossed the border! The report astounded us. Even after a pact had been concluded between Germany and Russia, no one believed that the Russians would attack the Poles from the rear. And now it has come true!

[Page 35]

Everyone understands that everything is lost, that the Polish army will not hold out in these pincers, between the German hammer and the Russian anvil, and the question arises, "What is there to do?" To flee? Where to flee? The time is two thirty in the morning. Before dawn breaks, the Russians will be in town. We come to the conclusion that there is nowhere to flee, and that there is no reason for flight at this moment, because everything is lost. We sit in the dark room and wait for morning.

With morning, the town slowly awakens from its deep slumber. We go out to the garden, all of whose flowers and grasses are bathed in morning dew. The east is totally aflame. The last stars disappear, one by one. A fresh morning breeze rustles in the adjoining gardens. How beautiful the town is, in its dawn garments, when all of its houses and streets are bathed in fresh morning dew dripping from all the roofs and from all the trees. It is early, before the pampered veil of radiance has disappeared, when grayness and pink occur mixed together. Doors and windows are opened and the early risers appear in the streets. The knowledge of a Russian arrival spreads with the speed of lightning. People begin to gather and to argue. Someone casts doubt on the truth of the report, and argues that it couldn't have happened, but here come people who heard the radio declaration of Molotov last night. "And the Non–Aggression Pact between Poland and Russia – what will become of it?" they ask. And the answer is? "Molotov announced that he is abrogating that pact."

Suddenly there are explosive sounds, which come one after another. The townspeople think that a battle is raging on the outskirts of the town, and they hurry to hide in their gardens and cellars. Moments of silence. And again explosive sounds. After a few moments, it becomes clear that there is not any battle. The rabble has fallen on the storehouses of the Polish army, full of clothing, food and commodities. The soldiers guarding the storehouses throw hand–grenades but the crowds are eager for spoil. They emerge from the cellars and other hiding places, gather in the streets, pray without end and wait.

Eight hours later, an acquaintance comes and reveals to us with a whisper that there is a possibility of escape before the Russians enter the town. The Romanian border is open and there are still places available on buses, which will leave for

Romania in just a few minutes. The buses are waiting in one of the alleys, which is furthest from the center of the town. And if we hurry, we can yet obtain seats. We take our bundles and turn to go to the alley where the buses are parked. We arrive in time. There is still room. We sit on the buses and wait. Hearts pound. Will we really be able to escape? Will we really be in Romania in a few hours? The drivers believe that the way is still clear, and that we will succeed.

But why aren't we traveling? A quarter of an hour passes. Another quarter of an hour and we are still sitting on the buses and waiting. The buses are full. Poles and Jews. Young and old. Women and men, and even children, are gathered together. All of us are excited. Will we succeed? And why are we waiting? I get out to find the reason for the wait. It becomes clear that the police are preventing it. About ten policemen have gathered near the bus, and they firmly request that we make a place available for them as well. If their request is not honored, they will not permit us to travel. Places are cleared for them. The buses have been filled from one end to the other and perhaps even more than that, but they do not move from their spots. The police order that we wait. The poor policemen! They are without plans. They don't know what they should do. They also want to escape to Romania, but they are afraid to flee. The police have been undone. There is no command and no commander, so how can they even know what they should do. What is permitted, and what is forbidden? They attempt to phone the police commander in the large neighboring city, but they are unable to reach him because the connection is severed. Without a plan, they stand near the buses. They do not dare to join us, and they do not permit us to travel without them.

[Page 36]

The policemen! How different are their faces and their postures during these few hours! Even their height seems lowered. Their embroidered garments still shine and sparkle, and their weapons are still in their hands, but they are poor and forlorn, and all of their radiance has left them. In one day, all of their wisdom has been confounded and has dissipated, after having stood by them for many years. How clever were those discerning ones to see every Jewish store whose owners had locked up a few minutes after the appointed time, and not to see the Polish stores open a half hour or three quarters of an hour after the appointed time had passed! How did they know how to calculate the time in the days of riots and pogroms, and to appear always at the correct and appropriate moment in order to manage to arrest the *victims*! Now they surround the *Zhids* for whom they had shown contempt and had persecuted just yesterday, to consult with them because, at this moment, they tend to believe that the *Zhids* know everything.

Suddenly, the air is full of the roar of airplanes. The people rush to disperse and hide. Flights of airplanes appear in the sky and quickly disappear. This time, the roar is not similar to the roaring of the German bombers, which we heard for sixteen days from morning to evening. This time, the roar is weaker and the planes are faster. We understand immediately that these planes are Russian and that they are not bombers. They move about the skies of the town, coming and going. The civilians quickly become accustomed, do not get excited, and do not hide. But the policemen run from time to time to the nearby garden and lie prone there in the grass or under the bushes and return dusty and filthy after the planes have disappeared. Oh, my heart to the policemen! All their bravery and courage has deserted them.

The hours pass and we sit on the buses and wait. We become angry and get agitated, but we do not benefit from this at all. The policemen send agent after agent to all kinds of offices, and the agents go and return and go again, and we wait. Noon. One o'clock. Finally, the policemen decide to travel. The driver grasps the steering wheel, the autos move. But at this moment, one of the agents who had been sent to scout out the way on which we intend to escape, returns and announces that all of the roads have already been captured by the Russians. We get off the buses and begin to disperse. A Polish official severely curses the policemen and they stand mournfully and shamefully. They hear the agent's reproaches and do not say a word.

Afternoon. The town is feverish. All the stores have been locked and the streets are full. The Polish army has left, but the Russian army has not come. There is not even a single soldier in town. The Ukrainian peasants from the nearby villages come to the town equipped with sacks and clubs. They walk about the streets and look at everything while their eyes express hatred and anger. Someone spread the rumor that the Russians would not come, but the Germans would, and the rumor passed from street to street. Jews were walking about worried and frightened. The Jewish youths are speaking of the need to establish self–defense, because there's no way of knowing what will happen at night. The looks of the peasants going around the streets of the town do not prophesy good things.

[Page 37]

Opposite the Post Office building stands a Polish worker who says that the Germans are gradually coming nearer. He swears that he has seen them with his own eyes, two hours ago, at some distance from the town, along with several German tanks. People ask him if he is not mistaken, and maybe he saw Russian tanks. No, no! He saw German tanks; a small Nazi flag was flying over every tank. By the life of my head! They gather around him, hear his story, and their hearts are full of panic and trembling. Whom to believe, and what to think? Who has come? The Germans or the Russians? My heart tells me that the story of the Polish worker, about German tanks that he saw outside the town, is a complete falsehood. Indeed, the Germans are not far away, but according to the information received from the radio, it seems reasonable that the Russians are advancing with the consent of the Germans, who are evacuating the Eastern region, which had already been conquered by them. There is no reason, therefore, to imagine that the town, which sits near the Russian border, would be conquered by the Germans. This, reason argues, must be correct. But the heart is suspicious nonetheless.

Pioneer Youth Reports about a Member who is Making Aliyah to the Land

Alarming reports begin to arrive from adjoining villages. It seems that the Ukrainian peasants are preparing for something. At this moment, no government exists in Skalat or in the vicinity. In the Ukrainian villages, they think that 'the strap has been undone,' and that the time has come to wreak havoc against both the Poles and the Jews. The peasants are convinced that the Germans are coming. They believe it because they desire it. One of the peasants, with whom I had the opportunity to strike up a conversation, explains to me that there is nothing like the Germans for honesty and for a fair attitude toward the population. They are mighty and righteous and they are friends of Truth to the Ukrainians. He continued that his entire village prays for the coming of the Germans, but is afraid of the Russians, that they will rob the peasant of his land and everything he has, that they will hand it over to the *Zhidiks* – the word the peasant uses for us. Jews managed to gather around him while we conversed – worried and fearful, but with the double worry about those same peasants who walk about in the town laughing but silent. Jews gather together in groups to share news. They confer and decide to spend the night in camps. The residents of several houses will gather in one apartment and will stand watch in shifts.

[Page 38]

The sun sets. The western sky is aflame. Evening comes slowly, a delicate, lovely evening of the beginning of Autumn. The famous autumn of Poland arrives with its sweet warmth and with an outpouring of golden radiance. Choruses of stars twinkle in the deep firmament and the sickle of the crescent–moon appears over the town. Skalat is covered with a garment of tender darkness. The streets of the town radiate light. The period of darkness has ended. The inhabitants, who for three weeks have not seen an illuminated street, stroll at their pleasure and move in the streets. Even the mood begins to change favorably. People come who testify that they saw squads of Russian tanks at a distance of several kilometers from the town. It seems reasonable that the Russians directed the bulk of their armies toward the large cities, and that the town situated on the side was automatically captured. The inhabitants, whose souls had been depressed by the specter of German occupation for the entire day, breathe a sigh of relief, not only Jews, but also the Poles. The Ukrainians generally are not satisfied. They looked forward to Hitler. After the feverish hours of the day, the evening brings a bit of calm. The man, dusty from the street, says, "It is good that the Russians are coming – it is good that we have been saved from the hands of the Germans..."

The night is heaped with terrors and much fear. Shots and distant explosions shook the silent city. We did not close our eyes. We sat in groups, listened and waited. Where are they shooting? And who is shooting? All kinds of theories were expressed. But the prevailing opinion was that something was happening in one of the nearby villages. We sat. We heard the shots and waited for the morning, with impatience and nervousness. The hours cranked by lazily. It seemed as if the night would never end, the moments advancing with excessive slowness in order to antagonize and provoke us. The night is expiring. The stars are covered with a thin and airy veil of mist. A slight wind blows through the garden and rustles the dawn. The sound of shots disappears. There is much silence all around. The sky becomes gray. The east brings dawn. Morning has arrived. The news comes to us that in one of the neighboring places our Jewish brothers and sisters, who dwell among the Ukrainians, experienced a very hard night.

With morning, our neighbor, the sergeant, returns. How much has he changed during a few hours! His face is as white as lime. Despair is in his eyes. At first he avoids us and is silent, but finally he begins to speak with his voice trembling and tears in his eyes. Poland is lost – the fault of our officials and our generals. What a disgrace, what a reproach! The officers fled and advised us to disperse. I am a soldier and I certainly know that sometimes one is forced to surrender – but does one disarm this way? through panic and confusion? When an officer flees, does he say to his soldiers, "Do what your heart desires?" Do army men surrender this way? Is this why there was chatter for years about military honor and bravery? Where did all these officers and cadets go? Who permitted them to flee like mice, and to leave us like a flock without a shepherd? Why did they not at least assemble us and explain to us that we were compelled to surrender? And why did they not arrange the surrender through order and honor? Do what your heart desires! May darkness take them! They received salaries. They wore shining uniforms. They spoke haughtily – but finally escaped like contemptible cowards. They didn't even know how to surrender honorably. Poland is lost. Tear after tear falls on the sergeant's cheeks. We comfort him. Poland will arise. In revival, a nation that dwells on its land will not perish. He listens, but does not accept consolations.

[Page 39]

After a few hours, the first red flags appear in the town. They are raised above the municipal and governmental buildings and offices, and a large crowd gathers and looks on. A group of youths performs a demonstration. Two *minyanim* pass through the streets and shout, "Long live Stalin! Long live Voroshilov!" The local Communists take government into their own hands and organize a militia. A Jewish youth goes around in the streets and announces that he was sent by the command of the Red

Army to organize the Soviet government in the town. He appeals to the citizens and requests that they stand at his right hand. He explains that the Russian army has come to the aid of Poland, and then ends his speech with the words, "Long live independent Poland!" The people hear this and it's obvious that they do not believe it, except for a few fools. In the afternoon, Russian tanks and several trucks full of soldiers arrive in town. The people who are standing on sidewalks look at those coming out of curiosity, but without enthusiasm. The Russians sing melodious songs and, with their caps waving in their hands, greet the inhabitants of the town who have, with handkerchiefs and hats, returned greetings to the arrivals. Some strike up conversations with the soldiers, and they announce to all of us that they are going out to fight against Hitler. We ask with surprise, "Against whom?" And again they announce, "Against Hitler! Against Germany!"

SKALAT. Days of Transition. Days of Changes. A regime goes out and a regime comes in. Glimmers. A government ends and a government is born. The flags of Poland were lowered, and the red flags were waved. The Polish eagle came down from its greatness, and the Soviet star inherited its place. Those above were below, and those below were on top. The Polish policemen, the fear of the Ukrainian village and the Jewish street are confined to barracks, and urchins of the Children of Israel go about the streets with a red ribbon adorning them, and their pride is on the rifle. The Polish officials, rulers of the town and its guarantors, have fled. And of those remaining, their radiance has departed and their honor has flown away. A Ukrainian serves in the position of mayor, and he publishes announcements and issues orders.

Days of Transition. There is confusion and disorder. You want to – you open your store. You don't want to – the store is closed. The peasant wishes – you can buy his produce with Polish gold coins (Zlotys). If you don't wish – you are obliged to pay him with salt, with gasoline, with matches, with sugar. The fools still believe that the Red Army has come to help Poland, and that the area of the Russian conquest will be returned to the Poles after Hitler is defeated. Consequently, the Soviet regime will not be instituted in the area of conquest, and the orders of life will not change. Someone floats rumors such as these, and the fools believe, but anyone who has eyes and a brain understands that there are 'no bears and no forest,' that they did not intend help, and that they did not think of conquest as temporary.

[Page 40]

Daughters of the Akiva Movement in Skalat

An Atmosphere of 'Between Sessions.' The streets are full of peasants who come to the town equipped with sacks and armed with curses and clubs. They have heard that it will be possible to 'disappear' a bit and to enjoy some anarchy. They go about disappointed. The Jews act naively and ask, "What are these sacks which you have brought?" The peasants blush and stammer about sugar and salt they had hoped to buy. Sugar and salt. Russian soldiers and officers circulate in the streets of the town and people gather around them. The soldiers tell of wonders and miracles in the Soviet Union. The legislation of Stalin shines for all the nations of the Soviet Union, and contributes a protective wall for all of them. Everyone receives employment and can support himself honorably. It is possible to buy food and clothing most inexpensively, and without any limitations.

The economic and cultural situation of the Soviet Union is excellent, and all the states' populations are happy and satisfied. If you are not lazy, and you have the desire to roam the streets and linger a few minutes near any group, which gathers around the soldier, you will be surprised and astounded. You will imagine that you have not heard the stories of a few soldiers but the story of one soldier. The same words, the same phraseology, the same details, the same tone. By my life! These Russians – either all of them think according to one template, and their thought is collective, or someone dictated to them exactly what they have to say and how they are required to say it.

[Page 41]

Days of Vacation. Regarding the stores, a few of them are closed but most of them are open. But in the open ones, there is almost no merchandise. They say that tomorrow or the day after tomorrow, the closed ones will be opened, and their owners will be compelled to sell the stock. They say that tomorrow, or the day after, 'normal' life will begin, and everything will return to business as usual. For the time being, Jews stroll in the streets and circulate in endless conversations and smoke cigarette after cigarette. Days of transition, days of anticipation. A regime dies and a regime comes in. What was ended is finished. The present? Woe to this present! What is hidden in the bosom of the future? What?

In the nights, a deadly silence rules the town. After eight o'clock, it is forbidden to go out into the street. The militia is very strict about the hours of curfew, and one who goes out onto the street after eight returns mostly in the morning, after he has spent the night in jail. We sit in our rooms or in the garden around the houses, bring up memories, and chatter endlessly. In the sky, stars burn. And in the desolate streets the men of the militia stroll. In the villages surrounding the town, there is much ferment, and every night 'miracles' occur there. The peasants relate to the new authorities with suspicion, and there is reason to believe that they are not happy. On one of the nights, a doctor was summoned to one of the villages. The Communist propagandist, who had traveled to the village, had been beaten murderously by the peasants. Multitudes of the Ukrainians are dissatisfied. They hate the Poles, but they did not look forward to the Russians. A different 'redemption' was promised to them and their hopes for 'Redeemers' were so close. They heard the thunder of their artillery and listened to the humming of the airplanes. And somehow a strange error occurred. The liturgies were switched, ' and the cards were mixed up. They had waited for the Germans, but the Russians had come. Someone had deceived them and mocked them. So they gnashed their teeth and their glances were dark. Their wrath blazed and their lust for revenge enflamed and agitated them.

Every tongue speaks in praise of the Russian soldiers. They are good. They are courteous. They are merciful. Those who remember the army of Czarist Russia say that the Russian soldier has changed his skin. He will not curse, will not get drunk and won't molest the girls. He knows how to read and write, and his manners are good. His uniform is plain but clean. In the Russian army, Jews constitute a large percentage. The young Jewish men have already managed to assimilate completely. They will speak Russian, but will not understand Yiddish. The Jewish way of life – who has mentioned it? 'The old ones' have not managed to forget everything. They speak Yiddish, and childhood study still percolates in them. At the close of Yom Kippur, a high officer greets and blesses the owner of a restaurant in which he will eat dinner. "May you be blessed with a good year! Next Year in Jerusalem!" And on the first day of *Sukkoth*, a group of soldiers, strolling in the streets, greets Jews returning from *shul* with shouts of, "A good Yom Tov, Jews! A good Yom Tov!"

Are the Jews happy? Are they satisfied? The Jewish Communists emerged from their hiding places and there is no limit to their happiness. Just as there is no limit to the joy of the Polish and Ukrainian Communists. When the Russians entered suddenly, to the astonishment of all the people who were convinced that the Germans were coming, the Jews rejoiced greatly at the first moment. The Poles also rejoiced, and only the Ukrainians were sorry. But the Communists were few in the town, and the

[Page 42]

first moments passed quickly. Was the Jewish population of the town happy? Was it satisfied? No and no! In his innermost thoughts, a simple Jew asks, "What's your opinion? Are we lost forever? Is there hope that we will yet see life, and yet be human beings?" And a Jewish woman wipes her tears and says, "I will not send my children to school where they will yet learn that there is no God but Stalin, and that Voroshilov and Molotov are his prophets." The Jews of the town suffered not a little in the days of the rule of the Poles. Polish officialdom persecuted them, suppressed them, expelled them from their positions and from their occupations, and related to them with hostility and contempt. The truth is that the Polish administration in the border regions did not excel in excessive political insight, was not blessed with broadmindedness or with the talent to accommodate a different future for Poland.

A story is told about a Polish military officer who sent a car to Tarnopol without any concern for the cost of fuel or the effort in order to buy an item in a Christian owned store, even though it was available for purchase in a Jewish owned store in the town. The cost of fuel amounted to much more than the price of the article that was purchased. The story showed the deep animus of our Polish neighbors against the Jewish townsfolk.

And there is the tale of officials who invited Jews to their offices and said to them, "If you do not fulfill our demand and contribute such and such to a Polish cause, you must surely know that you dwell in a border region, and we have the power to expel you from here on the basis of the 'Law of the Border Regions.' The Jews of the town suffered in the days of the rule of the Poles. There was no joy and no satisfaction in the stories of the wonders of the Russian soldiers, as they were just more made-up stories leaving the future painted in dark colors. The Jewish townspeople think about their future with much worry, especially related to trade, their main livelihood in the conquered areas, which would be destroyed. Without trade, Jewish merchants would become superfluous persons, hungry for bread, for whose lives there would be no reason. The possibilities of getting settled in other branches of livelihood would be very limited. The children would no longer be able to be educated in Torah, and without Judaism, they would be no better than the Goyim. No satisfaction, and no tranquility. The faces express worry and the glances show trembling. How would life get along? What would the near future bring? Days without deeds and nights without sleep. They turn from side to side. Their worries would not allow them to fall asleep. Those would be days of transition and changes, days of anticipation and trembling.

The stores have all been opened. Everyone buys, Russian soldiers, refugees, inhabitants of the town, peasants. The ravenousness of buying and hoarding has seized people. It is not important what they buy. The main thing is to buy! Shirts, suits, garments for the peasants, shoes, suitcases, sugar, flour, tea, everything. And they buy. In another few days, the entire stock will be sold and the stores will be empty. Then it will be impossible to acquire new merchandise – something that every merchant understands. Prices will keep going up. There is already a shortage of certain commodities. The Russian soldiers comfort the people, don't worry, everything will be in abundance. No coffee? There will be coffee! No sugar? There will be sugar!

In the first week, the new authorities would publish their announcements in three languages,

[Page 43]

Ukrainian, Polish and Yiddish. After that, only Ukrainian and Polish. Now the Jewish Communists are already content with only Ukrainian and Polish. The Jewish Communists rejoice and explain, which Jew doesn't understand Ukrainian or Polish?

In the town, there are several owners of farms, Jews and Christians. The government performs judgments against them. They arrest the owners. They show them contempt. All of their property has been confiscated. And if you ask which of them did they especially torment, and who was chosen to be the scapegoat? Any one of the inhabitants of the city, Jew as well as Christian, would answer, so–and–so the Jewish owner of the farm. Anti–Semitism? God Forbid! The reason is very simple. They try not to anger the Polish public. They do not take into account the Jewish public. And what is the fate of the farms that have been confiscated? Have they been turned into collective farms? God forbid. They divided the horses and cows among the peasants. And the mighty stock of grain and silage vegetables and other food commodities, which were found in the farms? They were crushed and disappeared in a few days. Farms fly away. Farms arrayed in exemplary fashion, gloriously destroyed in one day.

The Grina Kloiz –the Green Chapel Study House – in Skalat

[Page 44]

How the Judenrat was Established in Skalat

By Eliezer Degan

The first pogrom in Skalat, the day after the conquest of the city by the Germans, was held at the initiative of the Ukrainian intelligentsia. Four hundred of our residents were put to death by the Germans and the barbaric, bloodthirsty Ukrainians. The permission to kill Jews was given only for one day, but the human beasts, the Ukrainians, continued in their rampage in a partisan manner together with the special commando groups of the regular German army. With a variety of excuses – the search for hidden weaponry, army deserters – they conducted searches in the houses of Jews, and many of the residents of our city perished in this rampage. It is fitting to remark that all of the calamities, which descended on our heads in the first week of the city's conquest, primarily affected the men. Only a few women were affected.

At this opportunity, it is incumbent upon me to mention a good and humane act, which an anonymous German soldier carried out. Early in the morning, on the first day of the pogrom, this German soldier entered our house and announced, "Today a great pogrom will be perpetrated in your city in accordance with the demand of the Ukrainians, who are known for their cruelty. My advice to you is to hide until the anger passes." In his presence, we were able to mask off a side room in the apartment by moving a cabinet, which hid the entrance door. In that masked off room we hid – my father, of blessed memory, may the Lord avenge his blood, and I – while the German remained at his post in the apartment for two consecutive hours. When the Ukrainian murderers entered and searched for men in the apartment, he answered them in German, "Everyone is gone!"

One day, in that first week of the conquest, a German soldier, a commando, entered our apartment to search for weapons and fugitives. In the course of carrying out the search, he got up on a chair, looked at the cabinet, and to his surprise saw the door behind the cabinet. A cry of joy burst from his mouth. He was convinced that he had indeed found a rare treasure. The intervention of my older dear sister, Chaya, may the Lord avenge her blood, saved us, and we fled to the cattle barn, which was behind the house. At that instant, Yarmyszyn, a famous Ukrainian murderer, who had been chosen by the Germans to serve as the acting mayor of the city, passed by and noticed us. He was furious that we were still alive, and he did not cease reviling and cursing us.

For two hours, we sat in the attic of the barn. Suddenly, my sister Chaya of blessed memory, appeared, with a frightening message. The Ukrainian, from whom we had escaped, was sitting in our apartment and wanted to talk with us. He promised that no evil would befall us. Though we did not have much confidence that he would keep his word, we decided to come down and hear what he had to say. We were terrified, but he attempted to calm us. He presented himself as appointed mayor, and by the power of his office, he told us that we had until noon the next day to supply him with 150 workers to carry out certain tasks. He held out the threat of a second pogrom, if the requested workers did not appear at the designated hour near city hall.

[Page 45]

Horrified and seized with fear, we went out to notify the Jews of the community. We were received with cold stares. No one believed the word of the Ukrainian, who purported to be the mayor. The suspicion was that a trap was being laid. The next day no one came except for the two of us – my father of blessed memory, and me. At the appointed hour, the Ukrainian appeared and was astonished. "Where are the workers?" he shouted. We attempted to explain, but without success.

Yarmyszyn was angry and infuriated. He summoned the police and gave them an order to bring 300 men. In accordance with his order, they went from house to house and took all the men they could find. They assembled the men near the city hall. From there they brought us to the brickworks on the road to Horodnitza, gave us shovels, and commanded us to dig a pit. It was clear to us for whom it was intended.

Suddenly, two police officers appeared. They had been sent with instructions to bring us back to the city. We were brought to the Strustva building, divided into two groups, and told to clean the mounds of trash and papers in and around the building. The Russians, who had recently retreated from Skalat, had left all the garbage.

Before completing the cleanup, my father (z"l) and I were brought to the mayor's office. The Ukrainian mayor greeted us with rebukes and reprimands. He blamed us for not forcing the others to show up. According to him, it was a miracle that we were still alive, his words. This was not our fault we explained. It was the fault of the Germans who demanded us to perform labor, in order to prepare residential places for the Senior German Command who were about to arrive.

The mayor, with the power of his authority, demanded that we supply workers every day for different tasks. He promised a wage for the workers. Skilled workers were especially in demand, carpenters, locksmiths, and others. We were harnessed for labor, and we prepared a list of members of the community, according to the places of their residence, so we could be sure that all of them would bear the yoke, which the authorities had imposed. This organization of labor functioned efficiently, and the men received a wage. In the event that a man did not turn out, he hired another in his stead. When the demands of the Germans steadily increased, and it was not in our power to bear the burden by ourselves, we turned to a neighbor, Itsi Shtekel, and we asked him for his help in organizing the daily departure for labor. He worked with us, and the three of us continued in our labors for a full month, to the satisfaction of all the parties.

Suddenly, the skies darkened. The Germans imposed a random contribution upon the community. A large sum was demanded. It was compulsory to supply the money in a set time period. But this task was beyond the power of individual people. We called a general meeting of all the people of the community, in which a majority participated. At this meeting, the *Judenrat* was chosen. Nirler was elected as chairman. In this position, Nirler was saddled with an impossible task – the collection of funds to pay the ransom, which had been imposed upon us. To achieve the goal, he used different means, not always refined. He overcame every single obstacle until he succeeded in raising the sum demanded of the community, and even more, well before the deadline set by the Germans. That is the only praise that one can assign to him. To his credit, Nirler succeeded in preventing a new pogrom in the city.

[Page 46]

In the course of time, the Judenrat took a more inflexible stance. Their extortion methods were forceful. The local policemen – the German Schutzpolizei, the Ukrainian police, the Kripo criminal police all came and made various demands, and it was incumbent upon the Judenrat to supply them.

Three individuals in particular helped to develop the procedures of the Judenrat: Nirler, chairman of the Judenrat, the attorney Muni Lampert, responsible for the labor office in the Judenrat, and Zimmer, who functioned as liaison between the Judenrat and the head of the Gestapo in Tarnopol. Likewise very influential were Dr. Brier, head of the Jewish Police and a few advisers who acted as Nirler's right hand men. All these formed the policy of the Judenrat and its day–to–day operations.

My conscience obligates me to emphasize that the greatest failure of the Judenrat was in the matter of the "Contingent," the agreement of the Judenrat to present the Germans a list of people who were to be executed arouses repugnance and is worthy of public condemnation. I will never be able to understand the explanation for this abominable matter.

My father (z"l) was among the people who were elected to the Judenrat. He was never counted among the 'top brass,' in whose hands were the determinations and the decisions. He was a simple man all the days of his life, and in his simplicity, he also struggled in the Judenrat. Secretly, his soul cried at the fate of his brethren, the people of his city. Concerning his reputation, Dr. Berkowitz wrote, "At the time of the German conquest, I was together with Mr.Leibish Degen in the Judenrat. He never made peace with the awful distress in which we existed, and never trivialized the severity of the situation. Sometimes we argued about our situation under the rule of the German conquest. In the decline of faith, he saw the source of our catastrophe, and in its strengthening, hope for our deliverance through the kindnesses of the Holy One, Blessed Be He!"

[Page 47]

I was Saved with the Help of 'Aryan Papers'

By Tunka Raiz (Pikholz)

Skalat, July 1941.

The Russians are quickly abandoning their last positions in the city. The local administration collapsed, and everyone looks forward with worry to coming events. The trepidation is great. The new danger of a conquest threatens. The Germans are coming!

We knew that difficult days would be ahead of us. The odor of Anti–Semitism arises in our noses along with the knowledge of coming persecutions, conflicts, and discriminations. The reality would exceed our calculations. Even the hangman, in his distorted and sick imagination, could not imagine terrifying episodes of horror such as these.

We resided on '3rd of May Street,' on the main road through which the advance units of the S.S., who conquered the city, passed. The appearance of the troops is astonishing. They look proud, possessing confidence, dressed in splendor, 'the master race' upon its mighty chariots crossing the city.

The first victims were the members of the Schechter family. In their footsteps, a group of Jews was brought to the area of the river in the center of the city. Here the Germans tormented them. They commanded the Jews to enter the deep water. Curses were poured onto the heads of the unfortunate ones. Some immediately drowned, and others were taken out alive, because the portion of their affliction had not yet ended.

The Sabbath passed. The first victims are rolling in the streets of the city. A new day arrived – Sunday, silence! But suddenly cries burst out. Shots were heard. My father hurried to hide in the attic, because it was known that the men were the first victims. From the attic, through the cracks, my father followed the events happening in the market square. The Germans together with their Ukrainian allies cruelly forced the Jews out of their houses. Any attempt at resistance was suppressed with physical force. They tormented elders and children. The men were forced to clean military vehicles quickly, while their tormentors watched and laughed.

At the conclusion of the workday, Jews were brought to the *Bashta*, an ancient fortress in the center of the city. The Germans stood the Jews in rows and shot them. Their bodies were thrown in heaps. Hundreds of Jews lost their lives on this awful, bloody day. The next day, they buried the bodies in a mass grave in the Jewish cemetery of the city.

My family, too, offered up its first sacrifice on this day of terrors. My cousin, Zalman Messing, twelve years old, shared his fate with the rest of the slain of the city.

Several Nazis burst into our apartment, breaking down the doors, and stormed in upon us with shouts. I fled to my former neighbor – a woman named Marina. My mother fled to the house of the maid who had once served in our house, and my sisters found refuge in different places.

[Page 48]

The apartment remained empty, but not for long. Peasants, who had left the thanksgiving service in the church near our house, burst inside and took everything they could grab. They even removed the pictures from the walls.

I hid all day among the rose bushes, in Marina's garden. She cultivated these bushes as an additional source of her income. Shots rang out from the direction of the *Bashta*. I was still innocent. It did not occur to me that the townspeople and the Germans were now committing a massacre against my community. Suddenly, a solitary Russian plane appeared in the skies, and dropped a few small bombs. A tumult broke out among the people, but nothing happened. The bombing ceased, but the slaughter continued.

Here, hundreds of Jews were murdered

I did not return home for several days. Along with my sister Regina, I found refuge on the threshing floor in Marina's courtyard. We shuddered when we saw the German soldiers who attacked Jewish women at night. Certainly, desecration of 'the pure race' was a severe sin in Nazi Germany, but in Skalat, the desecration of Jewish victims was acceptable. Many Jewish women were raped, and then shot afterwards, to leave no witnesses and blur the consequences.

For two weeks, the anarchy continued. From then on, the civil administration began to get organized. The Judenrat was set up. The role of the Judenrat was to maintain the connection between the Jewish population and the German administration, and especially to fulfill all their demands speedily. The desire of the Germans was to find, in the Judenrat, assistance in the destruction of the Jews, and even to require it to carry out part of their heinous plan in their evil work. The first important function imposed upon the Judenrat was the 'contribution' – the collection of ornaments and jewelry from Jewish houses, including gold, silver, diamonds, and furs – for the sake of the German army, before its departure to the Russian front. This theft was in part transferred by the German officers to their wives on the home front.

[Page 49]

The Judenrat organized the distribution of bread among the poor of the community. A public kitchen was opened, which supplied portions of soup to the needy, and these gradually increased with the passage of time. The Judenrat took care to provide health services to the Jewish population and social assistance to the neediest.

During that period, I worked in the Social Work Department with the well–known teacher Rosa Pikholz and with Professor Frantzos. Our hands were loaded with work. We hurried to the aid of the young husbands and the Jewish youths, who were brought to the Kamionka Labor Camp, and worked there under very difficult conditions. Their situation was dire. They were hungry, poorly clothed, and lice–infested. Twice a week, we sent a wagon to the camp loaded with loaves of bread, fat, and fresh laundry. We brought back their dirty, lice–ridden clothing in order to clean it. The families assisted their relatives with our mediation. For individual people in the camp who lacked family, we made ourselves responsible for all their needs, within the framework of what was possible. The bread and fat that we supplied the people was given to us by the Judenrat. The work overwhelmed us. But we felt that it was in our power to lighten the load upon the unfortunate ones in Kamionka, who were condemned to slave away in hard labor in the stone quarries, hungry, and in ceaseless torment. There in the Kamionka camp Shlomo Perl perished, the second victim from my family.

We took care to provide the people in the camp with medical supplies. In this work, my good friend, Pinka Weintraub, who labored with endless dedication and with self–sacrifice in the municipal clinic, was of great help. She always stood at the right hand of the needy.

This work of ours was done without any salary, even though we too were lacking the means of sustenance. We too felt the pain of hunger. The smell of the good bread, which we supplied to the people of the camp who were hungrier and more unfortunate than we were, intensified this feeling of pain.

We had some valuable articles, which we were able to exchange for food, except that this deed was fraught with mortal danger. Hunger increasingly grew. No household escaped it: people, lacking the everyday wisdom of life for the need of this awful reality, and the poor, lacking any means of existence, perished from hunger. With no choice, they ate anything given, even garbage, which was left from any food whatsoever, such as potato peels. People exhaled their souls in the street. Hunger left its marks on many, in the appearance of their faces and in their movements. These did not request support from others. The spark of personal honor was still not entirely extinguished, and so too there were others to turn to. The shortage was the inheritance of them all.

This was how the winter passed for us. The spring of 1942 arrived. Different rumors were spread concerning an approaching *Aktion*. I did not yet understand the meaning of the word Aktion.

The most awful thing imposed upon the Judenrat was the duty to prepare a list of people who would be handed over to the Germans in order to put them to death. The Judenrat took upon itself the awful task. The list was put together especially including the poorest of the people, widows, orphans, homeless people – all those who appeared on the list of the welfare office, which was also run through the Judenrat. At first, knowledgeable people thought that the Germans would transfer the people to special camps. Our hearts refused to believe that the Judenrat had agreed to decide who would be the first victims, and chose them from among the neediest. A feeling of disgust filled me with regard to the Judenrat. I did not want to cooperate anymore in the Office of Social Work.

[Page 50]

At that time, the Germans began to organize a project for the collection of old household items. A special department for the job was opened, including a workshop and an office, using the former Mager family home. The people gathered bottles of every sort, and they were cleaned in the workshop. The items collected were sorted into a variety of categories. The director of this project was of Polish or German origin, one by the name of Malecki. I was brought into this department as Director of Accounts. This was very important for creating jobs and security, and was the best guarantee of livelihood for some few people. It was essentially an assurance that they would not be sent to the cruelly run labor camps.

Meanwhile, the rumors concerning the upcoming Aktion were circulating. The Germans demanded that the Judenrat provide them with 400 souls. The Jews searched for a way to escape the decree. They built bunkers, arranged secret shelters in different corners of houses, created contacts with peasants in the vicinity, and sought help in every place they could.

It is important to point out that despite the dilemma in which the Judenrat was caught up, the members believed they would indeed prevail over those who arose against us. We will live and we will overcome. Everything depended on the course of the battles on the Russian front. Perhaps a miracle would occur and the Red Army would inflict heavy losses on the German army.

My father built an excellent secret shelter in the basement of the house, but with a 'fat tail and a thorn in it,' meaning, something seemingly good but with a major drawback. Subterranean water flooded the basement, and blocked the air openings. It was impossible to remain there for long.

Finally, what we feared came to pass. The Germans came and demanded the quota of people, and our Jewish policemen, who acted under the auspices of the Judenrat, would be responsible for carrying out the order. Every policeman was given a list of people to bring to the Central Synagogue.

The silence of a cemetery descended upon the city. Everyone sought out a shelter in which to hide. People in panic fled from place to place, to neighbors, to blood relatives, out of the naïve hope that it would be more secure there.

My family hid in the attic of the dairy, which was at our house. The uncles and aunts, Messingov, Perlov, and their children, hid in the cellar. My sister, Regina, and I decided to remain on guard. We seized a position in the courtyard amidst a defensive excavation against air attacks, by the church, which was next to our house. This excavation also served as a privy for peasants who exited the church. A real public toilet in the vicinity of the place did not exist. A heavy stench filled our nostrils, but we stayed there until morning. A Polish neighbor served us as a liaison with the outside world. Every hour he appeared and told us what was happening in the streets. The Aktion continued all night.

The policemen got drunk before they left for Aktion, in order not to become depressed. They broke down doors, searched in cellars and attics, took terrified elderly men and women out of bunkers. Sometimes they seized young men and brought them to the collection point at the synagogue.

Shouts were heard from all around, wails of crying people who did not know why the hangman had chosen them. We stood guard and resolved not to allow them to take out our dear ones. We would defend ourselves, if necessary, even though no one knew how to accomplish that.

[Page 51]

Twice the Jewish policemen entered our house, and searched the cellar. They did not discover the bunker.

Dawn came up. The noise in the streets ceased. We breathed with relief. The family remained. No one was seized. My sisters, Shupka and Regina, had escaped through the cemetery to the neighboring village of Novosilka. I stayed in order to follow coming events, and to defend the family and relatives in the bunkers.

Suddenly, at seven in the morning, my sister–in–law, Manya Wallach, burst into our house, crying bitterly. Her husband had been killed in the first days of the

German conquest. Tearfully, she told us that her mother, my mother–in–law, had been taken. The policemen also had searched for her father, but he had successfully hidden. I left all of them, and I ran to the Judenrat to try to save her. After many efforts, I succeeded in finding a member of the Judenrat, the lawyer Munya Lampert. I sought mercy. He demanded ten thousand zloty and another two hundred grams of gold as a condition for freeing my mother–in–law, Freidel Wallach. We did not have such a large sum of money. My father–in–law had hidden the gold, and now with all the tumult and the confusion round about, we did not remember his hiding place. Without a choice, Manya and I went together and, as security, handed over any valuable object that we could round up in our house, textiles, coats, anything that would achieve our goal. Manya quickly returned with money and a gold chain in her hand, and waited to free her mother from the synagogue. It seemed as if everything had been arranged, and that there would be no further delays.

But fortune did not shine its face upon her. She was still waiting when the Germans arrived looking for the payoff. A convoy of trucks was waiting near the door of the synagogue. It was 4pm. At that hour, I was on my way home from the Judenrat building.

Suddenly, everything was silent. Every person had escaped to every secret corner. On the way, people warned me and advised me to flee, since the quota of 400 people had not yet been filled. Therefore, they would take anyone of any age or status and, absent choice, they would even take police officers for filling the required quota. I tore the ribbon of shame from my arm, which was embroidered with the Jewish Star, and without fear, I walked in the direction of the church. I was completely confident that no one would arrest me, although this crime carried an immediate death penalty for those caught.

For completion of the 'contingent' – the quota of people that had been set – a few were missing. The policemen bustled about, seized with frenzy in their search for victims. They detained and arrested Manya, my sister in law, who waited in the vicinity of the synagogue for her mother's release. Of course, they had not released my mother–in–law. All of them were loaded onto trucks, and were transported to an unknown destination, never to be seen again.

Deep despair overtook all of us. It was clear that our turn too would be coming. It was just a question of time. Like the spirits of ghosts, we moved around very depressed. All hope of being saved disappeared. We lacked a rear echelon, a base, or a homefront that would support us. Only a miracle could save us, and it tarried.

My father–in–law, Yitzchak Hersh Wallach, remained old and unfortunate. His eyes were wells of sorrow, filled with burning tears. He was a broken man. We brought him over to us and waited, crowded and pressed together in the small apartment, awaiting what was to come. We brought Hanna Perl, because she too had lost her parents.

Together with my sister, I moved about to obtain bread. Secretly, we reached former neighbors and here we exchanged different household articles for kernels of grain, which they ground at Marina's. We preferred the risk to the slow death from hunger.

[Page 52]

An Autumn Night. Fierce knocking on the door awakened us. A drunken Ukrainian peasant stood at the entrance and demanded that we bring out my sister, Shupka, who was 15 years old at the time. He was deeply in love, and demanded to know who would withhold her from him in the circumstances in which we were living? My father took his stand like a wild beast, and thus the struggle continued until morning. Only then did the drunken peasant sober up from his drunkenness, apologized, and even sent us a loaf of bread as a token of regret.

We received a loaf of bread, secretly, every day, from the baker, whose bakery was in the vicinity of our house. This loaf saved us from the jaws of famine. We also found other ways to alleviate our distress.

In the evenings, I found work for myself, managing the books of a German company whose influence was well known in the surrounding area. In these offices, the peasants would receive their salary, and more than once they whispered, "The Germans kill Jews. But they do not forego their brains."

Sometimes they took us for forced labor in the fields, and there we stole vegetables from whatever came to hand, but only in so far as what was needed to keep the family alive. This labor was beyond human strength. Our German and Ukrainian taskmasters found any pretext to intensify their curses and their cruel conduct. Sometimes they entrusted a pair of horses or oxen to me, and ordered me to plow. Gentiles who saw me in that state asked me more than once, "Where is your God?" I had no answer. One thing was clear to me, that one had to act, to struggle, and to hold out.

One night, Germans burst into our house. Their fearsome screams awakened us. They saw us, me and my sisters, Shupka and Regina. They looked and retreated, begged our pardon since it seemed to them that Jews resided here. We realized that it was incumbent upon us to create new identities for ourselves.

My sister, Regina, also worked for the German *Alt Schtuperfsung* Company, which employed Jews in the collection of old household items and trash. But they employed her in cleaning work. About this time, a supervisor for the company arrived in Skalat. His name was Mr. Nowicki, a Jew who seemed like a Gentile, using the subterfuge of Aryan papers. Nowicki was a rich man, an influential person among certain circles, and he had an unusual escape plan. His Jewish appearance was an obstacle for him. Therefore, he surrounded himself with friends who possessed an Aryan appearance. After we became friendly, he suggested that we flee together through the Romanian border. According to his plan, we had to approach the border in stages. We would obtain work in other cities, first in Chortkov, and afterward continue toward the goal of escaping. Meanwhile, Nowicki, in his supervisory role, left for Chortkov, and I began to deal with obtaining new documents, which would confirm my new identity as Christian. I decided to maintain the relationship between Nowicki and me.

It was no simple matter in 1942 to obtain documents such as these in Skalat. Our appeals to certain persons aroused suspicions among them. They simply were afraid to get involved in any way. Finally, I succeeded. A Ukrainian officer, whom I had known in joint work before the war, extended a helping hand. He discovered identification papers, in the local archive, that could be used. He also obtained a Christian prayer book for me, and even provided me with a Christian medallion. The new documents established that I was a Ukrainian girl by the name of Katheryna Lachoweczka, formerly Kachowa. It was difficult for me to remember my new identity. I repeated the new details over many nights, but nevertheless had trouble remembering. Fear paralyzed my ability to think clearly.

[Page 53]

My work in the managing of accounts with the Germans made it possible for me to have free access to official forms and governmental seals. I forged a document with the name of Katheryna Lachoweczka on an official certificate in the office. I sold a sewing machine and a few other articles in order to have some money for our getaway. Meanwhile, I waited for information from Chortkov. My sister, Shupka, was able to get new identity papers also, but my sister, Regina, struggled with the decision of what to do.

Meanwhile, the Germans began to gather all the Jews from the entire city into a small neighborhood, which stretched from my Aunt Malchiyah Bomse's house through the marketplace and the area of shops in Patzini to the Jewish neighborhood near the Great Synagogue. They brought all the Jews of Skalat, those from the neighboring towns of Grzhimalov and Podvolochisk, along with those from other surrounding villages to this constricted area. It was now occupied to the point of suffocation, and became the town's ghetto.

On the day of the opening of the ghetto, I received information that it was time for me to leave for Chortkov. I parted from my parents. That night I stayed over at Marina's, and with the coming of dawn, her son transported me to the train station in the city of Chorostkov. I saw terrifying sights along the way. I saw the Jews of Grzhimalov making their way toward Skalat. My heart ached at the sight of these unfortunate ones. Where would they find a resting place for themselves? What would they do in the new city? Certainly they would perish in the overcrowding, the hunger, and the cold, which were awaiting them in Skalat!

I strove with all my strength to remain alive. I was young. I aspired to save the remnants of my family members. If only I could be successful! I walked toward the unknown, to a new life. I felt great relief and confidence. I believed that I would succeed in surviving. As I entered the train, crowds of Polish and Ukrainian peasants, young and old, filled the coaches, all of them carefree, happy, and well dressed. I looked at their faces with envy, and I thought of my unfortunate family who remained behind. I pretended to look into the prayer book, and I recited prayers by heart. Despite the terror round about, it was wonderful to feel that I was a free woman, with no one pursuing me.

As we approached Chortkov, evening descended. "Where will I sleep tonight? Where will I stay tomorrow?" I had no idea. The search for lodging was very dangerous. Still on the train, I turned to one of the female passengers and, in my excellent Ukrainian, asked her about a possible place for lodging. She handed me an address not too far from the train station. Leaving the station, I turned toward the address that was in my hand. I entered inside. The lady of the house, an elderly Ukrainian woman, received me kindly, but not one unoccupied bed was left in the house. For lack of choice, I agreed to share a bed with her young daughter.

I was asked to explain my appearance here, and was ready with the story. I was afraid that they would seize me for labor in Germany, and so I fled from my city. Here they promised me work, which would shield me from being detained. My story was convincing. I remained in the place, but every night my sleep wandered. My worry did not leave me. I had to be ready for any new situation that might arise, to react quickly, and in a correct manner, to any surprise or complication. One thing I knew clearly was that, whatever my situation, I would not return anymore to my city, as it would become my grave!

[Page 54]

I walked around the streets of the new city like a free woman. The fear left me. My goal was clear. My mood darkened when I remembered the members of my family who remained behind me, who were sighing under the terrors of approaching death. "I know that you will live!" my oldest sister Matilda said to me before I left for the road. She showed me a hiding place in which she had hidden our ornaments, gold watches, rings, earrings, and other valuable articles.

The days passed. I looked for work, but in vain. Positions for women were rare. I believed that I would manage to obtain work, but reality slapped me in the face. And so, the first week passed in the new city. Meanwhile, it became known to me that a new Aktion had taken place. In this Aktion, my father, Tuvia Pikholz, was seized, as was my brother-in-law, Shlomo Bomse, and my father-in-law, Yitzchak-Hersh Wallach. More than three thousand people were seized and brought to the death camp in Belzec. This was in October 1942. They told me that my unfortunate father cried silently and found the strength to comfort others. His deep faith was for him and others a source of comfort. To date, I have never found out where, and in what circumstances, my father perished.

The next day after the Aktion, my sister, Shupka, went in my footsteps. She had gotten my address from Shuna Schar, with whom I had remained in contact. However, our paths diverged. On the day that Shupka reached Chortkov, I had left for Lvov. Shupka stayed with the same family to whom I had come first, and remained there during the entire period of the war.

The idea to volunteer for Germany, for labor in factories, took root in Nowicki's mind. I had a good knowledge of the situation and in what was happening. I listened to his advice, but making it happen was not so simple at all. Labor offices inducted people for forced labor in an orderly and organized fashion. Sometimes they kidnapped people on the streets, especially those who had attempted to flee from the threat, only to be sent to Germany for labor. I wanted to travel to Germany and work there, but my chances were poor. I walked around the streets of the city, especially on days on which they kidnapped young men and women for work in Germany. What stroke of luck. They never caught me! I planned a strategy. I turned to the committee that was impressing youths for Germany, and I requested to be sent as a volunteer. The step, in itself, had many dangers. I was bound to arouse suspicions. I took the risk out of a sense of great confidence that I would be up to the job. My personal documents, my secure stance, my 'good' facial appearance were all guarantees that I was indeed a Ukrainian woman and even a loyal patriot. As proof of my Ukrainian loyalty, I relied, among other things, on a 'familial relationship' to the lady of the house with whom I was staying. My story was convincing, and I was found fit for this important work.

They sent me to Lvov. The journey took all night. There was a huge camp for all those sent and who volunteered for work in Germany here. More than ten thousand people were gathered in this place from one month to another. In the bunk where they lodged us, there were four hundred women, most of them from the mountain regions of Poland. The filth here was unbelievable. Lice swarmed in everything, and even I did not escape it. Strict discipline prevailed in the camp. Frequent musters, medical examinations, constant disinfection, and meals exclusively at fixed times. All of these were an inseparable part of the schedule of our days. In the women's shower, men observed us and looked at us as beasts of labor.

[Page 55]

In this camp, a disturbing experience happened to me. It was a brush with death. Someone in the camp claimed he knew me from the years of our studies in school, in Tarnopol, and informed the authorities that I was a Jewish woman. The director of the camp and his helper entered the bunk and asked every woman of Jewish origin to leave the place. I froze in my spot. The director and his helper passed among the rows of women in the bunk and stopped near me. He ordered me to take my belongings and to follow him. I knew what was in store for me. Two days before, a Jewish boy who was discovered here was shot. The sentence was carried out publicly for everyone to see. That was a shocking scene. It seemed as if my fate was sealed. There was no way out.

With valise in hand, I entered the office of the director of the camp. He demanded that I show him my identity papers. After a basic inspection, he commanded me to pray in Ukrainian. I could not manage to remember even a single word of the prayer that I had repeated so many times. Out of fear, the words flew away from me. In no way was I able to draw them from memory, which now had betrayed me. I was silent. I was humiliated. My identity was clear to him from this point. One thing puzzled him. How had I succeeded in obtaining confirmation that I was Ukrainian, in the office of the Ukrainian Control Committee in Lvov, considered the holy of holies of the Ukrainian administration?

I had obtained the document in the simplest way. I had gone to the Ukrainian Control Committee, which was in the camp, and submitted two documents. Then I requested confirmation that I was indeed Ukrainian. One official tested me strictly. With impudent language, I turned to him and asked him to explain this scrutinizing of me, that if he didn't approve, I was prepared to leave the camp and forego my trip to

Germany and return home. My impudence had paid off. They were convinced, and immediately gave me a document confirming that I was a kosher Ukrainian. I still have the document to this day.

The director of the camp searched my valise. His eyes blazed with desire when he rifled through my articles. I saw his weakness, and suggested that he take several pairs of underwear and a scarf for his fiancée, if one existed. He did not object. Then I also offered him the money in my possession. My generosity worked, and he was convinced that I was indeed a Ukrainian woman. I received permission to return to the bunk.

I was at the point where I needed to decide whether to return to the camp and wait for the journey to Germany, or leave the camp entirely and get out of there. The director of the camp gave me the choice. I preferred the first possibility, despite the great risk, since remaining in Lvov would be more dangerous. My identity papers would be doubted, taken, and without appropriate documents, without money, and without work, I wouldn't be able to hold out in Lvov.

So with the first transport available, I left for Germany. They chose me along with another hundred women from the bunk. I was satisfied and actually happy. The train made its way in the direction of Leipzig–Turingen. The trip lasted two entire days. Apparently, I was not the only Jewish woman on the train. It was clear that the director of the camp had found a side source of income for himself, and that I was not the first Jewish woman he had dealt with in this way. In the evening hours, we reached Armstadt. They brought us to a camp in the vicinity of a munitions factory.

[Page 56]

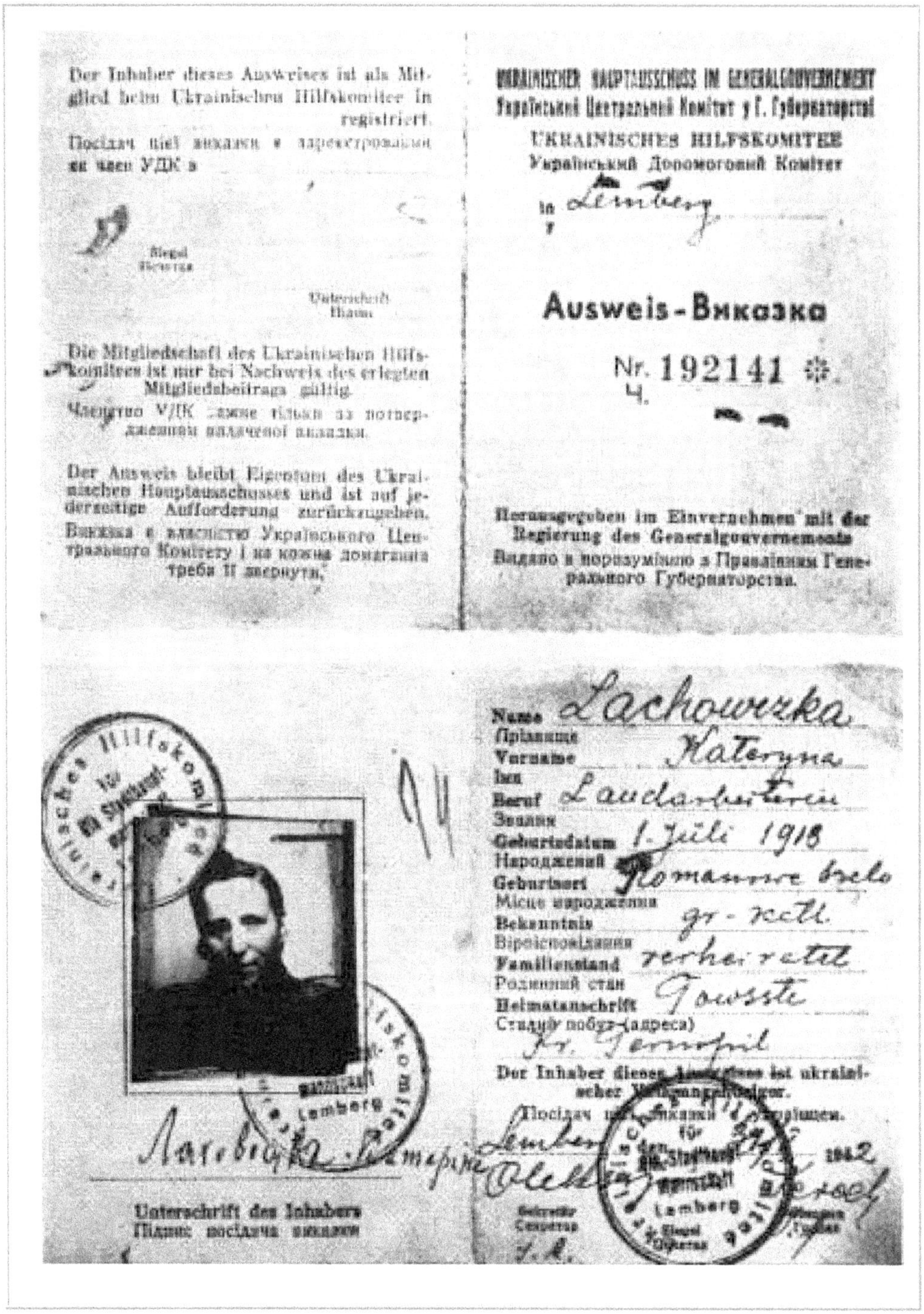
Der Inhaber dieses Ausweises ist als Mitglied beim Ukrainischen Hilfskomitee in registriert.

Die Mitgliedschaft des Ukrainischen Hilfskomitees ist nur bei Nachweis des erlegten Mitgliedsbeitrags gültig.

Der Ausweis bleibt Eigentum des Ukrainischen Hauptausschusses und ist auf jederzeitige Aufforderung zurückzugeben.

UKRAINISCHER HAUPTAUSSCHUSS IM GENERALGOUVERNEMENT

UKRAINISCHES HILFSKOMITEE

in Lemberg

Ausweis - Виказка

Nr. 192141

Herausgegeben im Einvernehmen mit der Regierung des Generalgouvernements

Name Lachowezka

Vorname Kateryna

Beruf Landarbeiterin

Geburtsdatum 1. Juli 1918

Geburtsort Romanowe Sielo

Bekenntnis gr.-kath.

Familienstand verheiratet

Heimatanschrift Gowste Kr. Tarnopil

Der Inhaber dieses Ausweises ist ukrainischer Volkszugehöriger.

Lemberg 1942

Unterschrift des Inhabers

Tunka's Aryan identity document

[Page 57]

Nine thousand workers were employed in Armstadt. There were workers from all corners of conquered Europe: French, Croats, Germans, Poles, Ukrainians as well as members of other nations who worked here. Women were in the majority. The residential bunks were three kilometers from the factory. Shod in wooden shoes, we were led to work daily like a herd of cattle. The food was meager and the plague of lice awful, and cruelly, they sucked my blood. I was unable to get rid of them. Even water and soap could not overcome them, and they always returned.

A new disaster threatened me. One morning, a young Christian woman named Tchobtoba from Skalat approached me in the camp courtyard. She was astonished. "What are you doing here?" she asked me. "How were you able to get here?" It became clear to me that in this labor camp, there were young Christian women from Skalat. What a disappointment!

During the war years, it was a disaster to meet acquaintances, Poles or Ukrainians. You were never able to know what trouble could arise for you from this kind of meeting. Frequently such a meeting led to denunciation. And then all your plans were for naught. But this time, fortune smiled on me. My sisters in distress from Skalat were indeed Christians, but they were as unfortunate and downtrodden as we Jews. That was my consolation. I did not think that they would hand me over, so, to make sure, I divided my poor ration of food with them. Sometimes I gave them one of my possessions, but eventually these sad experiences came back to haunt us.

Two months later, the bubble burst. One of the girls was not careful with what she said. With great speed, the information spread through the camp. They whispered about me, pried and asked. A few warned me to escape. All the while, the denunciations and slander had not reached the camp authorities.

Escape? Where could I go? Eventually, I felt that I excelled in the factory. The old mechanic, who had charge over one of the machines, was, it seems, a pacifist, and in the course of work, he would commit sabotage through slowdowns and even damage to the machines. We found a common language and mutual understanding in this task. Sometimes, he would secretly bring me soap for bathing, or meals in secret. The man endangered himself greatly, since helping foreigners was totally forbidden.

Under me, the earth burned. The worry about tomorrow took away my rest. I therefore rejoiced at the arrival of Christmas. We received three days of rest from labor. I decided to act. I wrapped the most important things, and staged a journey 'to my aunt.' The Ukrainian woman, Diminchuk, my sister in distress, decided to join me in this escape. Her sister was staying in Münster, in Northern Germany, and she decided to visit her. I felt that it was incumbent upon me to do something. Perhaps luck would shine on me in some other place.

We managed to slip away with no one from the camp noticing. My readiness stood me in good stead. I obtained two travel cards, and we entered the train. We traveled all night until noon the next day. The atmosphere of Christmas was all around us. We were hungry, but we didn't have food, and without food cards, it was impossible for us to obtain any. We were in a dilemma. German soldiers traveled with us in the compartment, on a short break from the front. One of them, a high official in the conquered territories from Poltava to Kiev, stood out in his appearance. In the course of a conversation concerning different personal matters, he declared suddenly that he was prepared to employ me in his office, which was in Poltava.

[Page 58]

Work Card, Side #1

[Page59]

Diese Arbeitskarte berechtigt nur zur Arbeit
bei dem genannten Betriebsführer und wird
beim Verlassen dieses Arbeitsplatzes ungültig

Arbeitskarte – Befreiungsschein*)

Work card, Side #2

[Page 60]

He needed a female clerk who was knowledgeable in the two languages, Ukrainian and German. His enthusiasm increased, and changed to more personal matters. The conversation ended with a proposal to marry me. I reminded him that the law forbade him from marrying a foreign woman, but he was not impressed with my words. Since he was a high officer, enjoying many privileges, he would be able to obtain a special authorization for this marriage from Hitler himself. And since all the obstacles were removed, he asked me to join him on his journey to his parents. I was confused. I suggested that he contact me when he succeeded in obtaining the appropriate authorizations. I handed him a fictional address. Nevertheless, not everything was in vain. When he reached his station and got up to leave, he left me his meat sandwiches as an expression of our friendship. A celebratory feast and the memories of that encounter put smiles on our faces.

We reached the labor camp in Münster. Horror seized me when four girls from Mantiva, a suburb of Skalat, recognized me immediately and greeted me. Again a defeat. And again, it would be necessary to flee to the unknown. I decided that on the way from here, I would get off at the city of Leipzig, but I advised my friend, Diminchuk, to return on the train leaving for Armstadt. She refused, and burst into powerful sobs. She was concerned about traveling alone because she was not knowledgeable about the roads, and feared she would be seized by the police and arrested. There was no choice. I accompanied her back, and returned to the camp.

The execution of the escape plan had to be postponed for another time. On December 31, 1942, a new opportunity presented itself to me. We received two days of furlough. With several pairs of undies, the one dress I was wearing, and without any articles to carry in my hands, I fled the camp. This time I chose to travel southward to the city of Wieden, in Bavaria. I received the addresses of several young Christian women from Skalat who worked as housemaids in private homes. These women were former friends from our schooldays. I had lived in neighborliness with several of them, before the war.

After some travel, I reached Wieden on January 1, 1943. It was a holiday. I did not meet even one of my town mates. It seemed that I couldn't find any of the addresses.

My staying here would be dangerous. I had destroyed my documents from the labor camp, in order to obscure traces of my escape. This time, luck was with me. I obtained a room in a hotel and food to satisfy my hunger. The redeeming angel on that day appeared in the guise of a strange man, a Czech who hastened to my aid.

The next day I met my girlfriends, Milka Hinda Boskovna, and Tuska Karbush. They received me with warm, open hearts. They too felt a great hatred for the Germans, and they therefore helped me to get settled in the place. At the labor office, they reported that I was a proper Ukrainian woman. I strengthened their account with a fabricated tale about the escape from the train, which led us to labor in Germany, especially because I wished to meet these girlfriends of mine. The local authorities indeed attempted to verify my story, but the chaos of the war helped me out, and they left me untroubled, and gave me work.

A German family took me in as a housemaid. A variety of jobs were given me. I saw to the cleanliness of the rooms, the kitchen and the bathrooms. I fattened poultry in the coop, and in the winter days, I saw to the central heating of the house. In the summer, I worked in the garden, and I even took charge of the shining and polishing of boots of the elderly German. The work was a lot, but it was good for me here. I lived alone in a clean room. I even was permitted to use the bathtub in the house. My Christian girlfriends from Skalat did not have conditions nearly as favorable. It was my good fortune. The ability to sleep alone in a room was a great and important privilege, too. I feared that sleep would betray me. I would make a sound. I would speak a word and it would end my life. Incidents like these occurred many times. A person shouted during sleep in his mother tongue. The pains and afflictions which you experienced by day could blaze a path for themselves during the nighttime hours. That was your last scream. It revealed your secrets publicly. And no one could save you from it.

[Page 61]

In the afternoon hours of Sunday, on the general day of rest, I would spend the time in the company of Milka Hinda. I was able to converse with her about many things. We even went to church together. She was a young girl who possessed a profound religious consciousness and prayed from deep within. I would observe her from the place where I sat on the bench in church. I felt the exaltation of her spirit during the service. I envied the simple faith and tranquility that enveloped her. With her fierce zealotry, she forced me to promise her that when the war would be over, I would convert and would be a faithful Catholic.

Time here improved my health, especially now, after I had tasted relative tranquility. But I felt the tension of life in different ways, with nervous agitation in my stomach and nasal polyps. I frequently had nosebleeds. I consulted an ear, nose and throat doctor. His treatment was very basic. In the course of my visit with him, he revealed himself as a sharp opponent of the Nazi regime. It was whispered that his wife was a Jewish woman, and that he was hiding her. Frequently and repeatedly, he would claim that the war would be over soon and that Hitler would suffer a defeat. With his help, I was able to obtain medical certification for Milka Hinda, which said she was forbidden, for reasons of health, to work in factories. This noble doctor, named Heller, was able to assemble a consortium of doctors to confirm this diagnosis and determination. Milka Hinda was then able to obtain work as a housemaid.

Dr. Heller even went further. For two weeks, he had us admitted to a German hospital. We feigned illness. We felt deep satisfaction that, in our time there, we were sabotaging the German war effort. During the day, we reclined on the porch of the hospital, and only during the doctors' rounds in the wards, did we get in bed. Nevertheless, we knew that we had to be careful not to stretch these strings excessively. I could not permit myself not to be okay.

A few months passed. I renewed contacts with my sister Shupka. She was living in Chortkov, and sometimes received news from home. Everything there was sad. In the spring of 1943, typhus rampaged within the ghetto, and many people died. Among the victims was my mother – Faige Pikholz – and many others in my family.

Before her death, my mother, beloved and unforgettable, managed to receive two letters, one from me, from where I was living in Germany, and one from my sister Shupka, in Chortkov. She was happy that it was good for us, and she believed with strong faith that we would get through the difficult period and would remain alive. With this knowledge, my mother closed her eyes forever. Dr. Sass, who was present by my mother's bed in her last moments of life, revealed these details to me after the war.

How was I able to succeed in getting a letter to my mother? Even this is an interesting story. My girlfriend, Tzurbotna, my workmate in Germany, was wounded in her hand. Four fingers of her right hand were cut off by a machine. As a cripple, she was freed from labor, and permission was granted to her to return to Skalat. I entrusted her with the letter to my mother. She stole into the ghetto, despite the danger, and personally handed over the letter from me, and so my mother knew I was alive. It is fitting to point out that this was an unusual and kind act by Tzurbotna.

[Page 62]

A day after my mother's burial, there raged a new Aktion. My two sisters, Matilda and Regina, were seized. Regina attempted to escape from a convoy of Jews who were being taken to death pits. She was murdered on the spot. Matilda also did not return.

At the time of one of the Aktions, my cousin, Manya Messing, was unable to escape into the bunker, due to having a broken leg. The Germans overtook her and shot her. My aunt, Tsila Messing, hanged herself in the bunker. Her husband, Nissim Messing, wandered over the fields for many days. He became deranged, until he was murdered. This is how they disappeared. They perished for their sin of being born Jewish. A sin that was too heavy to bear.

All my dear ones perished, and I alone remained. That was a terrifying thought. I cursed the day of my birth. It was decreed upon me to bewail my dear ones all the days of my life. Nevertheless, the will to live prevailed in me. I wanted to live and to tell the world about the cruelest crimes that were committed by human beasts. I wanted the world to know what they did to us. During many sleepless nights, I dreamed the dream of the future in which all of this would be revealed to the world.

On a Sunday afternoon, we received exit permission. We exploited that by meeting with young Polish people who were freed from POW camps in Germany. Many of them joined the Underground. There were Germans who assisted them, and supplied them with food cards. The work of the Underground charmed me. I helped to obtain food secretly, in order to distribute it among the captives who were fleeing from Camp Flossenberg.

One day, I discovered that the soap I was using was made from human fat. It was 'RIF SOAP.' After a while, I found out the actual meaning of the name was Pure Jewish Fat, or *Reines Judisches Fett* in German. I was astounded. It was so hard to believe, even if the truth was in front of you.

In the circles of the Polish captives, I recognized a Pole by the name of Andzhi Glud who, with endless self–sacrifice, hastened to the aid of any needy person. My situation worsened in those days. The danger that I would be discovered lay in wait for me always. Quickly it became known to me that the police had begun to take an interest in me, in the wake of a letter concerning my identity, which arrived from Skalat. There was no choice left for me except to flee anew. It even became necessary for me to change my name. Andzhi Glud came to my aid. It was he who saved me.

We decided to enter the covenant of marriage. From then on, I was called Antonina Glud. We resided in Neustadt. The traces of the past were erased. After the war, Andzhi was ready to make Aliyah with me to the Land of Israel, and to live there as a free man, but he did not live to accomplish that. Even he was going to disappear in the storm of the final days.

In 1945, I witnessed the downfall of the Germans. There was little joy in it for me. The deep feeling of guilt stayed within me, because only I had remained alive. And were it not for the expectation of the son who was about to be born, God knows how this all would have ended. I also felt a deep need to return to my home, and to discover the traces of Shupka, my youngest sister. Andzhi joined me in this journey.

[Page 63]

We stopped in Prague. There our son was born. Nineteen days after his birth, Andzhi was arrested by the Russians because he was a Polish officer before the war. His traces were lost forever.

I was left alone with an infant in my arms as I searched for a connection with my family. That was the beginning of a new struggle, but with totally different circumstances. In the capacity of Antonina Glud, I lived in Poland until 1948. The rise of the State of Israel aroused within me the desire to change my name, and I endeavored to leave.

My son bears the name of my family from my parents' home – Pikholz, in honor of
my father, of blessed memory, who always was sorry that he had no sons, and that
the family name would disappear forever.

Water–drawer in Skalat
(drawn by Tzipporah Hermoni)

[Page 64]

In the Struggle for Life
Thirteen Years Old at the Outbreak of the War

by Peretz Landesman

I was young when the war between the Soviet Union and Germany broke out in 1941. After the Germans conquered our town Skalat, they forced all the Jews to do hard labor. My father, Moshe Landesman, worked at cleaning machines. On the first day, everything went peacefully. The next day, they needed everyone to return to their work. The Germans threatened punishment on anyone who did not return. My father returned to work, and met with an accident. A truck driven by a German ran over his foot. His Jewish companions took him to the hospital. On the way, they passed some other Germans, who asked for an explanation of the matter. They explained to the Germans that an accident had occurred. Since crippled Jews were not urgently required, the Germans took him together with his companions to the cemetery, shot him, and ordered his companions to dig a grave and bury him.

We waited for my father all night. We didn't close an eye. Everyone else had returned, but he had not. The next day, they told us that my father had been murdered. Only my mother remained, and she had just been widowed with six children.

During the days of the first Aktion, I managed to escape from the surrounded ghetto to a village in the vicinity of our town. A gentile woman lived there who was a friend of the family. I thought that I would find my mother there. The gentile woman looked at me and didn't recognize me. I was very dirty. After much persuasion, she agreed that I could sleep over. Several hours passed. Her son, who was a Ukrainian policeman, returned from his post. She told him about my arrival and when the son heard this, he wanted to hand me over to the Germans. The gentile woman and her husband pleaded with him and asked him not to hand me over. I slept under a bench and the next day I fled. I went around in the fields, an entire 24 hour day, and I returned to the ghetto. Here I was told about the death of my mother, my sister Rivka, and my younger five-year-old brother David.

Several months passed, and a new Aktion was visited upon the ghetto. We entered hiding places in which we were able to secret ourselves, but the Germans found us with the aid of search dogs. They took us out. Our clothes were ragged, and outside much snow had fallen. A terrible wintery cold had taken hold. They brought us to the city of Tarnopol, and there they wanted to load us on a train, and to transport us to death camps. For some reason, they loaded us onto a trailer pulled by a tractor. My brother and I decided to escape at any cost.

We jumped and escaped. We turned toward the town of Skalat. The cold was fierce. We followed the road and sank into the mud. We were unable to walk on the road because the German traffic on it was so great.

We reached the town and sought refuge with one of the gentiles. But he did not consent to take us in.

[Page 65]

Another household agreed to harbor us after we promised to give them our money and our possessions, which remained in the ghetto.

In the morning, we left the house. We wandered about in the fields, and at evening returned to the ghetto.

Aktion followed Aktion, until the final Aktion came. The Germans made announcements about making the area *Judenrein*, Jew free. Every Jew who survived was obligated to present himself before the Gestapo. My brother Yaakov and I wandered around among the gentiles in villages whose inhabitants threatened to turn us over. Edible grasses and wheat, which had not yet ripened, were our food. We found nighttime lodgings in heaps of straw.

One morning we awakened and heard voices in German. It became clear that German soldiers had set an ambush for the partisans, who were accustomed to hiding here. To our good luck, the partisans did not appear that night. Had they come, we would have been burned up in the straw along with them. When the Germans were convinced that the partisans had not come, they left the place.

Our hunger grew from day to day. We were dirty, weary and scratched by grasses. We decided to stay away from the town, so that they would not recognize us, and instead we went to the villages such as Piznanka. At the approach to the village, I met a peasant riding a horse. I stopped him and asked him whether he needed a young helper. He was not in need of such a lad, but suggested that I go with him, and maybe others would have need of me. On the way, the gentile asked me about my place of origin. Following the advice of a friend, I told him that I was from Tomaszew Lubelski. And my name was Iwan Kovalchuk. I told him that my widowed mother lived with her many children in Tomaszew Lubelski, and that I was fleeing from a master with whom I had worked because he had been cruel to me.

When we reached the village, night had already fallen. To our luck, we met a peasant who was in need of a helper. He asked me details about myself and my family. I told him the same story I had told the previous peasant. He was convinced by my words and took me in for work. I would help him with farm work. The peasant's mother was from my birth city, Skalat, and she owned many fields. He would cultivate them and bring her a portion of the yield. When the harvest days arrived, the gentile asked me to join him on his way to Skalat. Fear overcame me. I was afraid someone would recognize me, but I was forced to travel with him.

What I feared, came to pass. Near the bridge, at the entrance to the city, stood two youths, gentiles, who recognized me and shouted that I was a Jew from Skalat. The gentile looked at me and continued to gallop. When he reached his mother's house, he told her what had occurred. They called for me, and interrogated me, asking if I was truly a Jew. I denied it. Even the peasant confirmed that I behaved like a gentile. They believed me. When we returned to the village, the peasant urged me to tell the truth and not be afraid. I revealed to him that I was Jewish.

For two weeks, he continued to behave decently toward me. Afterwards, things changed, and he did not give me enough food, and even began beating me. I wanted to run away, but the fall season was a bad time to leave. The cold was fierce. Eventually, the peasant himself decided to push me out.

I turned to other villages until I found a peasant who agreed to take me in, but on condition that the first peasant, with whom I had worked, would provide me with clothes. For lack of an alternative, I returned to him. To my surprise, he suggested to me that I continue to stay with him. I agreed, and remained with him, but only because the season was so severely cold. However, I lacked warm clothing. My clothes were torn, and my feet bare.

In the village, a widow would visit, who earned a living selling various articles. She was in need of a young helper like me. I told her about my bad situation. She took me to her village, which was located 30 kilometers from Skalat, the village of Kozivka. I worked very hard. In exchange, she gave me only scanty food and drink. Every day, I went to bring milk. On my way, I would meet young gentiles my age. There I met a youth with whom I became friendly. He told me that his uncle was in need of a worker like me. Maybe there would be a better place for me, I thought in my heart, except the uncle refused to give me work because, according to him, I was too thin. After struggling to persuade him, he consented to accept me. My condition improved, and I remained with him until the arrival of the Red Army.

[Page 66]

Theresienstadt

from "I Never Saw Another Butterfly"

Heavy wheels pass and travel on our foreheads
And engrave marks and pierce our brains
Only hunger dances around us silently
Children steal bread, ask troubling questions
And everyone desires just to sleep wrapped in silence

Heavy wheels pass and travel on our foreheads
And engrave and plow on our spirits
And years will not erase this

[Page 67]

The Mother of Daughters

by Hinda Kornweitz

When the battles between Germany and Soviet Russia broke out, many individuals fled eastward. I remained in Skalat, not because of any confidence I placed in the Germans, but because being the mother of two little girls, with a third daughter on the way, I was afraid that bread would be scarce in a foreign land. My firstborn daughter, Matilda, was 4 years old, a good and happy girl. However, on the first day of the conquest of the city, the Germans perpetrated horrors against the Jews who lacked defense. They killed without distinction, whether infants or the elderly. On that bitter and wild day, they killed my brother Hersh Tzvi Fisher. I was scared for my girls. I hid in the cellar of the Shapira family home, along with their neighbors and their children. The infants kept absolutely silent and did not cry, as if they understood what was happening around them.

After the pogrom, when we came back to our apartment, we saw destruction in every corner. Matilda's eyes reflected her fear. Her joy of life, joie-de-vivre, disappeared. Suddenly, she became an adult. She knew that it was forbidden to play in the street, and that it was incumbent upon her to be in close proximity to me.

Pala Tzipporah was one year old and did not understand anything of what was happening. My younger daughter Pala grew up quickly, because of our abnormal conditions, but she was very understanding and perceptive. When she was 3 years old, she understood the situation. At night, before the Aktion in April, we entered the apartment, and I said that I felt an Aktion was about to occur, and that we had to awaken the girls. Suddenly Pala answered that she was not asleep, but someone would have to awaken Matilda, "It's forbidden to forget her." Fate willed that in this Aktion, the Germans discovered our bunker and brought us to the Great Synagogue. There, they gathered us together before the violence and killing.

In my childhood, I saw the synagogue as a holy place, and now it had become a scene of horror. People, half-wild and frantic, alternately prayed and cried. In their grief, they begged that the earth would swallow them up. In the women's gallery, I discovered an attic, and I decided to hide in it. In the absence of a ladder, I asked Moshe Katzlov for help, and I went up with the girls, and with other tens of people. I had to work hard to pacify the adults among them, who feared that my girls would endanger our hiding place with their crying. I promised them that my girls would be quiet and would preserve our safety. The girls lay down day and night, and did not utter a sound.

[Page 68]

Berel the Rabbi's Son, and the Brave Teacher from Skalat

From Abraham Weissbrod's *Death of a Shtetl*

The order is given, "Strip! Arrange the clothes in a heap!" The Jewish policemen press and urge the people to move quickly. Anyone who disobeys is beaten with murderous blows. On the ground we spread a colored paper rug. There are paper money notes that the people have torn into pieces so they would not fall into the hands of the murderers. Children weeping, the cries of the *Shema*, Hear O Israel, mingle with shouts of "Hurry! Hurry!" And the heap of clothing gets higher and higher! Men, women and their children stand as naked as the day they were born.

Berel, the Rabbi's son, was stubborn and refused to strip. A German landed him a blow on his head, and he fell to his knees bleeding. He further absorbed several kicks in his belly. He cried "Shema Hear!," groaned, and died upon a heap of gloves which were drenched with blood. The German rolled the corpse to the mouth of the grave.

Roza Pikholz
(second from left)

[Page 69]

And already there are rising the muted throes of death. Berel, the Rabbi's son, the first of the martyrs from Skalat, lay in the grave, dressed in shrouds of red and, in his bosom, a *tefillin* bag, which he did not let go of.

And suddenly Roza Pikholz, a teacher in the high school, arose and faced the naked crowd, "I call upon you to be brave. We are innocent people!" The Stormführer interrupts her, "You are not human beings!" and slaps her on the cheek, "and now continue to speak, whore!" And she pours out her anguish and rage upon the heads of the murderers, "Your end is near, forests of hangings are awaiting you!" The German was already unable to bear this, and he shot the naked woman in the heart. Just like that, she was lying dead on the ground.

[Page 70]

Belzec

All the people of Skalat who were seized in the 'contingent,' and in the days of the first and second Aktions, were sent on freight trains to an unknown forest. Only at the conclusion of the war did we hear the name Belzec, a concentration camp, one of the most awful in the Nazi Satanic Kingdom.

Here our dear ones were put to death.

From the camp of horrors only a few lone individuals were left alive. Here is the testimony of one of these sufferers, as was recorded by the Jewish Historical Commission in Poland, in 1946, and it was transcribed from the book *From the Chapter of the Holocaust*, published by Reuven Mas.

[Page 71]

Belzec:

The Testimony of Rudolph Rader

This is the only testimony of a man who was in the Belzec death camp, escaped, survived and reported reliably about everything that he saw. Rudolph Rader was born in 1881. He worked in the manufacture of soap. Before the war, he resided in Lvov, and remained there until August 16, 1942.

There was not yet a special ghetto in Lvov. A few streets were set aside only for Jews. It was, therefore, the Jewish quarter in which there were several streets included from the Third Quarter, like Panienska Street, Wanska, Ogrodnicka, Salonczna and others. Here we lived an unquiet life with constant oppression. Already two weeks before the expulsion from the ghetto, everyone spoke about the approaching catastrophe. We were in despair. We already understood the real meaning of the word 'expulsion.' We had heard that a prisoner who had worked in a destruction team in Belzec had escaped. He had worked at the time of the establishment of the death factory, in the construction of the gas chambers. He told of the 'bathhouse,' which was truthfully only a building designated for gassing victims. He said that, of the people who would be brought there, none would return.

It was also rumored that a Ukrainian, who had worked in the destruction of Jews, told his girlfriend what was being done at Belzec. The girlfriend was alarmed and saw an obligation to secretly make this information known in order to warn those who were about to be put to death. In this way, stories about Belzec reached us.

These reports concerning Belzec were about to turn into facts on the ground. They were the cause of great anxiety and fear. In the streets of the Jewish Quarter, several days before the roundup, people were already terrified, and without guidance or leadership, they asked one another "What can one do? What can one do?"

Early in the morning of August 10th, patrols surrounded all the entrances of the streets of the quarter. Gestapo, S.S., Sonderdienst Special Services, moved in groups of six. Each group of six circulated several steps into the streets.

Many Ukrainian military men were there to assist these Germans. Already two weeks earlier, Major General Katzmann, the chief executioner of Lvov and Eastern Lesser Poland, had distributed sealed documents containing genocidal plans to the labor camps. There were a number of Jews, too, who had received the documents at the *Commisarium*, an official office near the Smulka Square Plaza. There were not many 'lucky ones' like these. The majority of Jews looked with deadly fear for some sort of refuge, a hiding place, a place to escape to, but not one of them knew what could be done to save him or herself.

[Page 72]

Meanwhile, patrols circulated for several days, going from house to house, from corner to corner. For a small number of people, the Gestapo examined their documents and left them in place. For others, there was no mercy. Those who did not have documents, and those whose documents had been confiscated, were forcibly expelled from their houses. The Germans did not allow them to take any clothing or food with them. Instead, they gathered the Jews together, and anyone who resisted was shot to death on the spot.

I was in my workshop, but I didn't have any documents, so I locked the door and didn't answer when I heard them knocking. The Gestapo men broke down my door, and they found me hiding. They hit me on the head with a whip, and took me away with them. They pushed us into electric trolley cars. The crowding was so great that it was impossible to move or breathe. They transported us to the Janowian Camp.

This was already evening. They gathered all of us together in a wide field, in a closed circle. We were about 6,000 people. They commanded us to sit down, and it was forbidden to get up to move, or to extend a hand or foot. From a tower, they directed a floodlight upon us. It was as bright as noon. We sat very crowded, while we were surrounded by armed murderers. We all sat together, young and old, men, women and children of various ages. If someone got up, it was probably because that person preferred to be put out of their misery quickly. A few shots were heard, and then there was silence.

We sat like that all night. A deadly silence prevailed. No one cried, neither the women nor the children. At six in the morning, they ordered us to rise up from the wet grass, and to arrange ourselves in rows of four. Then a procession of the condemned began moving to the Klifarovian Station. The Gestapo and the Ukrainians surrounded us in a thick ring. Not a person was able to escape. They brought us to a plaza at the train station. There was a long freight train already waiting for us. The train had 50 cars. Loading us into the cars began as soon as they opened the doors. The Gestapo men stood on both sides. In their hands, they held whips, and they struck everyone, as they passed, on the face and the head. Every one of us had marks on the face and bruises on the head. The women cried bitterly, as did the children while clinging to their mothers. There were mothers with infants near their breasts among us. There were smaller and bigger children, young women and old women. We were knocked about by the Gestapo men, who hit us without mercy. People pushed one another. The train car doors were high up, so it was necessary to climb to go up. One person would make another fall. We hurried because we wanted this part to be over quickly. A Gestapo man with a machine gun sat on the roof of every car. The Gestapo men counted up to a hundred in every car. All of this was done at great speed, so that the loading of thousands of people on the cars took less than an hour.

In our shipment, there were many men who had worked and had all kinds of work documents. These were seemingly 'safe' documents.

Eventually, the Germans sealed the train cars. Pressed into the other bodies of trembling people, we stood crowded almost one on top of another. Suffocated and hot, we were close to madness. Not a drop of water, not a crumb of bread. The train finally moved at eight in the morning. I knew that in the locomotive, there were only two Germans working, a mechanic/engineer and a worker who kept the fire burning. The train traveled quickly, but to us it seemed that it was traveling forever. The train stopped three times, at Kolikova, at Zolkiev, and at Rawa-Ruska. These stops were required, it seemed, for arranging the route of the trains and the changing of the track. At the time of these stops, the Gestapo men would come down from the roofs of the cars but would not allow anyone to approach the train. They did not allow people who wanted to offer water through the small, screened-in windows, to the people faint with thirst, to come near the train.

[Page 73]

As we traveled, no one uttered a word. We knew that we were traveling toward death, that there was no chance of being saved. At first, complete equanimity prevailed. No weeping was heard. All of us were thinking about only one thing - how to escape. But there wasn't any opportunity. I noticed that the car, in which we were traveling, was entirely new. The window was so narrow, that I wasn't able to squeeze through it. In other cars, it seemed as though it might be possible to break through the doors because we heard several moments of shots fired at escapees. Not one person spoke to another. No one tried to calm the women who had begun to cry. No one stopped the children who were now crying bitterly. We all knew we were traveling to certain and awful death. We wanted that certainty to be over. Perhaps some had escaped, I don't know. Perhaps it was possible to attempt to run away from the train.

Near the afternoon, the train reached Belzec Station. This was a small station. Around it stood small houses. The houses contained the living quarters for the Gestapo men and the Ukrainian railroad workers. There was a small post office there. Belzec is located on the Lublin-Tomaszow railroad line. It was 15 kilometers from Rawa-Ruska. At the Belzec Station, the train was moved to a side track, which led one kilometer further, straight to the death camp. The side track passed through fields. On both sides of the fields, the area was totally clear. There wasn't one building.

The entire area around Belzec was occupied by S.S. men. It was forbidden for anyone to appear here. The Germans would shoot any civilians who mistakenly entered the area. The train would enter a courtyard whose length and breadth was approximately one kilometer, surrounded by barbed wire fencing and iron nets, which were placed, one upon another, at a height of two meters. The wire was not electrified. When the train entered the gate, the guard would close it and then enter the tower.

[Page 74]

Then the 'reception of the train' would begin. Several tens of S.S. men would open the cars with shouts of 'Raus von hier! Get out! Raus! Out!' Just as the S.S. did when the people boarded the trains, they would drive the people out of the cars with whips and curses. They would force the people to jump, all of them, old and young. They had to jump a meter's height down to the ground. People would break arms and legs. Children would be wounded. Everyone fell from the car, all of them dirty, weary and frightened.

The German engineer who drove the train would get down out of the locomotive and 'assist' with hard blows and shouts, expelling people from the train cars. Afterwards, he would personally enter every car and inspect it to see whether anyone remained. He especially knew every trick that people might do under the circumstances. When the train was empty and had been secured, he signaled with a small flag and drove the train out of the camp.

An elderly German with a thick black moustache – I don't know what his name was, but I would recognize him immediately – would appear. His look was that of an executioner. He was in charge of moving us into the camp. The road from the station to the camp was a two-minute walk. For four months, I always saw this murderer perform the same ritual. The people would enter the courtyard through a wooden gate, covered with barbed wire. A tower stood nearby. Inside there was a guard with a telephone. There were always several S.S. men with dogs.

Aside from the S.S. men, there were also *Zugsführers*, platoon leaders to greet the trains These were the overseers of the Jewish workers in the death camp. They were dressed without any insignia of the camps, so it was impossible to tell to whom or what service they were accountable or belonged. The sick, elderly and small children, those who were unable to walk on their own, would be placed on stretchers, and were made to sit on the edge of deep graves which had been dug. There, the S.S. agent named Fritz Ihrmann would shoot them, and afterwards push them into the grave with a club. Ihrmann was an expert in the murder of old people and small children. He was a high Gestapo agent who had black hair and an expressionless face. Like the others, he lived in Belzec, near the station, in a small house, entirely alone, and, like the others, with no family or wife.

Early in the morning, Ihrmann would appear in the camp. He would remain there throughout the day and receive the death transports. Immediately, after taking the victims out of the cars, some guards would herd them into a square, which was surrounded by other guards. Here Ihrmann would speak. There was a deadly silence. He would stand near the crowd. Everyone waited to hear. Suddenly, hope would arise in us – "If they speak to us, perhaps we will live, and perhaps there will be some work. Perhaps despite this..."

Ihrmann would speak in a loud, clear voice. "You are now going to get bathed. Afterwards, you will be sent to work." That was all. The people were joyous, happy that they were going to work, and there was handclapping. I remember these words of his, which used to be repeated every day, in most instances three times a day, during the four months I was in the camp. That was the moment of hope and illusion. The people would momentarily sigh with relief. Complete silence prevailed, and the entire crowd advanced in silence. The males went straight through the courtyard to the building on which a sign in large letters said, 'Bade und Inhalationsraume,' Bath and Inhalation Rooms. The females went about twenty meters further, to a large bunk that occupied an area of 15 by 30 meters. In this bunk, the women and girls had their hair shaved. They would enter without knowing what the room's purpose was. Again, a quiet moment prevailed. I knew afterwards that when a few moments passed, they would have the females sit on wooden benches in the middle of the bunk and eight Jewish barbers, automatons who were as silent as a tomb, would approach in order to shave their hair completely to the scalp. Little girls who had long hair would go first, before the others, to have their hair shaved. At that moment, the women would grasp the entire truth, and not one of them, nor any of the men, who had already gone to the chambers, had any doubts. Small girls who had a little bit of hair went with the men directly to the gas chamber. All of them, young and old, men, women and children, went to their death, all of them, except for a few men chosen as essential professionals in the camp.

Suddenly, in a transition from hope to absolute despair, the females would break out into wailing and shouting.

[Page 75]

Many women would become irrational, seemingly deranged. Others would go silently to their death, particularly the young women. In our transport, there were thousands of educated people, many young men, but the majority were women. It was this way in every transport that came afterwards.

I stood at the side, in the courtyard, along with a small group of people who were left for the digging of graves. I looked at my brothers, my sisters, my acquaintances, and my friends who were being led to their death. At the same time, they led the women, naked, shaved, like cattle to slaughter, without counting, moving them quickly. They were already destroying the men in one of the chambers. Shaving the women took approximately two hours. The preparations for murder and the murder itself took a similar amount of time.

More than ten S.S. men would urge the women on, with whips and sharp pikes, to go forward to the building in which the gas chambers were located, and then up three steps to the vestibule. And the policemen would count the people, up to 750, for each chamber. The policemen would then stab the women who resisted entering the chamber with pikes, and blood was spilled. Then they would push them into the killing room. I could hear the locking of the doors, the screams and shouts, the cries of despair, in Polish, in Yiddish, bloodcurdling crying from the mouths of women and children, and, afterwards, one awful joint scream. This horror lasted 15 minutes. The motor worked for 20 minutes. Then there was silence. The guards would open the doors from the outside and I, along with the other workers like me, who were left from previous transports, would approach the work without any expression on our faces.

The fate of every transport was like the fate of the transport in which I had arrived. The people were ordered to strip their clothes. They would leave the clothes in the courtyard. Ihrmann would always speak craftily and always say the same thing. The people were always happy at that moment. I saw the same spark of hope in the eyes of every new arrival. It was the hope that they were being sent for labor. However, in a moment, the Germans would begin to grab small children from their mothers' arms. The elderly and sick would be thrown on stretchers. The men and the small girls would be lead by shouts and curses, further and further from the rest of the people, straight to the gas chamber. The naked women would be cruelly directed to another bunk where they had their hair shaved. I knew exactly the moment at which all of them would finally understand what awaited them, the fear, the despair, the screams, the awful wails all mingled with the sound of the orchestra. The men, who were prodded with pikes or stabbed, would come to the chambers first. Meanwhile, there were people in the first chamber who had been waiting and suffering this torture for two hours. There was such great overcrowding that it was difficult to close the doors. Only after all six chambers were full did they activate the machine.

The machine was large, a meter and a half by a meter. It was an engine with wheels. The engine roared with a great whine while operating at high speed - so quickly that it was impossible to distinguish between the spokes of the wheels. Two guards operated the machine. It worked exactly 20 minutes by the clock. After 20 minutes, they would stop it. Immediately, they would open the doors of the chambers from the outside, from the side that led to the plaza, and there they would throw the bodies on the ground. In this way, they accumulated a huge pile of bodies, several meters high. The guards were not particularly careful at the time of the opening of the doors. We did not notice any odor. We did not even once see any tanks of gas. I only saw cans of benzene. Every day, they would consume from 80 to 100 liters of benzene.

After the people were asphyxiated, the policemen emptied the chambers of all the bodies. Most victims were in a standing position, looking as if they were asleep. They were not yet blue, but blood would spew here and there from the wounds that had been caused by the guards with pikes. Their mouths would be slightly opened, their arms contracted, sometimes pressed around their chests. The bodies, which were located near the doors, would fall out automatically like puppets when the doors were opened. Behind the gas chambers was a road of sand that absorbed blood and liquids from the corpses. We dragged the bodies along this road.

When the machine once malfunctioned, they called me in, since I was known as 'the expert of ovens.' I looked in it and saw glass pipes leading to every single chamber. The machine produced a vacuum that drew the air out of the chambers. Then the benzene produced carbon monoxide, which asphyxiated the victims. The cries for help, the shouts and screams of despair of those enclosed and being suffocated in the chambers would continue for 10 to 15 minutes, at first with loud and penetrating sounds. I heard awful screams and cries in all kinds of languages, because there were Jews there not only from Poland, but there were also transports of Jews from outside of Poland. Afterwards, the screams would become quieter until the chambers would become entirely silent. We would drag the bodies of people who had been alive just a short time before, with the aid of leather straps, to huge common graves, which were ready. The leather straps had buckles, which we would place on the hands of a corpse. Its head would often be stuck in the sand, and so we would pull. The guards ordered us to place the bodies of small children on our shoulders and carry them to the mass graves. When we were dragging the bodies, we would interrupt our work of digging graves. When we were digging the graves, we knew that in the chambers, thousands of our brethren were being murdered. In this way, we were compelled to work from early in the morning until evening. At dark, our workday was completed because the 'work' was only done by the light of day. The orchestra, too, would be playing from the morning to the evening.

After a while, I already knew the entire area pretty well. It was located in the midst of a young pine forest. The trees here grew close to one another. In order to minimize the penetration of light, the Germans tied these trees to one another, and in this way multiplied the density of the trees in the place where the chambers were located.

The Germans stretched wire over the roofs and placed vegetation upon them, with the intention of hiding the area from surveillance by airplanes. Near the bunks was a small courtyard surrounded by a wall of boards three meters high, between which not even a crack was left. The boarded walkway led to the chambers in such a way that it obstructed anything the victims might see, other than straight ahead. The building in which the gas chambers were located was low, broad and long, constructed of gray concrete. Its roof was flat and covered with tarred material. Above the roof, there was yet another roof of netting, which was covered with vegetation.

Outside the building there was a large flowerpot with multicolored flowers. Side doors led to the gas chambers. These doors were made of wood. Their width was a meter each, and pushed to the sides using handles. Without windows, the chambers were very dark. The ceilings of the vestibule and chambers were lower than ordinary rooms. Their height was no greater than two meters. On the wall opposite the entrance of the chamber were two doors which opened by pushing them outward. They were two meters in width. These were the doors, through which we would take the bodies out, after asphyxiation.

[Page 76]

On both sides of the gas chamber building there were graves, full or empty. I saw a complete row of graves, which were filled and covered with sand. After a while, the graves would sink. An empty grave always had to be ready.

There were two bunks for the extermination workers of the camp, one bunk for general workers, and the second bunk for 'professionals.' The two bunks were similar to one another. Each bunk contained 250 workers. Platforms inside were built in two levels. The platforms were constructed of boards, with a small board at a slant, sort of like a pillow for the heads of the workers. Near the bunks were kitchens. A little further was the storehouse, the administration area, a laundry, a sewing shop and, at the end, well-ordered bunks for the guards.

I was in the Belzec death camp for four months, from August until the end of November 1942, during the period of mass asphyxiation of Jews. My few companions in calamity, those few who were in the camp longer, told me that there were more killings during this time than before. The trains arrived every day without interruption. In most instances, there were three trains per day. In every train, there were fifty cars, and in every car about a hundred souls. In the event that the transports would arrive at night, the victims would wait in the sealed cars until six in the morning. Usually, at Belzec, between 10,000 and 15,000 Jews would be killed every day.

Sometimes, the transports were larger and they would arrive more frequently. Jews came from many places - and only Jews. At no time did another type of transport come. Belzec served as a place of extermination exclusively for Jews. Only the Gestapo guards and Zugsführers surrounded the area during the time that the victims were exiting the train cars. There were Jewish workers several steps further into the courtyard, ready for helping the victims strip off their clothes. Those workers would ask in whispers, "Where are you from?" The answers were whispered back, "From Lvov, from Krakow, from Weiliczka, Jaslo, Tarnow, etc." I observed this scene every day, twice, three times a day.

In the transports that came from outside of Poland, there were principally Jews from France. There were also Jews from Holland, Greece and even from Norway. I do not remember a transport of Jews from Germany. On the other hand, there were Jews from Czechoslovakia. They would come on cars similar to those in which they brought the Jews of Poland, but the Czechs came with baggage, and they had been allowed to bring food with them. Our transports from Poland were usually full of women and children. In the transports from outside the country, there were primarily men and very few children. The parents were apparently able to leave their children in the care of their countrymen, and to save them from their own awful fate. The Jews from outside would come to Belzec without any knowledge of what was about to happen to them. They were certain that some form of labor was awaiting them. They were dressed like cultured people. They were well-prepared for the journey. Yet the attitude of the German murderers towards these people was the same as it was towards people in the other transports, with the same system of murder. They were exterminated with the same cruelty and died in the same state of hopelessness. Approximately one hundred thousand Jews from outside the country arrived during the time that I was in the camp. Almost all of them were exterminated.

They would shave all the women before murdering them. They would not put them into a bunk. The rest of the women would wait in front of the bunk, naked, barefoot, even in the winter, and in the snow. The women would be crying with despair. At that moment, shouts and pleas would begin. The mothers would embrace their children. I would be horrified every time I saw this spectacle. They would lead a group of women who had been shaved out, and others would come and tread upon the multicolored hair, which would cover the entire floor of the bunk like a soft and high rug. After the shaving of all the women from the transport, four workers would sweep all the hair with brooms made of poplar wood and collect it in one big pile, up to a half meter in height. Then they would put the hair, into sacks of simple cloth, and place them in storage.

The storehouse of the victims' hair, underwear, and clothing was located in a special bunk, not large, approximately seven by eight meters. There they would collect the clothes and the hair for 10 days, and then they would separately load sacks with clothes and hair, and a freight train would come to take the spoils. People who worked in the office told us that the hair was sent to Budapest. A certain Jew, the attorney Schreiber, who was from the Sudetenland, worked in the office, and he would pass along this information. He was a decent man. Ihrmann promised Schreiber that he would take him along when he traveled during his furlough. One time, Ihrmann went away for a brief vacation. I heard Schreiber ask Ihrmann "Are you taking me with you?" Ihrmann answered – "not yet." In this manner, Irhmann would deceive Schreiber, who was later exterminated just like all the rest of the people. Schreiber told me that every several days, they sent an entire trainload of sacks filled with hair to Budapest. Aside from the hair, the Germans also took sacks filled with gold teeth.

On the road, which led from the gas chambers to the graves, in an area of several hundred meters, stood a few 'dentists' with forceps. They would stop every worker who dragged a body. They would open the mouth of the corpse, check for and remove any gold. Afterwards they would throw the gold into a sack. There were eight dentists. These were usually young men, who were left over from transports, just for the purpose of this work. I knew one of them close up. His name was Zucker. He was from Rzeszew, Poland. The dentists lived in a special small bunk together, along with the doctor and the pharmacist. At dark, they would bring the sacks filled with gold teeth to the bunk, and there they would refine the gold, and melt it into the shape of bars. A Gestapo man, Schmidt, would guard them. He would beat them when their work was done too slowly. They had to complete every transport within two hours. The gold bars were one centimeter thick, a half centimeter wide, and twenty centimeters long.

[Page 79]

Each day, they would bring valuable articles, such as money, dollars and jewelry out of the storehouse. S.S. men would collect this plunder personally, and put it in suitcases, which workers would carry to the Belzec Station Command Post, guarded by one of the Gestapo men.

The station was not far. Twenty minutes by foot. The concentration camp, that is, the place of killing in Belzec, was subject to the authority of this Command Post. Jews, who worked in Administration, would tell us that they would transfer every shipment of gold, valuable articles, and money to Lublin, where the Head Command was located, and whose authority the Command at Belzec was subject to.

The clothing, which they removed from the unfortunate victims, would be collected and transferred to a storehouse. There, ten workers were required to undo the seams of every garment with particular meticulousness, under the supervision of S.S. men, with the threat of a whip. The S.S. men would divide the money, which was found in the clothing, among themselves. Special S.S. men, always the same ones, were sent in for this inspection. The Jewish workers who arranged the clothes, and the undoing of seams, were not able to take any money for themselves, nor did they want to. What interest was there for us in money or jewelry? We were not able to buy anything, and we had no hope of remaining alive. Not one of us believed in a miracle. The Germans would conduct an exacting inspection of every worker. Frequently, we stepped on dollars that were thrown down on the floor, but we did not pay attention to them. We didn't even touch them. There was no benefit in this. Once, a shoemaker took five dollars intentionally and openly. They shot him and his son dead immediately. He went to death willingly. He wanted his life to be over. Death was certain. Why suffer more torture for an extended period of time? The dollars at Belzec served us in the event we were ready to die such an easier, instantaneous death.

I belonged to the fixed group of workers at the camp. In all, we were 500 men. Of the professionals there were about 250. Another 200 worked at jobs in which there was no need for professionals – in digging graves, and dragging bodies. We dug pits and common giant graves and dragged bodies. Professionals, too, were forced to participate in this work, after the completion of work in their profession. We dug with implements. There was also a machine, which dug and removed sand from the soil. That machine was used to heap sand next to the graves. A mountain of sand would be created, which would be used to cover a mass grave after it had been filled with bodies.

[Page 80]

Approximately 450 men worked regularly in the digging of one mass grave, which usually took an entire week. The most awful thing for me was the order to leave bodies at a height of a meter over the full grave and to cover the victims with sand. Thick black blood poured from the graves and flooded the entire area like a lake. We were forced to climb over these mass graves, in order to reach the next mass grave. Our feet wallowed in the blood of our brethren. We walked over the graves full of bodies, and that was the most evil and awful thing.

At the time of this work, Schmidt, the murderer, guarded us. He hit and kicked us if any of us did not, in his opinion, work quickly enough. He would order the worker to lie down, and would lash him with a whip. Schmidt would order the person being beaten to count the blows, and if the victim made a mistake, he would give him an additional twenty five to fifty blows. The person being whipped was usually not able to bear 50 blows. The victim would reach the bunk with difficulty and, the next day, he would expire. This scene would be repeated several times a day.

Every day they would kill up to 40 workers by shooting them. The doctor would present a list of people who were weakened, or the Oberzugsführer, the main supervisor of the prisoners, would present a list of 'offenders,' such that every day 30 or 40 prisoners were exterminated. At lunch hour, they would be led to the grave and shot. Every day, the Germans would supplement the list with the same number of people from a transport. The administration office created a list of previous and new workers, and calculated how many they needed for the number of working prisoners to remain at 500.

We knew, for example, that Jewish slave laborers had built the camp and installed the asphyxiation machine. Not one of that group remained alive. It was a miracle if some of the workers at Belzec remained alive after five or six months.

The same two guards always worked at the machine. When I entered the camp, I found them occupied in this work, and when I left the camp, they remained in the same place. The Jewish workers had no contact with them, or with the other guards. When people from the transport would ask for a drop of water, the guards would shoot Jewish workers for offering it.

Already at three-thirty in the morning, the officer of the guard would pass by the bunk at night, knock on the door, and shout: "Get up! Get out!" Before we were able to get up, the murderer Schmidt would burst in and chase us out with a whip. We would run out with one shoe in hand or barefoot. In most cases, we would not take off all our clothes before sleep. We would lie down even with our shoes on, because in the morning we didn't have a chance to get dressed.

[Page 81]

It was still dark in the morning, when they would awaken us. To create light was forbidden. Schmidt would move around in the bunk and would hit right and left. We would get up, unfortunate and weary, to the point of exhaustion, just the same as when we lay down to sleep. Each one of us received a thin blanket. We could cover ourselves with it, or spread it out on the platform. At the storehouse, they chose old rumpled rags for us to wear. If someone complained, he would receive a slap in the face.

In the evening, they would turn on the light for half an hour. Afterwards, they would put out the light. The Oberzugsführer would circulate with a whip in his hand and would not permit us to converse. He would speak with us in a low voice.

The workers in the camp were mostly men, whose wives, children and parents had been exterminated by gassing. Many had obtained a *tallit*, a prayer shawl, and *tefillin*, phylacteries, from the storehouse, and when the Germans locked the bunk at night, we would hear from the platforms the whispers of prayer. We prayed the *Kaddish* in memory of the victims. Afterwards, there was complete silence. We did not complain. We were completely depressed. The fifteen Zugsführers lived with illusions, but not us.

All of us were people devoid of will. We were one body. I remember a few names, but very few. There was no value to knowing who a person was or what he was called.

I knew that the doctor was a young man who had lived beforehand near Przemysl. His name was Jakobuwitz. I also knew a merchant from Krakow. His name was Schlissel, he and his son. A Jew from Czechoslovakia, his name Elbogen, who had owned a bicycle shop. The butcher, Goldschmidt, was known from the restaurant at Karlsbad called the Hanika Brothers. One was not interested in the other. Life had passed us by when we were working mechanically.

At noon, we would get lunch. We would approach two windows. At the first one, we would get gravy, and at the other, a half liter of soup with grits, that is to say, water. Sometimes there were potatoes in the soup. Before the meal, we were required to sing songs, and again in the evening, before drinking coffee. At that time, we could hear the screams of those being asphyxiated in the gas chambers, while the orchestra played.

The S.S. men lived in Belzec and, in this place of killing, without wives. Even at a time of a feast, there were only men. This is how it was until October, when a transport arrived from Zamoszcz, with Jewish women from Czechoslovakia. In this shipment there were several dozen women whose husbands worked in the death camp. It was decided to keep many of them as workers. Forty were designated to work in the kitchen, in the laundry and in the sewing shop. It was forbidden for them to see their husbands. They peeled potatoes in the kitchen, washed pots, carried water. I do not know what their fate was. Certainly their lot was like that of all those confined to the camp. These women were all educated. They had come with their baggage. Some had a little bit of butter. They gave us what they had. They helped the men who worked in the kitchen or in its vicinity. They lived in a special small bunk.

[Page 82]

A *Zugsführerin* supervised them. During work hours, I would see these women conversing among themselves. I would repair the ovens everywhere and see them as I would go around the entire camp. They were not beaten like the Germans beat us. Their work would be finished toward evening, and they would arrange themselves two in a row and stand in line to get soup or coffee. As with us, the Germans did not take the women's clothes from them and did not give them striped clothing. It was not worth their while to institute a uniform costume for such a short period.

They sent the women straight from the cars, with their clothes, and without shaving their heads, to work in the shops and in the kitchen. Through the kitchen windows, they were able to observe the death transports which arrived at the camp every day.

Slaughter of the victims filled the camp space each day, and it was usual to see mass fear and mass murder daily. But aside from this, there were isolated instances of personal torment. At Belzec, there never were *appells*, or appeals. There was no necessity for them. The awful scenes took place without any advance notice.

It was near the 11th of November, and already cold, with mud covering the ground. During a storm, a transport arrived from Zamoszcz, one of many. In this transport were all the members of the Council of Elders, the Judenrat. When they already stood naked, according to the usual procedure, the men were led to the chambers, and the women to the bunk for the shaving of hair. The chairman of the Council of Elders was ordered to remain in the courtyard.

While the guards led the transport to extermination, the entire entourage of the S.S. men gathered around the chairman. I don't remember what his name was, but I saw that he was a middle aged man, pale as a corpse, and totally quiet.

The S.S. men ordered the musicians in the orchestra to go over to the courtyard and to wait for instructions. The orchestra, in which six musicians took part, would usually play in the area between the gas chambers and the graves. They would play without interruption on instruments, which had been taken from prior victims. I was then working as a plasterer close by, and I saw the entire episode. The S.S. men ordered the musicians to play. They played the violin, the trumpet and the accordion. The music lasted a while. After a short time, the S.S. men stood the chairman of The Council of Elders of Zamoszcz near a wall and beat him until blood flowed. They used whips whose tips were lead. They intentionally hit him on the head and in the face. Ihrmann, the fat S.S. man, Schwarz, Schmidt and several guards took part in the violence. They ordered the victim to dance and jump during the beating, with the accompaniment of the music. After a time, they brought him a crust of bread and forced him to eat during the blows. He stood, covered in blood, somber and serious. I didn't hear him make a sound. The torture of this man lasted seven hours. The S.S.

men stood and laughed. "This is a more important man, the chairman of The Council of the Jews!" they shouted loudly and fanatically. Only at six in the evening did Schmidt lead him to the grave. After all the torture, they shot him in the head, and pushed him by his leg into the pit of bodies that had already been asphyxiated.

There were also other unusual instances. A short time after my coming to Belzec, they chose a young man from a transport. He was a specimen of health, power and youth. He amazed us with his quiet spirit.

[Page 83]

He looked around and asked almost with jocularity "Does anyone escape from here?" That was enough for one of the Germans. This young man, almost a boy, was then tortured until he was almost dead. They then stripped off his clothes, and hanged him upside down on a scaffold. He was left hanging for three hours. He was powerful and continued to live. They took him down, placed him on the sand, and with clubs stuffed sand down his throat. That was how he died.

Sometimes, transports larger than usual would arrive. There were occasions when instead of fifty cars, sixty or more would pull in. One time, not long before my escape, in November, they forced 100 of the new arrivals, who were already naked, to labor in the burial of the corpses. The Gestapo men realized that the designated workers who were in the camp were not sufficient to place all of the many corpses into the graves. They chose only the young men from the transport. During the entire day, these youngsters dragged the corpses to the graves, and were prodded on with whips. They were not given even one drop of water. They were naked in the snow and cold. In the evening, the murderer Schmidt, led them to a grave and shot them with a pistol, one after the other, to the last one. I did not hear cries. I only saw how they tried to be the first in line for death, these remnants of the living and anonymous, devoid of deliverance.

The camp was entirely under the watch of armed guards and more than ten S.S. men. Not many of them were active, but a few stood out at every step for their special cruelty. They were really wild beasts. Some murdered and beat 'in cold blood,' but others still enjoyed the murder, which they committed. Their faces looked overjoyed. I saw them happy during the time that they looked at people, naked and pierced with pikes, who were led to the chambers. They looked with pleasure at the despairing human apparitions, particularly at the young men.

In the most lovely small house near the Belzec Station, the head commander of the camp lived. That was the Obersturmführer, whose surname I do not remember. The name was short. He came to the camp infrequently. He would appear in connection with some incident. He was a murderer, tall in stature, broad-shouldered, forty years old or more, with a simple facial expression. His appearance was that of a murderer from birth. A beast in human form.

Once, the death machine malfunctioned. When informed about it, he came riding on a horse. He gave orders to repair the machine, but did not allow the removal of the people from the gas chambers. They would choke and expire for several hours more. His legs were bent, shaking in anger as he shouted. Even though he would appear infrequently, he instilled fear in the S.S. men. He lived alone, with a guard attendant who served him. The guard would transmit reports to him daily. This head commander, and many of the Gestapo, did not have a fixed connection to the camp.

The Gestapo had a dining hall of their own, with a cook who was brought from Germany to cook for all of them. Their families never came to visit them, so each of them lived alone. They raised goats and ducks.

[Page 84]

People reported that, in the spring, they were sent baskets full of cherries, and received wines and liquor daily. At one time, I repaired an oven there. Two young Jewish women worked in cleaning feathers off the slaughtered geese. They threw me an onion and a radish. I also saw a village girl who worked there. Aside from them, only guardsmen-attendants were there.

Every Sunday, they would bring the orchestra and arrange a feast. Only the Gestapo men would assemble there. They ate greedily and drank. They would toss remnants of their food to the musicians. When the commander would appear in the camp, on a few occasions, I saw the Gestapo men and the policemen trembling with fear.

Aside from the head commander, four other murderers were in charge of the Gestapo men, and supervised and directed the entire murder operation. It is difficult to describe greater murderers. One of them, Fritz Ihrmann, was approximately thirty years old. Scharführer Schtab, the supply director of the camp, was an expert in the murder of children and elderly by shooting. He committed the most cruel deeds quietly, as if he were made of stone. He would be silent and behave with secrecy. Yet every day he would speak in front of the victims to tell them they were going to a bathhouse and to labor. He was a person with complete criminal consciousness.

The Oberscharführer, Reinhold Faix, would commit his deeds of cruelty in a different manner. He was from Gabluntz on the river Niese. He was married, and the father of two children. His manner of speech was like that of an educated person. He spoke rapidly. If someone did not understand his words immediately, he would hit that person and would shout at the sky like a madman. Once he ordered the kitchen to be whitewashed. A Doctor of Chemistry, a certain Jew, worked at this. The whitewasher stood above, on the edge of a ladder, near the ceiling. Faix ordered him to go up and down every instant, struck him with a whip in the face until blood poured from it, and it became swollen. This was how he did his work. Faix gave an impression of being mentally unbalanced. He played the violin. He ordered the orchestra to play the tune, *Goralu, Czy Ci Nie Zal*, without letup. He would order people to sing, to dance, and would torment and strike them for his enjoyment. He was a mad beast.

I don't know which of them was the crueler, and more fearsome – whether Faix or the Fat Murderer, or the short swarthy Schwartz who was from the interior of Germany. He would examine the guards to see if they were cruel enough towards us, and if they were hitting us hard enough. He supervised us at grave digging. He did not allow a moment of rest. With a roar, he would chase the men from the graves and prod them to go to the chambers, to the place where the piles of corpses waited for their trip to the deep graves. There he would gather us, and then run us again to the graves. The men waited at the edge of the graves, and with looks of madness upon noticing the children, the elderly, and the sick in the pits, waited for death. Schwartz would force them to look at the corpses and the blood, and to breathe the odors of decay. They wished for the instant the bloodthirsty Ihrmann would finish them off with gun shots. "Hands down!" he would shout, and derive much enjoyment from these acts of cruelty.

The young Volksdeutscher, an ethnic German, Henni Schmidt, was also apparently a Latvian. He derived even greater enjoyment from his cruel work. He spoke German in a strange manner, instead of "s" he pronounced a "t", not "was" but "wat".

[Page 85]

In the Belzec Death Camp

[Page 86]

With the guards, Schmidt spoke Russian. He did not want to leave the camp even for one day. Flexible, nimble, thin, with the mouth of a robber, always drunk, he moved around from four in the morning to the evening, all over the camp. He beat his prisoners, looked on with attentiveness at the tortures of the victims, and enjoyed this spectacle. "This one is the worst murderer," the prisoners would whisper among themselves, and immediately they would reply to one another "all of them are the worst." In a place where they would go out of their way to torture the people, there he would appear the first. He was always present at the time of putting unfortunate victims in the chambers. He would listen to the penetrating cries, which would arise from the awful chambers at the time of the asphyxiation of the women. He was 'the living spirit' of the camp, the most depraved and bloodthirsty beast. He would look at the profoundly weary and sad faces of those returning in the evening to their bunks with delight. He honored each one with a blow to the head with his whip. If one of us would slip away, he would chase after him and beat him. These Gestapo men, and the others who did not stand out, were some 'species of strange beasts.' Not one of them was human even for an instant.

From seven o'clock in the morning until dark, they would beat the people in all kinds of ways. At dark, they would return to the small houses, which were near the station. The guards stood during the nights on watch with their machine guns. By day, the Gestapo men would go out to receive the death transports with festivity.

The greatest holiday for the murderers was Himmler's visit. That was in the middle of October. From the morning, we saw that the murderous Gestapo men were working in a manner shrouded in secrecy. On that day, the entire process of the murder of thousands of people lasted less time. Everything was done very quickly. Ihrmann announced, "A high-ranking personality is about to come. There must be order!" They did not say who was about to come, but everyone knew, and the guards whispered among themselves about this.

Near three o'clock in the afternoon, Himmler came with Major General Katzmann, the head murderer of Lvov and the region, along with a subordinate and ten Gestapo men. Ihrmann and the others accompanied them, and showed the guests the chambers. The workers were occupied in taking the dead to the graves where they gradually accumulated an awful heap of young and entirely small corpses, the bodies of children. While the prisoners dragged the corpses, Himmler watched for half an hour and then left. I saw these Gestapo men happy, in a blissful state, from a successful visit. They were very satisfied and were laughing. I heard them talking about advance payments.

I am unable to define the mood in which we lived – neither my own mood, nor that of the prisoners who were condemned to death, nor what we felt when we heard the cries of the children or the awful screams of the people being asphyxiated every day.

Three times a day, we saw thousands of people who were close to derangement. We too were near madness. Day after day passed upon us. We ourselves did not know how, but we did not live even a moment with illusions. We perished a little bit every day, together with all the transports of people who had another moment of the torture of illusion. Complacent and despairing, we did not even feel hunger or cold. Everyone awaited his or her turn, and knew that we would be subjected to torments that were beyond human strength, and would then perish. Only when we heard the cries of the children – "Mommy, I was a good boy! Darkness! Darkness!" would our hearts be torn to pieces. And afterwards, we would again stop feeling.

[Page 87]

At the end of November, I had already concluded four months of my stay in the killing place, Belzec. The murderer, Ihrmann, notified me one morning that much tin was required in the camp. I was by then swollen and covered with bruises, the pus flowing from the wounds. The Gestapo man, Schmidt, had struck me on both sides of my face with a club. With a mocking laugh, Ihrmann said that I would travel under guard to Lvov to bring the tin. "Don't escape!" he told me.

I traveled by auto with an escort of four Gestapo men and a guard. In Lvov, I remained in the auto, after a day of loading tin, under the guard of a certain murderer. The rest went to spend some time in the town. I sat for several hours without interest and without movement. I noticed by chance that my guard had fallen asleep and that he was snoring. With a spontaneous movement, without thinking about it even for a moment, I leaped from the auto. The murderer was still sleeping. I went up to the sidewalk and pretended for a moment that I was searching for something near the tin. Then very slowly, I walked away. On Legions Street, there was a great deal of traffic. I covered my face with my hat. It was dark in the streets, so no one could see me. I remembered where a Polish woman, my landlady, had lived. I went to her. She hid me. It took twenty months for the wounds, which were over my entire body, to heal. Not only the wounds. I had witnessed horrifying events, which made even my rest incredibly tense. In dreams and while awake, I heard the screams of the tortured victims, and the cries of the children. I kept hearing the roaring of the motor. I was unable to tear the awful facial expressions of every one of the murderous

Gestapo men from my mind. I remained in this condition until the moment of Liberation.

When the Red Army expelled the German murderers from Lvov, I was able to go out into the world to look around me without fear. I could breathe pure air freely, and, this time, the first time since my German captivity, I could think about what had happened, and I began to experience feelings. There awakened in me a strong desire to see the place in which the Germans had asphyxiated two and a half million human beings who wanted very much to live. To live!

After the passage of some time, I was able to travel back to Belzec. I spoke with people who lived in the area. They told me that in 1943, the transports had gradually decreased. The center of the extermination of the Jews had been transferred to the gas chambers at Auschwitz. In 1944, they dug open the pits, poured benzene on the corpses, and incinerated them. Black smoke blew over tens of kilometers around the huge bonfires. The wind carried the stench great distances, for long days and nights, for long weeks.

And afterwards, people who lived there said the Germans had ground up the bones and the wind scattered the dust over fields and forests. The machine for grinding the bones of the victims was put together by Shpilka, the prisoner from Janowska Street, who was brought to Belzec for that sole purpose. He told me that he had already found the mounds of bones. But all the buildings had disappeared. He succeeded in escaping and surviving afterwards. He now lives in Hungary. He recounted this information to me shortly after the liberation of Lvov by the Red Army.

[Page 88]

When the production of 'Chemical Fertilizer' from the bones of millions of people was finished, they covered the excavated graves with earth. The Germans then very diligently straightened up the area of the grounds, which was drenched with blood. The German predatory beast covered the Jewish graves of the millions in the Valley of Killing in Belzec with verdant greenery.

I soon parted from the people who had reported this information, and went on the road, which had been known to me as 'the side track.' The track did not exist any longer. The field led me to a fragrant living pine forest. A deep silence prevailed there. Amidst the forest was a large, bright forest field.

The Command of Murderers at the Belzec Camp

[Page 89]

In the Ranks of the Partisans

*The capture of the city of Skalat,
one night, by the Kovpak Brigade,
in July 1943, plus the joining of the
Partisans by a group of Jewish
young people, that night, left echoes
in Holocaust Literature. We have
gathered all the material, which has
been published on this topic – a
moving experience, still remembered
by many of us.*

[Page 90]

With the Kovpak Men to the Carpathian Mountains

By Baruch Amitz

In the days of the German's destruction of our town, we young men and women awakened and warned everyone, especially those who cherished illusions and who put our community to sleep in the face of the coming danger of destruction.

Confused and stunned, we searched for guidance and direction. We sought a directing hand, but it did not exist. "Where are the leaders?" we asked ourselves. We realized that we had to act on our own. We decided to flee to the forest and to organize ourselves there.

The first pioneers – Shalom Schechter, Ya'akov Orenstein, Kuperschmid, the Brick brothers, Yaver and others – who made the decisive step and escaped to the forests, under especially difficult conditions, paved the way for those who came after them.

We reached the forest from the Ghetto, from the Skalat labor camp, and later from the Kamionka labor camp. We had left behind the bodies of our families in Belzec, and in the mass graves in the fields of Novosilka, near Skalat.

The days of terror were gradually farther behind us, but we still felt fear within our hearts. Without a homefront, surrounded by loneliness and dread, we continued to feel the cruelty of life as we waited for the hour of liberation.

When we arrived in the forest, we encountered many hardships. We wandered from one hiding place to the next, worn and battered, lacking weapons, and isolated.

Even though there were some individuals, here and there, who did not try to deceive us or sell us out to the Germans during this dark time – and it is forbidden to forget them – they were very few. Remembered for their kindness, *Zachur La Tov*, are the people of the small village, surrounded by the *Ostra–Mogila Forest*.

Every night our people, Fishel Feinstein, David and Herschel Shapiro, Pisi Sass, Shamki Epstein, Mottel Brick, Nadzya Weinzaft and others, would drag dried tree branches into the bunkers in the forest, drag sacks of potatoes, or dig and perfect the bunkers.

I remember how with Nadzya Weinzaft and Mottel Brick, we entered the village of Horodnitza in the middle of the night and took spoils from a rich peasant known as a Nationalist Ukrainian. When we came to his home, he was so terrified that he handed over everything we wanted–food and clothing. We also wanted weapons. Though we were certain that he had large quantities of weapons and ammunition stashed somewhere, we didn't find any.

[Page 91]

Many of us felt compelled to take food and clothing from the peasants by force. To achieve that, we constructed 'rifles' made of wood and, in that way, instilled fear in the peasants. We would steal into the peasants' fields at night, take potatoes and other foods hidden in their cisterns, in order to quell our hunger. Our raids increased the hatred of the peasants towards us, with additional intensity.

We felt orphaned and abandoned, but we knew that we were the last of the Jews of Skalat, and that our obligation was to avenge the blood of our loved ones. It was clear to us that our going out to the forest was not yet equal to the image of the partisans who fought the German enemy. Our task was, therefore, to win the status of fighters worthy of the name. To make that happen, we needed weaponry, but weaponry did not exist. After several months of wandering among the thickets of the forests, we reached the conclusion that we would not be able to hold out for much longer in our circumstances.

In the second half of 1943, reports reached us of Partisan activity in the forests nearby. We did not know with any clarity who the Partisans were, but we searched for ways to get in touch with them. The Partisans paved the way for us. After a difficult battle with the Germans, they captured Skalat. We decided to join them at any cost.

Our appearance in the Kovpak Brigade aroused the attention of all the partisans – especially the Jewish partisans. After a crushing three–month journey, we stood solemnly, arranged in two columns, to receive weapons. We were about eighty people from Skalat and the vicinity. Only a small handful of our entire town merited this honor–status. Our pride was immense.

In the order of the day, the partisans informed us of their intention to organize and set up the 'Seventh Squad.' This was a team solely made up of Jews – soldiers and commanders. I still remember the words of the commander of the Squad. He spoke to us in Yiddish.

"Remember! We, here, represent the Jewish People. We will carry ourselves honorably. Let us not embarrass our Afflicted People. Our presence as a brigade, as a separate Jewish unit, serves as testimony and proof that not all the Jews were led like sheep to the slaughter!"

We were so energized by these words, and by this solemn assembly, that tears flowed from our eyes. We received weapons, and that very night we, the Jewish Seventh Squad, took part in a battle at a Ukrainian village near the Zabroch River. It was our first battle, face to face with the Germans. In this encounter, we destroyed several German positions and killed several tens of Germans. And we took away weapons and ammunition.

Our heroic stand in that first battle instilled in us a feeling of bravery and valor. On the day after the clash, when General Kovpak was informed of the details of the battle and of our active participation in it, he approached us and blessed us with his words:

"Honor to you, sons of Maccabees!" This was, in our eyes, the greatest appreciation that we could receive from a Russian commander – to be seen as Jewish fighters and avengers.

The road ahead of us was still long. Our main goal was to sabotage and damage the petroleum refineries in the Carpathian Mountains. Overcoming difficult and complicated situations, we reached the summit of the Carpathians. And there, we fought under especially difficult circumstances against special German mountain regiments. Yet, we had great success in carrying out our mission.

[Page 92]

I do not have any doubt that we, the group of Jewish youth from Skalat, proved ourselves to be fierce and courageous fighters.

The wall of the fighters in the Museum of Yad Mordechai
In the seventh row from the bottom, on the right side, Skalat is mentioned

[Page 93]

Fire Caught the Forest

*From Gad Rosenblatt's book **Fire Caught the Forest**, an excerpt that relates to the young people of Skalat, who joined the partisans under the command of General Kovpak*

The sun came out and dried the earth, and birdsong could be heard through the trees. We did not manage to get even a bit of sleep, since we were attacked by the Germans here. Not far from this spot was the town of Skalat. When our arrival in the forest became known to the Germans encamped in the town, they came out to attack us. Our men of the Third Squad and the Lankin Cavalry killed many German soldiers, and caused the ones still alive to flee in every direction.

With a smile, Chartchik told me about the battle. In the ripe grain that covered the fields stretching from the forests to Skalat, chains of Germans marched and combed the area looking for Jews. They paused every few steps, kneeled on the ground, and opened fire upon the field and forest in front of them. The commander of the Third Squad had given the order not to open fire until his instruction to do so. Our men crouched in a ditch dividing the forest from the fields of grain, with their fingers on the triggers of their machine guns and submachine guns. Chartchik said that quiet nerves of steel were required. Imagine! Our men watching the Germans in front of them a distance of four hundred, three hundred, two hundred meters, and still waiting to open fire on them – until Karpanko would give the signal, a loud whistle, and, all over, our weapons simultaneously opened a hailstorm of fire, and mowed down the attackers and the grain together. As one, the fighters of the Third arose and, with a great shout, spread out over the Germans. The remnant of the German troops began a panicky retreat. A few succeeded in reaching the town. At their heels, the Third Squad and Lankin's Cavalry pursued, and entered the town to battle with the German garrison force and the Ukrainians of the civil administration. Our men of the Third burned, damaged and destroyed everything, while Pavlovsky took large quantities of liquor, wine, sugar, oil, butter, flour, meat, articles of clothing and leathers. During the conflict, they encountered a detention camp of Jews fenced in with barbed wire.

They set the Jews free, and immediately the Jews showered the partisans with kisses and tears of joy.

I stood at the crossroads and saw the men of the Third Squad when they returned from the battle, clothed in new uniforms, and wearing boots, which they had looted in Skalat. They were marching and singing and the forest rang with their voices. We only had two killed and several wounded.

We moved back into the forest and finally reached the military staff. Patti and I went to see the Jews who had been liberated in Skalat. Near there, we found more than one hundred men, women, and children, young and old, sitting and eating in the shade of trees. I approached one of the men and asked him in Yiddish how he was doing. I asked him to tell me about the camp and about the people of Skalat. He told me that, in the city, there was a camp, where the people had worked at forced labor. From time to time, the Germans would find people from among them and 'transfer' them to an unknown place. Theirs was the last group imprisoned behind the barbed wire fence, waiting for their sentence, until we came and liberated them.

[Page 94]

The survivors were confused, excited, and sad. They didn't know whether they should rejoice at their deliverance, or to cry bitterly over the hundreds of their loved ones who had perished. When they fixed their gaze upon me, I saw fear in their eyes. All of a sudden, I realized that I was dressed in a German uniform from my head to my feet. My explanation pacified them. Patti circulated and talked to them. It was clear that many of them wanted to join our brigade, particularly the young people among them. I wondered what would happen to the old people and the children. In our situation as a wandering brigade, engaged in incessant battles with the enemy, it would be impossible to have them join us. And Patti believed that they would be able to remain alive by finding refuge with the local peasants or in the forests.

When I returned to the camp, Eli Shcharbata told me that he had been called to the staff, to meet with Kovpak and Rodaniov. They explained to him that they had decided to organize all the liberated Jews from the Skalat labor camp into a special squad. But these Jews would need preparation and intense training until they would be fit enough to enter the ranks of the partisans. He also told me that Kovpak and Rodaniov were appointing me as Commander of this Squad. Shcharbata had requested a delay until the evening in order to consult with Patti and with me. Patti believed that there was no alternative but to forego our belonging to the Third Squad – which was dear to us, and which had absorbed us so well – and to devote ourselves to setting up the new Jewish squad. I too was of the opinion Jewish honor should stand above everything, and that it was important to devote ourselves to turning these people into soldiers, and into worthy partisans. Before meeting with the command, we agreed on the following suggestions for the structure of the squad: the Commander of the Squad – Yoel Shcharbata; the Political Commissar – Chaim Vitshin (Patti); the Commander of Section A – Gad Rosenblatt; the Commander of Section B – Adam Cooper; the Commander of Section C – Zisi Chaitchik. The new members of this squad were very weak and needed to get stronger. They also needed to acquire battle training and travel discipline. We suggested that three section commanders be appointed, instead of the usual two, that every section should have twenty–five men, and that each section be divided into two sub–groups. We also decided to ask the command to transfer all Jews from the first troop into the new squad. This reinforcement would aid us in solidifying a fighting and stable squad. In addition, we decided to submit a special request – to favor our group, which had been expelled from the brigade, and to join it to our national squad.

Toward evening, Shcharbata returned from the staff, rejoicing and very encouraged. He told us they had agreed to everything, and consented to all the requests. In addition, they recommended providing automatic weaponry, arranging transportation, and special treatment in all aspects of the squad, such as favoring the squad with status equal to the other partisans.

We brought all the people of Skalat into a special area of the forest, which was set aside for us. Shmuel Fishfaider was appointed quartermaster, and he, Shcharbata and I approached the staff to take delivery of weapons and the means of transportation. We received sixty–five rifles and ten wagons for transportation of supplies and ammunition. We also began arranging an internal organization, and placed the people into sections and sub–sections. The entire squad numbered seventy–five men, including ten young women. I set up a special camp for my section, and began training my men in the care and use of rifles and grenades.

[Page 95]

The day ended, and the sun set over the Zabroch. In all the expanses of the forest, campfires were lit, each section with its own campfire. I too lit a campfire, and I sat with the men of my section all around me. The fire lit up the darkness, and their hearts warmed. I was happy to sit with them, as brothers in arms engaging in the work of revenge, as one "teaching the Sons of Judah the bow." As I scanned the faces of the men of my section, I asked myself: are these the people who were liberated three days ago from the camp in Skalat? Were these the same people who, only a few days ago, were 'bond slaves' condemned to death, imprisoned, enclosed and waiting for the redemption of death? They had changed their clothes, shined their boots, straightened their statures, and now a spark of hope was in their eyes. Their entire look said 'freedom!'

I introduced the two commanders of the other sub–sections: "These are your commanders," I said, "who will lead you in the battles which are anticipated for you. They are veteran fighters who have already been tested in many firefights. It is essential that you listen to them. We, the men of the command, will ready you and aid you in overcoming the difficulties of becoming partisans. Fortune has smiled upon you and brought the Brigade to Skalat, to battle the enemy and to liberate you. Now, you, too, have weapons to strike the Nazis, to kill the murderers of our parents, our children, and our wives, the destroyers of our people. Guard your weapon from every patrol! Use it properly to shoot your target! Don't disappoint us! Don't disappoint us! Don't disappoint the name of the squad or its honor with deeds that oppose the laws of the Partisans! Remember that the mission of our Brigade, military unit number 00117, is the fulfillment of order No. 200, which prohibits taking anything from the civilian inhabitants of the place of battle, neither food nor clothing. Remember that anyone who transgresses this order commits a capital offense!"

During the conversation, I was asked, "Where will we be directing our movements, and will we pass through Skalat a second time?" I replied that the norm in the Brigade is never to ask where we were going. The route of the journey and the plans of action were exclusively bound by the military secrecy of the Commander. And our hearts were energized by our conversation.

Afterwards, they erupted in a lively songfest, when one of the veterans raised his voice and began singing one of the Songs of the Partisans, which were beloved by us. The song was about a young Partisan who fell slain, there on the rocky soil, in a virgin field. The rest of this veteran's companions followed after him. And the echo of the forest carried the sounds of the song as far as the mountains of Zabroch and its forests.

Only a few minutes passed, and the roaring of airplane engines assaulted our ears. Five airplanes flew above the river to the forest opposite. The sounds of bombs thundered, and the rattle of machine guns sawed the air. The planes circled above and shot without let–up. From the forest and from the river below, we heard the cries of the wounded.

[Page 96]

I crawled and reached a bush near which I had left weapons and clothing. The airplanes, which had completed their murderous work, disappeared. I hurried to the camp in the forest. In my heart, I sensed bad things to come. I reached the squad, and my world became dark. The field was cut by craters the bombs had made. Several wagons were smashed, and the horses lay with their bellies torn open. On every side, screams of the wounded burst forth. The remaining people lay terrified, shocked, and powerless. I began to assemble the men of the squad and to organize help for the wounded. Among the wounded were Shcharbata, Adam Cooper, Zisi Chaitchik, Fima Galfand, and many others. Almost all of the leaders of command had been affected. We laid the wounded on the wagons that remained intact, and sent them to the medical department of the staff.

Surely, bad luck! So many wounded among us, and this, only a few days after our victory and reorganization. There was no free time to devote oneself to anything other than the Partisans who had emerged safely from the bombings and held muster. In the line stood forty–five men. All the commanders of the sections and sub–sections were wounded. Only the Political Commissar, Chaim Vitshin, two sub–section commanders, and I were left uninjured

I was still standing with the Partisans when the squad courier appeared and informed me that the Commander of the Brigade, General Kovpak, and the subs, Polkovnik and Varshigora, were approaching us. I was in a state of confusion. A meeting would happen suddenly, in such terrible circumstances, after the bombing, when the squad camp had been destroyed, and all around was chaos. I had not managed to calm my mind, and here Kovpak was striding toward me, while he was leaning on his shepherd's staff, and next to him Varshigora and Bazima. I gave an order to stand at attention. I straightened myself and reported to them regarding the forty–five men arranged in a row, and about all the rest who were wounded and had been sent to the medical camp. "The Seventh Squad, Major–General, are arranged at your command."

"Squad, stand at ease!" ordered Kovpak. He stood and surveyed the men, was silent a bit, and afterwards he said:

"It is imperative that you know that we are soldiers, and ahead of us is a difficult, long road. I understand the difficulty of your becoming accustomed to that, but there is no alternative. It is incumbent upon you to be Partisans, like all the rest, or not to be in the Brigade. Those who seek to part with us are entitled to do so, and we will assist you to get along in this environment, just as we have already arranged for many of you, from the day you left Skalat. The weak, and those who are afraid of the difficulties, may leave the rank. But those remaining are obligated to follow all the laws of Partisans. Many of you were wounded, but we will try to help you heal. During a bombing, one should get down on the ground and lie motionless. From now on, Comrade Grigory Rosenblatt will command you, and as a political commissar, Comrade Patti Vitshin will continue to serve.

Kovpak handed the command over to me and went on his way with the men in his staff. I asked Patti to speak with the men of the squad and encourage them a bit. I took the list of my soldiers, to see whether there were any among them with a military past, in order to appoint them to positions of subsection commanders. I found two who had served in the Polish army. I took them out of the circle of those reclining in conversation, and persuaded them to accept the position. They were afraid to take upon themselves such a responsibility, especially with untrained people, but eventually they accepted their new posts.

[Page 97]

The squad courier informed me that in another two hours we would be going on the march. I went over to the medical department of the staff to visit the wounded. I found almost all of them there, except for Shcharbata and Fima, who had been only lightly wounded, and requested a wagon to take them to the squad.

Patti requested five new wagons from Pavlovsky, in place of those that had been damaged in the bombing. Pavlovsky was angry about the request, but eventually ordered the wagons turned over to us. In addition, three wagons of wounded were added to our supply train.

At dark, we left the forest. We moved in behind the Ninth Squad of Bakradza. The entire way, we kept an eye on the sections so that they would not lag. We made sure that every one of our men would travel, in turn, for a quarter hour, in a wagon. And because of this action, the Partisans were able to rest through the journey and were greatly encouraged. Patti and I decided not to ride on our horses. We tied them to the wagons and went on foot, with all the rest, during the entire journey southward (Rosenblatt).

[Page 98]

Echoes of the Holocaust
of Skalat in Russian Literature

In **Men of Pure Conscience**, *Varshigora, Kovpak's assistant, relates the story of the conquest of Skalat by the Partisans.*

Also below is a chapter of **The War of the Jewish Partisans in Eastern Europe**

by Moshe Cahanowitz

Regarding the rescue of the remnants of the Skalat Ghetto, in East Galicia, by the legendary Partisan commander Major General Kovpak, we have two confirmed sources: Russian and Jewish.

A Russian Witness:

Skalat remained engraved in our memory because of an additional incident. Miraculously, there still was a Jewish ghetto in this settlement in the summer of 1943, or, more accurately, only a remnant of it. Beyond the barbed wire fence, there were Jews who were craftsmen: tailors, shoemakers, leather workers. The Germans delayed putting them to death, but kept them barely alive with starvation rations, and forced them to work for their needs. More than three hundred people – among them women, children, and the elderly – were freed from their slavery by the youths of the Karpanko Squad. A great multitude of broken and tormented people attached themselves to the Third Squad and followed after it. Their appearance in our camp brought us to great confusion. We knew that if they remained in the city, they would all be killed the next day by the Fascists. But, at the same time, we did not have any way of taking these unfortunate souls with us. We were a military unit, carrying out a complicated march. Would weak elders and women be able to hold out under the tribulations of our war march? But there could not be any other alternative. During the night, we thought about their fate. Kovpak ordered Pavlovsky, who was appointed to oversee matters of the physical stock, to use a number of wagons for the weak. The healthier ones were obligated to keep pace behind our marching line.

The Commander and the Commissar left the solution of this new worry for our next encampment (Varshigora 427–428).

According to the assistant to the commander of the brigade, Piatro Varshigora, many of the Jews of Skalat were wounded in the German bombing of the forest encampment, the day after their rescue. The bright clothing of the Jewish women revealed the location of the Brigade's encampment to the German bombers. The following is Varshigora's dramatic description of the development of decisions in connection with the survivors of Skalat:

Kovpak came to the refugees' encampment. The unfortunate people were still shell shocked as a result of the bombing. After a few moments, I heard his order: "Get up, arrange yourselves in rows!" These strange soldiers stood in two rows. On the right stood pious elders in their kapotes, long, black, Chasidic coats. The women stood in the second row behind the older men. Several held the hands of older children. And on the left were young girls. Along the rows strode the elderly commander, for whose head the Fascists had promised fifty thousand gold pieces. He explained to the people, while stroking his cane, how to be careful and to be protected from the enemy's bombs. "Please listen to what I'll tell you, and please look." He removed his hat and the rays of the sun, which came through the tree branches, lit up his bald head.

[Page 99]

"I have grown old and bald in wars. I have seen some things. I have seen death in my lifetime, more than once. Therefore, you can rely on me. The most important law in war is never attempt to prevent it. March toward it with power. War, too, is a coward. It does not adversely affect the brave. And an airplane is not a matter of war. Why flee from it? Lie down quietly. One must camouflage the bright headscarves and dresses. How to camouflage? Very simple. Break off a branch and cover yourself."

Kovpak broke off a tree branch, took a girl from the ranks, grasped her hard, stood her before the row, and put the branch in her hand.

"And now look and see!"

The girl covered herself with the branch. A whisper of excitement passed among the people who, only yesterday, wandered around seized with panic and trembling at the time of the bombing. In the ranks of the youths, laughter could be heard. The older men shook their bearded heads as a sign of agreement, as if reading the Torah.

While looking at his new military units, the commander faced them with a favorite expression of his: "Did you understand? That's it!"

After he returned to survey his new recruits, he thought for a moment and said, "Now I want to have a serious conversation with you. We are men of war. We march toward serious matters. Even though I take pity on you, I will not be able to gather all of you into my troop. Let each person weigh his or her strengths on their own, whether he or she will be able to fit into the life of war. Is this more than you can bear? Decide for yourselves. I ask you to choose. Everyone who wishes to and is able to bear arms will remain. Those who hate Fascists may remain. And those who do not fear death and who are ready to sacrifice life for the Motherland will remain! But for anyone for whom this is not in harmony with his strengths or spirit – do not go with us! I'm telling you plainly, do not go with us! We will help all those who wish to remain here. We will divide you among the villages. We will hide you among the civilians. We will leave food for you.

But if you enter the ranks of our unit, you will swear a loyalty oath, and if you violate your oath, you will receive a punishment. This should not be seen as an insult, because, with us, there is one law for everyone, for the Russian and for the Ukrainian, for the Tartar and for the Jew. Think this over until the evening. Consult with your elders. Toward evening, I will send my command to you. And now, disperse!"(Varshigora 432–439).

A Jewish Eye Witness:

When they entered the city, the Kovpak Partisans took control of the German warehouses, destroyed the buildings of the German institutions, blew up the bridges, and all this was done with the active help of the local Jews. When the Partisans began preparations to leave the city, nearly all the Jews asked that they be taken too. But the Partisans refused since, according to their words, soldiers, healthy people, were essential for them, and not Jews from the camps who dragged their feet with difficulty. Nevertheless, about thirty Jews from the camps, who were healthier, followed behind the Partisans, and in no way wanted to remain in a place where certain death awaited them. The soldiers drove them away with clubs, but they continued to follow. After several attempts, they received weapons and, after the passage of several days, they were joined to the Partisan unit. The majority of the Skalat youths died in the great battle in the Carpathian Mountains (Weissbrod, *Death of a Shtetl*)

[Page 100]

After the tightened German encirclement, when routes of retreat and movement for Kovpak were blocked by greater German forces, fierce firefights broke out during the crossing of the Lomnitz River, near the city of Dlatin on the River Prut. Kovpak lost a sizable percent of his fighters. In those encounters, many Jewish youths who had joined him on his march, especially those who were liberated from the Skalat Ghetto, fell in battle (M. Cahanowitz).

[Page 101]

Jewish Fighters in the Kovpak Brigade

by Chaim Vitshin

Chaim Vitshin, the author of this note, was Political Commissar in the Seventh Squad in the Kovpak Brigade. This squad was made up of
the young people of Skalat, who joined the Partisans. This note is taken from The Book of the Jewish Partisans, published by The National Kibbutz

The Germans blocked the road near the town of Skalat. Gathered in the town was a very large contingent of armed local police from the Shoto and Miezhibozian S.S. units for Galicia, for whom this battle would be the first taste of combat.

The march to Skalat was very difficult. All night, a driving rain fell, and the roads were muddy. The Partisans wallowed up to their knees in mud, and the horses pulled the baggage with difficulty. Toward morning, we entered a grove and stopped to rest. Wet to the bone and weary, we tried to kindle campfires in order to warm up a bit. We succeeded but with difficulty. The wood and the kindling were very wet. But after about half an hour, we stood, hundreds of Partisans, in small groups around campfires, and we dried out our clothes.

Toward morning, shots opened up around the grove. These were scouts who approached the enemy posts and tested their positions. The shots did not arouse particular attention. We were accustomed to shots. On the contrary, *quiet* would arouse suspicions. At ten, the battle for Skalat began. The Third Squad, under the command of Karpanko, and armed with sub–machine guns and machine guns, was sent to the battle and was joined by Lankin's Cavalry. The command of the brigade underestimated the strength of the enemy units, and sent only two squads toward them.

The Partisans set an ambush in the high standing grain, which extended from the grove to the boundaries of the town. The enemy marched forward, with upright posture, through the standing grain, with the goal of attacking the brigade that had encamped in the forest. This mixed multitude of pogromists, dressed in shining uniforms, with the accompaniment of obese and beer–bellied gendarmes, moved very slowly and cautiously through the high grain, thinking that they would surprise the Partisans weary from the night march. In order for the "harvest" to be more efficient, Karpanko ordered his men not to open fire, except at a smaller, closer range. Lankin's Cavalry did not participate in the ambush. They were camouflaged at the edge of the grove, and their job was to block the path of the retreating enemy. The attackers, who were cautious and tense when they entered the standing grain, showed signs of fatigue. However, their tension lessened. They believed that the battle would begin in the forest and, for that reason, started to gather on a dirt road, which led between the fields of standing grain to the forest. Karpanko set the ambush from two sides of the road. The Germans and the Ukrainians now marched on the path in a procession and at a quick pace.

[Page 102]

When the column approached, fire poured out from close range, by one hundred submachine guns and tens of machine guns. The Nazi defeat was absolute. The Germans were mowed down by rapid fire. Those who succeeded in escaping, at this stage, attempted to flee through the standing grain in the direction of the city. Lankin, who had been viewing the battle from the forest, struck. As agreed, Karpanko ceased fire, and Lankin's Cavalry leaped with a gallop after those escaping. When Lankin reached the town, he did not encounter any resistance there. The Germans who had succeeded in escaping from the battle with their lives, and from the hooves of Lankin's Cavalry, got into their automobiles and fled from Skalat.

Meanwhile, the Third Squad also reached the town, and two units took control of it. A large amount of plunder fell to the hands of the Partisans. Pavlovsky, director of our physical stock, was especially happy. Located in a storehouse in Skalat, was a very large stock of sugar and butter. All the wagons were ordered to load at least a sack of sugar and two chests of butter. After several hours, Karpanko and Lankin returned with their soldiers, now dressed in new German uniforms, and singing joyfully after they had managed to sip a respectable mouthful of German 'rum.'

The road southward was open. In order to prevent the enemy from recovering from its loss, we left the Skalat grove in the afternoon, in the light of day. The mood was jubilant. The comfortable and refreshing weather, after a night of rain, and the victory over the Germans made us forget the difficult night march, which had preceded the fighting. My squad left, first in line. But the entire time, thoughts troubled me concerning the fate of the Jews who had been liberated from the labor camp in Skalat. Zoshia Chaitchik and Yosef Gorenstein, who participated in the battle, and broke through into the town, told me about their liberation. What would be their fate? Would they exploit the opportunity to escape into the forests in the area? Or would they remain in Skalat and wait for the return of the Germans who would annihilate them? The Partisans told us that the Germans had left weapons in the town, and that the Jews had led them from position to position to uncover the weapons. It incensed me that our Ninth Squad had not participated in the battle, and that we had not come into contact with the Jews of Skalat. Grisha Rosenblatt, Yoel Shcharbata and I, now in the Ninth Squad, were three of the Veterans of the Jewish Unit from the forests of Tzumani.

We thought bitterly that we would not abandon these Jews. We would distribute weapons to them and lead them to the forest. I marched, and pain burned in my heart. Was destruction to be the fate of these Jews? A fierce despair assailed me. I looked at those Partisans marching around me, men from distant Tomsk, from Siberia, from Leningrad, and from the Caucasus. Among them were fifty–year–old seniors and seventeen year old youngsters. With what confidence they marched, and they showed no fear of the absolute destruction stalking them. Many of them could have stayed at home. Who is making them march, I wondered, only the elderly commander? Was there something special in his power or in his ability to lead hundreds of men into battle, to marches and to severe tests? There is no doubt that some idea united this camp. I conversed with these men, who were simple people, collective farmers and industrial workers. I did not discover in them anything exceptional. Those who marched here were not stronger, certainly not brighter or more understanding than my destroyed brethren.

[Page 103]

And I asked myself: why would thousands of Jews not march with me here? Behold, around me moved hundreds of men believing in their future, yet here I was, the Jew who carried in my heart a heavy feeling of guilt that no outcry could assuage.

Night descended. I attempted to free myself from the pressing burden of my thoughts. Indeed, we had spoken much about these concerns within the Jewish ranks in the Tzuman Forests, and, since then, many months had passed. The winter had passed, and the summer of 1943 had arrived. During this time, we had crossed thousands of kilometers, we had reached Kiev, and had encamped in the hinterlands of Homel. We had conducted bitter battles with the Germans. We had sabotaged trains and had sown fear in the hearts of collaborators with the Germans. We were certain that the Jewish people had ceased to exist. We did not have knowledge of Jews outside of this adversity. We understood that all of Europe was an execution block and a graveyard for Jews.

The sudden knowledge that the Partisans, who had participated in the battle and conquest of Skalat, had liberated many Jews from the labor camp, aroused excitement in our hearts, and, at the same time, gave us a feeling of impotence. We were so close to them. Maybe we would be able to save them. We hadn't been able to come in contact with them. Though I went out on this march at the head of the column, it wasn't until the next day that I discovered that the Jews liberated from the camp in Skalat had been walking behind the column. They numbered close to a hundred people and among them were numbers of young women. The appearance of their faces, their poor clothing, their weak eyes, and the uncertain marching stood out against the background of the men who were marching in front of them. It brought us to tears. We wanted to embrace them, to kiss them, and to cry out in a loud voice, but I felt that they were in need of a different treatment. There was a compelling necessity to impress upon them that we were upright Jews capable of fighting. And though tears choked in my throat, I greeted them with an encouraging smile. We presented ourselves as Jews. With our appearance, their eyes lit up and their bodies straightened. There was a rustle of admiration among them. They stood around us, hardly believing their eyes.

At that moment, we were unable to stay with these broken Jews. We were forced to return to our squad. We encouraged them and called to them to walk in our footsteps to the nearby encampment. They were not accustomed to a march. After one night, weariness overcame them, but we encouraged them. They were embarrassed at their weakness and at their slow walking. We prayed in our hearts that the brigade would reach the encampments and that they would possibly be permitted to rest. The appearance of these Jews in their ragged clothing, shattered and broken, after their time in the German Labor camp, did not encourage the Partisans to want to help them. In fact, those in the rear–guard of the brigade either ignored or browbeat them. It would require a concerted and immediate effort to prevent their expulsion from the protection of the brigade. However, with our appearance, the Partisans did not dare to insult them. But we did not want to rely on the 'politeness' of the Partisans, so, on the way, we met with the staff and requested that the liberated Jews be allowed to stay and march with us.

[Page 104]

With the losses suffered by the brigade in the Carpathian mountains, we received orders to retreat, and to move to the region of Glushkavitz, which was in Belarus. We wanted to take the Seventh Squad, but those who had come from Skalat did not want to go with us. Many of them wanted to go through the mountains to Hungary, and others planned to return to the Skalat region and to take it back. In vain, we urged them, but they stayed firm (Vishkin).

General Kovpak
(third from left, in the company of his officers)

[Page 105]

The End of Skalat

The Town in which the Years of My Youth Transpired

by Dr. Hillel Zeidman

Skalat was a small shtetl in East Galicia, in the region of Tarnopol, not far from the former Polish–Russian border. Skalat was the center of its district, and the headquarters of the governor. Around it were no less than seventy villages, and the peasants of the villages would come once a week, on Tuesday, to the fair in Skalat, sell their produce, and buy vital supplies in the shops. Jewish merchants would buy the harvests of grains, and Jewish shopkeepers would sell supplies, as was usual in a Jewish town. The Jews lived in relative tranquility, would marry off sons and daughters, and would 'await deliverance.' As the burdens of earning a livelihood became heavier with higher taxes, the weight of such pressures distressed the Jews.

In the villages and in the town, cooperatives were formed with the goal of 'liberating' the peasants from the Jewish merchants. Anti–Semitic societies arose which preached a boycott of the Jewish merchants. Often, Jews experienced harassment and persecution.

Through an Expectation of Certificates

Nevertheless, life flowed somehow in its old channel. Most of the Jews of the city were Husiatyn Chasidim, and there were four Husiatyn study houses in Skalat. The Jewish younger generation was already pro–Zionist, and for the most part aspired to go to the Land of Israel.

Some of them had already traveled there, and the remainder prepared to go. Essentially, they were ready at any time, but they awaited travel certificates that were distributed only sparingly. Skalat, a border city, was captured by the Russians after the outbreak of the war in September 1939.

Conditions gradually became more severe. Not because the Soviet regime was anti–Semitic, but because, in aiming its arrows at commerce and the bourgeoisie, it unintentionally adversely affected the Jews.

When Permission was Granted the Destroyer

But in some way, 'they got along' and continued to await Deliverance. Instead of Deliverance, the Germany–Russia war broke out, and at the beginning of July 1941, Germans had already taken the town.

The Germans indeed gave permission to the Destroyer, the Ukrainian pogromists, and a pogrom immediately broke out against the Jews. The Ukrainians did their work with an especially awful cruelty. The pogrom lasted several days. More than 200 Jews from elite households and families were murdered. The Ukrainians' slogan was 'Revenge against the Bolshevik Jews.'

[Page 106]

Afterwards some calm returned. It was very bad. There were persecutions, hunger, seizures to labor camps – whose meaning was death. The people suffered, gritted their teeth, and hoped to endure the days of starvation. But they did not endure.

A Clean Euphemism for Impure Acts

In the summer of 1942, the Germans began to remove elderly people from the city. No one knew to where they had 'disappeared.' Afterwards, they began *Aktziot*, the Aktions. This was the euphemism for the awful murders in which millions of Jews were exterminated. They did not say 'pogroms,' they did not say 'killings,' only 'Aktions,' or 'deportations' or 'expulsions,' and so these more neutral terms replaced the real descriptions for these evil deeds, and this terminology has remained through the present day.

On October 20, 1942, the Ukrainians, under the leadership of the S.S., spread out over the Ghetto and seized Jews. Yet, before this, an order was given that all the Jews from the nearby towns, from Podvolochisk, Grzhimalov, and others, and even from the small villages, were obligated to move to Skalat. Apartments did not exist for several thousand Jews from the vicinity. Therefore, the new 'residents' rolled around the streets, or several families lived in one room, in crowded and awful conditions. These Jews were adversely affected first.

Three thousand Jews were seized and rounded up in that Aktion. The S.S. men and the Ukrainians pressed them into the synagogue. They held them for two days, without food or water in awful crowding. Afterwards, they took them to the train. They ordered them to stay several hours on their knees on the extensive earthen area in front of the station. Afterwards, they pressed them into cattle cars and transported them to Belzec.

It is Better to Die among Jews

The remaining Jews were taken for hard labor. They thought that the matter was concluded, and that those who remained would continue to remain. Strange information circulated in the Ghetto. People told of wonderful dreams, from which they concluded that deliverance was already not far off. However, on November 9th, a second Aktion came and, again, 1500 victims were caught. Again, the Germans and Ukrainians gathered them into the synagogue, with the accompaniment of blows and shots, and eventually these Jews were also sent to Belzec.

Then people began to escape back to the villages to hide with the peasants, with acquaintances, old friends, with money bribes, much money. The Ukrainians searched for them, and when found, seized and shot them. Many were unable to bear the constant fear of death and returned to the city. They wanted to live among Jews. But if it was decreed for them to perish, all they wanted was to be among other Jews, together with all of them.

The people were registered for labor and continued to hope that, from now on, they would remain alive. The days of Passover approached. Spring appeared in the land and, with it, the Red Army approached. The Jews absorbed the information about the Russian advance. Since November 1942, there had been only silence.

But on April 7, 1943 (Nisan 2, 5703), disaster came again. Suddenly, the Ukrainian murderers came with the S.S. men, surrounded the Ghetto, and took away its young and old. Again, they dragged 2,000 Jews to the synagogue. Among those seized to die was the Rabbi of the community, Rabbi Yitzchak Rosenblatt.

[Page 107]

Deliverance is Approaching and the Trouble is Near

Scenes of terror occurred in this Aktion. The people already knew what it meant, and they wanted to live. People hid on the ground, between the graves in the cemetery, they fled to the forests, hid in holes, in cellars, and in the attics of the houses. A vicious hunt took place for the unfortunate Jews. The Ukrainians immediately shot those attempting to escape. Gentiles, residents of the city who initially hid Jews, informed. Pursued and hunted, few people were left of what was once a large, thriving community.

When Passover came, information arrived concerning the advance of the Red Army. It was spring in the world. Nature began blossoming and awakening to new life and, together with it, weak hopes for deliverance were awakened in those remaining. They thought: 'if they've let us remain until now, they will let us remain for the future also, and we will already live to see the end.'

But the wicked enemy did not think this way, because he plotted in his heart to go to the ends of the earth to uproot the Congregation of Israel to the last man, woman and child.

Psychological Preparation for the End

On the first day of the Festival of Shavuoth, June 5, 1943, our enemies expelled the remaining handful of Jews who were seized in their hiding places in Rodvalutzisk, Rimliv, Tarna Roda, Satanov, Kodrintz, Toist and the villages back to Skalat. And again, they gathered for a cruel hunt of all the remaining Jews still in Skalat. Now there was a group of Jews who had come from other places and did not have a place to live, who lodged in the Synagogue. This made it easy for the murderers to find them. There, into the synagogue, they pressed all of the last Jews of Skalat. They imprisoned them inside and surrounded the synagogue with a cordon of strict guards from the Ukrainian militia. Two days and two nights, they held the Jews, with awful crowding, without water, without food and without air. Outside, shots could be heard without letup. Those were shots aimed at Jews who tried to escape when they were discovered somewhere in their hiding places, or Jews that the children of the Gentiles had informed on, handing them over to the Germans. So the last remnant of Jews was brought to the synagogue, including those who had succeeded up until then in concealing themselves from the eyes of the Destroyer. The S.S., along with the Ukrainians, searched and scoured all the holes and hiding places, and it was not possible to conceal oneself from them.

The Jews in the synagogue, numbered at about 700, waited only for their end, with a shudder of death, with hunger and suffocation. Children cried. Women fainted. Men lost their minds.

Suddenly, Berle Walowitz ascended the Bimah, wrapped in his tallit, his prayer shawl. He was the son of Rabbi Benjamin Walowitz, who had already been killed in the first pogrom, by the Ukrainians. A great *Talmud–Chacham*, a scholar, and a discerning man, he said, "Jews! We are standing before the end. Recover, do not lose your minds!" And he began saying, along with the congregation, the Confessional. Afterwards, he said words of Torah in the matter of martyrdom, in the cause of *Kiddush Hashem*, the Sanctification of the Divine Name. Thus, he stood for an hour, on the Bimah, and from him flowed biblical verses and statements of the Sages of blessed memory. The congregation awakened as if from a nightmare, and listened to the words of Berle, the Rabbi's son. He was very honored in the entire city. The Council of the Jews had made all efforts to save him. And surely, he had remained for that reason to the end.

[Page 108]

To the Graves which They Dug with their Own Hands

Without warning, the gates of the synagogue opened and wild shouts were heard, "Out! Out!" No one deceived himself with false hopes with regards to where they might be going. They were already so depressed and despairing from the crowding and the choking, from hunger and from thirst, that everyone pressed toward the gates, in order to be the first to leave.

Outside waited a gang of Ukrainian militia men under the lead of S.S. men. The congregation was ordered to stand in rows, 5 by 5, and to march. Through a cordon of a guard of militia men, who supervised so that no one escaped, the procession of 700 Jews moved ahead, the last remnant of the community of Skalat and the vicinity. The Gentile neighbors went out into the streets to look at this spectacle, and waited for the moment when they would be able to storm into the empty Jewish apartments and carry off the spoils.

Then they did not lead the Jews to the train, nor to Belzec. There were transportation difficulties, and an insufficient number of railroad cars. Outside the city were the fields of Novosilka, on the way to Rodwalitziska. The fields had belonged to the estate owner, Yosef Tenenbaum. The Germans had led some Jews there a few weeks earlier, and had ordered them to dig pits. They had told the Jews that the pits were for storing potatoes for the winter. The Jews did not know they were digging their own graves.

To those same pits, they now led these 700 Jews. They stood them at the edge of these excavations, and ordered them to strip their off clothing, so that the clothes, which were destined as spoils, should not be stained with blood. Berle, the Rabbi's son, refused to strip naked, and remained wrapped in his Tallit. The Ukrainians and Germans struck him with murderous blows, but he did not give in, and finally they killed him with a gunshot, while he remained dressed. This also was the fate of a young woman, Margaliot, who refused to strip her garments. Yosef Tenenbaum, the former head of the community, pleaded for his life, while promising to show the murderers a treasure of money that he had hidden, but to no avail. They shot him as well.

The Groaning Graves

The Ukrainians only had pistols, and their shots did not always kill their victims. Even the wounded were pushed into their graves while still alive. The Ukrainians and Germans completed their work and departed, while the living remained in the graves, their limbs entwined with the flesh of their fellow Jews. An awful struggle with death took place in the mass graves.

Peasants from the neighboring villages heard the cries and groans from the graves. They came near and saw hands and feet struggling to emerge from the soil, and awful sounds arising from the graves. The peasants were unable to bear the sounds, and they approached to take out the living. Among them was the 17 year old daughter of David Epstein. He was hidden in the city somewhere in a cellar. A certain peasant recognized her and brought her to her father. She told her father what was being done in the mass graves of Novosilka. Meir Greenfeld, also, lay secretly in a pit not far from the graves, and saw and heard what was being done. For more than three days, groans and cries arose from the graves, until the people slowly perished, and the sounds of their voices were finally stilled. To this day, the peasants call the place, 'the Groaning Graves.'

There still remained a handful of Jews in Skalat, about 50 men and women, who worked in a labor camp at the edge of the city, cut off from any connection with the world, and working in crushing labor. A month later, June 20, 1943, the majority of the Jews in this camp were also exterminated and another month later, on July 27, 1943, the S.S. cut off most of the Jewish remnant from Skalat and all the neighboring towns.

[Page 109]

The Remnant that Remained for Deliverance

There remained only about thirty Jewish souls. Some were hauled away to Russia as deportees or soldiers, a few fled to the forests to join the Partisans, and several were hidden in villages with friendly peasants. They returned to Skalat after it was liberated by the Red Army, but liberation did not come to them. Nearby, all the houses of the Jews had been seized by the Gentiles. A Jewish house passed from hand to hand for 50 to 100 zlotys, extremely inexpensively. A few houses, slightly larger, which remained intact, were grabbed by Gentiles. A Jew was unable to receive anything in return. Ukrainian gangs also fell upon the Jews. It was said that the regime was not anti–Semitic, but nevertheless, there was no place for the Jews. And, to this day, not a single Jew remains in Skalat.

They went to Lower Silesia, and can be found today in Galiwitz or in Bytom. But some of them traversed a farther road. I found several of them in Fahrenwald, and in Munich, and in Neufriman. They look forward to reaching some faraway secure shore. Not one of them has a relative or redeemer in Poland or in Europe in general. Several of them have relatives in America, or in the Land of Israel, and they look to them for help. They hope to leave the D.P. Camps in Germany, where they live as Displaced Persons, as soon as possible, to reach any place of rest. The majority of them lift their eyes to the Land of Israel. They are tired of wanderings, of oppression, of isolation, and of living in exile (Ha Boker, 3 Elul, 5706 (August 30, 1946). *[Page 110]*

The school, named for Y. Krol, adopts the community of Skalat

A student reads the scroll of perpetuation

Hadassah Katz brings up reminiscences in the Adoption
Ceremony

[Page 112]

We are Adopting a Community that was Destroyed

By Arela Asheri, 7ᵗʰ Grade

Skalat! I hear a voice shouting inside me. How is it different from the rest of the towns, the little shtetlach? Aren't there small houses with red roofs in Skalat? Aren't there verdant fields and people working them with love and with dedication? Is it unique?

No...no! It was a town like all the towns. Wheat fields surrounded it, and churches adorned it. In it were people who tasted the taste of hate and love, laughter and pain.

The pampered children of Israel traversed its streets. Most of them are no longer alive. A few remained, and their wounds have not formed scabs. Did they have mothers who they would embrace and hold close to their hearts?

There was a mother, but they do not remember her. Sometimes they think about the appearance of her face, the color of her eyes and hair, and perhaps she is still alive and searching for them?

They are seeking an answer that they will never uncover. They are certainly picturing her in their imaginations. But all their memories of the small house, there in the town of Skalat, are wrapped in fog.

And perhaps this too is for the best. For if they would remember everything, their brothers and sisters, their mothers and fathers, these sights would pursue them all the days of their lives, sights of the loved ones who hovered between life and death. And what is the reason for life? Behold there is neither relative nor redeemer close by. They are alone, even though they certainly have wives and children.

Many people were sentenced to death. Why? Because of their Jewishness? Because of the superstition that Jesus of Nazareth was murdered by the Jews? And since that time, so many years have passed. But if we assume that the Jews crucified

Jesus, they crucified only one person, not six million. Yes! Six million were murdered. A legendary number. Six million were murdered. And why? Was there a reason for the murder of those Jews? What was the sin of the million and a half children of Israel who were murdered before the eyes of their mothers, of those infants and sucklings who were slaughtered and asphyxiated?

One community, the one that we are adopting, cries out to me, stands before my eyes. And I see its streets and its beautiful, destroyed houses, its dead children, and its dry fields, through the curtain of distance. The Destroyer descended upon all of them.

[Page 113]

Their lives were bitter. Those solitary remnants that remained for deliverance, out of thousands, stand before my eyes.

From afar, the ruins of the town cry out to me. Do Jews still live there? That town would remind them of frightening sights of those difficult, awful days. Who knows, perhaps one of the murderers still lives there? The Ukrainians certainly seized their places, and they did not love them. Perhaps the town again blossoms and flourishes? But it does not seem probable that life would flow in the old channel. Or perhaps piles of ruins are still standing there, a remembrance of a vibrant life for which such a great price was paid.

And perhaps, if they had not slaughtered so many people, if they had not burned them in furnaces, there would then have been a more beautiful, better, purer world.

The Choir of the Krol School at the Ceremony of the Perpetuation of the Community of Skalat

[Page 114]

מגילת־ההנצחה

בית־הספר _____ ב־ _____ במדינת ישראל

מצהיר בזה חגיגית, כי ביום ___ לחודש _____ תשכ"___ קיבל עליו את המשימה הקדושה

להנציח את קהילת _____ (בארץ _____)

שנחרבה בשנות השואה על ידי קלגסי הנאצים הטמאים וגרוריהם.

תלמידי בית הספר, בשיתוף עם הרשויות החינוכיות ועם ארגוני
הקהילה בארץ ובתפוצות, ובעזרת הוועדה הארצית להנצחת הקהילות
שעל יד יד־ושם בירושלים, יעשו כמיטב יכולתם וימשיכו במפעולה
שהחלו בה להעלות לזכר עולם את הקהילה הנ"ל בחייה ופעלה, עד
לשואה וכן בסבלה, מאבקה וכליונה בתקופת החורבן.

על החתום :

מנהל(ת) בית הספר _____ מחנך(ת) הכיתה _____

פני התלמידים המנציחים : א) _____

ב"כ ארגון הקהילה : א) _____

נציגי הוועדה הארצית להנצחת קהילום: _____

מגילה זו נתקבלה ביד ושם למשמרת עולם.

The Scroll of Perpetuation

The school named for Y.
Krol in Petach Tikvah, in
the State of Israel,
solemnly proclaims that
on the 22nd of the month
of Teveth 5728, it has
taken upon itself the
sacred task to perpetuate
the community of Skalat,
in the land of Poland,
which was destroyed in
the years of the Holocaust
by the impure, evil
soldiers of the Nazi regime
and its accomplices.

The students of our
school will continue the
remembrance in eternal
memory of Skalat. They
undertake this act in
cooperation with the State
Educational Authorities
and with the Communal
Organizations in the Land
of Israel and the Diaspora,
with the assistance of the
National Committee for
the Perpetuation of the
Communities of Yad
Vashem in Jerusalem, in

its life and its work, as
witnesses to the suffering,
the struggle, and the
annihilation of the town of
Skalat, during the period
of the Holocaust.

Signed:
Principal of the
School_____
Educator of the
Class_____
Representative of the
Participating Students

_____

Proxies of the
Organization of the
Community

_____

Representative of the
National Committee for
the Perpetuation of the
Communities_____
The Scroll was Accepted
at Yad Vashem for Eternal
Safeguarding.

[Page 115]

Mr. Dov Aloni, Representative of Yad Vashem, greeting

[Page 116]

At the Ceremony of Perpetuation

From: *That Conflagration*

By the Poet, Chaim Guri

From that conflagration which burnt your tortured, charred body,

We have borne a torch–fire, giving light to our soul.

And with it, we have kindled the flame of freedom.

With it, we have gone into battle upon our soil.

Your pain, which has no equal,

We have poured into iron hewers and sharp–toothed plows.

Your humiliation, we have turned into rifles,

Your eyes into a lighthouse

And ships, into battles in the night.

[Page 117]

In the Expanse of the Soviet Union

By Ar'el Asheri

With the outbreak of war between the Soviet Union and Germany in June 1941, and the advance of the German Army eastward, a few families from Skalat escaped to the interior of the Soviet Union. Similarly, transferred to the interiors of the country, many of the residents of the city were conscripted into the Red Army, out of a suspicion of lack of loyalty.

In the Soviet Union, they encountered suffering and afflictions, another story of the enormity of the Holocaust and its terror.

[Page 118]

In the Land of Cold and Frost

By Mordechai Or

Very little has been written about the fate of the Jews who fled for their lives to the Soviet Union, or of those who were drafted into the Red Army with the outbreak of the war between Soviet Russia and Nazi Germany.

In June 1941, many Jewish youths from Skalat were conscripted into the Red Army, along with Ukrainians. With the outbreak of fighting, there were Jewish families and lone individuals who fled.

At the beginning of the war, the Red Army suffered severe defeats and began to retreat eastward in disarray. The German Air Force struck the routes of retreating soldiers, as well as multitudes of Jewish refugees from eastern Poland, under a hail of terrible bombings.

Settlement after settlement in Western Ukraine fell into the hands of the cruel conquerors. Trembling seized the Jewish population, while the nationalistic

Ukrainians rejoiced and served as a fifth column for the Germans who were drunk with victory. The enemy controlled the air without restraints and sowed destruction and annihilation.

The night bombings of the city of Tarnopol made a frightening impression on me. Suddenly, illumination bombs were dropped, one after the other, in the dark of night, and by their light Ostroskigo Street could be clearly seen, with many soldiers and refugees retreating in fear through the narrow bridge, some on foot and some in wagons. The crowds were routed by the retreating tanks, and hurt by the merciless enemy bombing from the air. We hoped that the Soviet Army would succeed in stopping the damage and in stabilizing the front near the Zabroch River.

In Volochisk, we found terrified Jews who were afraid of opening their hearts to strangers. Even the waters of the Zabroch River did not have the power to stop the advancing German army. We were weary and drained from wandering on the roads. Hunger pressed. The supply of food was absolutely chaotic. Sometimes food was in abundance, and sometimes we starved for entire days.

Signs of desertion were obvious among the conscripted Ukrainians. Several impatient Jews were not able to hold out. In their naivete, they believed that the violence was not so terrible, and that it would be possible to exist even under the rule of the Germans. They bribed Soviet Officers and disappeared. Later, it became known that Ukrainians had killed them before they managed to reach Skalat, their destination.

The panicky retreat lasted about two months, day and night, on the routes of suffering in eastern Ukraine and its forests. We reached Kiev. There, they separated me from the remainder of the Jews of Skalat, and I was stationed at a mobile military hospital together with a Jew by the name of Y., who was from the environs of Zalshitzikr. I was sometimes sent westward in the direction of the front, to find out the fate of the rest of the mobile hospitals from Eastern Galicia.

[Page 119]

On our way, we picked up wounded. We offered them first aid and transferred them to the rear. The severely wounded breathed out their souls far from their families and their dear ones, and for lack of time and means, their bodies were sent to the pit without any formalities of ceremony. The appearance of the dead made a shocking impression on me.

My companion in trouble, Y. Mazlashatziki, became friendly with me and, in his bitterness, he opened up his heart to me. He was shocked and depressed by strong longings for his wife and his small son. In his despair, he had ceased eating. In view of his difficult psychological situation, I tried to encourage him. I brought him his food, and really forced him to eat. Many times, he attempted to influence me, at the time of the retreat. In different places of encampment, he insisted that I should remain with him until the arrival of the German army, in the unrealistic hope that we would succeed in returning home to live our lives in peace in the bosom of our families. With difficulty, I succeeded in moving him away from that vision. But his sickness, caused by the death of his family, gave him no rest. Sometimes he would urge me anew to remain with him and to desert. In one of the encampments in Eastern Ukraine, he began to negotiate with two wounded German captive POW's, saying that he would remain with them until the arrival of their army. Meanwhile we received an order to retreat because the German Army was advancing. When I realized that my friend Y. was missing, I searched for him in the forest, shouted and called his name. There was no sound and no one answering. Our trucks began to move from their places. Suddenly, I discovered him conversing with two captives. I informed him that we were moving, but he was firm in his belief that these nice Germans promised him that they would serve as advocates for us if we remained with them. With great difficulty, I convinced him that these friends would be the first ones to murder us. With great effort and breathlessness, we caught up with our caravan.

Meanwhile, several severe incidents occurred. A young Soviet soldier from our unit hid his grenades in the forest, apparently with the intention of falling into German captivity. A court martial sentenced him to death, along with several of our wounded comrades who were executed when it became known that they had shot themselves in order to get away from the front.

At the end of August 1941, an order was received that all former Polish citizens were to return their new uniforms immediately, including our personal boots from home, and we were issued old, patched uniforms instead. Immediately a rumor spread that we were about to be sent to the front. My friend Y., a sworn pessimist, continuing in his usual way of thinking, said that it would be a shame to give good clothing to those who were to be used as cannon fodder, and that was the reason they dressed us in these rags.

We were put into a closed military automobile, and traveled on a circuitous path through the forests. According to the direction, I discerned that we were traveling east, and I comforted my friend that his prophecies were dark. After several hours, we reached a military camp of conscripted soldiers from western Ukraine. From this camp we continued to Priluki, a city east of Kiev. Trains began to arrive there with west–Ukrainian soldiers who had been sent far away from the front, and, like us, were suspected of a lack of loyalty.

To my joy, I found several Jews from Skalat there, Yosef Rotstin, Izir Felshner, Philip Goldstein, Moshe Schechter, Max Sapir, Lunk Margolis and Izir Bomze z"l.

At the beginning of September 1941, they put us on board a freight train, and we were transported to Siberia. The trip, in closed cars, intended for cattle, took over two weeks, while our food was especially scanty.

On the 17ᵗʰ of September, at dusk, we reached the Yurga Station, a far–out village east

[Page 120]

of Novosibirsk. After a march of five kilometers, we reached the camp that was intended, apparently from the start, for forced labor.

An electrified fence with guard–towers around it surrounded the camp, which consisted of several bunks. Our spirits were depressed. My friend Y., who did not stray from me, added oil to the fire when he whispered to me that in the darkness near the gate, he had seen an N.K.V.D. man from the security police with his rifle aimed at us, while standing on guard. That implied that we were imprisoned, through no fault of our own, lost and forgotten, and that no one even knew to where we had disappeared. In the darkness, we reached a bunk that housed about 500 men on platforms, four double–statures high, without mattresses or blankets. The worn out coats served at night as a mattress and blanket, both. The people of the place looked upon us with pity in our summer uniforms and doubted whether we would hold out in the Siberian winter, where the temperatures reached minus–50 degrees centigrade. The food was inadequate, as the suppliers had conspired with the command and had stolen from the meager conscripts' portions. Because of my education, I was asked to serve as the head clerk in the office of the command. It was easy work and at a suitable salary as well. It included food in abundance and warm clothing. The main reward was dwelling in a warm bunk. However I turned that down and recommended Y. for the job, instead.

The administration in the camp was more severe than in the brigades of forced labor camps, and in large measure even worse from the point of view of work conditions, as well as the quantity and quality of food, and vital supplies. Rising at five in the morning, we would go out about ten kilometers on foot, in snowstorms and burning frost, to a railroad station to work at loading and unloading of heavy weights of coal, gigantic beams of wood, machine parts, and more. Similarly, we worked at digging ditches in the frozen Siberian soil for foundations of a factory. The work lasted until eight in the evening. The men worked with their meager strength, in order that their daily bread rations, which did not exceed 800 grams, not be further reduced. It was a kind of frozen cereal of grain mixed with potatoes and bran. Its nutritional value was very low. The cold forced us to work so that we would not freeze. To our increased distress, they would sometimes awaken us at night in order to unload freight trains that arrived during the night hours. We would work until morning light, and afterwards would continue to do our regular jobs, as if nothing had happened. The hunger and the lice ate us ravenously. Swollen with famine, many began to scavenge in the garbage cans from the need to diminish their hunger.

The strength of the men, mostly Ukrainians, and a minority of them Jews, gradually diminished. After two months of crushing labor, almost without food, without the possibility of bathing, without any change of clothing, about six to seven of the men began dying daily. When 'the water reached my neck,' I handed over my wrist watch, my only keepsake from home, to a Soviet officer, in exchange for the possibility of working in the nearby village as a civilian. I settled myself into working in the office of a tank factory and I wasn't subject to military discipline. From then on, I worked in a heated room, and I began to recover.

In addition to the bread ration, the commanders of the section received a bucket of cabbage soup three times a day. Most of the commanders divided the soup among their men, while leaving little bits of potatoes for themselves. The results were deadly, and many perished. In my unit, I instituted dividing of the soup in rotation, so no man would be deprived. Thanks to that, not one person died while I stood at the head of the group. It is especially important that I mention Izyo Felshner, who worked in the kitchen, for the brewing of tea in the camp, and who more than once shared his piece of bread with me. The fierce cold and the hunger left their mark on the men and did not spare the Skalaters who did not benefit from working in the kitchen or other services that had advantages. Izyo Bomze became sick and died prematurely. Moshe Schechter became weak but lived to be liberated.

[Page 121]

When the complaints of the people of Yurga, who were afraid of an epidemic plague, reached the authorities in Moscow, and it became known that out of a brigade of about 1000 men, only 300 men remained alive three months later, and of them about half in human condition, the authorities ordered the camp closed. The commanders were imprisoned. Some of those remaining alive were transferred to a labor camp in the city of mines, Stalinsk. I worked there, for a time, in the office of a large restaurant. The food was abundant, and for fellowship, I relied in a steady manner on a group of Jews from Tarnopol and its surroundings.

I suffered in Siberia in this way only four months, but I will never forget that difficult period.

[Page 122]

From Skalat, through Cheliabinsk, to the Skies of Kibbutz Degania

By Ze'ev Reuveni

The Conclusion of the Second World War

Cheliabinsk. The capitol city of Ural, May 1945. The Second World War has come to its end. The citizens of the Soviet Union are weary from the war and the prolonged suffering. They celebrate the great event together, with the entire Free World.

The Jews of Cheliabinsk celebrated the end of the war with mixed feelings. Among the Soviet Jews were many Jews from Eastern Europe, particularly from Western Ukraine.

The overwhelming majority of the Jews of Cheliabinsk who had reached Ural during the war in 1941 were single men who had served in the Polish Army, and who, after the German attack on the Soviet Union, were conscripted into the Red Army. Over the course of time, the Russians kept the Western Ukrainians from the front by questioning their loyalty, especially if they were Jewish. Those who were distanced were organized in semi–military organizations, and were conscripted to labor in heavy industry.

We worked in tank factories, and manufactured replacement parts for planes and other military equipment in order to assist in hastening the victory over the Nazi enemy. We worked with energy and dedication because we knew that this was a war against a common enemy who would decide the fate of the Jewish people, even though we did not imagine the magnitude of the catastrophe that had been visited upon our people.

Every day, we saw long columns of heavy tanks that were destined for the front. Soldiers and officers from the Armored Corps arrived at our workplace to receive the new equipment, to load them on flatcars, and to leave for the front. Frequently, I received an answer in Yiddish from soldiers who wished to emphasize their Jewish origins. In one instance, an officer with the rank of major told me that he had been wounded three times, and that the army wanted to transfer him to the rear. But he had not agreed "because how is it possible to stop fighting?" From many Russian officers and soldiers, I heard that the Jewish soldiers distinguished themselves in exemplary self–sacrifice, bravery, and in their fierce desire to triumph over and to destroy the German enemy. I was very happy when I heard Russian soldiers telling me in Yiddish, sometimes haltingly, that they were Jews, and several of them had already received medals of distinction for their daring and dedication in battle. The Jewish Major, who had been wounded three times, told me that the number of Jewish officers and soldiers who had received the distinction of *Hero of the Soviet Union* was proportionately greater than those of other nationalities. After the war, I found out that the Jewish fighters took fourth place after the Russians, the Ukrainians and the Belarusians.

We, too, the workers and heavy industry laborers, whose task it was to supply the equipment needed for victory over the enemy, received prizes and certificates of distinction.

[Page 123]

In Cheliabinsk, similar to other places in the Soviet Union, in places where there were Poles and Jews, Polish citizens from before the war, formed organizations named the *Union of Polish Patriots*. The goal of these societies was to generate economic and moral help for Polish citizens. But the most important goal was the concentration of all one's powers towards the war effort and the annihilation of the enemy.

The Historic Meeting

The *Organization of Patriots* would meet in the evenings, after the work day, and read news from the Russian press. After the conclusion of the war, we regularly received the Polish daily press from Warsaw.

After the war, one of the newspapers, *Trybuna Ludu*, the People's Platform, the newspaper of the Polish Workers' Party, printed articles sympathetic to Zionism and to the aspirations of the Jewish people to rebuild their lives, which had been destroyed by the Nazis in the Second World War.

One of the articles that particularly impressed me was similar to a Zionist speech that the leaders of Polish Zionism would voice before the war. After reading the newspaper with the enthusiastic Zionistic article, I could not find rest for my stormy soul, and my desire was to disseminate the article. I knew that this was a dangerous adventure. On the other hand, this was an official Polish newspaper, and what was permitted to a worker's Polish government was also permitted to an organization abroad. In every way, I knew that one should not postpone a wonderful opportunity like this, and I read it in front of the public, for groups of Jews, but Poles were also listening.

I began to read the article regularly, but when I reached certain places, I amplified my voice and began to read with much excitement about the possibility of new life on the soil of our ancestors. In the newspaper, *Na Ziemi Ojcow*, those words were explicitly used. I read the latter part of the article in an excited manner. In this last part, the author wrote with great enthusiasm about Palestine as a national home for the Jewish people since, for 1800 years, the people had suffered from life in exile, depression, poverty and persecution. "And the time has come," this Polish Gentile wrote, "that the Jewish people also should obtain its inheritance in the Land of its Fathers." The emphasis throughout the entire article was on "the Land of the Fathers."

In the midst of the audience sat a young Jew who saw himself as a Politruk, a political leader responsible for the political education of his followers to the official Communist Party line, even though he had been an ardent Bundist in Poland.

I finished my task, and completed the reading. The article made a strong impression on the listeners. After I completed the reading, an unusual silence prevailed, and only the Politruk approached me, raised his voice, and asked me angrily from whom I had received permission to read a Zionist article at a meeting of the organization. He even threatened to report me to the authorities. That worried me very much. Indeed, I had read an article from an official Polish newspaper, but my emphasis at the time of reading, and the applause of the audience, could all put me in deep trouble with the authorities.

The chairman of the organization intervened, calmed the 'law abiding one,' and told him that I had read an article from an official newspaper of democratic Poland. The matter was not reported to officials. But I was

[Page 124]

left in fear, because I realized that they were liable to imprison me for Zionist propaganda and prevent my exit from Poland. My fears and tension did not dissipate until I left Cheliabinsk.

The Conversation with the Manager

After the historic pact between the Soviet Union and the provisional government of Poland concerning repatriation had been signed, I registered at the appropriate office and filled out a special form. Usually, the returnees received liberation from their labor and an exit permit without difficulty. Despite this, there were instances where the managers of factories and vital projects, particularly those of defense value, attempted to prevent the exit of engineers and other experts for a certain period. I waited more than a reasonable time to be liberated from my position as a regular engineer, and as a tutor responsible for youths working in military factories. I was worried. My colleagues, in other workplaces, had already been freed a long time ago and had received exit confirmation.

The Russian Engineer who Understood Our Aspirations
(Seated – second from left)

One day, early in June 1946, I was invited to the office of the Manager. At the beginning of the conversation, I was very agitated, but the good words of this intellectual Russian calmed me. The Manager, a veteran engineer from Leningrad, had been transferred in the days of the Siege of Ural, and served as chief engineer for the project on which I worked. In the course of time, he received the position of Manager of the project.

[Page 125]

The conversation was far from formal and turned into a pleasant and friendly dialogue. The engineer, Mr. Volkov, said, "I have heard that you are leaving us. Too bad. You have learned to work well, and you would be able to advance in rank if you wanted it. We would be prepared to fund your studies in Moscow or Leningrad. Is it bad for you with us?" I attempted to explain to the engineer that I had left family at home, and how important it was for me to get back with deliberate speed since there was no way to know their condition after the Holocaust. Perhaps, in spite of this, they remained alive and in need of my help. The engineer, who did not believe this was possible, listened to my words with a slight smile on his lips, and said, "Do you truly believe that someone remains alive? Isn't it known to you that the Fascists exterminated all the Jews, and that the remnants are only a few solitary individuals?" I answered, sorrowfully, "Yes, Piotr Ilrionovitch. I know very well what the Nazis did to the nations of the world, and especially to the Jews. And despite this, I still have a spark of hope that remnants of my family remain alive."

The conversation lasted about half an hour or more. I did not have any doubt that the noble Russian was relating with sympathy to my case. He turned to me, not as to a worker of his office project, but as one who is speaking to a son of the Jewish people after the terrible Holocaust.

As our conversation neared its end, the engineer turned to me with words that I was unable to understand at the time. That a Russian man, in an official position, could speak in such a fashion with one of his workers was unheard of. The engineer turned to me, as if he was speaking to the representative of the Jewish People. At the conclusion of his words, he said approximately this, "Beautiful. If you wish to travel, it is left to me only to wish you success. But I do not think that you will find a home and family in Poland. The fate of the Jewish People in the lands of the Nazi conquest, and especially in Poland, is well known. Look, it is not an accident that the overwhelming majority of the Jews of conquered Europe were concentrated and exterminated in Poland. I understand that you will continue from Poland to Palestine, which is the hope of many Jews. Fine, but in Palestine, Arabs dwell. How will you get along with the sons of Ishmael?"

I was silent. I was astonished and surprised. I thought, "maybe the Bundist had informed on me, that I had read the article about a national home in Palestine?" Never had it occurred to me to discuss, with this distinguished Russian Gentile, pleasant and good, my dream of reaching Israel. I had not given even the slightest hint about this. After a number of seconds, he continued speaking and concluded with a parting blessing, "Travel in peace, and may you succeed, you, and the sons of your People, to establish your independent state in the Palestine of your ancestors. Be well and a good journey."

"Thanks very much, from the bottom of my heart," I said, and we parted.

The last parting words of the engineer were said with true Russian warmth, and when he parted, he was moved. I knew that his words were sincere. I was very moved by his words. I felt a psychological need to be alone for a number of minutes. A strong hope filled me that, indeed, I had succeeded.

Goodbye Cheliabinsk, Hello Our Brethren, the Sons of Israel!

In mid–June 1946, seven hundred Polish citizens, most of them Jews, were crowded onto a long freight train. Many were young people, but there were also aging parents. In every freight car, a group of comrades and friends were together. Indeed this was not a regular passenger train, but despite this, we were satisfied that everyone had found for himself enough room to arrange his belongings to his satisfaction.

[Page 126]

The Russian landlady had packed my things for me, since I didn't have time for that. A female friend of mine from Bialystok lay sick for many months in the hospital, and the doctors advised her not to travel because she was liable to endanger her life. The patient, herself, whom I had dealt with all the time, with the sanction of the organization, and as a friend, did not make peace with her fate and wanted to leave in order to reach the Land of Israel. I did everything to obtain approval for her to leave. After much effort, I actually succeeded in bringing her to the depot, by carrying her on my back. She was very weak, and did not believe that she would live to complete the trip. She had a personal nurse, who was always prepared to provide first aid or to administer an injection. In Poland, she had joined Gordonia, and had been active in Bricha, smuggling and arranging illegal immigration. Today she is married and lives in Ramat Gan.

Another young woman, a tuberculosis patient, whom the organization had supported, was supposed to leave with us according to our plan. Since, in the opinion of the doctors, she did not have enough strength to leave for a long journey, we took her to a suitable institution, and she remained in the Soviet Union. On the day of my departure, I was able to bring her a certificate of approval, a *Potiuvka*, which allowed her to be placed in a home for the disabled in Troitzk, at government expense.

A Russian Jew, who worked with me in one building, arrived at the station to depart with me. He was an engineer who more than once asked me how it was possible to join the Poles, in order to leave Russia. The question occupied me, whether I would prefer to remain in Poland or continue on my way to Palestine. My answer was clear and unambiguous: to go home to the Land of Israel.

At that moment, the face of this Jew actually lit up and, with tears, he said to me, "Too bad that we cannot join you, but this is our fate. I have a request for you. Send regards to my mother and my sister in Tel Aviv. He handed me the address. We were silent. The two of us stood with tears in our eyes and parted.

Apparently, already there had begun an awakening of the Jewry of the Soviet Union. The Russian Jew left me with slow, heavy steps. While I hurried to the railroad car, raindrops began to fall, and it was a sad moment upon the heart. I turned my last glance toward the Russian Jew, the representative of the *Jewry of Silence*. I entered the car, where my companions offered me drink. I didn't want to drink. I settled myself down and sank into thoughts about the large and precious Jewish community, an honorable and important aggregation which was keeping silent, and whose future was very murky. There was no way of knowing whether and when it would join its people in its land. Who knows what will be the fate of the Jews of Russia? Will this people arise to national redemption and join its brethren? Would that it should happen!

A sharp, drawn–out whistle interrupted my thoughts, and another whistle, and yet another, and the train moved. Slowly, as we moved away from the city, I said goodbye to Cheliabinsk. To our Jewish brethren I added another prayer: "See you in our Land. Amen!"

The Border and the Inspection

After an exhausting and long trip, we reached the inspection point. The passengers prepared their documents. Police of the N.K.V.D. entered the car, greeted us, and requested our papers. I must remark

[Page 127]

that the behavior of the policemen was somewhat unexpected, polite, courteous, and far from official. It was rumored that there were instructions from the authorities to treat us nicely, because the work we had done in the military industry was exemplary and that we had helped defeat the enemy. Despite this, there were those among us who were afraid. Maybe they would search for gold, watches, jewelry, or other items. There was a good reason to assume that they were *Raprarientz*, a division of the oppressive secret police, and that for us to fear the worst was justified, but there were no searches, and everything passed peacefully.

We crossed the Russian–Polish border. We reached the Polish village of Kashivda – the meaning of the word is *deprived*. At this station, we had to wait a long time. A number of passengers got off the train and went into a nearby grove for their personal needs. We saw Poles who stood in the vicinity of the train. They formed groups among themselves and ganged up on us while saying, "They are returning here. Too bad that Hitler didn't manage to exterminate all of them." Some did not content themselves with words, but signaled to us with a hand on the neck. We appealed to the passengers to return to the train and not to walk around, because we were in mortal danger. All the passengers returned to the train except for three young men. We searched for them but did not find them. All the efforts to find these companions ended in failure. Also, an energetic appeal to the manager of the station did not return them to us. We received an answer that this was not his business and that, in a number of minutes, we would continue the journey. The young men were already no longer alive. The murderers lay in ambush for prey and found it. There were some who refused to enter the train without the absent companions, and only after urgings and pleas that the number of victims was liable to increase did the people return to their cars. At one of the stations, the bitter information was reported that the three young men were murdered in Kashivda. Now, the companions were reminded that, indeed, they had heard three shots, but they hadn't wanted "to open a mouth to Satan."

The 'Wives' Parted from Their 'Husbands'

With contained pain and deep sorrow, after the murder of the three, we continued on the way and saw suspect types who reminded us of the murderers from Kashivda. They went around, particularly at the railroad stations, and lay in wait for victims.

At last, we reached the final station, Wroclaw. The city was ruined beyond repair, and our people found doubtful refuge in destroyed and half-destroyed houses.

Young couples who had registered in the city of Cheliabinsk, at the office of marriage registration, in order to enable a son or daughter of the couple to leave the country, parted with handshakes and with words of thanks. These were fictitious marriages. There were also couples who received, in the course of time, encouragement for legal rabbinic confirmation of their marriage, with a halachically proper marriage canopy and sanctifications.

My 'wife' also parted from me and joined Hashomer Hatzair, and I joined Gordonia. We transferred our certificate from the office of marriage registration in Cheliabinsk in order to enable a Latvian girl to exit the Soviet Union and join her family in the Land of Israel. The Baltic lands had been annexed to the Soviet Union and, therefore, only with the help of marriage confirmation with a Polish native was it possible to leave the Soviet Union.

I arrived at Lodz and received a position in the chief leadership of Gordonia, 'The Young Maccabees.' After a brief time, I was sent to Lower Silesia, and I received a position as head counselor and coordinator of the school of the children's camp of

Gordonia in Niemci. Our final goal was to arrive with 200 children making illegal Aliyah to the Land of Israel. The children were Survivors of the Holocaust and a portion of them had been repatriated from the Soviet Union. The children, who were accepted at the camp, were between the ages of 6 to 16, and some were also of a more mature age, serving as counselors and teachers.

[Page 128]

We divided the camp into groups according to age. The largest was a group of adolescents aged 16 and upwards. The rest of the groups were smaller. Every group had its own counselor and a teacher. In certain cases, the counselor also served as a teacher. In the morning hours, the groups were organized into study classes.

The work in the camp proceeded according to a fixed, orderly, daily routine. In the camp, there was a female doctor and two assistant nurses who worked very hard because the children, Holocaust Survivors, required constant, serious treatment. They had been brought from the concentration camps, and from different clandestine places, with severe illnesses. They suffered from a variety of symptoms and required serious care.

We received aid in medicines and food from the Joint Distribution Committee. The budget was guaranteed, and the children received nutritious food, as well as clothing, and shoes, in a well thought out way. We stayed in this place close to three months.

At the end of the summer of 1946, we packed our belongings and went out, in a few automobiles, to the Polish–Czech border. Several hundred meters before the inspection point, we got out of the automobiles and waited for the command to move. Men of the Haganah and the Bricha, worked hand in hand with the border officers. We received instructions from the Commander of the Bricha, the Illegal Immigration, that we should be vigilantly on guard. We arranged ourselves in groups, and at the head of each group, we placed a counselor. He waited for a signal. Suddenly, we heard the Commander's voice, "Gordonia, go up forward!" We marched like an army. Behind us walked a number of parents who would not part with their children. We consented to allow them to advance along with their children's groups.

We Cross the Border

As we approached the border, officers, soldiers, and border guards left their posts and only the Commander of the Bricha remained. He gave us a short command, "Forward!" We crossed the border without incident into Czechoslovakia. The inspection was superficial. They did not search much. The inspection and searches were essentially done of the parents. We got into the autos that waited for us, and drove to the Czech village of Bromov.

In the village, there was a German P.O.W. camp. The P.O.W.'s had been transferred to another place, and the bunks renovated. We settled down into that place. In the vicinity of the camp, there were more German P.O.W.'s, but there wasn't a more suitable place for us, so we remained there. The Germans closed themselves in, and did not go out of their bunks. The people of the Joint, 'Ministering Angels' as we called them, received us very warmly and cared for our health. They served us food and drink without limit. This was our first meeting, face to face, with the people of the Joint. It is hard to describe in words their dedication and their desire to help. The women of the Joint carried the small children in their arms, hugged them and kissed them. One who has not seen the dedication of the people of the Joint to the children of the remnants of the Holocaust, does not know what love of Israel is.

[Page 129]

We hadn't even managed to rest when, behold, there was an announcement over the loudspeaker to prepare for inspection. This was the first inspection of Gordonia in this place, in the German P.O.W. camp, on Czechoslovakian soil. The children of Israel, Survivors and remnants of the Holocaust in the hundreds, were gathering in the shadow of our national flag, in order to prove their fierce desire to begin life anew, in spite of everything.

The bunks of the German P.O.W.'s were not far from where we stood. From the windows, the Germans looked upon the Hebrew flag flying and announcing 'the Jewish People live!' This was the revenge that the Children of Israel were able to take on the Germans for the great suffering that they had caused. The revenge of children, who with their own eyes had seen the deaths of their parents, their brothers, and sisters, and whose only great sin was that they were the children of the Jewish People. This is the revenge known in our literature as 'Revenge of the Covenant.'

With the conclusion of the inspection, the command was given, "Forward march!" Hundreds of children and youths marched in clean clothing in an orderly way around the camp, with a powerful song in their mouths, 'The Flag of the Camp of Judah.' The Germans saw this with their eyes, amazed, and asking, "Are these the remnants of the Jewish People which was exterminated?"

We stayed only a number of weeks in Bromov. Before we left, important visitors reached us, people of the Joint, the Bricha, and representatives of the Red Cross. They were received in the office of the Director of the camp, who was a Czech and managed the camp. In the office of the Director sat an important official who filled out different forms and prepared documents for us, and whose help we needed in order to continue our journey. The next day, we parted from Bromov, after an emotionally festive inspection, and went out on the road. We did not know the next stop. We traveled on a train. Two cars were designated for us. The entrance of strangers into our cars was forbidden.

When we were near Vienna, at the station just before the capital, we got off, got into autos which were waiting for us, and were taken to the Rothschild House. The Rothschild Hospital in Vienna was destroyed in the war, but the Jewish community decided to refurbish it and prepare it as a lodging place for 'remnants of the sword.' This was a temporary station, because we knew that we had to continue on the way.

I left for the city, in order to visit the grave of the visionary of the Jewish State at the cemetery. Immediately at the entrance to the cemetery, I found the family grave of Herzl. I was deeply saddened by the desecration of the monument by its many visitors, with their inscriptions of names on it, profanation of the sacred. I stood silent near the grave and I thought that, perhaps now, after the awful Holocaust, Herzl's dream would materialize, and that the State of Israel would arise. At that moment, it did not occur to me that we were very close to the establishment of the State, which would transfer Herzl's remains to the eternal capital of Israel, Jerusalem.

When I returned to the Rothschild House, I found out that we were divided into two groups, the children, who were essentially Survivors of the Holocaust, who would be transferred for recovery and rehabilitation to Schtrobel, and the youth and the adults who would continue on their way in an unknown direction. After many travels, and transitional stops, we reached Saalfelden in Austria, in the American Zone.

[Page 130]

COMITÉ INTERNATIONAL DE LA CROIX-ROUGE

DÉLÉGATION A *Prague, Jiřina Opletala.*

5

Signature du délégué:
Signature of Delegate:
Unterschrift des Delegierten:
Firma del delegato:
Firma del delegado:
Подпись делегата:
Podpis delegata:

Dr. O. Lehner, Chief of the
delegation of the CICR
in Czechoslovakia

Cachet de la Délégation:
Delegation stamp:
Stempel der Delegation:
Timbro della Delegazione:
Sello de la Delegación:
Печать делегации:
Pieczęć delegacji:

Empreintes digitales (obligatoires)
Finger-prints (compulsory)
Fingerabdruck (unerlässlich)
Impronte digitali (obbligatorie)
Huellas digitales (obligatorias)
Отпечаток пальцев (обязательно)
Odcisk palca (obowiązkowo)

Photographie (facultatif)
Photograph (optional)
Lichtbild (nach Belieben)
Fotografia (facoltativa)
Fotografia (facultativa)
Фотография (необязательно)
Fotografja (dowolne)

Under Auspices of the Red Cross in Prague,
toward the Continuation of the Journey

[Page 131]

Saalfelden and Manual Toil

In Saalfelden, there were different pioneer youth movements. We would go out to work, which was assigned to us by the camp management. We would carry out the work on a contractual basis, and would receive a wage in money or in food. In the evening hours, we organized a variety of cultural activities.

It was reported to us that we should reach Italy, which was the last stop before Aliyah. The children of Schtrobel from the first group had already reached Milan. We waited for the order with impatience. The days in Saalfelden were numbered.

During this period, we increased the cultural work and, especially, the study of the Hebrew language. Everyone studied Hebrew, the language of the homeland. We read newspapers that arrived from the Land of Israel, and carried on fluent, flowing conversations and lectures about real matters.

The manual labor of the members of Gordonia made an impression on the people of the camp and many followed in our footsteps to seek work. Manual labor in the Saalfelden camp changed the atmosphere, and changed the attitude of the camp management and the American officers towards the Jews. The American officers told us that they had not believed we'd be qualified to fulfill all that was required of us, and that they wouldn't need to invite workers from the outside. The officers joked that they wouldn't allow us to leave Saalfelden, since they had no chance of getting workers like us. Thus, we became professional workers.

In the continuation of our journey, we would have to reach Italy, so we began to investigate which roads to use. As usual, rumors circulated. We got reports from different sources that the route would be comfortable and that we could travel by train directly from Salzburg to Milan. There was a second possibility that we would walk most of the distance on foot.

The Continuation of Illegal Immigration from Saalfelden to Milan through Innsbruck

In the last days of December 1946, we received an order to be prepared for the continuation of the journey, which was not especially easy. We were told to react with absolute silence to any questions we might be asked in connection with the continuation of the journey. They forbade us to take letters, notes, pictures, or anything that was liable to identify us. We were not to disclose the origin or the name of anyone.

One evening, we left for the journey. There was the Commander, a man of the Bricha, who was revered by the entire American officer corps, and ruled the area. 'Comrade Arthur' distributed travel cards to us, simple slips of paper with numbers on them. This was the power of the commander of the Bricha. Several adults, parents of the children, wanted to join the journey. The Commander explained to them that the journey would be difficult, and advised them to wait for another opportunity, but after much deliberation, he relented, and we left with a number of parents – many of whom were quite mature.

We reached the station of the train that waited for us. The train workers helped us board, and took care that no strange passenger would join us. The Commander had organized everything beautifully. We traveled on the train for several hours. Finally, we got off and continued on foot to a place where trucks awaited us and brought us to Innsbruck, a Bricha point on the Italian border. This was the last stop on the way to Italy. We made the rest of the trip on foot. The walking was good but dangerous. For the few adults, it was difficult. It was no accident that the commander opposed taking them. We walked in snow, half a meter high or more. One woman, the mother of three children who took part in the journey, had great difficulty walking. At a certain point, she sat down in the midst of the snow and didn't want to get up anymore. When I approached her and asked her to get up, she didn't answer. I invited a counselor to help me get the woman up, and she began to mumble in Yiddish "Loz mich shtarben, kinderlach," Children, let me die. One of the counselors, a Bricha man who was experienced and strong, approached us. He took the woman on his back, as though she were a sack of flour, and continued on the way. The children excelled in quick, easy walking, and we walked in a long line. The counselors guarded us well, watched that we did not lag in walking, and helped the weak to advance. The relationship between the counselors and the illegal immigrants was really very special. Every one of them was a father and mother at once.

[Page 132]

Tired, thirsty and somewhat fearful, we approached the border point, which was in the French zone of conquest. There was very loud barking of dogs and, after that, shots interrupted the silence of our march. The order was given by the counselors to lie down and not utter a sound. We lay down in the snow. The shots accompanied us to the Italian border, and we kept falling, getting up and continuing. Suddenly, we saw a house. Someone took the trouble to explain to us that we were already in Italy. In that house, we were to rest. We advanced cautiously in silence.

The house had an expansive threshing floor full of grains. We were given permission to take off our outer clothing. We took off just what was possible to take off. We shook the heavy snow off of our clothes and socks, and the load was lightened for us. We hung our socks and coats on nails or on heaps of straw for drying out. We felt great relief, and there was respite for us because we felt that the danger had passed. We had crossed the border successfully. We were happy.

Our young men, from the Haganah and the Bricha, walked around as if they were at home. Suddenly, the owner of the house, a woman, entered with several of our young men. In their hands were pitchers full of warm drink, and they distributed cups to us with great speed. The woman provided a full cup to everyone, and did this with a broad smile on her lips. It was obvious she was very satisfied.

The drink was free. We drank much. Everything was ready in advance. This was the most delicious drink we had ever tasted, even though to this day, I do not know what we had, tea or milk, but it was good, and very tasty. And, it was a *hot* beverage. We were unable to stay in this house for much longer, since it was near the border and we had to depart before daybreak. We did not manage to rest. Soon an order was given to get dressed and be ready for the road. Autos arrived.

We traveled less than an hour. We got out, and went over to *other* autos. Then we continued on foot until we reached 5 Via Uniona Street in Milan. This was the Jewish community building. In this building, there were groups of the remnants of the Holocaust, who were also being brought to the Land of Israel. We entered the courtyard, which was full of refugees with bundles and large suitcases in every corner. We went up to the second floor.

[Page 133]

They brought us to the dining room. We ate and drank, but we were tired and just wanted to sleep. Some among us fell asleep at the table. We were then brought to a corner in one of the rooms, lay on the floor to rest, and fell asleep immediately. After a brief rest, the counselors awakened everyone, and we were told that from now on we would be allowed to speak and to sing. We were free.

We Reach the Institute in Salvino

We traveled from Milan to Salvino, which took two hours. We reached Salvino in the evening. Salvino was an exemplary village among thousands, and the Shtzisaupoli Institute was intended for Fascist youth. Mussolini had visited this place. There was a special room for him at the time of his visit.

Our eyes lit up at seeing a clean and orderly place. Every corner was exceptionally clean. The tables were set with everything good, fruit, drink, hot rolls, butter, cheese and more. This was a special place. The young children who had been in Schtrobel had arrived here a while ago, and looked different, since many had been sick from malnutrition and the difficult conditions of the concentration camps or other hidden places. It was difficult to recognize these children. They were dressed in beautiful holiday clothes, clean and polished, joyous and happy, as if they had been reborn. The community in Milan, *The Center for the Diaspora*, and also the institutions of the city, took care to supply the Institute with all its needs.

At the head of the institution, *Young Gordonia–Maccabee in Salvino*, stood a soldier of the Brigade, a person who worked with unusual dedication for the Aliyah of the children to the Land of Israel and of overcoming the need for the transit camp.

The children in the Institute studied and worked, and prepared themselves for Aliyah. The pupils were responsible for the cleanliness of the house, the courtyard, and the restrooms. Even the youngest children learned how to tidy their rooms. Life in the house was based on service. Indeed, there were workers and hired employees, but those were professionals. I was assigned to organize the school. At the Institute, there were two hundred children. The children studied almost all subjects, but textbooks were lacking. The teachers worked with exceptional dedication, and, in different ways, they enabled the students to acquire the basics of the Hebrew language and other subjects. By the time of Aliyah, most of the children had acquired the language and spoke Hebrew. This was the greatest achievement of the teachers and the counselors. Salvino was the last step before Aliyah.

We Make Aliyah

We were fifty young people. Twenty graduates from our Institute Salvino–Gordonia, twenty members of Hashomer Hatzair, and another ten people from Hashomer Haleumi—all of them knowing Hebrew, and all of them ready to join the ranks of the Haganah. We received an order to be ready to move. We were not told when we would make Aliyah, but it was hinted to us that it was forbidden to speak about it. We would not be able to take bundles, only small briefcases containing our minimal personal needs and nothing else.

A few days before Rosh Hashanah 5707, we reached Rome and awaited instructions. On *erev Rosh Hashanah*, the person responsible for the planning of our Aliyah arrived and invited us to meet. In this conversation, he did not reveal the secret to us, but according to some hints, we gathered that we would fly on a special flight.

[Page 134]

On *Tzom Gedaliah*, the Fast of Gedaliah, the 3rd of Tishrei 5707, early in the morning, the Emissary arrived and announced that, in another hour, we would leave for the road. The only document, instead of a passport, was the approval from the Red Cross, whose special agent had signed the documents while we were in Bromov, in Czechoslovakia. The practical value of this approval was negligible. It could not even have served as an identity document.

Since I was responsible for the undertaking, a special file was given to me. I also received a large sum of money, part as payment for the flight, and a second part for special expenses. I was to hand over the balance to the agent of the Haganah when we arrived in the Land of Israel.

According to Aryeh's instructions, we presented ourselves as a group of students who were flying to India. We left in two elegant tourist–taxis on the way to the Fortress of Rome. Not far, at the southernmost point, we had to find a military airfield a number of kilometers from the Fortress that had been in use in the days of the Second World War.

We saw American soldiers following us, so we changed the route. Instead of approaching the airfield, we approached the Cemetery of the Slain of the Second World War, to conceal our real objective. We entered the cemetery. A Star of David marked the graves of Jews who had fallen in battle. Aryeh jotted down several fictitious names on paper, approached the guard, and asked how to find their graves. Obviously, the graves were not located. But the guard received his reward and was satisfied. Our escort was even more enterprising and found the grave of an unknown Jewish soldier, ordered us to shift to silence, and stood by himself near the grave praying silently. The guard was happy that we had found at least one grave. And, again, an order, and we went out to the road. The soldiers who had followed us had departed, and the performance had succeeded.

We continued searching for the airfield. The guide and I had instructions on how to find the place. Tired and nervous, we moved around until we found a deserted and wide lot. We knew that this was the place. We had to wait half an hour for the arrival of the plane. It was 7:30 in the evening. Suddenly, a motorcycle approached us. Two Italians approached, and asked us what our business was in this vicinity, and how they could assist us. The guide knew Italian, and explained to them that we were tourists, and that we were waiting for buses that would take us back to Rome. The Italians departed.

We were worried by the encounter, but we knew that they were merely civilians. We received an instruction from the Counselor to hide the briefcase containing the money and the documents. I put the briefcase behind a tree and placed a stone on it. Suddenly, we heard noise, and we knew that the plane was arriving. We took up a position, everyone in his place. It was already dark. We lay down with flashlights, in order to signal the plane. The plane landed with tremendous noise. This was a military plane loaded with military cargo for Cairo. In that moment, another motorcycle approached with an armed police officer. The policeman interrogated one of the two pilots, and also questioned me. We received the order to board, and one by one, the 'students☐ entered the plane on their way to 'India.' The guide handed me several instructions and departed from the place. My turn came to enter the plane. I was the last of the 'students' and, due to the panic and excitement, I could not find the briefcase with the money and the documents. The situation seemed desperate. Part of the money was destined as a payment for the 'hitch–hike.'

[Page 135]

I knew that if I didn't find the briefcase, we would not reach our destination.

After a search, and moments of suspense, I found the briefcase and managed, at the very last minute, to enter the plane with the help of the co–pilot, a Dutchman. The policeman, rifle drawn, still continued his argument with the first pilot. Suddenly, the pilot drew his pistol. The policeman lowered his rifle, marched backwards and shouted, "This is not oaky!" but the plane lifted up, and we took off. A mighty song burst forth from our mouths: "We are making Aliyah to the Land!" *We were like dreamers* (Psalm 126 – *Shir HaMa'a lot*).

All Are Dead

We took off at 8:30 in the evening. At 12:30am, we reached Athens. Even here, we experienced hours of trembling. The pilot explained to us that, after we refueled, we would continue on the way, and that at 6:00 in the morning, we would reach the 'Skies of Kibbutz Degania.' The pilot warned us not to speak, only to lie down. "You are dead," he said. "There is no one on the plane, just military cargo."

The co–pilot stood at the entrance of the plane, and did not allow the inspection team to enter, due to the military cargo that was aboard. He even showed them an authorization to prove it to them. A deliberation ensued, and of course, as before, the pilot had the upper hand. We continued on the way. It is hard to describe the joy on the plane, and the cries of "Long Live the State of Israel!" that echoed in its cabin.

Our joy was not yet complete. We knew that the English were liable to send us to Cyprus, or to prison, or even return us to Italy. However, our excitement grew. We were on the way to the Homeland. Was it possible that the Exile was behind us, and the Land so close? Behold, a few hours ago, we were there in the Exile. The expectation grew and increased, another hour, another half hour, a quarter hour, we were very near. At 5:55am, our plane circled in the skies of *Emeq Yezreel*, the Jezreel Valley. The plane made a turn, in order to reach the Degania at exactly 6:00am. Then the plane landed. We did not sing. We did not speak. We were paralyzed. We saw healthy young men standing on automobiles, grabbing us straight from the plane, one by one, and departing with their autos.

The Curfew and the Searches

The Haganah announced a curfew, in order for us to reach a secure location. We saw Haganah men in uniforms and thought that these were British soldiers. The Kibbutznik from Masada explained to us that these were our young men who wore uniforms of the British army, thereby preventing the British and the Arabs from approaching the area, so that we could reach the farms. With the passage of a quarter of an hour, we were already in Degania. A second group reached Masada, and a third Sha'ar Hagolan. At 6:30am, we were on the farms. They immediately dressed us in work clothes. We entered the dining room, ate breakfast, and went out to work. My wife and I were at Masada.

At 7:30am, the English reached the farm to search for 'illegal' immigrants, and found veteran kibbutzniks with English identity documents in their pockets. The followers of Ernest Bevin did not know the secret power of the Jew in his war to burst through the gates to reach the Land.

For us, the path of afflictions had come to an end. We had come home! *"And the children have returned to their land!"* (Jeremiah 31:17).

[Page 136]

The Trial

In 1966, a group of Nazi criminals, who had operated in the region of Tarnopol and local towns like Skalat, were made to stand trial in Stuttgart. Among the accused were Müller and Roebel. We bring here the bill of indictment against Müller and, so too, from the verdict. Our thanks to Dr. Yosef Karmish, and to Mr. A. Brand from Yad Vashem in Jerusalem, both of whom helped us to obtain these sources. Special thanks to Ms. Ruth Langutzky for the translation of this material, from German to Hebrew, without any monetary remuneration.

חורשה
ע"ש קדושי קהילת
סקאלאט
והסביבה

Grove Named for the Martyrs of the Community of Skalat and the Vicinity Monument in Memory of the Martyrs of Skalat in the Forest of the Martyrs

[Page 137]

The Bill of Indictment Against Müller

Skalat:

A city in the region of Tarnopol

Place of the seat of the Landskomiser

   1. July 6, 1941. A pogrom was conducted by the Ukrainians – Müller, vv Bl.189 (Reisel Epstein)

2. On August 30, 1942, 'The Immigration Aktion' was conducted. About 500 elderly and sick were gathered together, by Jewish policemen, and were transferred, the next day, along with 60 additional Jews, into the hands of the SIPO in Tarnopol. The victims were assembled in the synagogue, and were transported to the railroad station. There they were forced to kneel on the ground, despite the rain, which had not ceased falling all that day. Later they were loaded onto trucks, and brought to the concentration camp in Tarnopol. This Aktion is known by the name of the 'Aktion of the Quotas,' since there was a need to transfer a certain quota in every transport, and sometimes there was a need to gather additional Jews for filling the required quota.
Müller, EAIII Bl. 44, 51, 84, FF
Müller vv Bl. 189 (Reisel Epstein)

3. On the 21/22 of October 1942, after Rosh Hashanah, 'The Cruel Aktion' or 'The Great Aktion' was conducted. In it, 3000 Jews were brought to the synagogue and then transported to the railroad station. Before this, about 1,000 Jews from Grzhimalov, Podvolochisk, and other locations in Skalat were forced into the Skalat ghetto. During this Aktion, many incidents of shooting occurred.
–Müller EA III Bl. 45, 51, 105
Müller vv Bl. 189 (Reisel Epstein)
Bl. 206 (Dlugacz) Bl. 192 (Witrakiwetz)
Bl 134 (Ben Porath)
Müller EA III Bl. 84/85 (Anna Chrein –Trif)

4. On November 9, 1942, 'The Little Aktion' was conducted. About 1,000 victims were taken out of the city in trucks and were executed by shooting while standing in front of graves dug in advance. Among the victims were women and children. Searches for Jews were conducted and, when they were found, they were assembled in the synagogue or next to it. Apparently, many of the victims were Jews lacking labor permits. Younger Jews who were seized in these searches were brought to ZAL Chalobotchk. Jews who attempted to escape through the windows of the synagogue were shot by men of the guard.

[Page 138]

–Müller EA II AS Bl. 377, 385 (Czerwny)

Müller EA III Bl. 45, 51, 87, 106

Müller vv Bl. 208 (Dlugacz) Bl. 189 (Reisel Epstein)

5. On April 7, 1943, several days before the Passover Holiday, an additional Aktion was conducted. Again, searches were held in the Ghetto. The victims were shot to death outside the city, on a hill near the village of Novosilka. There were several hundred victims. This Aktion is known as 'The Weeping Graves.'
–Müller, EA III Bl. 107, 51/Weissbrod, Kiwetz).
Müller vv Bl. 135 (Ben–Porath) – not Eyewitness.

6. On June 9, 1943, the Ghetto was finally liquidated. The surviving remnant was hurried once again to the synagogue, and from there were transported to the shooting–hill near Novosilka. A few succeeded in hiding in the town before the beginning of the Aktion, or by hiding in the forests.
–Müller EA III Bl. 51, 87, 107
Müller vv Bl. 92 (Zharkover) Bl. 135 (Ben Porath)
Not Eyewitness, vv. Bl. 21 (Hofmann)

The Aktions at Skalat were reconstructed in detail in Abraham Weissbrod's *Death of a Shtetl* (Yiddish), Munich 1948.
–Müller EA III Bl. 42 FF

The liquidation of the Labor Camp at Skalat, known as Kamionka, came afterwards in July 1943.

In context with the number of victims: In the census of the residents from the Skalat region in the year 1931, 89,215 residents were counted. Of these, 45,631 Poles, 34,752 Ukrainians, and 8,486 Jews, of whom 7,037 dwelled in the cities.

[Page 139]

The Destruction of the Jews of Galicia

Particularly in the Tarnopol Region

A Segment of the Verdict Against Roebel and Müller

1. First Wave of Extermination

1 In the fall of 1941, the first wave of extermination of the Jews of Tarnopol took place. It was considered relatively light compared to the later waves.

Many Jews were arbitrarily shot to death next to graves prepared in advance, at the command of the KdS and carried out by the men of the Department of Deportation.

The winter of 1941–42 constituted a kind of calm period in which crimes took place mostly against Jewish properties, and not against the Jews themselves. The arbitrary mass murders still did not arouse any suspicions by the Jews of the area concerning a complete genocide against Galician Jewry. Jews were required to hand over all money and precious metals, along with all furs that were in their possession. This came to be known as the 'Aktion of Fur' during December 1941. Anyone who refused or attempted to evade this demand was in mortal danger.

2. Second Wave of Extermination

2a. The strike against the Jewish population in Spring, 1942, revealed the methodology for the first time. That occurred when the Belzec extermination camp, in the zone of the conquest of Galicia, was built for the purpose of the mass murder of thousands of Jewish victims. The Germans then moved ahead with the wave of Aktions that inundated the entire region, and slowed only for a brief time through the summer of 1942.

The sign of recognition, in those early Aktions, was the categorization of the victims. Cases of the indigent, elderly, sick, and orphaned, those lacking social backing and lacking value as members of a labor force, were liquidated in the first blow. The Committee of the Community, the Judenrat, was responsible for arranging lists with the names of these victims for the Germans.

The huge number of victims from the city of Lemberg alone, at the time of the Nazi invasion, was about 160,000 Jews. These victims activated the extermination machine at Belzec in a full reception and tempo that made it impossible for the camp to absorb transports of victims from other districts. As a result, extermination and mass killing was perpetrated in those other places by shooting.

[Page 140]

2b. The Aktions in the Tarnopol region were always carried out using the same method. First, they harnessed the Jewish Committees of the Community to draw up lists of names of the victims. Later, when the objectives of the Aktions and their outcomes became clear to everyone and the Jewish population refused to obey, they refused the appeals of the Communal Committee to present themselves at the assembly places. Then the gathering of the victims at the assembly points was accomplished with a cruelty and barbarity that cannot be described.

Equipped with weapons, curses, and whips, the Extermination Services, with the accompaniment of Jewish police, Ukrainian lawmen, German soldiers and Gendarmerie, burst into the houses of the victims and forced them, with cruel blows and shots, to hurry to the gathering places. There, they were ordered to bend to their knees or to crouch on the ground, in their underwear only, for hours or even days, without moving a limb. Then they were taken to shooting places that were euphemistically called, by the S.S., 'Immigration Points,' places where mass graves had been dug for the victims in advance. These were dug by men of the Construction Service, which consisted of Ukrainian and Polish staffs, similar to the German Construction Service, which operated in the boundaries of the Reich. The Shooting Commandos, firing squads, mostly composed of men from the Deportation Department of Tarnopol, were located near the mass grave excavations.

O 4/20 -55 -1

Schwurgericht bei dem Landgericht
Stuttgart

Strafsache gegen
Paul Roebel , Hermann Müller und Andere

wegen
Mordes (NS-Verbrechen in Tarnopol)

Ks 7/64 = 12 Js 1403/61 Staatsanwaltschaft
bei dem Landgericht
Stuttgart

Urteil vom 15. Juli 1966   Band:

The Title Page of the Verdict against Roebel and Müller

[Page 141]

In exceptional cases, security forces were added, such as policemen, gendarmerie, and Ukrainian militia, which generally served only for guard purposes, and also as Shooting Commandos, even though, with regard to them, different instructions existed.

Under guard, they ordered the victims to form groups, about 30 to 50 meters from the open graves, and to wait in place. In this way, they did not withhold from them the terrifying and protracted scene of mass execution ahead of them until their turn came. They were sent in small groups to the edge of the graves, while opposite them riflemen were positioned according to the number of victims. There was no resistance. Isolated individuals, who dared to try to escape, were killed on the spot by these murderers.

Before their last steps to the edge of the open graves, the victims were ordered to strip completely. In 1943, this was certainly the procedure. It is possible that, even before that, this is how the Germans customarily operated. Then the victims were told to face the corpses already in the graves, and to stand in front of 'their' riflemen. At a signal, the riflemen shot into the skulls of their victims and, with a swift kick, threw them into the mass graves.

To victims who were a complete family, they allowed this last stand together. More mature children were ordered to step like adults to the edge of the graves. Infants were left in the arms of their mothers. The mother was shot first, and at the moment she buckled under, they aimed and shot the infant.

There were instances where the shots missed their target and sometimes it was possible to discern limbs moving or to hear groans. Seldom did they redeem such wounded with an additional shot. But, generally, those unfortunates suffocated under the next to be slain, or at the time of covering over the graves – something that was also carried out superficially.

Since the bodies of the victims swelled very much, and their graves usually lifted up a few meters – only later subsiding – it was possible to close the graves, finally, after only a few days.

The men of The Shooting Commandos were subjected to difficult psychological depression. The terrifying human suffering, which occurred before their eyes, was so awful that the internal callousness toward the Jews, which they had adopted for themselves, did not always hold up for them. In order to subdue any weakness or human bonding, and to ease forgetfulness, alcohol began to play a considerable role. The men of the Commandos were given alcoholic beverages to drink, liberally, before, during and after the executions. Toward the end of the Aktions, when most of the riflemen were absolutely drunk, the poorly aimed shots became more frequent, and the cruelty increased even more.

Already at the time of this focused Aktion against the Jews and, later, after the reduction of the Deportation Department, all of the Deportation Department men were tied to the goal of mass exterminations, unless they were mustered for another important activity.

Aside from the place of execution, only a negligible power in the Deportation Department remained. Usually, those were only three female typists.

Before the Aktion, in a choreographed manner, the Commander of the place would convene a session in which the details of carrying it out were decided. The commander of the place would receive his instructions from the KdS in Lemberg that, for its part, received instructions from the SSPF, or the governor of the District, who decided on the time and place of the Aktions and handed it over to the Deportation Department for carrying out.

[Page 142]

The instructions of the KdS, among others, established the staffing of those carrying out the activity, and also the evaluation of the number of victims that were, for the most part, minimal.

The function of the Commander of the Deportation Department, in coordination with the instructions of the KdS, was to execute the maximum number of Jews in the shortest amount of time. There is no evidence that, within the authority of the Commander of the Deportation Department in Tarnopol, there was ever the ability to determine, on his own, the number and place of the victims of the notorious Aktions.

If it happened that Aktions occurred at the very same time in several places, the Commander of the Deportation Department transferred his authority to his appointees, who substituted for him. He was sufficiently mobile and could arrive by automobile at any place he wished to follow up on personally, and with his own eyes, to observe how his subordinates had carried out the extermination orders. There were instances where he personally commanded the Aktions. He did not content himself with following from the side, but participated with his own hands as a rifleman at the mass graves. In doing so, he fulfilled instructions, which said that a Commander was to serve as an example to his subordinates.

3a. Arranging the matter of substituting for Jews who were vital as a labor force when reaching the third wave of extermination:

For the time being, with difficulty, HSSPF Krieger and SSPF Katzmann were able to agree to keep alive those few Jews who were especially valuable for the war economy, such as professionals in the military realm of the arms and weapons industry. For psychological reasons, their families were also temporarily left alive.

As far as they were concerned, the total extermination of the Jewish population, and its removal from the face of the earth, constituted the highest, most exalted command, more important than anything. In this idea, they were of one mindset with the head leadership.

Katzmann did everything to reduce to a minimum the number of Jewish workers in German workplaces and projects. He was alarmed and fought, not only against the contemptible broadmindedness of the civilian labor managers, but also against the frequent readiness of the management, and even the army, to comply with the requests of many Jewish workers, and with the excessive use of labor permits bestowing a certain security upon Jews.

Katzmann, in his appeal to the KdS Supreme Field Command 365, and the Armament Corp in Lemberg, wrote on November 6, 1942, "Concerning the speedy release of Jewish professionals from the labor process, as a supreme mandatory principle." He demanded the immediate replacement of Jewish professionals with German ones for his projects and labor positions. He accused the German army of "encouraging Jewish parasitism through the issuance of special permits, without any inspections," as is expressed in his report of June 30, 1943, directed to Krieger HSS.

With extremism and severity, he began personally arranging the replacement of Jewish professionals with Aryans, without encountering any further opposition at all. He reported about this, personally, as follows,

[Page 143]

"Since the management has proved its ineffectiveness and inability to overcome chaos, the matter of the replacement of the Jewish workforce has been transferred to the hands of the S.S. and the commanders of the police."

The personal and energetic intervention of Katzmann, a sign of his power, possessed a sharp, decisive significance for the Jewish population. These labor permits were the only hope of remaining alive for their Jewish holders, since the Aktions of Spring 1942 left the unemployed Jews with deadly terror and fears.

In the city, in the district of Lemberg, tens of thousands of unemployed or semi-employed Jews were sent to the slaughter. Rumors about this terrible misfortune traveled terrifyingly around the expanses of the country, something that had the effect of making these permits even more coveted and sought after. Many Jews who were unable to obtain employment in German projects or labor jobs attempted to save their lives by forging permits. The matter was revealed in an inspection conducted by the police forces.

"In their thousands" – as Katzmann emphasizes in his report of June 30, 1943, holders of such forged labor permits were sent to 'Special Handling,' meaning, to execution. Now there was a probability that the SSPF men and their subordinates would closely scrutinize those individual vital Jews who remained, and separate them from the rest of the Jewish population. Those Jews who lacked utility and who were deprived of rights and protection, would surely be caught up in the mass wave of extermination, which was planned to be carried out during the second half of 1942.

3b. The Third Wave of Exterminations: Mass Extermination in Belzec

In the summer of 1942, the technical forecasts for the extermination of Galician Jewry were published. Already at any early stage, it was clear that with the existing conditions at Belzec, and even with additional help from Lemberg, they would not be up to the task.

The solitary bunk, which stood at their disposal at Belzec, and whose interior was made of tin, was capable of killing only about 150 people at a time with poison gas.

In June 1942 they erected, in place of this bunk, a massive stone building that contained six gas–chambers, with which it was possible to simultaneously gas about 1,500 people. From then on, the absorption of relatively large transports, which were liquidated within a few hours, was made feasible.

The seizure of the Jews, in great numbers, by the men of the Deportation Department of the Armed Security Forces wasn't a problem. The problem was transport. The distance from Tarnopol to Belzec was more than 200 kilometers. The main issue was that the network of railroad tracks of the East was in the middle of the battle area, which constituted an especially difficult problem.

[Page 144]

Himmler, with the help of his assistant, the S.S. Commander Wolf, sought the aid of the Reich Transport Ministry.

His appeals had results. He was promised a free field of action and, on July 19, 1942, he issued an order, in a letter to Krieger, the head of SSPF, that "the transfer of the entire Jewish population under the Administration will be carried out, and they will be liquidated by December 31, 1942. From that date forward, it will be forbidden for a person of Jewish origin to be found in the area, unless he will be found in one of the concentration camps in Warsaw, Krakow or Czestochowa, Radom or Lublin. One should abolish, by that date, all the positions which Jews are still holding, and only in instances in which there is no possibility to abolish a position, should one not transfer its Jewish holders to one of the concentration camps."

This order was the basis of an extermination of tremendous dimensions, which swept over all of Galicia, and which continued from the beginning of July until the end of December 1942. This horrible wave left an especially small number of Jews in isolated ghettos only. Beginning July 22, 1942, ten thousand Jews per week were murdered in the Belzec extermination camp.

S.S. Commander Wolf, Personal Adjutant to Himmler, wrote a letter on July 28, 1942, on this subject to his colleague, Albert Ganzenmoller, the Under Secretary of State at the Reich Transport Ministry. Wolf wrote that in accordance with the agreement between the management of the Eastern Railroad and the security forces in Krakow that beginning July 22, 1942, a train with 5,000 Jews from Przemysl to Belzec would be instituted twice a week. A short time after, the railroad complex passed from Przemysl through Lemberg on its way to Belzec.

In an August 13, 1942 letter of thanks, Wolf also expressed the satisfaction of the S.S, "Fourteen days from now, from day to day, a train departs carrying 5,000 of the sons of the Chosen People to Treblinka and, with this, we have achieved the acceleration of the process of the transfer of this population. I have been in contact with those concerned with the matter and everything is being carried out without frictions and with maximal security."

Those logistics concluded the need for the Shooting Commandos, and for a while the activities of the security forces changed. Now the emphasis was placed on packing the transports. The place and times of the Aktions were fixed in accordance with the timetable of the Eastern Railroad. Having established a fixed timetable for the transport trains, it became possible to carry out a number of Aktions at the very same time. The number of victims was determined according to the capacity of the transports.

3c. The Carrying out of the Aktions of Transports by the Deportation Department of Tarnopol

The first order, pertaining to the activities in the framework of the third wave of extermination, reached the Deportation Department in Tarnopol only at the end of August 1943. Until then, the Belzec camp, despite the expansion of its capability, was occupied because of the crowding together of transports from Lemberg and from other places in the region.

The Deportation Department was assigned to ship tremendous transports to Belzec from August 28 to the middle of November. These transports came, this time, from those places, which, because of technical difficulties, they had bypassed in the course of the previous Aktions.

[Page 145]

The transport activities were generally carried out in great haste. The reason for this was not a result of the large number of Aktions carried out within only a few months, and not even a result of the exacting inspection of labor permits, which were signed anew, and known as "The Aktion of the Seals." Now such particulars were viewed as a waste of time. The principal reason for haste was due to the fact that the current Jewish population had begun to evade the claws of its murderers. The Jews began building countless hiding places to which they disappeared at the first signs of an Aktion. Ones who did not succeed in hiding, but instead lingered in their apartments for as long as possible until found, were forcibly taken to the places of assembly.

It became clear that the Germans had a difficult time gathering victims. Valuable time went to waste – especially in this period – as they were obliged to gather the majority of the Jewish population by the end of the year, packing the capacity of the transports to the maximum. Now the transports were carried out in sudden and energetic Aktions, which gradually became frequent and did not leave the Jews time to hide.

The gathering of the victims therefore became several times more terrifying. From then on, the soldiers of the Deportation Department and their helpers spurred on the terrified Jews with all their means, and with their full staffs, in order not to lose time. Jews now were forbidden the opportunity to take their clothes or any food at all to the places of assembly. Anyone who remained behind, whether he wished to continue to live, or whether he attempted to flee, or whether the reason was illness or old age, was ordered to be shot on the spot.

It became the job of the Committee of the Community, the Judenrat, to gather corpses from the houses and from the streets. At places of assembly, the victims were subjected to terrifying conditions. Lacking everything, they were exposed to awful psychological and physical suffering. For hours, and sometimes for days, they had to kneel or crouch on the ground without moving a limb. While they were subjected to this horrible crowding, they were left to the worst conditions of severe weather. Everyone knew that if he even moved a limb, he would risk lashes or being shot. In instances in which the victims were gathered into enclosed places, they would pack them in with shots until there was no possibility of sitting down.

In addition to the blows and gunshots was added the torture of withholding any food or water from the unfortunate ones, including women and children. The children were the ones who suffered most. When they later pushed the tired and dirty victims, after days of waiting under terrifying conditions, into the railroad cars, their suffering was made many times more severe. Without mercy, they packed the victims into the trains under a hail of blows and shots. It was impossible to sit or to lie down and the transport lasted an entire day. They threw the corpses of those killed into the cars, onto the heads of the victims, and then closed the doors upon them, crushing the limbs and the bodies of the last ones pressed in, without any consideration. They even closed over the especially narrow, few air holes in the train cars with nails. Sometimes, particularly in the burning heat of the severe month of August 1942, the foul condition in the cars caused a situation where most of the victims suffocated during the journey of terror.

The lack of air, the awful suffering before and during the passage, the lack of water or food, regularly caused numerous deaths, which enabled for the victims who remained alive a little more room. Sometimes, the corpses served as places to sit. Despite these barbarous terrors, the will to live was not extinguished, especially among the young people.

[Page 146]

Though the shaky condition of the cars provided opportunities for escape, the only escape route that remained was jumping from a car during the journey. Very few succeeded. Many breathed their last breath either from being shot by the guards, falling under the wheels of the train, or from wounds that were inflicted on them in the leap from the cars.

Despite this, another opportunity became possible for a small number of men, those whom they had designated for the notorious *Zwangsarbeitslager*–ZAL–L (ZAL–Lemberg) a slave labor camp, which was on Janowska Street in Lemberg. It continued its operations after Belzec had been abandoned. For this, they were provided death by a different method. The Aktions, which were conducted on the Jews, left their awful imprint upon the non–Jewish residents of each place, even though they apparently knew very little of what occurred.

In the weekly and secret *News of the District*, which was edited by the Chief Department of Propaganda of the Administration in Krakow, the Germans attempted to allude cautiously to death camps and associated activities in front of the Governor. In the September 24, 1942 weekly report the following was described, "At this hour, Aktions of 'Transfer' against the Jews are being conducted, in all the areas of Galicia. On account of the great extent of the Aktions, it is impossible to totally hide these activities from the local population."

On October 16, 1942, the following announcement in Lemberg was in the *Weekly News*:

The good mood of the residents of the place was muted by the continuation of the conscription of the labor force for the Reich, and also because of the continued transport of Jews. The Aktions of those transports, which are being taken against the Jews, which do not align with the behavior of a cultural nation, surprisingly cause the comparison of these methods of the Gestapo to those of the G.P.U.

The conditions in transport trains are so terrifying that it is impossible to prevent the escape of Jews. As a result of these escapes, the hunt for the escapees is taking place, and cruel shootings echo in the transfer stations. Likewise, it is known that the corpses of Jews who were shot by the Germans are left for days in the streets. In spite of the fact that all the Germans in all expanses of the Reich, including the foreign populations, are convinced of the correctness of the liquidation of the Jews, perhaps it would be better if the matter would be carried out secretly without it arousing such great repugnance."

This principal and basic extermination was supposed to leave alive, according to the intention of the management, only those Jewish forced laborers on the roads and in concentration camps, and exceptionally vital Jewish professionals for the weapons industry, or those who served the army and who underwent an especially exacting re–education. Temporarily, in accordance with the instructions of the management, members of the Committees of the Community, and policemen, or officials of the administration of the Jews, and members of their families were also left alive.

Unintentionally, and in opposition to the design of the murderers, some Jews were left alive who, for technical reasons, had not yet been located, or those who succeeded in hiding in the Ghetto itself, or outside it, and thus succeeded in evading the Aktions.

These Jews returned to the ghetto with the drop in the wave of exterminations, not only because of their desire to be near the remnants of their relatives and acquaintances, but also because these Jews found themselves more secure between the walls of the ghetto than in Aryan areas. There was the great danger that people on the outside would, for a reward, inform on them, thus causing the escapees to be sentenced to death for the misdemeanor of having left the ghetto.

[Page 147]

All told, the Jewish population by November 1942 had lost about 255,000 people who had fallen victim in the Aktions, which had occurred in the second half of 1942. To this number was added an unknown number of those killed in concentration camps and in crushing labor. The ghettos had been almost emptied of their inhabitants, due to the mass extermination and to the considerable number of Jews who were taken to forced labor camps, or those who were held separately from the remnant 'lacking usefulness.'

4.The Pause of the Winter 1942–43: The fate of Jews vital to the war effort

Despite the desire of the S.S. men, the Ukrainians and Poles were not qualified to fill the places of the Jewish professionals in the weapons industry.

Already in the course of the wave of extermination in the second half of 1942, serious disruptions had occurred in the supply of weapons, in the economy, and in the war industries, due to the loss of Jewish professionals. The matter reached the point where the most urgent work no longer operated on the timetable.

On September 18, 1941, the governor of the region warned, while writing to the OKW, "Keeping the Jews away is causing a situation where the potential of the Reich has gone down greatly, and the supply to the front and to the S.S. troops will be forced to cease for a while." The situation was significant, even to Himmler's Supreme Command, for the course of The Final Solution of the Jews of Galicia by the end of 1942. For Himmler's part, it was necessary to leave the minimal number of the most vital Jews alive while they were operating in few places.

In light of the primary priority, which the S.S. men gave to the extermination of the Jews, the demands of the HSSPF and the SSPF, concerning leaving vital Jews alive, seemed suspicious and not serious. In intense arguments, which they carried on with the men of the Wehrmacht, the S.S. men succeeded in reducing, to a bare minimum, the number of vital Jewish professionals.

By August 29, 1942, at the beginning of the mass destruction at Belzec, the governor of the District of Galicia in the "News of the Week" warned:

The labor force in the District is being exploited to the maximum. The matter stems from the severe shortage of Jewish professionals. It was incumbent upon the District of Galicia to prepare everything within less than a year, while in its possessions was a labor force poor in its professional capacity, as opposed to the rest of the districts. Therefore, the war economy was damaged more than in other places by the Aktions against the Jews.

The basic question, whether to give preference to the liquidation of the Jewish People over the war effort, has been solved by preference of the matter of the liquidation of the Jews, for political reasons. Despite this, one should take into consideration the steep decline in the ability of staying–power in the war effort, in the affected areas. I hereby declare that the results of this decision will be clearly felt in Galicia."

Despite the predicted worsening of the situation, due to the extermination of the Jews in the second half of 1942, the Wehrmacht relinquished its demand for the war effort, and thereby submitted to the S.S. ambitions for exterminations.

[Page 148]

In conversations which were conducted between its men, the OKW and the leadership of the S.S., it was decided to transfer the Jews who had worked until then under the command of the Wehrmacht, to the HSSPF, and from then on to call them, "Hard Labor Prisoners of the HSSPF."

Now Katzmann was able to filter out anew, and without anyone disturbing him, those Jews who had remained in the weapons industry against his will (November 1942 Katzmann's Report S.100). Jews who were not connected directly to the weapons industries were fired immediately without even worrying about filling their places.

To the restricted circle of Jews whose talents were impossible to replace, armbands were supplied, on which were printed the letters 'R' and 'W.' The R and W Jews were housed in barracks which were built for them by the HSSPF and which were called JULAG, Jewish Labor Camp. In the Tarnopol Ghetto, a special quarter was set aside for JULAG. The management of the place was entrusted to Untersturmführer Richard Rokita, the legal proceedings against whom have not been completed and therefore have been severed from the main trial. From here on, Katzmann 'separated the straw from the kernel.'

In their multitudes, even the families of the professional Jews who had remained alive until now were sent off for extermination, and all those Jewish officials, Committees of the Community and other workers who had survived in the diminished ghettos, were now proclaimed superfluous and ready for extermination.

A matter of the past, no longer considered, was whether for reasons of propaganda, the Germans would keep the families of the Jewish workers from destruction, so as not to trouble Aryan workers with pain and sorrow. From now on, there was no longer a need to take the matter into consideration, since the end of the few professionals who still remained alive was already visible. There was no longer a need even for the Committees of the Community, since the communities had been almost totally exterminated.

Despite the proceedings, the individual imprisonments, and the murders, the winter of 42/43 constituted a last pause for Tarnopol Jewry. It was caused by the destruction of the Belzec camp, so that there should not be any incriminating traces or evidence. At the end of 1942, all the buildings were demolished. All the installations were removed. All incriminating traces were gathered and burned.

The Jewish Labor Commandos were ordered to exhume the hundreds of thousands of corpses from their mass graves and to incinerate them with the help of huge wooden logs immersed in gasoline.

In the spring of 1943, a young pine forest occupied the place of the notorious Belzec Extermination Camp, in which over 390,000 people were murdered, an especially modest estimate.

The hope, which the remaining Jewish remnant cherished during the relatively quiet winter of 1943, was that the Germans would not adversely affect the most vital workers in favor of German victory. But that hope was absolutely shattered. Already, at the beginning of the winter, Himmler had succeeded in pushing forward his position, that all Jews must be liquidated without any consideration of possible damages. Logic and expediency no longer were in play. In a speech that he gave in April 1943, in Kharkov, in front of the S.S. Commanders, he expressed his outlook in a few words:

As good nationalists, our motto is 'Purity of Blood,' and this is the first time that we have turned it into deeds. The question of Purity of Blood is not identical to Anti–Semitism.

[Page 149]

It is the equivalent of searching for fleas. Getting rid of fleas is not a *weltanschauung*, an outlook, a world view. It is a question of cleanliness. Anti–Semitism, to us, is not a question of outlook, but a matter of cleanliness. The problem has almost come to its solution. Soon, we will be free of fleas.

The army men and commanders of armaments gave up on their demands for leaving a Jewish professional labor force in especially vital places, in the face of Himmler's abysmal and blind hatred. Also contributing to this was the weak and submissive character of their commander in the OKW, the General Field Marshal Keitel, who was a total follower of the authority of the leadership of the NS. He gave his consent to Himmler, early in November 1942, in the matter of the immediate removal of all Jews employed in German positions. Therefore, Himmler's order removed the last serious obstacle to the total destruction of the Jewish population in the region of Galicia.

5. Last Wave of Extermination

A few more months passed until the Deportation Department in Tarnopol received the order to begin the final extermination. After the demolition of the Belzec Camp, there was a need to return to using the Shooting Commandos, and for that reason, they waited until the main part of the winter.

And then the Aktions began, from March through June, and they repeatedly struck in the town, 'until the last wick was extinguished.'

Everything happened in a similar way to the previous shooting Aktions, except that this time the victims were forced to strip their outer garments at the time of assembling, and then to strip completely near the graves.

The methods of gathering the victims became more barbarous and cruel, since the victims, in the bitterness of their despair, held together their hiding places with their fingernails, and only with great difficulty was it possible to find them.

In page 24 of a report from June 30, 1943 to Katzmann's staff:

At the time of the Aktions, we encountered especially serious problems. The Jews had indeed not escaped from the place, but they hid in every possible hole and corner, in order to evade the decree. They entered sewer pipes, hid in chimneys and privies. They attempted to fortify themselves in subterranean tunnels, in cellars serving as bunkers for them, in the cleverest hiding places, in floors, in grain–heaps and in furniture.

Only in a few places did the number of victims amount to the same number as in the previous Aktions of the fall of 1942, and quickly subsided afterwards.

The immediate victims of the present Aktions were Jews of R and W. After these Jews, the Germans exterminated the Committees of the Community, and policemen, and their families. With the conclusion of the Aktions, the ghettos were cleaned out in a short time, and every Jew who was discovered was shot to death.

6. General Numbers

At the conclusion of this extermination push, there was officially not a living Jewish soul in the region of Tarnopol nor in the expanses of the district of Galicia.

More than 41 Aktions were credited to the Deportation Department in Tarnopol, in which between 34,000 and 40,000 victims were murdered.

A tremendous but unknown number were killed in pogroms, in concentration camps, and in lone individual Aktions, or as a result of the frightening suffering prevailing in the ghettos. Death still waited for 21,156 Jews who were in 21 remaining labor camps.

[Page 1590]

Katzmann reported that: "For the security men, there still awaited serious 'ants'-work' in the attempt to discover Jews, who camouflaged themselves or hid."

Katzmann's men engaged in their liquidation, during the summer of 1943, by shooting small groups of Jews who were seized. Their number does not appear at all in Katzmann's list of victims. The number of victims from Katzmann and the National Socialists in Galicia's extermination policy, is estimated, up to the date June 27, 1943, at about 434,329 people.

[Page 151]

The Trial, Half a Jubilee,
Twenty Five Years Later

By Y.B.P.

"Mr. Witness," the Chief Justice began his words. "Is there any family relation at all between you and the Defendant Müller?" This question sounded like a macabre joke, as if it was not of this world, in which the sad and the ridiculous were mixed. The question was one of the least pleasant inscribed in my memory from that trial in which I testified against the heads of the Gestapo of Tarnopol. The Court was in Stuttgart, and the trial took place in February 1966.

After I replied to the Judge's question, with not just a little astonishment, the Chief Justice explained to me, apologetically, that legal procedure obligates him to ask that question, even though it is certainly not pleasant for the witness.

I happened to testify at the Stuttgart trial almost by chance. About two years before the trial, I had submitted testimony with the Israeli police, after I had encountered an advertisement in the newspapers. It did not occur to me that this testimony, which I had submitted in Tel Aviv, would bring me, in days to come, to testify in front of the Court in Germany, a country that I did not rejoice in re–visiting after I had left it in 1947.

Müller had been the head of the Gestapo in Tarnopol, and he bears the responsibility for the liquidation of the Jews of the district of Tarnopol. He had personally supervised most of the Aktions in Skalat.

Before there was a Ghetto in the town, I had worked in the delivery of newspapers. My father was also involved in this work, and I helped him bring the German newspapers principally to unsafe places, which did not usually endanger me, when I was a boy, 11 years old. As a result, I encountered Müller, at least twice before the Great Aktion, when I would bring the newspapers to the Shofo building, which was in the house of Dr. Kron.

At the time of the Great Aktion of October 1942, I was seized, and brought to the Great Synagogue, and there I saw Müller conducting the work of the liquidation of the Skalat Ghetto. I saw Müller shooting into a crowd of people who were gradually being trampled in the synagogue. Since not many were left alive who were able to bear witness against Müller with direct testimony, the Israeli police, who elicited the statement from me, thought that my testimony possessed importance and that it was in my ability to aid in his conviction. The principal problem, which was liable to influence the admissibility of the testimony, stemmed from the fact that I was 11 years old at the time of the Aktion.

About two years passed since I had submitted my statement in Tel Aviv, and the matter had been forgotten from my heart, when suddenly it was reported to me that I was to travel to testify in Germany. Since I was a soldier in regular service, it was not convenient for many reasons, but my commanders related to the matter with much understanding, and my trip was authorized.

[Page 152]

I was scheduled to be a witness the day after I arrived in Stuttgart. I asked to testify in the Hebrew language, for reasons of both convenience and principle. The matter caused a bit of a burden for the legal authorities, since most of the witnesses testified in Yiddish, Polish or German, and they had to engage the rabbi of the city to interpret. He was an Israeli serving in the rabbinate, temporarily, of course.

Ten Germans were standing trial. Of them, I recognized at least three: Müller, Roebel, the commander of the Kamionka and Skalat camps, and his assistant, Meller. Even though their facial appearance was well–etched in my memory, I was not qualified to identify any one of them, considering the 24 years, which had passed since then. And, more than that, they were wearing new, different clothes, not their Nazi uniforms. To my good fortune, I was not asked to identify Müller. I mainly testified against him. During the trial, I was also asked about Roebel.

After I was sworn in, and after the Chief Justice had asked a series of questions, I was asked to repeat before the Court the main points of the testimony, which I had submitted two years earlier in Israel. Immediately, it became clear, as expected, that the focus of my testimony would be in the matter of Müller's shooting into a crowd at the synagogue, on the day of the Great Aktion. These shots were bound to hit people, although I was not able to testify clearly who was hit by them, even though I had seen people wounded and killed inside the synagogue. After I had concluded my testimony, the examination began in which the defense attorney opened.

As expected, the defense counsel began with the weak spot of my testimony, my age, and the time that had elapsed since then. Among the rest, he asked me how I could claim with such confidence that the man who fired was indeed Müller. I replied that, "as of today, I don't know who Müller is," and it became clear that the scoundrel had absolutely changed, wearing eyeglasses and, he wasn't called Müller at the trial. But I always saw him in uniform and with a hat. I was able to establish that the man I saw shooting was identical to the man I saw in the *Schutzpolizei*, at the time that I was bringing the newspapers there. This answer invited, on the part of the defense attorney, a question that I expected to be asked. "Mr. Major," (that was my military rank in which I appeared in court) – the defense attorney turned with quite transparent cynicism – "you claim that you were delivering newspapers. Can you mention to the court the names of the newspapers which you delivered?"

I understand German, and since I had expected this question, I had refreshed my memory about which newspapers I brought to the Germans, before the trial. I had an answer prepared immediately. I allowed the interpreter to translate the question calmly, and after thinking for a few seconds, I began to count a long list of the words of filth, which were used by the Nazi press, beginning with the *Völkischer Beobachter* and ending with the *Stürmer*. While I was counting the newspapers, one after the other, I did not take my eyes off the defense attorney. I was impressed that he did not particularly enjoy my answer to his question, which was intended to trip me up. The whispers emanating from the benches of the jurors told me that this had not been a successful question.

The defense attorney's follow up question was also rather foolish. At the time that I testified about the manner in which Müller had shot, I had said that, according to the angle of fire, the bullets were bound to hit people. The defense attorney bore down on the term 'angle of fire,' which the interpreter had translated as *Schusswinkel*. He argued that it was a professional term, and that as a boy, I could not have known either its meaning or its essence, and that as a military man, I was inventing it now, just as I was inventing the entire story, in order to mislead the court.

[Page 153]

I immediately replied that the defense attorney was correct, that 'angle of fire' is a professional term, and that I recognize it only now in such a capacity. But in this there is no contradiction to the manner in which Müller had shot, and that when I mentioned 'angle of fire,' I intended to concretize for the Court the certainty that Müller's shots had hit people.

After that, I was asked another long series of questions about Müller and Roebel. The defense attorney concluded with a question in which I was asked to describe the Great Synagogue in maximum detail.

I knew the Great Synagogue well, and I remembered with detail and great precision not only its walls, its ceiling and its windows, but also the content of part of the fresco paintings that covered the walls and ceiling. All those details, and even the smallest, I described with specificity.

When the turn of the Prosecutor came, he asked me only two short questions: "When did you last see the Great Synagogue?" I replied "In October 1942." "Did you also then see the Defendant Müller shoot in the synagogue?" I replied "Yes!" With this, my testimony ended.

The Court session was concluded, and the Prosecutor invited me for a conversation in his office. Among other things, he explained to me that the Defense attorney's question about the description of the synagogue had served the prosecution. He said that my detailed description brought credibility to my testimony about Müller's deeds, especially since the defense would attempt, at the time of the summation, to weaken the effect of the testimony with the argument over my young age, and the amount of time elapsed since then.

On the following day, I left Germany, but with no further thought of revenge. I also doubted the measure of severity that is expected for the defendants in a German court. My doubts grew even greater when I found out that the Chief Justice was a Jewish apostate, a Jew who had converted to Christianity.

I found out that Müller indeed was sentenced to life imprisonment. This Müller had brought destruction upon most of the Jews of Skalat, and upon all the members of my family. Was it made easier for someone that this evil murderer was sentenced to life imprisonment? I doubt it very much. It is probable that one who ascribes the supreme value of justice will come thereby to some small satisfaction, but only partially. It seems to me that the significance of this trial, and its importance, is far beyond the justice that was done for the sake of the ones who were murdered.

[Page 154]

Will and Testament
from the book *Wars of the Ghettos*

By Tzipporah Birman

Everything is lost. This is our fate: to atone for the sins of the previous generations.

We have mourned them all, have ached for their loss. The most awful event which was liable to occur in history has come upon us. We have seen. We have heard. We have ached. Now it has been decreed upon us to be mute for eternity. All the bones will not even be brought for a Jewish burial. It is difficult. There is no plan other than to fall with honor, together with the thousands who went to their deaths, without panic, without fear. We know: the Jewish People will not be destroyed. We will arise to resurrection. We will grow and will flourish, and will avenge our spilled blood.

Surely, with this I turn to you, Comrades, wherever you are: you are responsible to avenge. Day and night, I do not keep silent from the command of revenge. Avenge the spilled blood, just as there is no silence for us, face to face with death.

Cursed is the man who will read this, sigh, and return to his day's work. Cursed is the man who will shed tears, and mourn for our souls, and say "enough!" Cursed is the man who will read this, sigh, and return to his day's work.

Not this we demand of you! We, too, did not mourn for our parents. Silenced and keeping silent, we saw the corpses of our dear ones, who were shot like dogs, lying there.

We call to you: avenge, avenge without mercy, without sentiments, without 'good' Germans. The 'good' German – for him, an easy death, but with death, may he be killed eventually. They, also, promised the Jews right to their eyes: "You will be shot last."

This is our demand, the demand of all of us. This is the burning demand of people who tomorrow, it's probable, will fall on those falling, will fight with might and fall with honor.

To avenge, we call upon you, you who have not been afflicted in the hell of Hitler. That is our demand, and you are obligated to do it, even with mortal danger.

Our crushed bones will not know rest, scattered in all ends of Europe. There will be no silence for the ashes of our bodies, strewn to the wind, until you take our revenge.

Remember this and do it: it is our request; it is your duty.

[Page 155]

Epilogue

[Page 156]

The Last Jew Who Saw Skalat

Witness: By Fischel Goldstein

In 1967, I left Poland to visit friends from Skalat who lived in Lvov, Ukraine. A policeman, a friend of the Skalaters, agreed to take us in his automobile for a one–day visit to Skalat.

The journey from Lvov to Skalat took two and a half hours. A paved road, wide in expanse, which branches off eastward to Kiev, crosses the cities and villages: Zlochov, Zaburov, Tarnopol, Borokivilki, and Kolodiovka – until you come to Skalat.

Skalat – a destroyed city. Nothing remains in it from the days of its past. The destruction, which the Germans wrought upon the city remains as is. The Russians did not attempt to rehabilitate the city at all from its ruins. I traveled from Mantiva to Kariba and almost did not see that I was in the midst of a city.

Author of the sketch, on the right, in Skalat, in 1967, near a fence made of tombstones

[Page 157]

From the former 3rd of May Street, in the heart of the city, you can distinguish the train station, which is outside the city. The entire area, which had been highly populated, is newly empty of houses.

Which houses still stand on their foundations? The Starusta Building now serves as a school for *kolkhozes*, collective farms. A workshop for wheat is now in the house of Kron, the lawyer. The post office is located in its repaired building, so too the hospital. The Sokol Athletic Society is now a municipal culture house.

On 3rd of May Street, a few houses still stand: The Tenenbaum House, the Teller House, the Rosenzwieg House, the Kosovsky House, the Mager House, the Gelbtuch House, the Grobman House. And so too, the huge business house near the City Hall.

Near his Pre–War Store Stands Fischel Goldstein and the new female salesperson

The well–known quarter, Haftzini, was totally destroyed. The marketplace stretches in a portion of the quarter, just as it was in the days of Polish rule in the town.

Not a trace remains of the Catholic Church, which stood not far from here, and glorified the city with its beauty. A number of solitary houses stand out at a distance not too far from here.

In the street leading to Horodnitza, solitary houses stand from their former days – the Katz House, the Muni Pickholz House. Desolation and emptiness are all around.

The railroad station has kept its character and its form. The same very old building. Only freight trains now visit the station. Passenger trains no longer arrive. What was once Yosef Weintraub's house, south of the train station, still stands, complete as it was.

[Page 158]

Gentiles and Russian officials reside in the houses of the Jews who left in order to survive. The population of Skalat is now scanty. In total, there are 1500 people in the entire city.

There are only four stores. A store selling meat and sausages is in the house that Rozya Bernstein lived in. A business selling electrical appliances is in the Rotstein house, opposite the Ukrainian church. In the home of Zolnadzyah, there is a grocery store. And at Grobman's, a restaurant has opened.

The municipal garden near the school is completely destroyed. In it is a collection of memorial stones, which were brought here from the nearby Jewish Cemetery.

The city is poor. The clothing that the people wear is old. Progress lags here by hundreds of years. The city has contracted so much that not even a police station is located here. But there is one movie theatre. The people of the city earn their livelihood from the *kolkhozes*, the collective farms, in the vicinity, and also from the limited commercial sector.

The memory of the Jews of Skalat who were exterminated comes up in every conversation with the gentiles of the place. They mention the names of Jews who helped them. They express sorrow for everything that happened, and describe the 'Journey of Caravans' of Jews to the death pits. For a brief moment, it seems that the disaster, which befell us, pains them. They would want to return to the days of the past. They justify themselves that the fault is not on them for the disaster which befell us. They bring up Dr. Chilkowski as an example of humane behavior of Christians toward Jews in the days of the Holocaust.

They may say what they say. There is now not even one Jew in Skalat. The Holocaust here is absolute. There remained here only poor and paltry signs of the life of the Jews in days past.

They turned the Jewish Cemetery into a stadium. The monuments were removed and sold to gentiles for construction purposes. The fence surrounding the Starusta is built from memorial stones from the cemetery. Even the sidewalks on Pilsudski Street are paved with memorial stones. The soil of the cemetery, with its many graves, moves and shakes without let up. And during a soccer game, one of the players stumbled, and he fell into a gaping grave.   .

Today the old cemetery fence surrounds the stadium. They straightened the area of the cemetery with the help of tractors. The bones of the dead were collected and buried on the spot. With a huge press, the ground over the graves was flattened. All those details were made known to me by my friend from childhood, Kravitz.

The magnificent synagogue from former days still exists. Its appearance is like a burnt–out ruin. Broken windows are covered with boards. A workshop for frames is located inside. The business is not large. Three people in all work there. A toilet was installed in a corner of the synagogue. The paintings and decorations that once adorned this holy sanctuary are still visible on the ceiling.

The area around the synagogue is empty and deserted. There is no longer any trace of the many synagogues which were here, all around. They have disappeared completely.

At some distance from the city, stretch 'the pits' – the mass graves of the Jews of Skalat. The spot is hard to find. All of it is covered with wild growth, trees and grasses. It's impossible to find any sign of a grave here. A person passing by the place would not think that a multitude of people is buried here. The Gentiles who accompanied me here stood silent. The sorrow of this place was recognizable even on their faces.

[Page 159]

A shocking experience awaits the person who visits Skalat, so many years after the Holocaust. This is the city in which I was born. I knew it in each stone and in every spot, and now I do not recognize it. I stood for a moment at the place where my house once stood. Nothing was left of it. Only the kiosk in which I had worked stands in its place today. In its entrance stood a Russian girl who even found it proper to apologize to me, and to remove from herself any guilt for the changes that had occurred.

There indeed was a town, and its name was Skalat. It no longer exists.

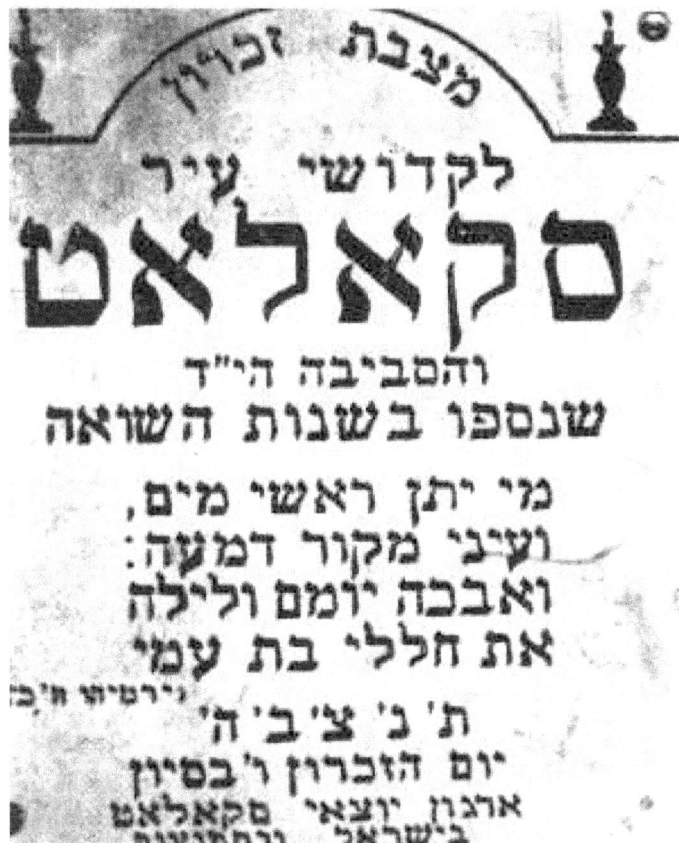

מצבת זכרון

לקדושי עיר

סקאלאט

והסביבה הי"ד

שנספו בשנות השואה

מי יתן ראשי מים,
ועיני מקור דמעה:
ואבכה יומם ולילה
את חללי בת עמי
ירמיהו ח'כ"ג

ת' נ' צ' ב' ה'
יום הזכרון ו' בסיון
ארגון יוצאי סקאלאט
בישראל והסביבה

A Memorial Monument to the Martyrs of the City of Skalat and the Vicinity,
May the Lord Avenge their Blood, who were Swept Away during the Years of the
Holocaust

Would that my head were water

And my eyes a fountain of tears

That I might weep day and night

For the slain of the daughter of my people

Jeremiah 8:23

May their souls be bound up in the bond of everlasting life

Memorial Day, 6th of Sivan

The Organization of those Originating from Skalat in Israel and the Diaspora

[Page 160]

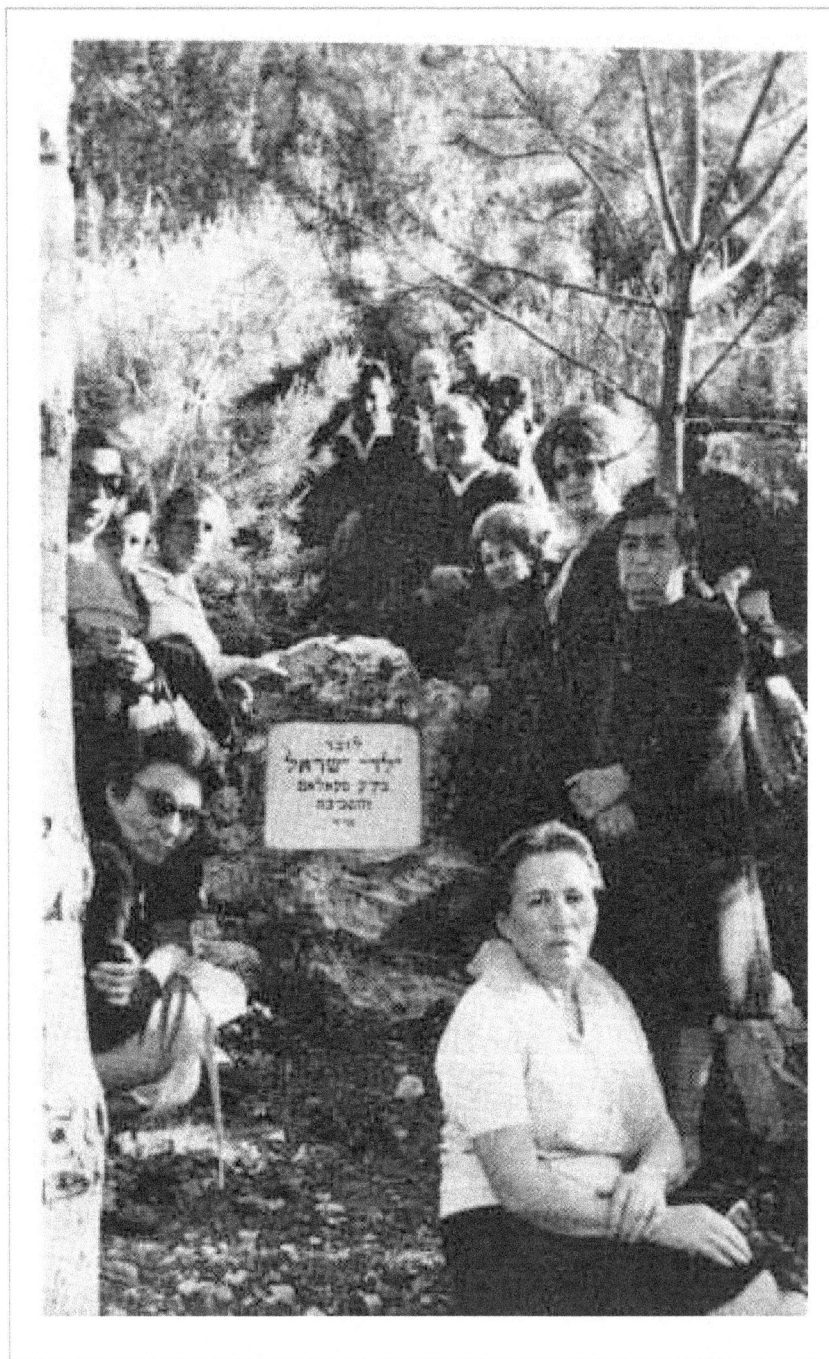

*The Memorial Monument to the Children of Skalat in The Forest
of the Martyrs*

DEATH OF A SHTETL

By

Abraham Weissbrod

I. Kaplan, Editor of the Yiddish Text

**Published (in Yiddish) by the Central Historical
Commission of the Central Committee of Liberated Jews
in the American Zone of Germany
Munich, 1948**

**English Translation
Arranged by Lusia Milch and Joseph Kofler**

**English Text and Additional
Testimonies of Witnesses
Edited by Lusia Milch**
U.S.A., 1995

The original Yiddish book can be found at:

https://www.yiddishbookcenter.org/collections/yizkor-books/yzk-nybc307412/es-shtarbt-a-shtetl-megiles-skalat

Or

https://digitalcollections.nypl.org/items/88f86ce0-996b-0134-a15b-00505686a51c

TABLE OF CONTENTS

List of Appendices

[Page i]

Introduction

A half-century has elapsed since Abraham Weissbrod wrote his book describing the extermination of the Jews in the small Galician town called Skalat.

Of the few of us who survived the slaughter, those of Abraham Weissbrod's generation are no more. Those who were then young, a dozen or two teenagers, and the few surviving children are the last living witnesses to the catastrophe which befell the town of our birth. It will be far less than fifty more years before there will be no one left to say - "We were there. We saw what happened. We remember the suffering and we still carry the pain of our losses." As I have grown older, this thought has given me no rest. During various contacts with other survivors, I realized how many of them were preoccupied with the same thoughts. When speaking to my children and to others of their generation, I also became aware of how much they wanted to know everything that happened to us and how urgently they needed a record to pass on to their children.

But the questions of the young people and our answers to them proved more painful to handle than I had anticipated. The prospect of reliving my personal tragedy in writing made it impossible for me to pick up a pen for forty-five years. Some events of the Nazi era have marked me indelibly: the mounting dread, the hopelessness of our situation and above all the **'actions.'** Those shall be with me to the end. With time, however, I had begun to forget the names and the details of the daily nightmares of Skalat in those days. It is with these reflections in mind that I turned to Abraham Weissbrod's book.

Living in a small town, naturally our families knew one another well. The author's mother, Amalia Weissbrod, found me sitting on the ruins of my home, near the marketplace of our town, on the day I finally came out of hiding. Having recognized me, she addressed me in Yiddish, "Vus tiysty du?" (What are you doing here?). I looked up and answered her in Ukrainian "Bihrne ya zhydivka, no ya zabula hovoryty po zhydivski" (I swear, I'm Jewish, but I forgot how to speak Yiddish). Terror and loneliness had blocked out the Yiddish language in me and made it impossible for me to form the words in the tongue of my parents and my community. She stared at me in disbelief and said, "So young, all alone, how did you survive?" Tears flowing, we slowly made our way to her place. She took me in and that night as I went to sleep, for the first time in a long time, I felt safe.

I was in Skalat during the Nazi occupation and there lost my entire family. At eleven years of age, I was old enough to understand the terror and the overriding necessity to run and hide in order to escape the killers' bullets. For that reason, I share the anguish and passion with which the author relates the events which led to the annihilation of the Jewish community in Skalat. At that young age, there was also, of course, much that I was not privy to, especially the dealings between the members of the Jewish Council, i.e., the Judenrat, and the Gestapo headquarters in Tarnopol, as well as between the Jewish Council and the German and Ukrainian administration in Skalat. Since each survivor knows only his or her part of the terrible puzzle, there is much in Abraham Weissbrod's book from which we, who lived those events, have also learned. Obviously, only those who jumped from the trains, witnesses at the mass shootings and the very few wounded who came out of the graves, could tell us what went on there. Others supplied details about events in the Skalat ghetto, the camp and the woods. We are, therefore, indebted to the author for the amount of information which he collected and passed on to us.

When one reads the story of the destruction of the Jews of Skalat, it seems that although the town was small, it was typical of what took place in thousands of other towns both small and big. Even if this book were the only record left of that tragic time and place, one would still be able to know the circumstances, the Nazi aims, the process and the final result of that unprecedented evil. In Skalat, a small Jewish community was persecuted then incarcerated, extorted, tortured and finally with a few systematic **'actions,'** brought to an end.

Abraham Weissbrod's recollections of the events and the testimonies of other survivors were shaped into a book and printed in Munich (Germany) within two years after our liberation. There was not yet, at that time, much printed material on the period subsequently known as the Holocaust. But even now after half a century of accumulated information, one still can't understand how that which took place, could have occurred. Often we, the survivors, can't comprehend the events which we experienced. It is precisely because the horror of that period was so extreme, that future generations may be tempted to doubt its authenticity. There are also those whose anti-Semitic and malicious intent is to rewrite the facts and to deny the truth of the Holocaust period, as some "revisionist" writers of our time have already done. We think it is imperative, therefore, not only to make the book available in English and thus accessible to a broader reading public, but to add to it additional personal testimonies which could only be obtained from the remaining survivors, in order to further substantiate the verity of these events.

[Page ii]

With that in mind, the task of obtaining an English text was undertaken. In addition, personal testimonies were solicited. Contact was made with survivors from Skalat in the U.S., and in the Spring of 1992 a group of survivors met in Israel. Dates, names, and the accuracy of events were verified. The book was considered from a perspective of fifty years since it was written. Those who gathered felt that with the exception of some obvious repetitions and a few pages of philosophical ponderings, stated from a personal perspective and therefore deleted from the edited version, Abraham Weissbrod's book depicts faithfully the destruction of the Jews in Skalat and, therefore, should stand as written.

All agreed with the view expressed by Buzio Eisenstark. With the exception of the creation of the State of Israel, where some Skalat survivors rebuilt their lives, and also those who did so in the U.S., there are no bright rays in the sad saga of the perished Jewish community of Skalat.

We join in Abraham Weissbrod's desire that this book serve as a memorial to the Jewish victims who perished in and near Skalat and also as a legacy to our children, grandchildren, and to future generations who must undertake the difficult task of educating themselves about this tragic period in our long history.

Lusia Milch nee Rosenzweig
New York, 1993

[Page iii]

Introduction to the Original Yiddish Text

(1948)

With Death of a Shtetl, the Central Historical Commission in Munich begins publication, in book form, of more extensive works by individuals who describe the *khurbn* [1] of Jewish settlements, as well as their own experiences under the Nazi regime.

It is superfluous today to speak of the importance of such works. Innumerable Jewish communities were uprooted or cut down with the most refined cruelty, leaving no documentary trace or memory of their destruction. In countless *shtetls* [2] as well as in the larger towns, it is impossible to determine the locations of the Jewish mass graves, to say nothing of the dates of the **'actions,'** [3] or other details of what befell the Jews before their extermination. The existing written history of the *khurbn* is now focused mainly on the testimony and descriptions of the few survivors. All testimony - each detail, including hearsay - is important at this stage. And it is especially welcome that a person who survived the *khurbn* devotes himself to compiling a broader description - a monograph - of the annihilation of an entire community, as in this book.

Abraham Weissbrod has shown the courage, in writing this book, to erect a monument to his birthplace, Skalat, a *shtetl* in Eastern Galicia. Even under the Nazi regime, he began to gather his material: to question people and to clarify many of the details regarding the Jews of the town. His work became much broader after the liberation. He threw himself with all his energy into collecting more and more reports. He gathered data from among the few who returned to Skalat. He also traveled to find other Skalat survivors and to record their experiences. He corresponded with many more. He doggedly researched each event of the occurrences in the town and the fate of almost every individual. Thus the author succeeded in assembling the work that lies before us. And though the book is limited to Skalat, it throws light on the destruction of many other Jewish settlements in Galicia and in other parts of Poland, where events transpired in a similar manner.

In relating the various events and experiences, Abraham Weissbrod demonstrates great descriptive powers. At times he even evokes admiration for his artistry. Weissbrod is also no stranger to the satirical writer's style, which, within the context of this book, introduces a lighter note and a certain liveliness.

The author also demonstrates a marked tendency to philosophize. Deep reflections and psychological insights frequently accompany his recounting of the events themselves. Perhaps the author's insights and, still more, his conclusions suffer from the emotional involvement resulting from our proximity to the events. Yet his reflections add much poignancy to the content of the book. They underscore for the reader the issues of that wild and tragic time and encourage us to think more deeply about those events. We're living close in time to the events described, therefore to a still-smoldering atmosphere due to these events. Hence, we cannot expect the author to maintain a cold, measured tone nor complete objectivity when dealing with the torture of his relatives in the Skalat Ghetto and in the nearby camps nor complete objectivity when dealing with the behavior of some Jews who held leading positions in Jewish institutions. In some cases we may differ with the opinions of the author and his judgments about these persons. It is also possible that some of his other views may be open to correction. However, in regard to his relating of the facts themselves and of his own actions, there is nothing to give us pause. Here we can see plainly that the author writes with deep integrity, that every event he relates bears the seal of his conscience, of his own painful experiences and, more pointedly, of his feeling of social responsibility.

[Page iv]

The literature of our latest *khurbn* is yet so small and the *khurbn* itself so horrible that the need to preserve the eyewitness accounts becomes a veritable commandment of our times. We must, therefore, approach such a work as *Death of a Shtetl* with our fullest attention, especially since its materials were gathered so carefully and with a sacred devotion. The book itself was written as though it were a holy obligation.

This work is truly an important contribution to the recorded history of our great catastrophe. May Abraham Weissbrod's work be an example and a model to our survivors, and for each of us, a reminder to devote our time and strength to erect similar memorials for the many, many murdered Jewish communities.

J. Kaplan

[Page v]

In Memory of the Shtetl
(Foreword by Abraham Weissbrod, 1945)

The *khurbn* of Polish Jewry is a bloody inscription in the martyrology of the Jewish people. Every city and *shtetl* in Poland where once Jewish life pulsated became, during World War II, the site of the greatest tragedy and martyrdom.

The Jewish cities and towns have died out.

They were destroyed and buried along with their Jewish lives, even along with their Jewish cemeteries. Now one cannot find even a trace or memory of a Jew in the small Polish towns. Only the tattered remnants of the *khurbn,* dispersed and wandering among strangers, in search of a home and a future, know the horrible details of towns which became slaughterhouses. Every individual who survived is a major living witness to the monstrous crime of the extermination of the Jews. Every individual shtetl is a monument for all time: a document of tragedy and sacrifice. Each collapsed hut, each foot of earth, each stone stained with Jewish blood shouts and asks: "WHY?!"

If and when we ever learn the tragic sum of the total destruction of the Polish-Jewish shtetl, each town would still have its own specific history: retain its individual path of pain, reflecting the diversity within the overall martyrology. The human suffering of that time is So boundless that when one attempts to recount it today, it seems to many almost inexplicable and unbelievable.

Today, as I detail the tragedy of a small *shtetl* in Galicia, I find myself motivated by two   considerations:
1. Based on my own experiences and on materials I have gathered, I wish to describe the end of Jewish life in the average Galician *shtetl* because as soon as Hitler planted his boot on Galicia, events involving the Jews followed a similar pattern. I also wish to describe, in this book, the Jewish struggle in the Galician *shtetl* the battle and its end.

I wish to relate how a Jewish community once flourished in Skalat where later the people were subjected to so much suffering and how they died - to the very last. The great tragedy of this little town must be set down objectively: free of exaggeration, embroidery or self-aggrandizement. In telling the brutal truth, one must also relate errors and weaknesses. This, however, should not be considered a desecration of the memories of our martyrs but should be viewed as an effort to provide an accurate illumination which will serve as a moral warning for present and future generations.
2. I intend this description to serve as a monument to the murdered Jewish people of Skalat. There will be far less written about Skalat, its environs and approximately 5,000 Jewish inhabitants than about Warsaw, Kaunus *(Kovno)* or Vilnius (*Wilno*). The Skalat Camp and its four hundred prisoners is not as notorious as, for example, Treblinka, Auschwitz or Majdanek, but the fate of this small community, in its

crushing and silent tragedy is, in its smaller way, just as inexplicable and equally horrible. The destruction of any such town requires deep psychological insight and profound penetration into the metaphysics of suffering and death.

*****

A divine mystery, a bloody specter, envelops the past of my *shtetl*. As we memorialize our martyrs their spirits rise, commanding us to remember and demanding: **DO NOT FORGET US!**

My *shtetl* died.

I am now far from my home but I still hear the pitiful sobs rising from the mass graves I still hear the last gasps of my father, of blessed memory, in one of those graves, who gave up his innocent soul amid all the other martyrs: relatives, friends and companions of my town. I still hear the echo of their sacred final cry: *Shmah Yisroel!* [4] It is an echo that drives one to madness.

My account of the sorrowful history of the life and death of my *shtetl* is but the anguished cry of the thousands who perished there. How weak, though, are words when compared to the sacrifice of the martyrs. The Jewish shtetl is no more. All that is left is memory. Therefore let this modest work stand in place of a tombstone for my vanished home, Skalat, and in memory of all the martyrs. May they finally find peace in their graves.

[Page 1]

1. The Shtetl As It Was

Two kilometers outside the town, at the edge of a wood, a giant stone erupts from the earth. It is a tall, broad, gigantic boulder. From afar its smooth and semi-circular form gives it the appearance of a huge, bald human head. A number of smaller stony mounds lie scattered about, like dwarfs at the foot of the gigantic boulder. Nature itself apparently determined the name of the town, since in Slavic languages *skala* means boulder.

Over generations a settlement grew here. The soil of the Podolia [5] region is fertile and from earliest times drew large numbers of settlers. The first colony quickly grew into a hamlet, the hamlet into a village, the village into a small town, and finally into the bigger town, Skalat, which was eventually surrounded by seventy-two dependent villages. Among forests and fields, between valleys and meadows, the huts grew, the people multiplied, and, under the biblical mandate: *by the sweat of your brow* people toiled and their labor provided sustenance.

The river Zbrocz flows through the area and, some twelve kilometers from Skalat, marks the Russian border. It passes through Podwolczyska, Tarnorude and many other villages. The town Skalat, in the Tarnopol district of Galicia, formerly part of Poland, has its own history of battles and victories, of Tartar and Cossack invasions, of fire and blood.

Four massive XVII Century towers, with red tile roofs, rise from each corner of the surrounding huge town wall. Nearby stand rows of small, old fashioned, twisted little houses. In a few places one also sees separate huts, scattered chaotically and bent toward the earth. In the central marketplace, opposite the church, a handful of hunchbacked houses huddle along the Picynia Section which, itself, is a remnant of a great fire some fifty years earlier, when only this one little area miraculously survived. Along it are spread the small adobe houses, leaning against one another and exposing the thickly-growing moss through their rotted out shingle roofs. Here also are the few dingy, large driveway houses with clumsy, diamond-shaped roofs, and broad overhangs supported by posts. Here and there, on the main street of the town, are a few single-story houses with grey zinc roofs.

In contrast to them stand the buildings of the *shul* [6] , the city hall, the post office, the courthouse and, at the town's outskirts, the large Sokol [7] . These buildings, a blend of the highest achievements of modern technology and provincial architecture, stand proudly as though they were skyscrapers. The Roman Catholic Church in the marketplace, the Greek Catholic Church in the Gmina Section and the *shul* in the Bath area stand out prominently from all the other buildings. They inform all who approach from afar that here in Skalat, God is worshiped by three religions: those of the Jews, Ukrainians and Poles who have lived here, side-by-side, for hundreds of years. Old traditions were woven into newer times. The three groups bought, sold, bartered, conducted commerce and lent each other money. Whatever different historical or political winds might have blown outside, they, more or less, got along among themselves.

In 1939, out of approximately 8,000 inhabitants of Skalat and its peripheral areas (Mantiawa, Preczepinka, Krzywe, Nowy-Swiat and Ksiezy Kat), some sixty percent were Jews who lived, mostly, in the center of the town. The Jewish population consisted of some small traders, craftsmen, businessmen, and a few professionals and officials, There were also students of the Torah, beggars of the older generation and ordinary unemployed do-nothings. It can be said that in its high rate of unemployed Jews, Skalat was a typical *shtetl*. It was one of the oldest Jewish *shtetls* in Galicia, where Jews had settled in the sixteenth century or earlier.

[Page 2]

At the end of the nineteenth and beginning of the twentieth centuries, there was mass migration to America. due to poverty, hunger and the lack of opportunity. Further impetus was provided by anti-Semitism and the wave of pogroms in Russia. In later years, hundreds of Skalat families received aid from their relatives overseas. This helped to ease the poverty in the town. Skalat *landsleit* [8] established a large orphanage named after one Louis Rosenblatt. They also assisted in setting up the co-operative bank and the free-loan society which helped the Jews through critical times.

Jewish life flourished in Skalat. Institutions and organizations participated actively in the town's social, cultural, religious and political activities. Though Skalat was nominally an orthodox. Hassidic town, the younger generation followed the paths of progress and national, secular education in addition to religious instructions. All political parties, from the extreme left to the extreme right, were organized and exerted their influence on the young. The *shtetl* was no different from other Polish towns and the people here engaged in a daily struggle for existence and for human rights.

According to the rhythms of history, the tangle of world politics, and the constant changes in political regimes, the Jews of Skalat experienced times both good and bad. At first there was the old Polish kingdom, followed (in 1792) [9] by the Austrian rule, then in rapid succession came the First World War (in 1914), the Ukrainian "Lightning War" (of 1918-1919) and the Polish restoration of(1919-1939). With the advent of the Second World War came the (1939-1941) Soviet occupation of Galicia, then the (1941-1944) German occupation with its tragic consequences. Finally there was the return of the Soviets (in 1944), but this time to a town without a Jewish population.

On its fateful, painful road, Jewish Skalat experienced many regimes and all sorts of troubles: insecurity, hunger, tortures and persecutions. Yet it survived the worst times and revived. It remained for the German madman to become the Angel of Death: the executioner of this *shtetl* and of all the *shtetls* of Poland. Now it is time to relate the facts of the life-struggle and destruction of Skalat!

[Page 3]

2. On the Eve of the Fire

When Germany attacked the Soviet Union, on 22 June 1941, the people of Skalat had been living a more or less normal life. The Soviets had instituted a certain calm and order during their 22-month rule of Galicia. The Poles, formerly the lords of the land who had lately lost their political independence, gritted their teeth and endured the occupation, or the so-called "Red Exile." The Ukrainians, who had long had an appetite to rule this land and who dreamed of full sovereignty, reacted to the Soviet rule with hatred while appearing to accept their regime.

The Jewish population found itself in a very uncomfortable position: between the hammer and the forge. On the one hand they adjusted to the new regime but, on the other hand they feared "what the Gentile neighbors would say," that is, how the Gentiles would view that adjustment. Anti-Semitism had been rooted in the souls of their non-Jewish neighbors for many generations. Now it had a fertile soil in which to flourish. The arrival of the Soviets provided the fuel that fed the fires of the Jew-Haters. "Commie Yids" had been an old slogan in Polish politics and now the Jews "were being chummy with their old buddies, the Bolsheviks..." - so went the popular anti-Semitic rationalization.

Everyone could find work now and life was both good and bad, depending on one's position under the new regime. It was quite understandable that the Jews were able to adjust more easily to the new life, since the Soviet regime trusted the Jewish population more than it did the Gentiles. A significant portion of the Jews - the workers, the artisans and the working intelligentsia, therefore, took on leading roles in the economic and social life of the town. They held important positions in cooperatives and in communal and public institutions. No one group could have adjusted better to the newly created conditions of life than the Jews.

Yet, the radical change in the social and economic structure left the vast majority of the Jews without a way to earn a living. Among them were businessmen, small traders and craftsmen. There were also the opportunity bereft unemployed of a typical provincial town. The number of prosperous Jews and *"burzhuyis"* [10] was very small. All of these *declasse* Jews were desperate to obtain formal positions because the watchword of the new order was: *He who does not work does not eat*. In addition this, middle class, the former house owners and traders, made a strong effort to find employment in order to obtain a work-card, which protected one from being considered "non-productive" and therefore exposed to various troubles, including exile to Siberia. Regardless of whether it was out of necessity or simply as a cover-up, the impoverished and declasse Jewish population made every effort to work and be productive. The reshuffling of one's social standing took place overnight, one might say. This phenomenon had, without doubt, some positive value in the social, egalitarian restructuring of Jewish life.

The Ukrainians and Poles, living as farmers on their own land, did not experience a particularly disturbing effect on their accustomed life styles. For that reason, they had no need to find new employment or sources of income. No peasant stopped being a peasant. "Our people left, our people will return" was the familiar, meaning-filled folk-saying among the Gentiles. Their tragedy was rather of an ideological or nationalistic and territorial nature. They lived peacefully, waiting for better times and better conditions. In regard to the Soviet regime, the Ukrainians and Poles were weak and powerless. With respect to the Jews, however, in spreading anti-Semitic poison and in preparing the soil for the eventual slaughter, they were quite powerful -virtual giants. Despite their own national tragedy, the germs of envy, hatred and anti-Semitism grew and increased among the Gentiles into a powerful force which confused the minds and consciousness of both the masses and their leaders. That was why they could hardly wait for the Germans to arrive. Better the Germans than the Soviets, thought many Poles. And the Ukrainians saw in Hitler a Savior, the creator of an independent Ukraine.

[Page 4]

3. The Knives are Sharpened...

From the first days of the war, the town was gripped by a wild, nervous mood. Instinctively we knew that momentous events were about to occur. The radio brought alarming reports: *Heeresgruppe Sud* [11] under Von Runstedt was advancing on the regions of Galicia and Wolin. Soviet authorities sought to maintain the calm of the civilian population, while preparing themselves to evacuate. During the first days of July, 1941, the Soviets began their orderly withdrawal from the town.

They were accompanied by some 200 Jews, mostly workers, craftsmen and some who simply had good sense and a clear vision. I stress "clear vision" because very few Jews fully understood the danger awaiting them. On the contrary, no matter how fatally foolish it may now appear, there were some, mainly among the more affluent, who thought that living with the Germans might be easier than with the Bolsheviks. Realistically, where was one to run? To Russia, the Red Hell? Or, at least, that was how those Jews assessed the situation. Another part, the majority of the Jewish population, simply thought: how can we leave our homes and go off into exile? And so the Jews left their fate in the hands of God and to the future.

On 3 July, the Soviet civil administration, the police and the armed detachments left the town. Only a few soldiers remained behind to carry out specific assignments and the town was left without a government. On the deserted streets, underworld characters and various peasants from the neighborhood sought opportunities for robbery and other adventures.

At the first signal of the impending conflagration, the beginning of agitation and turmoil occurred - even before German jackboots marched into town. A peasant named Hilko Kory (some say he was called Krupa) said to the Jews: "Wait. Just wait, you kikes. Hitler's coming soon and we'll slaughter you all like chickens!" A Soviet soldier, hearing of the incident, was outraged by such talk. He tracked down the peasant, dragged him off into the fields and left him there dead. The incident enraged the already excited peasants and provided the village of Krzywe with an excuse to carry out an act of vengeance on the few Jewish families living nearby. They murdered them all in a beastly fashion. Blaming his death on the Jews, the executed peasant was declared a "holy martyr."

The peasants in town and in the surrounding villages were stirred up. They began sharpening their knives for the coming slaughter. At midnight on Friday, 4 July, we heard the continuous sound of machine guns and the detonations of exploding grenades. At 2:00 AM the first German patrol arrived on motorcycles, surveyed the neighborhood and called out over loudspeakers: "Ukrainian brothers, awake!" There really was no need to rouse them as they were already wide awake, ready to help the German soldiers -especially in robbing and killing the Jews, who were fleeing in all directions. At 5:00 AM on Saturday, 5 July, the regular German troops arrived. Joy was widespread among the Ukrainians. They dressed in their holiday clothes decorated with ribbons in the blue and yellow of their national colors. Ukrainian flags decorated their houses and here and there fluttered red banners with the Nazi swastika. Carrying floral bouquets, and with songs on their lips, Ukrainians came to greet their German liberators. They danced and kissed in the streets.

Later that Sabbath morning, some Jews walked openly and unhesitatingly to services, carrying their prayer shawls, as though nothing had happened. Others, - in truth, very few - went off to admire the German military equipment. Today it sounds incomprehensible, but some Jews were convinced that so cultured a people as the Germans would not harm anyone. Besides they believed that now they would be more secure: before there had been danger from the enraged *goyim*, [12] but now there would be law and order.

[Page 5]

At first they seemed right: the German military harmed no one. On the contrary, they spoke in a friendly manner to the Jews, boasting of their swift and heroic deeds against the Reds. These Jews later argued with others: "Fools, what are you hiding for? Are they harming anyone?" Some affluent Jews, though not all, naively thought that even if the worst were to occur, it would not affect them but the "Eighth Company." [13] Therefore, these people felt, let the Socialists or Bolsheviks worry, but not the well-off. The Germans themselves know that the prosperous ones were also victims of the Red regime. The new rulers would probably return the land, the confiscated wealth and the nationalized houses. Thus some deluded people reasoned. They quickly learned, however, how such foolish optimism had clouded their minds.

At around 10:00 in the morning, several battalions came to a halt in the *shtetl*, while other troops continued their "triumphal march" eastward. The Commander of the SS brigade, so that his troops might "have some fun," gave the order: *Tzen minuten schlachten Juden!* [14] The soldiers passed the order on to each other and quickly leaped from their automobiles, tanks and other armored vehicles and ran to the very center of town. Sweaty, begrimed from the long ride, in shirt sleeves with the cuffs rolled up, they ran about like wild wolves, firing their guns. First they assaulted Jews encountered on the streets. The first victim was Efraim Diener, [15] hose beard they cut along with part of his face. The bullets fired at him missed, miraculously. The murderers were in a hurry and left the victim, who had fainted, on the ground.

Peasant children and some of their elders ran after the raiders, pointing out *Jude!* [16] *Jude!* The town was thrown into turmoil and gripped by panic. Germans ran after the fleeing Jews, shooting at them constantly. They chased Mordechai Orenstein (the milkman) and his wife down to the riverbank and drove them into the water. They fired at them until their bodies sank, leaving only red stains on the surface. Then some Germans, led by Ukrainian peasant children, ran among the houses, shooting at each pointed out Jew. Other soldiers raided homes: ostensibly searching for weapons and hidden Bolsheviks, while robbing, defacing and destroying the contents of the homes. The allotted ten minutes sufficed to turn the town upside down, to leave some twenty Jews killed and an equal number wounded. Some were slightly wounded and others seriously. The Jews sought to hide wherever they could. Their homes, now unguarded, fell prey to the Ukrainian peasants and the Polish town hoodlums, who rioted for hours afterwards. They stole whatever they could, and beat, unmercifully, any Jew that they found.

This was but the prologue to the slaughter of the following day, conducted entirely under the direction of the newly appointed Ukrainian administrators.

[Page 6]

4. The Historic Meeting

Over the generations in Galicia, the Ukrainian village and the Jewish *shtetl* had been in relatively friendly contact. The Jews had no territorial designs in the area. The Ukrainians suffered under Polish rule almost as much as the Jews did, which tended to bring the two peoples together in the common struggle for their minority rights and for the preservation of their national identities. Leaders of the Ukrainian folk movements often spoke out in sympathy with the Jews, and in elections to the Polish Sejm, [17] Jews and Ukrainians ran jointly in some areas while in others the Ukrainian press at times urged its readers to vote for the Jewish slates.

Thus, who would have predicted that these same Ukrainians would turn so viciously against the Jews, their centuries-old neighbors? These repulsive deeds were carried out not by benighted individuals among the Ukrainians, nor by fascist terror groups. These heaven-offending acts were the work of none other than the *UNDO*, [18] the leading organization of the Ukrainian people in Galicia and its official representative for many years.

The UNDO organized the first pogroms in almost every town and village in Galicia involving the entire Ukrainian community in this enormous, bloody event. With the exception of a small group among the older generation which was disgusted by the savage behavior of its sons, the balance of the Ukrainian population now shares the burden of guilt for the destruction of Galician Jewry. Established facts, documents and eyewitness testimony will prove that it was they who were the killers of their age-old neighbors. This chronological review of events in the single shtetl of Skalat also reveals parallel patterns in other towns. Everywhere it was the Ukrainian people who carried out the mass murders. The same criminal hand was at work.

Already on Friday evening, (although some say it was Saturday evening), the Ukrainians in town held a secret meeting to consider the new situation created by Hitler's victorious march. The meeting was attended by the elite of the Ukrainian populace. All segments were represented from priest to peasant. The lively meeting was opened with the singing of the Ukrainian national anthem, "Shehe Ne Vmerla

Ukraina," [19] and quickly turned to matters of state. Such questions as organizing a Ukrainian militia and selecting persons for public positions and institutions were considered. Various opinions were expressed about their work, with an eye towards the fulfillment of their aspirations in the future. An important question arose about the attitude of Ukrainians toward the Polish population.

The most important question on the floor, however, was: what is to be done with the Jews? Those who were there, one after the other, took the floor. Whole pages were quoted from Hitler's Mein Kampf and from Alfred Rosenberg. The conclusion reached was that the Germans were to be supported in every way, because only they were the true liberators. "We must gain the Germans' confidence," said one of the speakers. "Hitler is right. The Jews are a menace to the world. They are like a bone in our throats as well, so let there be an end to them!" In a vote, the majority supported the proposal of a pogrom against the Jews. Those who were there understood that it would be necessary to obtain permission from the Germans. Hence, a three-man delegation was chosen on the spot to go to the Military Command in order to obtain permission for a 24-hour slaughter of the Jews. Such a full day's work, they believed, would suffice to end the Jewish presence in Skalat.

One of the main spokesmen at the meeting was a well-known personality in town, the Greek Catholic priest Canon Onuferko. He had long been involved in business matters with the Jews and used to boast of having been a Judeophile all his life. He spoke Yiddish fluently. It was of him that local Jews

[Page 7]

would say: " A hen that crows and a priest who speaks Yiddish should both be sent to the chopping block." The folk expression was quite apt. In addition to the priest and his wife, among the others at the meeting were Judge Politila, Maruszszuk (a blacksmith), Bilyk, Jaromiszyn, Chruszcz, and Wilczynski, all well-known people in Skalat and its environs.

On the following day, the Ukrainian delegation led by Canon Onuferko appeared before the German General Staff carrying a signed petition, requesting permission to carry out an anti-Jewish pogrom. They were welcomed by an aged general who, with deeply-furrowed brow, wondered about their demand. He had other considerations in mind: he agreed that the Jews should be slaughtered, but in a planned fashion. First, however, their physical labor could be useful to the military machine. The general gave permission for a pogrom, but only of eight hours duration. He also said, with a warm-looking smile, that women and children should be spared. The delegation thanked him heartily, bowed deeply, and departed.

The Ukrainians immediately called a general meeting of all their community activists, including their newly organized militia. Those attending decided to make the necessary preparations to execute the plan.

The German military authorities sent a report to Berlin, enclosing documents which demonstrated "justified" local hatred of the Jews. That petition, along with hundreds of similar petitions from Ukrainians in various other cities and villages were later released to the press by the German ministry of propaganda so that the world might see that it was not the Germans who were slaughtering the Jews, but the local populations who were demanding the right to carry on their own pogroms.

[Page 8]

5. The Pogrom

On Sunday, 6 July 1941 [20] (11 Tammuz 5701), at about 11:00 AM, organized gangs set out across the town. The Ukrainian militia, armed with rifles, and civilians, carrying sticks, went from house to house calling Jewish men and youths to come out to work. Wild shouting, curses, resounding slaps, the wailing of women and the cries of children were heard from Jewish homes, while German soldiers stood about on the street joyfully watching the spectacle.

The Jews, thus drawn out, were forced to perform tasks that only sadists could have devised. One group was ordered to uproot some small trees with their bare hands. Since that could not be done, those Jews were beaten to death. Others were ordered to crawl on all fours, gathering stones in their mouths, and then, crawling further, to deposit the stones into pots. Still others were forced to clean privies with their bare hands, sweep streets with their hats and to perform other senseless tasks during which scores of Jews were further tortured and finally put to death. Some of the Jews were assigned to the German military units, where they slaved, as in the days of Pharaoh, while being beaten about the head with rifle butts. The Jew, Chaim Szrencel, already badly beaten, was thrown to the ground and was run over by a truck, which crushed his bones. The victim, writhing in pain, was finally shot through the heart by a soldier.

Terrible acts were perpetrated near the water-pump in the marketplace. There, some Ukrainians forced the spout of the water pipe into a Jew's mouth and kept pumping the water until he drowned. Leib Jawer, an imposing Jew, tall and handsome with a silver-grey beard, had his legs broken by assassins wielding iron rods and then was placed under the pump for a "cold shower," as the murderers so wittily termed it. The victim pointing at his heart, for he could no longer speak, pleaded to be shot and to end his suffering. The wild-eyed bystanders, laughing and enjoying the show, egged on the killers: "No! No! Let him live a while longer! " A mob of peasants then attacked the victim, ripping hairs, one by one, from his patriarchal beard. The near dead body was again placed under the water spout, his mouth forced wide open, and water pumped into him until he drowned.

Rabbi Benjamin Wolowycz [21] was tied behind a horse and then the Germans, Ukrainians and other peasants, standing on the sidewalks, whipped the horse into a gallop. At first the Rabbi ran, but he soon fell and was dragged, bloodied and tortured, as far as the towers, were he gave up his soul. His body was carried into the tower and tossed onto the growing pile of corpses. A similar fate was that of a certain Friedman [22] (son-in-law of a tinsmith from Grzymalow), who was tied behind a moving vehicle and dragged through the streets until his body became an unrecognizable mass of flesh: red and black from blood and dirt. Dr. Leon Fried [23] was dragged to the public privy near the bathhouse. There he was ordered to jump into the cesspool, where he was shot. Many Jews were shot by Ukrainians, who then stole their shoes and searched their pockets for other booty. At the same time, village peasants roamed the streets of the Jewish sections, robbing the houses.

The main collection point for the victims was amid the four old towers in the center of town. It was there that the great bloodbath occurred. The Ukrainian police led Jews, in groups of thirty or forty, to the tops of the towers and ordered them to jump, while firing automatic weapons at them. [24] The martyrs met their deaths with screams of pain and with cries of Shmah Yisroel! Throughout, the Germans photographed the slaughter, and the photos, with appropriate captions, were later sent on to Berlin to prove that it had been the Ukrainians who were killing the Jews and not the Germans. There amid the towers, more than three hundred people were murdered, including thirty children and youths.

[Page 9]

Similar horrors took place at the cemetery. Groups of newly-captured Jews were forced to bring the dead there and bury them and then were shot themselves as soon as they completed their work. It was told of Isaac Binsztok, son of Szyje-Nuty Binsztok, the butcher, that among other corpses he had to bury his own father. While reciting the Kaddish, [25] he was shot down and fell on top of the just-filled grave. At the cemetery alone, approximately 150 people were slaughtered. By 3:00 PM the death toll had reached five hundred. [26] Who knows how many more victims there would have been that day were it not for an air attack by Soviet bombers, which scattered the killers across the fields. Some village peasants were in the midst of preparing an attack on the synagogue. The bombing, and the few resulting casualties among them, caused a break in the slaughter.

For a few hours all was peaceful. Then the mob returned. Even though the allotted eight hours had ended, the slaughter went on for another two days, although on a smaller scale, and additional scores of Jews fell at the hands of the Ukrainians. On Wednesday morning, the Ukrainian militiamen dragged out the three Lastman brothers and Loma Gross, and shot all four on the grounds that they were Bolsheviks.

The slaughtered Jews were still lying around the towers where they had fallen. Then the Ukrainians dragged the Jews out of their hiding places and ordered them to take the unburied corpses to the cemetery. All day long, using horse carts, the Jews carried the corpses, wrapped in blood stained sheets and prayer shawls. Stiffened arms and legs and bloodied heads hung down from the carts and swayed to the rhythm of the wheels. Blood dripped along the entire length of the road to the cemetery writing in long red lines the tragic story of those snuffed out lives. It was the muted voice of the innocently shed blood which the cursed earth was thirstily soaking up.

Deep sorrow enveloped the town. Jews observed *Shiva.* [27] The surviving Rabbi proclaimed a community day of fasting and ordered the wearing of sackcloth and ashes as a sign of mourning for the martyred dead. The surviving Jews sent a delegation to the German commander, who promised to restore calm. The military authorities issued an order to the population to return all stolen items. Of course, nothing was returned, nor could the five hundred lives lost in the pogrom possibly be returned.

Meanwhile tragic reports began to be heard from the surrounding areas. The Ukrainians had conducted a pogrom in the neighboring *shtetl* of Grzymalow. There, they had driven some five hundred men, women and children into the river and machine-gunned them all. It was said that for days the river ran red with Jewish blood. In the village of Chmielisko, the Ukrainian peasants buried alive some thirty of their long-time neighbors. In the village of Turowka, the local Jewish doctor had his legs broken and was then impaled on the tines of pitchforks. In Tluste, a smaller town near Skalat, the Ukrainians slaughtered all of the Jews.

So went the Ukrainian twentieth century version of Saint Bartholemew's Night. We shall neverforget the partner and the right hand of the Germans. As it is written: Ye shall remember Amalek!

The great tragedy of Skalat had just begun.

Footnotes:

1 *khurbn* - Total destruction.

2 *shtetls* - Small towns.

3 **'actions,'** - Round-up of Jews for killing.

4 *Shmah Yisroel* - First words of the key Hebrew prayer. "Hear, 0 Israel, the Lord is God, the Lord is One."

5 Podolia - The flatlands of Eastern Galicia.

6 *shul(s)* - Synagogue(s).

7 Sokol - Sports hall in Skalat.

8 landsleit - Fellow countryman (Yiddish).

9 In 1792 - Dates have been added (not in original text). L. Milch

10 "burzhuyis" - Under the Soviets, denoting a wealthy person and having a pejorative connotation. L. Milch

11 Heeresgruppe Sud - A German battalion under Von Runstedt, which occupied Galicia in 1941.

12 goyim - Non-Jews.

13 "Eighth Company" - A phrase used to signify the impoverished masses, It is thought to have originated from the notion that long ago craftsmen and those providing services had to purchase permits of which the eighth-category was for the lowest occupation. L. Milch

14 Tzen minuten shlachten Juden! - Ten minutes for killing Jews.

15 Efraim Diener - According to my own and some other survivor's recollections, the first Skalat victim was Esther Fiszbach's son. L. Milch

16 Jude - Jew.

17 SEJM - Polish parliament.

18 UNDO - Ukrainian Nationalist Democratic Organization, the main Ukrainian political organization in Galicia L. Milch

19 "Shehe Ne Vmerla Ukraina...." - The Ukraine is alive...

20 Sunday, 6 July 1941 - Another version of Skalat survivors states that the main slaughter of the pogrom took place on Saturday, 5 July 1941. Isaac Butel (Birnbaum), the only survivor of the slaughter in the towers, did to the best of his memory, substantiate the Sunday date. L. Milch.

21 Rabbi Benjamin Wolowycz - Another version states that the rabbi's neck was broken when he was thrown from an attic and that he was then killed. I remember this version. L. Milch

22 Friedman - Some survivors of Skalat stated that another Jew, though no one remembers who was dragged to death by horses in addition to Friedman. L. Milch

23 Dr. Leon Fried - The eye witness account of Chajka Kawer nee Sass states that on Sunday, 6 July 1941, she saw Dr. Leon Fried, Berl Sass (her cousin) and M. Bernstein, lying decapitated near the public bath. L. Milch

24 As per Isaac (Birnbaum) Butel's testimony, he and the victims killed late in the day, were lead inside the towers and shot. L. Milch

25 Kaddish - Prayer for the dead.

26 I and other survivors remembered the number of pogrom victims to be around four hundred. L. Milch

27 Shiva - The observance of a seven-day mourning ritual.

[Page 10]

6. The Judenrat and its Institutions

After the pogrom, the *shtetl* was in shock. The Jews could not recover after such unspeakable experiences. The Ukrainians became the masters of the town and their vicious behavior continued to terrify the Jews. Each day hundreds of Jews were dragged off to do hard labor and in the process they were beaten and insulted.

Naively, the Ukrainians believed that their time had come. Under the protective wings of "Hitler the Liberator," young and old strove to join the militia and other administrative offices of the future Ukraine. Once established in their new positions, each tried to outdo the others in patriotism, expressed through hatred of Jews, and by beating and kicking the Jews, their neighbors and former friends. In this way they hoped to gain status in the eyes of their German "liberators."

A certain Nikolaj Bilyk was chosen from among the local Ukrainian activists to rule over the Jews. By the second week after the pogrom he had authorized the former cattle dealer, Leibisz Degen (to whom he was partial, due to their former business dealings) to form a provisional committee. This temporary body consisted of twelve members. Bilyk would come to the *prezes*,[28] Leibisz Degen, to demand a designated number of Jews for labor. Toward that end, the required number of workers would assemble early each morning at the marketplace to await their assignments. Jewish men and women swept streets, cleaned toilets and washed floors in various government offices. Some were also assigned to farms in the surrounding villages. A special store was established in the marketplace for Jews to obtain goods.

Four weeks after the pogrom, an order arrived from the German Security Service (SD) in Tarnopol, to establish a *Judenrat*[29] to serve as the liaison between the Jews and the German authorities. The Ukrainians asked Yankev Perlmuter to undertake the task of establishing the Judenrat in Skalat. Perlmuter refused. And no one else among the professional intelligentsia would accept the honor. After a few days of indecision, Meyer Nirler (a son-in-law of Jisroel Elfenbein) was placed at the head of the *Judenrat*. The other members were:

Yeshaye Zimrner -in charge of liaison with the regime and of securing provisions;

Dr. Berkowicz -treasurer;

Yosef Laufer -taxes;

Dr. Izydor Kron;

Eliezer Schoenberg;

Aszkenazi (the pharmacist);

Mot ye Parnes;

Jankef Scharf; and

Leibisz Degen.

Others in the town were drafted to fill various positions. Emil Orensztein and Mendyk Neiman worked in the birth registry office; Leon Brust in housing, Dr. Fried, Rosa Pikholc, MA, and Francoz in Social Aid, Doctors Gutman, Halpern-Berkowicz and Feeh in Medical Aid. Dr. Berkowicz and Nuchym Safir conducted the Jewish court. Later a Jewish post office was established under the direction of Moishe Gotlieb. The head of the Jewish police (the so-called order keeping service) was Dr. Josef Brief.

At first it seemed as though it might be possible to live from day to day: after all, the Jews were being allowed to tend to their own affairs. "We have a small Jewish Republic, under the sheltering wing of the Germans." The Jews even dared to jest. No one then could have even imagined that the *Judenrat* would eventually become a tool for extortion in the hands of the German murderers.

[Page 11]

On Saturday, 19 July, orders came from Tarnopol that the Jewish population of Skalat must pay a ransom of 600,000 rubles[30] within five days, i.e., by Thursday the 24th (29 Tammuz). Failure to meet the demand would result in tragic consequences. Jewish affairs in Tarnopol were then under a German named Faulfinger, and it was in his name that, on the same day, representatives of the Judenrat were summoned to the Regional Command Office where they received the harsh terms of the order. The delegation was also instructed to provide, by the same deadline, lodgings for twelve Germans, completely equipped with furniture, pots and pans, linens, etc. Faced with such a daunting assignment, the Judenrat established a large committee to carry out the tasks. Raising such a large sum would not be easy, but the tradition of "rescuing souls" was strong enough to breach the walls of impossibility. The committee began to tax the well-to-do and, in view of the danger, the Jews met their responsibility. The committee worked feverishly, night and day. Nirler, the chairman of the *Judenrat*, worked selflessly and with tremendous energy. By the appointed day, the required sum, plus a surplus, had been raised and a delegation took the funds to Tarnopol. The surplus remained as a reserve in the treasury. Lodgings for the twelve Germans, equipped as ordered, were also provided.

The main functions of the *Judenrat* in its early days consisted of: (1) providing 200-300 workers each day to the German and Ukrainian authorities; (2) provisioning the Jewish population, via a bakery at its disposal; (3) organizing the activities of these newly established administrative functions; and (4) providing "gifts" for the Germans who came almost daily to extort wealth from the Jews. Eventually it became necessary to set up a storehouse for the clothing, furniture and tableware collected by the *Judenrat* from the Jewish population to be handed over to the Germans on demand.

During the same period, on 16 July (*Tammuz* 20), an order was issued requiring Jews to wear white armbands marked with the Star of David on their right arms.

Members of the *Judenrat* were to print the word JUDENRAT in large letters on their armbands. The Jewish *Ordinungsdienst*[31] wore yellow armbands marked with its title. In addition, Jewish houses had to have the Star of David signs, for which the *Judenrat* paid a high fee. Life in the *shtetl* somehow became routine and, with minor changes, continued in this way until the beginning of Autumn.

On a certain day, before the High Holy Days, the *Judenrat* announced that all Jews were to report to the marketplace at 9:00 the next morning. No one seemed to know the reason for the order. Then Nirler came forward and explained to the crowd gathered that there was no need to fear, but that a certain number of Jews would be taken away for labor. Schneider, the German Kommandant[32] of the Skalat *Schupo*[33] then selected 200 young people and sent them off to Maksymowka for heavy labor on the rail line. Conditions there were terrible, but by the end of the month most had returned, having been ransomed from the Germans for large sums of money.

Simultaneously the Germans had also established a camp for Russian prisoners of war in the nearby village of Borki Wielkie. The inmates there worked extremely hard and had to subsist on a single daily ration of watery soup. The treatment which they received from the Germans was inhuman. The Russian POW's in the camp were exhausted, broken in spirit, and the mortality rate among them increased daily. The Jews would help them as much as possible. Secretly they would toss them pieces of bread and cigarettes. Such actions, when discovered by the Germans, were punishable by beatings and, sometimes, by shooting. The unfortunate POWs were starved to death. The Germans filled in their ranks with transports of Jews from Lwow and Stanislawow. The Skalat Jewish labor office had to supply Borki-Wielkie, each day, with 200 Jewish workers who were returned home by train each evening. On 24 December 1941, the Germans executed all of the remaining Russian prisoners and then established a forced labor camp exclusively for Jews. On that day the 200 Jews from Skalat did not return home: they were detained as the core of the new Borki Camp.

[Page 12]

The *Judenrat* in Skalat promptly organized a Women's Committee, whose task it was to bring aid to the Jews in Borki-Wielkie. Every other day the women would bring food there, consisting mainly of bread. During the extremely cold winter of 1942, they also supplied warm clothes, gloves and straw to serve as protective shoe-covers. By early 1942, the camp in Kamionki had been established and filled with Jews from Czortkow, Kopyczince, Trembowle, Mikulince, Chorostkow and Grzymalow. Soon thereafter camps were also established in Stupka and Romanowka. Food packages were also sent to the Jewish inmates there through the connections of the Skalat *Judenrat*. Because the camps around Skalat devoured so many lives, each city in the Tarnopol area had to supply a monthly quota of men, primarily youths, to replace the decimated ranks.

Skalat had liaison people, who communicated with the Germans. The *Judenrat*s from the surrounding towns, therefore, used these connections for such transactions as the ransoming of people (trading poorer inmates for wealthier ones) and bribing the Germans. Gradually the Skalat *Judenrat* became the center of trade in human lives and the *Judenrat* began to sink deeper and deeper into a vile swamp. At the same time, it was trying to be of help to the population. It established a home for the elderly and a soup kitchen for workers. Children received extra food rations: occasionally even portions of milk and cereal. The official ration per person amounted to 100 grams of bread, a few hundred grams of grain and a couple of kilos of potatoes. It was, of course, impossible to survive on those rations. The more affluent Jews purchased additional food on the black market. Some even managed to put aside reserves. The poor, on the other hand, suffered from hunger and deprivation. The main source of food was barter with the village peasants, who traded with the Jews for clothing and other goods. The social aid arm of the *Judenrat* helped out as much as it could. Financial resources were limited, however, as the collection of various goods and funds were imposed on the population.

As a method of building a steady source of income for itself, the *Judenrat* established two coffee houses, employing only its own people. These enterprises sold tea, baked goods, cigarettes and delicatessen, bought at high prices through connections with Gentiles. The two gathering places were known in the *shtetl* as *"batyarnyes*[34] a name indicating a clientele with little respect for money. They were also the places where almost all the "wheeler-dealers" of the *Judenrat* would gather to hash over and decide various issues of the moment.

In January of 1942, the Tarnopol SD issued an order to the Jews to turn in all fur coats within three days under pain of death. By the deadline, the warehouses were filled. The best coats were taken by the higher German functionaries and, a few days later, two wagons were loaded with furs for the *Winterhilfswerk*,[35] earmarked for German troops, fighting deep inside Russia. Some Jews had burned their furs rather than give them to the Germans. Having turned in the fur collars of their winter clothes, the Jews' outer garments were left with "comical collars" of raw buckram. This led to an ordinance that the collars be covered with dark cloth, which is believed to have originated with the *Judenrat* concerned with the aesthetic appearance of the people.

Nothing unusual occurred in Skalat during February and March of 1942, but in April the Jews were ordered to evacuate the main streets of the town as their homes had been assigned to select Ukrainian families. In the course of eight days, scores of Jewish homes were emptied and the expelled Jews moved in with people in the back streets.

[Page 13]

The first **'action'** occurred in May in Tarnopol. It was the so-called "contingent"[36] of the aged and weak. The victims consisted mostly of people from the hospital, the old-age home, and the forlorn children from the orphanage. The appalling news from Tarnopol brought panic to our *shtetl*. All sensed disaster to be close at hand.

Harvest time was near. The villages and the rural estates in the area heeded farmhands. The labor office at the *Judenrat* was assigned a daily quota of five to six hundred Jewish workers who went out to their work places guarded by the Jewish Ordinungsdienst At that time the Jews began to receive authorized work-passes with German and Ukrainian signatures, which were thought by their frightened bearers to be protection against eventual dangers. These *Ausweisen*[37] were arranged through the *Judenrat*: Such scraps of working papers were also available, at very high prices, to those who did not work. Pass-fever gripped the entire Jewish population. Anyone possessing a pass believed that it assured his very existence. The passes had some validity for about two weeks. After that they did not prevent anyone from being shipped off to the camp at Borki Wielkie. In July of 1942, the *Judenrat* was called on to supply a quota of thirty girls to the tobacco plantations at Jagielnice. The young women there worked under horrible conditions. After some time, their parents were able to ransom them. Miraculously for them, it was just a few days before some 400 other girls there were brutally shot.

So life went on in Skalat during the so-called "calm" days from July of 1941 to August of 1942. By contrast to later events, that was, indeed, the "Golden Age" under the German occupation.

[Page 14]

7. The "Live Contingent"

A year had passed since the first pogrom of 6 July 1941, but the wounds of that bloodbath had not healed. During that year, and under difficult conditions, the *Judenrat* had regulated our lives. After *Tisha b'AV*[38] the Jews of Skalat noted that the members of the *Judenrat* seemed particularly dejected. "Fellow Jews," they said, "things are bad. There is an evil hanging over us, and may God be merciful." This sad news spread like wildfire among the Jewish inhabitants. As tension increased, the nights became sleepless and the days despondent. What was about to happen? The members of the *Judenrat* held consultations and racked their brains, looking for a way out of the crisis.

Lacking any other options, it was decided to raise a large fund for the purpose of bribing the Germans and thus to avert the impending peril. The Jews contributed their remaining belongings. Within two days, the officials had gathered two valises filled with gold, silver, cash and other valuables. The Committee chose a delegation, headed by Nirler, which promptly set off for Tarnopol to meet with the Gestapo. How much of the treasure actually was given to the Gestapo is not known, but the delegation returned encouraged and satisfied. Nirler was missing a few teeth and the other delegates were badly bruised as well. This was probably due to their reception by the SS. They believed, however, that they had accomplished something for the common good. "It was worth it. We have saved the town, " they said. They had conferred with the Germans in Tarnopol and had accomplished much. Even in the future, no evil would befall Skalat, so effective was the gift to the SS and so successful was this delegation.

Hearing such tales of wonders and miracles somewhat helped to calm the nervous populace, which wanted to believe these assurances as true. At the same time the "protectors of the community" still wandered about, distraught. Secret meetings occupied the members of the *Judenrat*, day in and day out. At first no one else knew the real reason for their uneasiness, but eventually the whole story came out and this is what was revealed: the Germans had intended to carry out an **'action'** against the sick and the old. The *Judenrat* delegation to Tarnopol had arranged to have the matter placed into their own hands. "You need not come to Skalat," they had pleaded. "We will carry out the **'action'** ourselves. Just set the quota for us." Thus they came to terms with the chief of the Tarnopol Gestapo, *Obersturmbannfuhrer*[39] Muller, for five hundred souls to be delivered on 31 August 1942.

It was 30 August 1942 (17 Elul 5702). The inhabitants of Skalat, expecting no evil, strolled about the town. At about 5:00 PM, carrying prepared lists and accompanied by Jewish policemen, the "elite" of the town set out in pairs. They visited among the scattered houses and began dragging the aged grandfathers and grandmothers, the elderly parents, the orphans or other children considered to be sickly, plus the so-called "useless" Jews, i.e., the relief cases. Those collected were led to the synagogue, which had been designated as the collection point for these unfortunates. The *khapers*[40] even tried to deceive their victims, saying: "Come, Jews, have no fear. There's to be a meeting at the *shul*. It's a matter of state. Or would you rather have the Germans drag you there?"

It was no use crying or protesting -one had to go. Those who refused to go peacefully were taken forcibly by the militia. Those unable to walk were carried. Heart-rending scenes took place at the hospital when the sick were brought out. It is difficult to relate all the fearful scenes that took place. In the end, though, the job was done successfully. All night long the *Judenrat* members went around seeking searching in holes, in cellars and attics, and leading the aged and the sick to the *shul*. Very few of the aged succeeded in hiding, because: first, the calamity came unexpectedly; second, hiding was useless since the' catchers' were determined to fill their quotas. If a designated person was found to be missing, they took another family member instead. Every 'catcher' was responsible for his quota. They had already learned discipline and order from the Germans.

[Page 15]

Those who had not been directly affected by the calamity went about saddened and confused: just what was happening here? A small segment of the Jews thought that if people had to be sent to their deaths, the aged were the better choice since they had, after all, lived out their years! This type of thinking, though wrong and morally untenable, influenced the supporters of the *Judenrat*, whose members, they believed, were doing their best on behalf of the community. Such a twisted theory could only have arisen from the warped minds of the *Judenrat* members and their supporters. The overwhelming majority of the populace watched the bloody doings with horror, but they were too weak to resist and powerless to do anything about it.

By 9:00 that evening, when most of the victims had been gathered in the *Shul*, the building was surrounded with an augmented guard of the Jewish police "to prevent, God forbid!, any escapes" especially during the night when new victims were brought in. After completing their work, the *Judenrat* members gathered at their headquarters to review the day's activities. Liquor and cake had been prepared and these Jews rejoiced and congratulated each other; believing they had done no small thing: they had rescued the town. Their reasoning was: if not by us, it would have been done by the Germans, and how much more blood of the able-bodied would have been spilled. It is reported that council-member M. Lempert received a cash prize from the *Judenrat* for being the first to bring in all the people on his list: 100% complete! After the celebration, they telephoned the Gestapo in Tarnopol reporting that the job had been completed and that the Gestapo could come the next day to take over the transport.

All of this is hard to believe, but the surviving witnesses know it and report it, no matter how painful the truth. My mother, who was in the *shul* that tragic day, in place of her mother, my grandmother, whom she wanted to save, provides this eye-witness account:

"On the tragic day of 31 August (18 Elul), I was able to hide my mother, Eidel Jales, age 87. My mother was a treasure: well-read in the *Tzenereneh*[41] and other edifying religious books. She had borne three sons and two daughters. Some 40 years earlier, two of the sons had gone to America, and from them she received support until the outbreak of the war. In Skalat and in Tarnopol she had two daughters and a son, whose families included some twenty grandchildren and great-grandchildren. On Sabbath days the old woman was hard-put to decide which child or grandchild she should visit first. Almost every year, one of the American sons would come to do her filial honor.

It was a pleasure to hear her tell stories about the holy saints. She had a phenomenal memory. Despite her advanced age, she did not lack wisdom and cleverness. Generally she kept herself clean and in good health, as though she were thirty years younger. Every morning she would put on her spectacles and say prayers from her huge morning prayer-book, and then cook her breakfast. Later she would go out into the town to find out who might be sick or in need: for the one some preserves, for the other a few *zlotys*.[42] This she did because she felt people are not immortal and must during their lifetime store up fulfilled commandments and acts of loving kindness. She had long since prepared her burial shroud and a plot in the cemetery near the husband who had died twenty years before. 'Anyhow, if I'm called, I will go,' she used to say. 'It is now more near than far. Meanwhile, how dear to me is the joy I derive from my children!'

That fatal day, we said to Mother: 'Come, Mama. We will hide you. We won't let you go to the hangman's hands!' The old woman trembled like a leaf: she still wanted to live, or if she had to die then let it be at least in her own bed. 'My dearest children, don't leave me,' she said and went into the hiding place on unsteady legs.

[Page 16]

The *Judenrat* officials ran about all day like madmen: searching for her everywhere. They were incensed: 'How can it be that the old Jales woman hasn't been crossed off the list yet? Can you imagine the gall of such a conscience-less family, to hide away such a broken old woman? No, they won't get away with it! ' The militia came to me with an ultimatum, demanding: 'Are you turning over your old mother or not?'

'I don't know where she is,' I replied.

Then the policeman began to shout: 'If you won't hand her over, then you must come with us... You will bring harm to all of us! We must have the total number of people - don't you understand?' I did not understand. I felt it was better to go myself than to deliver an aged mother to her death. I cried, screamed, went faint, fought with the gangsters, refusing to go. But it was to no avail: they dragged me off to the *shul* as a hostage.

The *shul* was crowded, suffocating. Screams! Sobs! The old people sigh, cough, clamor and faint. All that time in the heat without even a drop of water. A few of the aged and sick, lacking stamina, had already died.

Hersz Siegal stood at the pulpit and recited the Psalms in a tearful voice. Our long-time neighbor and dear friend had been a part-time teacher, a religious instructor as well as a broker. He was a sensitive young man but poor and in tatters all his life. Lately he had become penniless and was supported by communal funds. Therefore he, too, was on the list of the 'useless' and, as such. he, his wife, and his two children had been dragged here.

'Mrs. Weissbrod, what are you doing here?' Hersz Siegal asked me. I told him all about my mother and learned of his troubles in turn. 'What do they want of me? -And why are my wife and children at fault?' These were questions I could not answer. I stood there, perplexed. Still I clung to the hope that within a few hours I would be released from this lions' den and that my mother, too, would be rescued. The members of the *Judenrat* were, after all, good acquaintances who would not permit such a shameful act as exchanging a daughter's life for a mother's. Meanwhile, Hersz Siegal and I wrote notes to our families and friends: 'Save me!'

Times passes. The hours fly by. Nothing is heard, nothing is seen. Evening approaches. Night comes: no rescuers appear. New victims, however, are brought in regularly. We surround them. asking what is happening in town. Faith in rescue becomes ever weaker, while fear of death begins to assault one's thoughts. What a night the other Jews and I spent there! Nights in hell could certainly not be worse. Dawn arrived. The red, blue and green panes of the tall *Shul* windows let in the daylight which revealed both the frightening reality and the dark thoughts of another world.

There were no replies from outside to the notes we had sent. Fearfully we awaited whatever the coming hours would bring. I had lost hope by now, and no longer believed I would be rescued. Meanwhile my old mother had found out what had happened. In her way, she experienced a profound dilemma: how could she possibly permit her own daughter to be lost? She wove together the strands of Fate and Divine Providence. The Master of the Universe must know what He is doing! She did not sleep all night and barely survived until morning to be able to ransom her daughter from the murdering hands.

[Page 17]

'My daughter I have come!' I suddenly heard my mother's voice. 'I, alone, will be the sacrifice for the family. Go home: you are younger than I.' Then she pressed into my hand a gold coin, worth $20.00, and whispered: 'Perhaps you will yet be able to ransom me.'

I did not want to go. Tears choked me as both of us, mother and daughter, stood there: frozen and mute. Moved by that solemn moment, both of us stood motionless, like deeply rooted trees. These tragic last moments together both broke and united our hearts.

'Go, my daughter -go before it is too late,' the heroic 87 year old woman warned. 'But try...perhaps you may yet be able to ransom me.' I can't remember how long we embraced.

A policeman led me outside, barely able to walk. My old mother remained in the *shul*"

*****

Promptly at 4:00 PM on Monday, a group of SS, led by *Obersturmbannfuhrer* Muller, arrived from Tarnopol with eight empty trucks to transport the "live contingent." The first truck stopped at the gate of the *shul*. The "gentlemen" of the *Judenrat* appeared, servile and obsequious at the feet of the German hangmen.

"How many have you gathered here, you shitty Jews?" Nirler waved his hands about and managed to stammer out a few words. The enraged German replied with a wild shout: "What? So few? Damn you! In one half hour another hundred Jews! Or else we will shoot you down, like dogs!" There were supposed to have been 500 people. At the last minute, though, it turned out that there were only 480. Somehow twenty had disappeared. It was said that *Shikale-ganif,*[43] a policeman, had permitted that number of people to ransom themselves and had let them out through the back door during the night. If the *Judenrat* could let people ransom themselves or replace their relatives with strong, young people why not Shikale?

The few Germans and the Jewish police spread out across the town and grabbed anyone they could lay their hands on. The half-hour chase brought in another eighty souls to add to the "live contingent."

Obersturmbannfuhrer Muller consulted his watch and waved his hand to indicate that there were enough. It was getting late. The doors of the *shul* were opened wide, disgorging the mass of hardly recognizable people: exhausted from hunger, thirst and heat. Pale, broken, stooped and bent, like living corpses, some pushed forward, some fell in a faint and some held each other's hands.

The militiamen loaded the people onto the trucks as though they were handling freight, packing them in tightly to achieve the fullest load, while the Germans cracked their whips overhead. The old people were carried and loaded with great effort. My great aunt, Fayle Jawer, 96 years old, was among them. She had spent the night in the *shul* with my grandmother, her sister-in-law. She was lucky. As they were carrying her onto the truck, she breathed her last. Her corpse lay packed in among the living but she suffered no more pain. When all the victims had been loaded aboard the trucks, one of the militiamen asked what should be done with the corpses that had been left in the *shul.* "Pack them in with the rest of them" came the reply.

"Move out!" the *Obersturmbannfuhrer* shouted, and the trucks began to move, to the sound of sobs and wailing. The 560 victims were taken to Tarnopol, and then, from there, to an extermination camp.

[Page 18]

*****

Supplement to this chapter:

Abraham Somerstein a former resident of Skalat, provides the following details about the '**action**' of 31 August 1942:

The first victim was Efraim Olesker, who was caught on the street. The "heroic" policeman called out joyfully and loudly: "Here's the first fish! "

Many people were freed for large sums. The ransom money was collected by Nirler and Eliezer Schoenberg. When Shikale-ganif saw that rich folks were buying their way out, he was outraged and out of empathy for the impoverished, let out about twenty of the poor people through the back door during the night. Of course, he did not take any ransom.

The close relatives of *Judenrat* members were exempted.

Shikale-ganif caught Josi Rothstein on the street and beat him brutally, shouting: "Will you give up your mother and father or not?" Rothstein panicked and revealed his parents' hiding place. They were found and dragged off to the *shul*.

Motie Rosenblat was taken hostage. As he wouldn't reveal, or did not know, his father's whereabouts, he was loaded aboard one of the trucks. He managed to escape by leaping off the train. Another Jew tried to follow his example, but was shot by the Germans as he ran.

Mrs. Munia Bernhaut of Skalat relates:

On the same day, an **'action'** took place in Tarnopol. The Skalat victims were taken, along with those from Tarnopol, to the Belzec extermination camp.

The *Judenrat* detained a separate group of privileged old people at the police headquarters, hoping the Germans would be satisfied with the number held in the *shul*, allowing the privileged ones to be spared. The Germans, however, ranted that the quota had not been filled and therefore these people were led to the *shul*. In addition, more victims had to be caught in the streets.

It was said that Muller, the Tarnopol Gestapo Chief, had remarked to the *Judenrat*, before driving off, "We shall return in six weeks." If so, that would have been advance warning of the great slaughter that came to be known as the "Wild Action."

[Page 19]

8. The Underground Community

The *shtetl* was horror stricken. There was fear that a new catastrophe might arrive at any moment. The population of Skalat had already heard of the Lwow evacuation **'action'** and its 50,000 victims as well as the **'actions,'** in other cities such as Tarnopol, Mikulince, Trembowle and Czortkow with their own slaughters. Everyone tried to devise a means of rescuing oneself and one's family before the inevitable next **'action.'** Everyone made every effort to be as prepared as possible.

In Skalat, as everywhere else, there was mass hysteria to devise hiding places, the so-called "bunkers." Jews became master-builders and engineers. They racked their brains, night and day. To find ways to make their hiding places inconspicuous and well-camouflaged. A subterranean world began to emerge under floors, in cellars and in gardens. Tunnels were dug and narrow passages, connecting cellars of the attached row houses, spread in every direction. Some of the hiding places were truly marvels of construction, including some that were built to fifteen meters below ground with provisions made for such essentials as air ventilation, water, toilets, brick storage areas, etc. Necessity awakened dormant talents in the art of construction. That sort of "engineer", however, would also be a craftsman, a brick-layer, and a common laborer. For the most part, these "specialists" built bunkers for the more affluent homeowners at high fees. Sand, lime, bricks, boards and other building materials became scare. Trade in these items grew frantic and prices soared.

A major problem for the Jews building bunkers was the excavated earth, which, more than once, betrayed the fact that there was an underground bunker. Where could the Jews dispose of wagonloads of dirt? The construction took place at night and upon arising in the morning, anyone could tell that a new bunker had been built nearby. To remove the tell-tale signs, people would work unceasingly and during the following nights, carry the earth in baskets or sacks, as far as possible outside the town.

The members of the *Judenrat* and their families came to realize that they, too, were in great danger. In other cities, many *Judenrat* members had been hanged for failing to carry out German orders properly. Thus their situation was obviously hopeless and preparations had to be made just in case. Because they had large amounts of money, each built virtual fortresses, equipped with various comforts and with storage rooms like Pithoms and Ramesese, crammed with provisions and beverages.

Skalat was a magnet for frightened Jews, because it was believed to be relatively safe. The stream of refugees from the surrounding towns and villages added to the housing shortage and worsened living conditions. Every house and each apartment was overcrowded and the crowding led to a lack of cleanliness and hygiene. Vermin proliferated. At night the Jews posted guards near their houses to alert them if anything happened in town. Every accidental noise, the barking of a dog, the stumbling of a drunk somewhere, not to mention a shot, sufficed to alarm and rouse an entire household to its feet. The slightest sound assaulted the nerves. People slept fully dressed so as to be ready to run instantly. Many people slept in bunkers, some spent the nights with Gentile friends, and others in fields. So the Jews passed their days in mortal fear.

Fear grew intense when it was learned that the Tarnopol Gestapo had ordered the surrounding towns and villages to become *Judenrein*.[44] All Jews were to leave their dwellings and move to Skalat. A deadline was set for 15 October 1942. The Jews saw this as an evil omen: a sign that something was about to happen. The Germans, it appeared, were bring the Jews to Skalat for the "Feast Day"[45] - some said, in jest, to make sure that everyone was present for the "slaughter-fair."

For two weeks, caravans of displaced Jews streamed into Skalat and the roads were clogged with horse-drawn wagons, piled high with domestic goods and belongings. The wagons were followed by pedestrians, sweaty, grimy and exhausted. As the deadline approached, the migration reached its high point and the appearance of the caravans grew more awesome. Some 4,000 Jews came to Skalat from Grzymalow, Podwoloczyska and the surrounding villages, all of them long-time dwellers, driven from their homes. The housing shortage and overcrowding became unbearable. People actually lived in the streets. Those who were better off among the newcomers were able to rent quarters from Gentiles, paying huge sums of money. Most found shelter with relatives, or simply with other Jews who wanted to help people in the midst of such turmoil. Twelve to eighteen people were crammed into small dwellings, like herring in a barrel. Hundreds of Jews made living quarters for themselves in the stalls of the bazaar, which had been left empty, robbed and ruined, after the first pogrom. Many also lived in the *shul*s, in the Houses of Study and small prayer-houses.

[Page 20]

The sudden addition of thousands of people changed the appearance of the *shtetl* beyond recognition. Hunger and poverty reigned. It was impossible to provide for so large a population. Inflation and the black market grew. Diseases spread and the mortality rate escalated. Not a day passed without an increase in the number of deaths. Charitable Jews, among the wealthier, helped significantly. Among many others, we must mention Tennenbaum of blessed memory, who helped the poor with a generous hand and at the risk of his own life. Much is told of his gentleness and of his good deeds. The Hasidic followers of the Rabbi of Kopyczince honored their leader's memory by sending food parcels to his son-in-law in Tarnopol.

However, panic and nightmarish fear continued unabated. Then, in mid-October of 1942, the order was issued to establish the ghetto All the Jews were to be squeezed into the few small streets between the marketplace and the *shul*.

The *Judenrat* had its hands full and was unable to deal with the new situation. The members were in constant consultations: mainly about a pending new catastrophe, whose arrival was almost palpable.

"What is to be done?" The question tortured everyone unmercifully. "What is to be done? What can be done?"

[Page 21]

9. "Jews, Do Not Worry"

One day the *Judenrat* held an urgent meeting. After much discussion and argument two opinions emerged.

Some councilmen, the more decent and conscience-stricken, argued for letting fate take its course: "As God wills, so let it be, but Jews themselves should not participate in the **'actions.'** Let all who can, hide; no other course is open to us." For the record, let us state that there were some councilmen, among them Dr. Izydor Kron, Dr. Berkowicz, and Yankif Sharf, who could not back the shameful actions of the majority and who opposed their colleagues on all vital issues. It must also be said that at the beginning, none of them could have imagined that the *Judenrat* would become a tool in the hands of the Germans. Once mired in that evil, however, and although fighting with all their might, they were unable to extricate themselves from the vipers' nest. Initially it seemed to everyone that the *Judenrat* members were not in as great a danger, but now survival became the supreme preoccupation, even for them. Faced with the real possibility of death, survival by any means was a temptation not easily avoided, although it cannot justify the sins that were committed. The so-called "opposition" was determined not to permit a repetition of the methods used by the *Judenrat* during the "Live Contingent" **'action.'** "Not only must we not carry out an **'action,'** but we dare not assist the Germans in the slightest way," they argued. Their position was: hiding and escaping wherever possible is the watchword of this tragic hour.

The other side took quite a different approach. Eliezer Schoenberg and his hangers-on demanded, categorically, that, as had happened in the earlier **'action,'** an agreement should be struck with the German authorities allowing the *Judenrat* to conduct future **'actions,'** on its own and to deliver the assigned quota, thereby at least saving themselves, their families, relatives and many other younger and "more useful" people. Therefore, they argued, the *Judenrat* must make the effort to collect another large sum of money. Councilman Schoenberg gave his assurance that, should the Gestapo agree to a contingent of, say: 2,000 people, he would undertake to supply 1,000. "We have enough people to spare," he claimed. "We won't need to take any of our local people: the town is full of ragged newcomers, who are sleeping in the bazaar and dying of hunger anyway."

Following a stormy debate, this proposal was adopted and the majority of the councilmen supported it.

The *Judenrat* quickly stepped up its activity. Heavy funds were levied against the better-off inhabitants; councilmen went from door to door collecting gold and other valuables. They also called in representatives of the newcomers, demanding that they raise large sums among themselves to rescue the group as a whole. With a view towards lowering the danger, the Jews did not stint. Perhaps it might yet be possible to counteract the evil decree, they thought.

The delegates Nirler, Schoenberg, Zimmer and Lempert went to Tarnopol. There they met first with the Jewish "fixer," who had connections with the Gestapo. He brought them up-to-date on the current situation. "Things are bad, " he said. "There's an **'action'** scheduled very soon in your town. But if you have the right proposal, try bringing it to *Obersturmbannfuhrer* Muller; you might be able to accomplish something."

The delegation met with Muller. Upon hearing their proposal about establishing a sum for the next contingent, which the Jews would assemble through their own efforts, *Obersturmbannfuhrer* Muller; shouted: "Wha-a-t?" and then began to speak more calmly. "What makes you think, all of a sudden, that something is about to happen in your town? There is nothing currently scheduled for Skalat. Come back in a few weeks and we will talk about it. Now you can go home quite calmly and reassure your people. Why worry for nothing, when all is in the best order? Just don't worry."

At previous meetings the Council had been used to receiving insults and whip lashings. This time Muller was like a lamb. "Our gift softened his heart," one of them said, while the others struggled with sorrowful thoughts, full of doubt and confusion. Yet all of them wanted to believe in a good omen, regardless of logic. The delegates prepared to return. "What do we tell them at home, in the *shtetl*?" they asked themselves. "What have we actually accomplished?" Their ears still rang with Muller's words: All is in the best order. Just don't worry. Was that such a bad message for the *shtetl*? Such words could really calm distraught nerves and spirits!

[Page 22]

During the twilight hours, when the delegation was expected back from Tarnopol, hundreds of Jews gathered on the road far out of town, impatiently awaiting the messengers who carried in their hands the fate of the *shtetl*. Due to particularly good news from the Russian front that day, the crowd was in an optimistic mood. Why always expect the worst, people thought, when the good might also come unexpectedly?

Coincidentally, some girl had dreamed that a group of Jews wearing prayer shawls was at services in the *shul*, and an old man, standing at the pulpit, blew the *shofar*[46] and informed the crowd that salvation would arrive on the 11th day of *Heshvan* - which was the next day! Perhaps salvation might begin today, starting with the good news that the delegation is about to bring.

"Jews, here come the delegates!" The long awaited moment had arrived. The horse drawn wagon came to a stop and hundreds of Jews surrounded the delegates. They listened to the report with bated breath and with joy. Triumphantly, the delegation quoted the very words of the Tarnopol Gestapo Chief: "Don't worry: nothing will happen in the town for the time being." And to this the messengers added: "Calm down, now, Jews. Drive away your fears. Don't spread panic. As you can see for yourselves, we are doing everything for your sake. In return we ask only for your understanding and cooperation."

At first, the good news assuaged distraught spirits. As evening came on, however, sobriety returned. Fear of the night brought back the gnawing unease. Guards were posted as before and people slept half-dressed, resting their weary bodies wherever they could. Most by now had become accustomed to such an oppressive life. Some terrified people would creep up to the windows of the councilmen's houses to determine whether they were at home. If so, that was the best sign that the night would probably be peaceful. If things looked really bad, they, the councilmen, would not spend the night in their own homes. Who else would know everything, if not the *Judenrat*?

Thus the overwhelming majority in Skalat went to bed that night in their own homes and with a feeling of greater security. Besides, it wasn't that simple finding shelter among the Gentiles time after time, or just wandering about all night long. In times of inordinate danger that might have been necessary, but not tonight, when the delegation had brought such good news. Some, however, hid this night too. Better safe than sorry. Self-preservation was the rule!

*****

Obersturmbannfuhrer Muller and his aides apparently understood that this would be the ideal night to conduct the '**action**' in Skalat. They had given the delegation such fine-sounding assurances that the Jews there were sure to be passive. An unexpected attack would certainly be successful.

The orders went down: "Everyone must be ready to leave for Skalat at 2:00 AM.."

Footnotes:

28 prezes - Chairman.

29 Judenrat(s) -Jewish Council(s) (the main liaison between the Jews in the ghetto and the Germans)

30 ruble(s) - Monetary unit of Russian currency.

31 Ordinungsdienst - Jewish police (order keeping service).

32 Komrnandant - Commander.

33 *Schupo* (Schutzpolizei) - Security police (Germans).

34 "batyarnyes" - Derived from the Yiddish word batyar (hooligan) and referring to two coffee houses in Skalat. under the German occupation. L. Milch

35 Winterhilfswerk - Campaign to provide warm clothing for German troops inside Russia during the winter of 1941-1942.

36 "contingent" - A quota of the aged and sick, rounded-up for extermination in Belzec. L. Milch

37 Ausweisen - Work passes.

38 Tisha b'Av - Ninth day of the month of Av, traditionally a day of fasting, commemorating the destruction of the Temple.

39 *Obersturmbannfuhrer* (Muller) - Gestapo chief in Tarnopol.

40 khapers - Catchers.

41 Tzenereneh - "Let's Go and See" book of prayers written in Yiddish and read mostly by women.

42 *zlotys*- Monetary unit of Polish currency.

43 ganif - Thief (Shikale) - most adults in Skalat had nicknames based on physical or character traits. L. Milch

44 *Judenrein* - Cleansed of Jews.

45 "Feast Day" - Saint Anne's Feast was annually celebrated in Skalat with a big fair. L. Milch

46 shofar - Ram's horn: trumpet call used during the High Holidays and special occasions of national emergencies or celebrations.

[Page 23]

10. The Wild Action

On 21-22 October 1942 (10-11 Heshvan 5703), Skalat endured the bloody tragedy which the Jews of our town called the "Wild Action," because of the cruelty and savagery with which the brutes carried out the 'deportation' during those two days.

Precisely at 4:00 AM, five busloads of armed and helmeted SS-men pulled into Skalat. They surrounded the town, and then waited calmly until the break of dawn. Three shots were the signal to start the **'action.'** Soon the air was filled with the wild cries and unintelligible bellows of the group-leaders and commanders. The Germans stood in full battle order, arranged in groups, strategically placed as though in a planned military maneuver. They behaved as though the "enemy" responsible for starting World War II and threatening the Third Reich were the Jews of Skalat, including the women and children. "Forward! Let no one escape! If they run then shoot -and shoot - and shoot again!"

All of the soldiers had, earlier, received rations of alcohol, which were provided before every **'action,'** as though to assure better results and make the 'work' easier, bolder and wilder. The Ukrainian militia, led by its *Kommandant*, stood to the side in two long rows, awaiting orders from the *Obersturmbannfuhrer*, who assigned two or three Ukrainian militiamen to each group of German SS-men. "Listen, fellows, work faithfully for the sake of our Ukraine and for the glory of the Third Reich," the *Kommandant* called, leading his men forward.

The shouting and shooting roused the *shtetl* from sleep. The people quickly realized that disaster had struck. Terror and turmoil reigned. People ran about, lost and terrified. Where does one hide? Where does one run? Most Jews did not have bunkers in their cellars and scurried to seek shelter with neighbors in shared hiding places - but by now it was too late. The Germans were running wild in the streets.

The newcomers had no hiding places at all. Some tried to escape, thinking that perhaps it might be possible to break through the ring, reach the "Aryan" side and hide somewhere in the open fields. They had nothing to lose and everyone could see their plight clearly.

Streets and alleys were filled with German and Ukrainian troops, rifles at the
ready. They were strategically waiting at every wall. The continuous sound of shooting,
the wild shouts from the Germans, the cries of children, the moans and groans of the
wounded - all combined into a terrible cacophony. Other Jews still tried to escape, as
the soldiers fired at them ceaselessly. The death toll rose minute by minute. Over one
hundred fell in the first moments of the slaughter, and the corpses were left lying in
the streets all around the town. Only a few actually succeeded in escaping the siege.
As the desperate running came to an end, the shooting quieted down. Now the wild
killers set out to grab victims from their homes. Jews hid wherever they could, but the
majority, lacking hiding places, and without hope or help, remained in place. They
surrendered to their fate.

By now there were almost 150 victims. The bloody prologue completed, the
cutthroats turned to their main job. From the Houses of Study and Prayer they
dragged the Jews and led them in groups to the *shul*, where they had already
crammed in hundreds of others. They dragged their victims from houses, from attics,
from cellars, from under beds, from closets, and from all the other mouse-holes. With
curses and shouts, they led them to the collection point under a hail of whip lashes
and with the prodding of gun butts. One woman, Tonka Bernhaut, while being driven
to the *shul*, screamed curses at Hitler and his 'Master Race.' The German leading her
would not tolerate the vilification. He drew his revolver and shot her, shooting again
when she attacked him with her fists.

As the **'action'** progressed, *Obersturmbannfuhrer* Muller made a deal with the
leaders of the *Judenrat* and the *Kommandant* of the Jewish police, Dr. Josef Brif, to
take an active part in the **'action.'** He solemnly promised that they and their families
would be spared. The Jewish police and some individual *Judenrat* members quickly
turned to their assigned work. Their main task was to help uncover the bunkers and
other hiding places. In the meantime, they got Muller to agree to release
those *Judenrat* members and their families who had been caught at the start of
the **'action.'** They were quickly released.

[Page 24]

The work proceeded under full steam. By noon the *shul* was packed with over a
thousand victims. *Obersturmbannfuhrer* Muller and his aide, Leks, were very pleased
with their Jewish helpers and did, in fact, spare the relatives of the council-members.
The Jewish helpers justified their actions with the view that since all was lost, one
must, at the very least, save one's own life and the lives of one's nearest. Neither Nirler
nor the Jewish police *Kommandant*, wearing riding breeches and highly polished
boots, shirked at their tasks. Just like the Germans, they ran about in their
shirtsleeves, cuffs rolled back, redfaced, sweating and excited wielding riding crops.
They ran helter-skelter, along with the manic German and Ukrainian butchers, from

house to house, from attic to attic, from cellar to cellar - dragging, tearing, beating and screaming like wild animals in imitation of their experienced masters.

It was characteristic that these Germans, virtuosos of atrocity and brutality, were simultaneously cowards. They even feared children who might put their eyes out in vengeance. If such a German had to search some hole in a cellar or an attic, he would send in a Jew while he stood outside, safe from attack. Some Jews would, indeed, uncover hiding places and drag out their own.

In a relatively short time the Germans managed to dehumanize their victims and some Jews did not escape the brutalization forced on them by the killers. The will to live, no matter how tragic the conditions were, perhaps explains the shroud of iniquity and cruelty which covers the mounds of corpses. "Meyer, Meyer! Do all that you can so that we may live! " - pleaded the mother-in-law of the infamous Nirler at that time. In this light it was proper to do almost anything to save one's own, even if it meant sending thousands of others to death. And both the mother-in-law and son-in-law did survive.

The '**action**' went on. The *shul* was packed: even the ante-room and the women's balcony. The officers of the '**action**' were forced to take out many people to make room for the newly-arrived captives. Under heavy guard, groups of wretched victims were taken to a wet meadow near the railroad station where the soil had always been soggy because of the swamps which once covered the area.

On the first day of the '**action**' 2,000 Jews were captured. Conditions in the *shul* became intolerable. Scores of swaddled children, some in sacks and some wrapped in sheets, lay, scattered, on the stone floor of the ante-room. They whined and cried ceaselessly. Infants screamed for their mothers' breasts. They shivered with cold and nervously tossed about their arms and legs. No one paid attention to them. Their own mothers had left them to God's mercies as they themselves ran to hide. For who would admit a mother and screaming child into a bunker? And how could one run with a child in one's arms? The youngest infants were forgotten in the great madness of the stampede. But the executioners didn't forget them...they shot them on the spot or brought them to the *shul* in little sacks.

The sanctuary was packed. No one was permitted to leave: not even to attend to bodily needs. Soon the stench became overpowering. None of this prevented the crowd from praying: people murmured prayers, recited Psalms, offered confessions. Motie Perlmuter wailed verses and the congregation repeated them in response. The cries and sobs of hysterical women rose from all sides. Most of the captives no longer had faith in the possibility of rescue. Many were sadly silent, biting their lips. Most of the older children understood what was happening but tried to keep their spirits up. They bore their pain and woe quietly and stoically, with a determination beyond their years. "What could be the sin of such little flowers?" someone in the crowd called out. There was no reply.

The '**action**' continued to rage in the town. Then scores of soldiers surrounded the *Shul* and the last groups captured during the day were brought to the meadow that evening. The quota that had been set by the Tarnopol Gestapo had not yet been filled. Three shots, fired in rapid succession, was the signal for a break, and the SS gang headed off to enjoy themselves at the *Judenrat* office, where a celebration had been prepared. Liquor, whiskey, wine and eggnog flowed like water. There were roasted and marinated meats, cakes and pastries. Pretty girls were also present. The caterers of the *Judenrat* busied themselves

[Page 25]

at the richly adorned tables, slavishly dancing attendance on the guests as though they were monarchs. Laughter was heard, music played: the night passed in song, dance and joy. All of this while 2,000 people suffered in the heat of the packed *shul* and in the cold of the meadow by the railroad.

On the second day, Thursday 22 October, capturing victims became more difficult. Nevertheless the required additional 1,000 victims, plus a surplus, were collected. Scores of bunkers were uncovered that day, some of them sheltering from sixty to seventy people.

Terrible scenes occurred in the meadow near the railroad station, where the victims were gathered. Everyone had to remain in a kneeling position. If someone moved, he was savagely beaten by the Ukrainian Hitlerites. Limbs ached and grew as numb as logs. The weeping of women and children pierced one's ears. Scattered about the very center of the large clearing lay scores of tiny children, pleading and crying. The weather was autumnal: bleak and cold. Night fell abruptly, heavy and dark. Bonfires blazed on all sides of the square, illuminating the terrible scene. The Ukrainians had built the fires for warmth and to keep a closer watch on the Jews. Constant firing into the air was another warning to those considering escape. The wretched victims lay down on the damp earth; hunger, cold and deathly fear coursed through the very blood in their veins.

By morning, many people were frozen and too weak to stand. Part of the crowd was almost naked, having been dragged from bed in their underwear. The people were miserable, staring blankly and hardly recognizable. They had already resigned themselves to their fate. Still, at times, some individuals tried to escape, although they were rarely successful. The Hitlerite guards shot down the escapees, and the toll of the dead and/or seriously wounded grew higher and higher. A few did manage to escape, but most were caught and returned by peasants without a conscience. Bloodied corpses were strewn about. Hundreds of peasant onlookers stood around, ostensibly watching sympathetically, but actually enjoying the Jewish agony.

All of the people in the *shul* were brought to the meadow in the afternoon of the second day. With the arrival of the last group of captives, at around 7:00 PM, the count stood at over 3,000. This, apparently, was the Gestapo's assigned quota. The full complement of German, Ukrainian and Jewish participants now gathered at the train station for the new task of transporting the victims.

Part of the *Judenrat* was otherwise engaged in town: making preparation for a farewell banquet for the Tarnopol SS-men. But some of the Jewish police were still busy, trying to effect a last-minute rescue of some of the *Judenrat* members' families, who had been swept up among the captives. The main intercessions were made on behalf of Dr. Gutman, bookkeeper Moshe Sas of Tarnoruda and Dr. Finkelstein of Podwoloczyska. The *Judenrat* negotiated the matter with Muller and Leks, the Gestapo representatives. The chief was in a very bad mood and kept cursing and shouting. As far as he was concerned the **'action'** was finished. But the members of the *Judenrat* were determined to save them, regardless of the cost and therefore they kept interceding. "For every Jew I free, bring me 25 others," Muller demanded, thinking this would make them desist.

"At your command, Herr *Obersturmbannfuhrer!*" replied a *Judenrat* member, who promptly turned to the police and gave the appropriate orders. Some of the Jewish police set off through the streets, with renewed energy, to uncover another bunker somewhere and to supply, quickly, the needed number of people. But after half an hour's raging through the town, they were barely able to gather up a total of 25 people. The German, Muller, stared in amazement at his Jewish "assistants." He dismissed only Dr. Gutman and his family and the bookkeeper, Sas. He would not free any others. He shouted and swore and would not listen to another word. The Ukrainian militiamen drove the newly-captured Jews into the human mass.

The last death negotiation ended the **'action.'**

[Page 26]

The system of trading Jews for other Jews was a usual practice for the *Judenrat*. The councilmen were always ready to do business for large sums. In addition there were always favorites and dignitaries to look after.

A locomotive pulled empty freightcars up to the station platform and the command was given to load up the victims. The soldiers drove the Jews into the cars. Amid shouts and blows, groups of 100 to 200 were crammed into each of the cars. The dead were also tossed in and included in the count. The cars were sealed and boarded up. In one hour's time, the long train was ready to depart.

At 9:00 PM, the transport moved out, leaving behind a bloody meadow, over which various items of clothing were strewn haphazardly. An army of peasants, with baskets and sacks, quickly attacked these "spoils." But this scene offended the aesthetic sense of the Germans: "Such bloody swine!" they shouted, and the peasants ran off quickly.

Obersturmbannfuhrer Muller and his aide, Leks, heartily thanked the Ukrainian *Kommandant* and his men for their devoted collaboration as well as the Jewish police, who stood drawn up in ranks like the strings on an instrument. They, in turn, saluted the departing German guests from Tarnopol, who rapidly climbed aboard their large buses. The *Obersturmbannfuhrer*, his aide, and the rest of the higher functionaries were seated in their limousines. Leks stuck his head out of the side window, stared coldly at the group of Jewish councilmen, and called out: *"Auf Wiedersehn!* We should return in four weeks!" He smiled sadistically and suddenly called out: "Come here, *Ober Jude."* [47]

Nirler stepped forward, listened to a few words and answered: "At your command, *Herr Chef!"*[48]

The limousines drove to the *Judenrat* offices, where the Gestapo-men spent another hour. They had time for a toast, a light supper and to receive attractive gifts before departing.

[Page 27]

11. After the Devil's Dance

The day after the "Wild Action," the *shtetl* was a shambles. Houses were ravaged and in ruins. Corpses of murdered Jews lay in the streets in every part of town. Jews, by now experienced in survival, were afraid to leave their hiding places. The first of those who had hidden, did not appear until just before noon. Only a handful from among the 3,000 victims of the **'action'** had managed to escape. Those who survived had been hidden in bunkers and other places or had been able to find refuge in the fields and forests outside the ghetto.

Hesitantly, people began to search for others. Wives sought their husbands; brothers their sisters; a mother her child. The small number of survivors were now a group of newly made orphans, widows and other lonely and broken souls. All of the 153 corpses found in the streets had been shot. As they were being buried, the survivors stood about as though frozen. Everyone knew that the catastrophe was not yet over: "We will return in four weeks," the murderers had said as they left and there was no reason to doubt their word.

In the bunkers of Skalat where the Jews had hidden, events took place that were beyond imagining. People told of seeing mothers suffocate their own children, to prevent them from crying and thus betraying dozens of others hidden there. And, in fact, many hiding places were discovered because of the sobbing of children. Some mothers used sleeping potions such as veronal to quiet their thirsty and starving children. Sometimes it happened that the dose was too strong and the children were silenced forever. There were more than twenty such incidents. People had been jammed into the bunkers like herring in a barrel, without air, without water and without food. When the **'action'** was over, they emerged dazed and exhausted. Their loved ones were gone, their houses pillaged, and they found themselves at a loss as to what to do next.

The *Judenrat* and others who worked with the Germans during the Devil's Dance were still dazed by their experiences and for days were unable to gain their equilibrium. The bloody scenes of the gruesome '**action**' continued to play out before their eyes and their deeds gnawed at their consciences. They tried to bury their guilt in a flurry of diversions. Duty called daily business matters needed attention and the *Judenrat* began to function as before. It was simple reckoning: the fact that the Germans had spared the members of the *Judenrat* during the '**action**' was the clearest indication they intended some kind of Jewish settlement to remain in Skalat and that something would yet be required of them. With these ideas they consoled themselves and others and turned to their work with renewed vigor "for the sake of the community."

Meanwhile, some of the Jews who had jumped off the train began to filter back. They reported that many people had jumped to escape. The transport guards shot down most of the escapees firing on both sides of the railroad tracks which led toward Lwow. Those who had succeeded in escaping spent the following weeks wandering in the fields and on the roads, in rain and cold. Peasants with no conscience or pity robbed many of them and then turned them over to the *Schupo* or the Ukrainian militia, from whose hands no one emerged alive. Some fifty of these *skotchkes*[49] made it back to town.

It was reported that the Skalat transport had stopped in Lwow, where the Germans performed a selection. Two hundred young men and women were sent, as laborers, to the Lwow forced-labor, extermination camp on Janowska Road. All the others were ordered to undress (to keep them from escaping) and taken in sealed boxcars to Belzec, the notorious extermination camp for Galician Jews.

At that time, I myself was in the Lwow Ghetto. By 12 December 1942, when I was dragged to the Janowska Camp, I found two of my townsfolk still there: Mordechai Tennenbaum and Yekele Berger. They told me that all the others from Skalat had perished during the "cleansing" that Wilhaus had

[Page 28]

conducted there. The "cleansings" were carried out via the so-called 'death races' which were marches around the large mustering square. The Jewish inmates were forced to run around the square at top speed. Whoever tripped or fell behind was dragged aside by the SS-men and, in camp terminology, were used as "fuel" for the crematory ovens in Belzec. These selections took place every few weeks. At times the Germans would vary the game by shooting into the running crowd. Scores would drop like flies. For the Germans this was a favorite diversion.

And that was the sum total of the "Wild Action" in Skalat, and its 3,153 victims. But this was not yet the end of the near-Biblical punishment awaiting Skalat.

[Page 29]

12. N.Z.L. (NIZL)

"NIZL" is not a mystical or symbolic designation, although in Ashkenazic Hebrew it means 'rescue.' In our town, the letters were the initials of Nirler, Zimrner, and Lempert, who were the pillars of the Skalat *Judenrat*. They thought of themselves as the protectors or saviors of the Jews and, indeed, their intimates and friends considered them their 'guardian angels.' It was the general population who began calling the *Judenrat* "NIZL," which, for some indicated wishful thinking, for a few hope, but for most irony, disappointment and distrust.

While the Jewish population of Skalat was still in shock from the "Wild Action," the *Kripo*[50] wandered among the empty Jewish homes, collecting all the household items, such as furniture clothing and valuables, to be sorted in the huge warehouses that formerly belonged to Bishel & Co., the egg export firm. The *Judenrat* was required to provide dozens of workers daily to sort these belongings of the deported Jewish families. Furniture overflowed the warehouses and was piled up outdoors, where it was exposed to the elements for a long time.

A few days after the "Wild Action," on 25 October 1942, the Tarnopol Gestapo ordered the Skalat town commissioner Ellenburg to reduce, immediately, the area of the ghetto and the *Judenrat* were required to participate in tightening the ring. More than three thousand Jews were compressed into a small area of the town. The Jewish Ordinungsdienst maintained regular patrols around the perimeter of the Jewish section, since crossing the line was punishable by death. Similarly, non-Jews were forbidden to enter the ghetto. Despite these restrictions, village peasants sneaked in to sell their wares at greatly inflated prices. The *Judenrat* and the Jewish police were exempt from these laws and were permitted to move freely. Some of them even lived outside of the ghetto. The NIZL's work fell into a routine. They were doing business and generally leading an easier life than their brothers in the ghetto. No one in their families had yet perished. During that difficult time, living was far easier for those who could lay claim to privilege and/or authority. Characteristic of this situation was the ditty that children would chant about a *Judenrat* member, Leibisz Degen, who lived a relatively normal existence with his family, was assured an income and, so far, suffered no hardships. A pious soul and not a mean person, and although a *Judenrat* member, no victims suffered at his hands. He kept repeating his simple, innocent refrain: "Dear God, as long as it doesn't get worse!" The children would chase after him through the street, chanting in a mixture of Polish and Yiddish: "Leibisz Degen cries loud and far Let things stay at least as they are!" How much tragedy and irony is reflected in that bit of doggerel!

The Skalat Jews were painfully aware of their danger. They felt themselves caught in a prison from which there was no escape. Day and night people were obsessed with one concern: where to find a secure bunker. And, indeed, they spent their nights building new hiding places, new mouse-holes. A few of the better off Jews paid fortunes for arrangements to hide with Christian families in town or in the villages.

Jews lived in constant terror. Fear of new slaughters denied them rest. Crowding, poor sanitation and sewage led to outbreaks of typhus, grippe, diphtheria and other previously rare diseases. The mortality rate kept rising. Rumors about forthcoming **'actions,'** abounded. The German town commissioner was alleged to have declared that Skalat must be made as *Judenrein* as all the neighboring towns and villages and that Jews would not be allowed to live because they had been declared "war criminals". It was said that only young, Jewish people, capable of work and confined to forced-labor camps, would be permitted to exist.

All of these second-hand reports produced confusion and increased panic. The *Judenrat*s demanded bigger and bigger payments from the Jewish population to cover the communal needs, and especially the bribes for the Germans, the Ukrainians and the *Kripo*. The NIZL traveled regularly to Tarnopol to see what they could learn from their contact man. Each time, though, they returned disappointed and still more confused - not knowing what to do. They had finally become convinced of the Germans' deceitful ways and also realized that there would soon be an end to keeping their own heads above water. At the same time, the *Judenrat* was required to provide contingents of laborers for the surrounding camps in: Borki- Wielkie, Romanovka, Stupka, Kamionka, etc., under the command of *Obersturmbannfuhrer*[51] Rebel. By then the camps were filled with thousands of Jews and Russian POWs, who were dying from exhaustion, hunger and thirst, as well as the blows and beatings of the Germans. While there were no crematoria in those camps, the living conditions were not different from those in the more infamous death camps. Here the SS-men brought on death by shooting, hanging and torture. The most one could hope to survive was around three months. The unremitting drain of people resulted in the constant demand for replacements, which the *Judenrat*s were required to supply on schedule.

[Page 30]

Again the Jews had to hide to avoid capture for the camps. The NIZL demanded large sums to ransom people and often those ransomed were replaced by the poor. There even were cases when the NIZL captured elderly, well-to-do people as a way to extort money from them. This was how they captured my own sickly 62 year old father for the Kamionka Camp. My mother, who survived, reports:

"I went to Nirler and to Eliezer Schoenberg to get them to release my husband. There I was beaten mercilessly and left lying on the ground for over an hour, bloody and unconscious. Eight days later, through great effort, influence and the payment of 15,000 *zlotys*, I was able to ransom my husband – exhausted and broken - out of the Kamionka Camp."

This was the situation in the *shtetl* before the "Little Action," which took place twenty days after the "Wild Action."

[Page 31]

13. The Little Action

Because the '**action**' of 9 November 1942 was more limited in scope than the earlier '**action**,' claiming only 1, 100 victims, it came to be known as the "Little Action."

Once again, unbelievable though it may now seem, there had been predictions of a miraculous salvation, over the previous two weeks. Mordechai Melamed, in a dream, saw his grandfather (peace to his soul) dressed in a festive white robe and wearing his *talis*[52] and *tefillin*.[53] His grandfather told him to prepare a celebration because on the 29th day of Heshvan, the Jews would be rescued! Salvation was at hand! Mordechai Melamed, a poor man all of his life, sold his last shirt, bought honey cake and liquor, had his wife prepare a Sabbath-*kugel*[54]and invited all the neighbors to share the bounty and the blessings. He was overjoyed to be the harbinger of the salvation that was to come soon.

But 29 *Heshvan* 5703 was the day of the "Little Action," in which Mordechai Melamed and his family were among the victims. At dawn on 9 November 1942 the *shtetl* was surrounded by troops of the Tarnopol SS-men, under the command of Reinisch. They proceeded with their task in the manner now familiar from the earlier '**action**.' Again they were joined in the '**action**' by the Ukrainian militia and the Polish-Ukrainian *Kripo*, as well as the Jewish police. The *Judenrat* still had enough influence to be able to rescue some relatives and close friends.

The raids lasted until noon when Reinisch realized that the *shul*, again the collection-point for the victims, was jammed with more than the assigned quota of 1,000 Jews. He selected 100 young and strong looking victims and had them shipped to the Hluboczek Concentration Camp, from which none returned.

The SS troops, their Ukrainian collaborators and the Jewish police stood around the *shul*, awaiting further orders. At 12:30 five large trucks from the Otto Heil company drew up. The Germans and the Ukrainians lined a path, forming a gauntlet from the door of the synagogue to the trucks, through which Jewish police would lead groups of twenty victims at a time. On their way through this gauntlet, the victims were brutally beaten, especially the aged and the women, who could not climb quickly enough aboard the high tailgates. Such savage beatings were supposed to facilitate the cramming of one hundred people, like sardines, into each truck. Five trucks, fully packed with screaming and sobbing people, soon departed for Tarnopol. Two hours later the empty trucks returned for the remaining victims. At the Tarnopol railway station, all of the captives were ordered to sit in the snow and anyone who stood up or moved was shot. Many among them, shivering from the cold, were only half-dressed or still in their nightclothes.

On that same day, there were '**actions**,' in Tarnopol itself, as well as in Zbaraz. Newly-caught victims were constantly being added to the crowd. Some 5,000 people had been brought to the railway station from all those places. Railroad cars were drawn up to load and take the Jews away. The assembly point was surrounded by SS-men, *Schupo, Kripo* and the Ukrainian auxiliary police -all gathered to herd the collected "cattle," as they described their Jewish victims. Some "kindhearted" SS-men, who could not stand the sight of tiny children shivering in the cold or huddling on the ground, nor the sound of their crying, would grab the little creatures in one hand and shoot them. They then threw the bleeding corpse aside, like a slaughtered bird.

Soon the loading of the assembled human mass began. Some SS-men drove the crowd into the open freight cars while other SS-men selected able-bodied men from the crowd and held them aside, although many of those selected did not want to part from their families. Tragic scenes occurred: hesitations, tears and mournful farewells. German whips or bullets quickly put an end to such tenderness cutting short their final leave-taking. Some young men left the assembly place of the "lucky ones" at the last moment and joined their families in the freight cars. Of the two hundred people who were picked, half were assigned to the concentration camp in Hluboczek, and the rest to Kazimirowka, near Zborow. Among those selected were a score of Jews from Skalat, in addition to the one hundred youths who had previously been selected in Skalat for the Hluboczek Camp.

[Page 32]

The entire trainload, including the Skalat Jews, went directly from Tarnopol to Belzec, the infamous extermination camp. During the trip from Skalat to Tarnopol and then the train ride to Belzec, several dozen Jews managed to leap free, but only a few lived to return to Skalat.

On the day after the "Little Action," just as after the "Wild Action," people remained in their hiding places, afraid to come out. Dead bodies were scattered in several places, many of them children who had tried to jump from windows and were shot like birds in flight. The brutalities during this **'action'** were much the same as those of the previous **'action,'** only the tempo was faster, allowing completion by noon. Again, the members of the *Judenrat* were not touched. They lived in a separate block, which the Germans bypassed in exchange for substantial bribes. A large group of victims of the "Little Action," about 25 percent, were children, a significant portion of the adult population having been taken earlier in the "Wild Action." Most of the young people had already been shipped to the camps around Skalat.

Again the survivors in the *shtetl* were left dazed: many found themselves alone, having lost their families. These people now preferred to be in the camps where they hoped to survive longer, and began to volunteer for 'deportation'. The *Judenrat* took advantage of this, demanding high fees for the privilege of going to one camp or another. In addition, there was a rumor that the situation had improved in the Kamionka   Camp   where   the *Judenrat* was   said   to   have bribed *Obersturmbannfuhrer* Rebel to ease somewhat the torturing of Jews. They supposedly also negotiated with him to establish a camp in Skalat itself, so that they might remain in town in the event the ghetto was to be fully liquidated.

A German officer, one *Hauptsturmfuhrer*[55]Bischoff, arrived from Tarnopol to confiscate all the Jewish belongings left after the latest **'action.'** Under his direction, Jews were ordered to gather all the furniture and household goods from the empty Jewish dwellings and bring them to the big warehouses, where they were sorted as before. A few days later it was all carried off to Tarnopol.

With great effort, and a large bribe of gold, the *Judenrat* succeeded in getting *Obersturmbannfuhrer* Rebel to establish the Skalat Camp (described later). His first orders were to establish within the camp a "demolition squad" in order to raze Jewish homes. The lumber and other building materials were to be gathered and made available to the Gentile population. They were to begin with the old Picynia section in the market square, to be followed by all the other Jewish dwellings which, after the **'actions'** and slaughters, now stood empty. Peasants roamed through the Jewish ruins, digging deep into the cellars, in search of legendary Jewish treasures. The City Council obtained official permission from Ellenburg, the German town commissioner, to sell the salvaged building materials, from the demolished Jewish dwellings. The peasants were able to buy these at very low prices, paying from 100 to 200 *zlotys* per house. After making such a purchase, the peasants would methodically take apart the Jewish houses, carrying the materials back to their villages where they would use them for their own construction projects. The very center of the town was leveled and the appearance of Skalat was changed beyond recognition.

[Page 33]

14. Aryan Papers

When talk began to circulate about the complete liquidation of the ghetto and each day Jewish survival became ever more difficult and hopeless, people began to seek new ways to save themselves. They began to focus their attention on "Aryan Papers."

If someone had a "good mug," i.e., a face with non-Semitic features, one could begin to think about trying to pass as an Aryan. Such a possibility was out of the question in a small town where everyone knew everyone else. For that purpose, people traveled to distant cities where, for the most part, they registered as volunteer laborers to Germany. The roles that people were forced to play on the "Aryan" side demanded imagination and ingenuity. Jews were working as German officials and in private institutions. They disguised themselves as priests, beggars, chimney sweeps, city toughs and street cleaners. Women passed primarily as maids and nurses and young girls worked in hospitals, school dormitories and nunneries. Hundreds of nets were constantly being spread by agents, informers or extortionists in efforts to catch these "impostors," and the number of victims turned over to the Germans by these criminals was very large. Nevertheless, a handful managed to pass the stringent ordeal. Someday these experiences will be remembered by weavers of Gothic tales, retelling their suspenseful stories.

In 1942, a dentist named Dr. Jan Slota settled in Skalat. He practiced there and developed a large circle of patients. Some time later, his wife bore a son. As was the custom, the baptism at the church was a major celebration. Eventually, an informant revealed that Dr. Slota was a Jew. His case was first referred to a medical commission, which confirmed that his documents were all in order. He even had a paper attesting that as a result of a venereal disease, he had been circumcised for medical reasons. This did not suffice, however. The suspect was sent to the Gestapo in Tarnopol for a more thorough investigation. He never returned.

His wife, realizing that they had been unmasked, quickly handed her infant over to a Polish woman, paying her a large sum to hide the child while she herself disappeared. Within a few days, the SS-men arrived from Tarnopol to arrest her. Unable to find her, they sealed the dwelling and, within a week, all the contents of the house were confiscated. The whole town buzzed with the tale of the audacious Jew. It was also resented by the Christian woman who was hiding the child. One day she bundled up the child and took it, herself, to the Security Police. "This is a Jewish child," she said. "It was left with me by Dr Slota's wife before she ran away." Security Policeman Paul, appreciating the noble act of the Christian woman, immediately rendered what he deemed a "just decision." He seized the infant by its feet and swung its head against a tree. This barbaric act was apparently unexpected by the God-fearing woman, who began to withdraw quickly. "Come back!" the German called to her. "Take this away...I'm not an undertaker."

The mother of the child wandered about for some time in Tarnopol, amid enemies and false friends, barely avoiding starvation. She only held on to the will to live for the sake of her child. When she learned that her child was no longer alive, she decided to end her own life by identifying and turning herself in to the Gestapo. "You killed my husband...you killed my child...now kill me too." They obliged her.

There was another case in Skalat which caused an uproar. For some time a high German official named Beltzen had lived in town and was the agricultural inspector for the entire region. He had shown great ability in his work, had an outstanding reputation with the authorities, and was in close contact with the higher German civilian, police and military officials. He established a magnificent home and led the life of a prince in the former dwelling of Joel Bauer, one of the nicest Jewish houses in town. He rode to all the farms in a carriage drawn by splendid horses and gave orders to all his subordinates who trembled at his glance.

One day a peasant, who had served with him in the army, recognized Beltzen as a former Polish cavalry officer with the rank of *Rotmistrz*. Suspicions quickly arose that Beltzen might actually be a Jew, and a secret investigation was begun. When the

Security Police arrived to take him to Tarnopol, he welcomed them with whiskey and wine, saying that the weather was cold and the trip back would be colder, so fortification was necessary. The Security Police were fortified and somewhat tipsy. Meanwhile Beltzen harnessed the horses, donned an SS-man's uniform, took his eleven year old son, and fled. They searched for him all over, even posted "Wanted" bulletins - but they never caught him. Beltzen (or rather Benzel, which was his real name) at the time of this writing lives in the British Zone of Germany.

[Page 34]

The German agricultural land commissioner, Hefner, had on his farm in Nowosiolka. a hired hand and the man's son of about seventeen. The farmhand, who was actually a Jew from the Stanislawow area, passed as a Gentile and worked on the farm for some time as a coachman. His work was quite satisfactory .In fact, he was considered to be an exemplary worker who specialized in raising pigs. One day, the peasants noticed that the driver's feet were too pale. They reasoned that a real peasant's feet weren't that pale, therefore he couldn't be a real peasant. Despite those suspicions, however, the peasants did not inform on him. When the Germans started to unmask "suspect Aryans," the Jew began to fear discovery of himself and his son. They both disappeared and no one knows to this day what happened to them.

The former Wagner company in Skalat had long employed a young man from Lwow named Rubel, who was in charge of purchasing clover for the entire region. His real name was Polak. He had converted some years before and was married to a Ukrainian woman. When the Ukrainian police came to arrest him, he fled, but then in his panic, climbed up a tree from which the police shot him down.

A young Jew, apparently from the town of Brody, worked as a bookkeeper in the Skalat division of the MTS shop.[56] He went under the name of Nabodny. The Security Police learned that he was a Jew, but he was lucky. When they came to arrest him, he was away on a business trip. The manager, Federovitch, informed him of the danger and so he escaped certain death. Nothing further is known of his fate.

For a while, the major activity in town among the Jews seemed to revolve around securing "Aryan Papers." Meyer Grinfeld, about whom more will be told later, was very involved in securing such papers. Here is his testimony:

"When the **'actions,'** intensified, it became clear that no one would be saved from death. I then began to think about ways to secure "Aryan Papers" for my wife and for others. Recalling that the files in the Town Hall contained the documents of emigres, I planned ways to get at those documents. I tried to establish contact with various officials, but none of them was bold enough for the task.

Time was growing short, so I decided to get to the files myself. Once inside the Town Hall, I located the documents and it occurred to me then and there that I could provide these papers to others, as well. I packed up original birth certificates, passes, citizenship certificates, etc., and I soon had a package weighing some 20 kilos (44 pounds), which I carried to the window, where I had left a ladder leaning against the building. I peeked out of the window and saw that the ladder was gone! Someone must have spotted it and taken it away.

I cannot describe the terror I felt, but I didn't dwell long on dark thoughts. I tried desperately to find an escape. until suddenly I realized that the guard (who lived near the town prefecture) had gone home. I waited half an hour more, then dropped the package out of the first story window and jumped after it. Fortunately I jumped well.

With the help of Yizkhak Bekman, a draftsman and engraver, we copied various official stamps, removed old photos from the documents, replaced them with new ones, and applied the proper stamps. In that way we set up a factory for false papers. During the course of three months we created papers for over five hundred Jews. They came from Tarnopol,. Czortkow and even from Lwow. They came from all over eastern Poland. With the large volume of work I found it necessary to return to the Town Hall a few more times. Every document required tax stamps from the town government, for which I paid the town official, Czapkowski, 250 *zlotys* each. For my part, I accepted from 500 to 1,000 *zlotys* for a complete set of papers, although in many cases I gave them away free. There were even cases where I bore the travel expenses, too.

[Page 35]

A typical story involved a man named Kowlentz, who came from Katowice, had been living in Skalat and wound up in camp. Kowlentz had managed to escape from camp and make his way to Warsaw. I was asked by Monias to make a pre-war Polish identity document for Kowlentz. He didn't ask for any other documents. Kowlentz needed the document when it was decreed in Poland that every Aryan Polish citizen must carry a "Kennkarte" (identity card), which he now had to obtain. When it came to filling out the forms, and lacking a birth certificate, he made up the first names of his parents on the spot: Joseph and Maria (since pre-war Polish identity documents did not list one's parents' first names). He now sent word to me that he needed a birth certificate with the indicated names shown as father and mother. While waiting, he worried about not getting the certificate and feared that I might be dead or at best that there simply wouldn't be a certificate available with the required names. How great, then, was his joy when he received the birth certificate from me and there, in black and white, were the names of his parents –

Father: Joseph. Mother: Maria. What a miracle!"

[Page 36]

15. Sobbing Graves

There was no end to the devastation. The horror-filled days of the now familiar **'actions,'** and 'deportations' came one after another, with sporadic intervals between them. Each time people were brutally torn from the *shtetl*. At first it wasn't even known where the victims were being taken. The remaining number of Jews in our town dwindled steadily and yet, though the constant fear of death remained with them, those still living continued to believe in some miraculous rescue. Throughout that period, Jews tried to retain hope even when all seemed hopeless. They had faith in the inevitability of a miracle! .

After each **'action'** was over, some of those who survived insisted that the tragedy had been a sacrifice which only God himself could understand and that now something good would have to happen. The arrival of the Messiah, they believed, is connected with suffering and renewal and that he is to come after days of audacity and injustice on Earth. But he is blessed who is sustained in faith and lives to see that blessed day which will come -which must come! It may seem strange and incredible but, as I have indicated earlier, before every slaughter there were dreams being interpreted and prophecies offered which, based on various signs and hints, foretold the exact day of salvation. Paradoxically, those very days turned out to be the days of the greatest **'actions,'** and mass murders. As a result, during that time people used to say to each other: "Wish me anything - except salvation."

The **'action'** of the "Sobbing Graves" about to be recounted also coincided with one of those "days of salvation" that had been predicted for the Jews of our town.

This time it was Berl, the son of Benjamin Wolowycz (the well-known Rabbi and leader of the orthodox Agudat Yisroel party), who had calculated by cabalistic numerology that salvation would come on 2 Nissan 5703. Berl was a dreamy young man of about twenty, who embodied all of the virtues. He was sensitive, a gifted preacher, a master of prayer, of Torah-reading and of shofar-blowing, as well as a profound scholar and a mystic. He was also familiar with the modern sciences, such as mathematics, physics, astronomy and philosophy - a truly outstanding young Jew. During the worst times of the German occupation, when Jews were left moaning and bleeding after each disaster, Berl consoled everyone. Several times he and my father spent hours studying the Torah and the cabala, and every time they found in the Eternal Sources not only consolation but some deeper meanings for our tragic fate.

And now Berl had discovered in the cabala that 2 Nissan would be the great day - the revelation of the Great Secret! Berl's message came as a healing for heavy hearts, a balm on Jewish wounds. The *shtetl* breathed more easily. Hope filled the sorrowful souls and strengthened their spirits. It was no small thing: Berl the Rabbi's son, that great mystic and student of the Torah, had said it himself! And isn't it time that the One On High should show mercy to His Chosen People? Salvation must come!

Incidentally, it was around that time that the Germans were suffering reverses in North Africa and it was also after the battle of Stalingrad. If the Ruler of the Universe were to provide the final push, there would be an end to our suffering! So the Jews waited impatiently, hoping for the coming of the blessed Second day in the month of Nissan. And finally, after much suspense the anticipated spring day arrived: 7 April 1943. The weather was sunny and fair, ideal for the fulfillment of the most beautiful dreams.

Suddenly the air was filled with the sound of gunfire, from afar and nearby. Frightened hearts knew that something terrible was happening. All of the previous slaughters had started in the same way.

On that day the order came down for the final extermination of the remaining Jews. The *shtetl* was to become *Judenrein*. Three trucks, jam-packed with SS-men had arrived from Tarnopol. Again they enlisted the aid of the local German garrison and the Ukrainian police. The *shtetl* was completely surrounded so that no one would escape. The murderers raced fiendishly through the streets and houses, like devils, searching for and dragging out people, pulling them by the hair and shooting at those who ran. Most of the people were too frightened and dazed and did not know where to run. "Come on, hurry or I'll shoot you!" the executioners shouted at their victims. After a half-day's rampage, nearly 700 Jews, men, women and children, were jammed into the *shul*. The building had by now become the usual assembly point during every **'action.'** Among the prey was Berl, the Rabbi's son...

[Page 37]

Some weeks earlier, the Jews in the camp had been ordered to dig three large pits in a field outside the town. They were told that the pits were to serve as depositories for phosphates to be used during the spring planting. It never occurred to any of the Jews that they were digging their own graves. On the contrary, they regarded the project as proof that they would be employed in the coming season, as they had been the year before. Now, though, in the *shul*, they understood the purpose of the pits.

The *shul* was so jammed that it was practically impossible to breathe. Packed as tightly as sardines, they waited in terror. Thoughts of death consumed them. Some recited the Psalms while others chanted confessional prayers. Some sobbed convulsively while others were as silent as stones. The *shul* was as hot as a furnace, sweat poured from everyone. Mouths were dry and tongues were leaden. "God in Heaven: be merciful!" Berl, the Rabbi's son, elbowed his way through the crowd and mounted the pulpit. Pounding for attention, he began to speak. "My masters, this is our Judgment Day. We are about to go to our death - but let us be strong. To die for the Sanctification of the Name is to attain forgiveness. We must not oppose His Judgment..."

He who had prophesied salvation for that very day now consoled the crowd with Holy Words, but he soon broke down. Choking back his tears, his voice grew weaker sounding like the spent murmur of a shofar - until nothing could be understood.

Sudden wild shouts from the Germans electrified the crowd. At the gate, SS-men began the preparations for the final march. Everyone's heart froze. The crowd grew quiet and in the silence that ensued it seemed that one could hear the approaching steps of the Angel of Death. The Germans renewed their shouting: *"Juden raus!*[57] *Juden raus!"* People started pushing toward the exit as though to a rescue, because everyone yearned for a breath of air. Blows from gun-butts and blackjacks rained down on the heads of the condemned.

Once outside, the Jews were lined up in rows of five. Seven carts drew up, carrying the deathly ill patients and the staff from the Jewish hospital. The victims were counted. In the vestibule of the *shul*, there were ten infants lying. The police brought them out to be included in the count. The Gestapo Chief, Herman Muller, said they were not to be counted, they were just to be tossed into the carts among the sick.

Now the column began to move, accompanied by wild shouting. Guarded on all sides by about a hundred Germans and Ukrainians, the procession snaked through the winding, narrow streets of their town, leading to their own Golgotha. Along the way were crowds of bystanders, watching the condemned with glances of questionable pity. Moving as slowly as the very old, barely dragging their feet, the condemned filled with dread, walked mutely in their own funeral procession. Here and there tears fell. The carts loaded with the sick followed in the rear, with the infants sobbing ceaselessly. Shots were fired into the air regularly, warning everyone against attempting to escape.

The column came to a halt before the three open mass pits and the killers began to prepare for the bloody job. The Jews were made to form a square. The infants and the sick were placed to the side, on the ground. The eighteen Jewish policemen were forced to participate in the work, in exchange for a promise that their lives would be spared. .Then came the first command: "Take off all your clothes. Place your clothes in one pile!" The Jewish policemen drove the crowd to undress quickly. Those who resisted were brutally beaten. The ground was soon strewn with torn paper money, ripped up to prevent the bills from falling into the hands of the assassins. The cries of children mingled with the prayer-filled shouts of *"Shmah Yisroel!"*, as ghastly scenes took place, while the murderers wildly shouted "Faster! Faster' Faster!" The mound of clothing grew higher by the minute as men, women and children stood stark naked, shivering in the cold.

[Page 38]

Berl, the Rabbi's son, stubbornly refused to undress. A German struck him several times in the head and he fell to the ground, bleeding. He was then kicked in the belly several times. He managed to stammer out a final *"Shmah Yisroel!"*, groaned and gave up his soul while lying on the pile of bloodied clothes. The Germans kicked the corpse over the edge of the pit from which there soon came the thud of Berl's fallen body. The Rabbi's son had triumphed at the mass graves: he was the first to fall at the hands of the murderers and now lay in his grave dressed in a red shroud. At his breast lay the phylacteries sack from which he never parted.

Janka Margolis, a Jewish beauty, also refused to undress. She was beaten to death but did not yield. The Jewish policeman, Kuba Migden, seeing his wife, child and mother-in-law standing naked and ready for death, voluntarily stood with them although, as a member of the police, he had been promised that he would be spared.

Some individuals, totally naked, fell to their knees before the killers, begging for mercy. Such pleas were answered with kicks to the head. The wealthiest man in Skalat, Joseph Tennenbaum, the landowner of the fields in which the slaughter was about to begin, pushed his way to the senior officer and implored his mercy in exchange for the treasure that he had buried somewhere. He was ready to lead the way to the treasure, when the blow of a gun-butt struck him down dead.

Suddenly the high school teacher, Rozia Pikholtz, began speaking to the naked crowd: "I call on you to maintain your courage: we die today as innocent people..."

"You are not people!" the SS *Sturmfuhrer* interrupted, dealing her a blow across the face. "Now you can go on speaking, you whore!"

The speaker continued, letting her anger at the German murderers and her pain pour out: "Don't think we are not enjoying vengeance...we know that your end is near. Whole forests of gallows await you!" This was more than the German could bear. A bullet pierced the heart of the naked speaker and her body fell to the ground. The crowd envied her the privilege of so painless a death.

Then came the next command. "Faster! Faster! Finish this off! Shoot them in groups of four!" First, over sixty infants and sick people were tossed alive into the pits, from which their cries arose. Ephraim Szpacirer, a policeman, threw his own two children into the pit and then jumped in after them. Then groups of four were lined up at the pits, one behind the other. Three SS-men fired a single pistol shot at each and, regardless of how the bullets struck, the victims were pushed into the grave -many of them still alive. As more bodies fell, the cries from the graves grew louder .

The bloody work went on for two hours without interruption. They sent for a machine gun to speed up the work, because the murderers were anxious to attend the prepared feast. This new murder weapon was equipped with long belts of bullets, and now groups of ten were placed at the edges of the graves to be cut down by the experienced killers, like ripe sheaves before the reaper's scythe. The machine gun spurted fire while the graves spurted fresh, warm blood. The piles of bodies grew larger in each of the graves. Cries of *Shmah Yisroel*! hung over them, mixing with the screams of the half-dead.

During this **'action,'** the Germans had ordered the entire *Judenrat* and their families to report to the *shul* at 1:00 PM. Some members of the Council went into hiding but the rest, particularly the quieter and gentler among them, such as Dr. Izydor Kron, Yosl Loyfer, Nuchym Safir, Leibisz Degen, Yankef Sharf and their families became victims of the **'action.'** They were forced to watch the whole slaughter and then to fill the graves and tramp down the bloody mounds of dirt on top of the still-moving people buried below. Finally they and the Jewish police were also lined up for the firing squad. Once again, horrendous scenes took place. Naked people fell at the feet of the Germans, who knew them, and begged for mercy. The Germans responded with derision and murderous beatings. The same machine gun that had wiped out the mass of Jews also put an end to the lives of the ghetto officials who had believed, right up to the last minute, that they would be spared.

[Page 39]

While the unceasing cries from the graves continued, the Ukrainians filled the third grave with earth. Then the killers fell like locusts upon the clothes: patting every garment, searching and turning out each pocket, looking for "Jewish gold" and other valuables. They finally loaded the clothes into trucks and drove off, leaving a sacrifice of three fresh, heaving graves, that rose and fell like waves. Inside those graves, beneath the mounds of earth, human beings with limbs entangled and not yet dead, were tearing at and biting each other. These victims were being denied their final rest. The graves groaned and sighed. The next day the peasants in the nearby village heard the far-off sounds of human groans and cries. On the third day, passersby again heard the sobbing and were convinced that the sounds came from the humans, not yet fully dead, lying in the poorly covered graves.

A few peasants from the village of Nowosiolka found David Epstein and told him what they had heard and seen at the graves. They had recognized his seventeen year old daughter, whose head had emerged from the earth and was calling for help. People went over there and indeed found David Epstein's daughter alive, as well as two other children who showed signs of life. The children died the next day. The girl, however, survived another week and told what had occurred under the earth: how living people among the corpses had shoved, bitten and clawed at each other. She also described in detail the entire course of the **'action.'**

The sobbing graves are to be found approximately three kilometers outside of Skalat, on the right side of the road leading to the village of Nowosiolka. Some one hundred meters beyond the graves there is a row of tall poplars in the middle of a field. From the distance one can also see a dark stripe, the edge of the Hores Forest, approximately two kilometers away.

And though the sobbing graves have been eternally silenced now, this place and thousands of similar places shall cry out to the end of time in their demand to be heard.

Footnotes:

47 Ober Jude - Chief Jew.

48 Herr Chef - Sir.

49 skotchkes - (Train) leapers (from Polish verb, skakac, to leap). L. Milch

50 *Kripo* - Criminal police, made up of Poles and Ukrainians.

51 *Obersturmbannfuhrer* (Rebel) - In command of all the camps in the Tarnopol region.

52 talis, talaysim - Prayer shawl(s).

53 tefillin - Phylacteries (used in morning prayers).

54 kugel - Pudding.

55 Hauptsturmfuhrer (Bischoff) - In charge of confiscating Jewish properties in Tarnopol.

56 MITS shop - Mashyno Traktonaya Stantziya - Machine and tractor, maintenance and repair shop (Russian). L. Milch

57 "Juden raus!" - "Jews, get out!"

[Page 40]

16. The Rebellious Tombstones

There was a new style of clothing in the villages around Skalat: the black-striped women's skirts sewn from stolen talaysim. The peasant market, however, suffered a shortage in parchment torn from the Scrolls of the Law, which shoemakers had long since learned to convert into lining and padding for boots and shoes. On the other hand, the market square and the streets among the Jewish ruins were littered with heaps of books and pages ripped from Talmuds and prayer books: free for the taking. Earlier, when there had been Jews working for Malecki in the "Raw Material Collection Brigade" which gathered large quantities of Jewish books for sale as scrap paper: they even had some exchange value -eight *groschen*[58] a kilo. But that trade ended after the last slaughter, when there were no Jews left to work at it. The books and torn pages were then used merely for packing materials in local stores, and as toilet paper.

Every Gentile knew by now that the Jews were to be totally exterminated -that no remnant of Judaism would be allowed to survive. It was, therefore, acceptable to destroy Jewish buildings and wipe out Jewish cemeteries. The local population seemed to take to that task with sadistic and vengeful joy. The elimination of the living having almost been accomplished, it was now the turn of the dead.

Gravestones, with their holy letters, torn from cemeteries now appeared as paving stones, scattered over stretches of sidewalks and roads. The anguished cry of the stones fell on deaf ears while the dead in the unmarked graves yearned for their memorials. The peasants stopped their graveyard expeditions only after a fatal accident when a tombstone fell on a grave-robber, killing him instantly. Frightened, they believed that the tombstones were rebelling when being dishonored. They feared that the stony strength and weight of the gravestones would inflict black and blue marks and painful wounds. They believed that the dead were taking vengeance.

Fantastic stories were told about the terrible and wondrous events at the Jewish cemetery. Some told of hearing groans and quiet sobbing coming from the graves while others claimed to have seen blood coming from them. A wall made of stolen tombstones had been set-up around the Town Hall. One morning, several of the stones were found lying on the street. The story quickly spread that corpses came out at night to reclaim their tombstones and, indeed, the wall around the Town Hall did appear to be shrinking steadily. Then the peasants stopped stealing tombstones from the Jewish cemetery.

While this brought peace to the dead, the living Jews felt powerless against the constant danger which they faced. Living in the crowded ghetto like chickens in a coop, they awaited their inevitable deaths. The unsatiated local rabble stared mercilessly across the ghetto at some nine hundred Jews who still drew breath there. In wonder, they shook their heads and said: "Can you believe it? They're slaughtered and slaughtered and still they're here! But you can smell the Angel of Death over there."

[Page 41]

17. The Final Struggle

After each '**action,**' the *shtetl* took on the look of a village fair. Some peasants came to determine the remaining number of living Jews, while others came simply to steal whatever they could from the emptied and not yet demolished homes. In the Pre-Passover '**action**' (April of 1943), many murdered Jews created unintended "beneficiaries" among the hundreds who had undertaken to hide Jewish possessions. Every Jewish death instantly enriched a local "helper."

In those final bloody days, when the last of the last were about to be exterminated, the remaining Jews of Skalat were crowded into thirty small houses. The passageways of streets and alleys were boarded up. The handful of remaining exhausted Jews lived in the most awful congestion and filth, above ground as well as below in bunkers. Every day and every hour of every day the Jews in the *shtetl* lived in mortal fear, anticipating the inevitable liquidation of the ghetto and their deaths.

The population consisted almost entirely of women and children, widows and orphans of previous '**actions.**' A small number of surviving men could be found in the Skalat Camp and in the other camps in the area. In fact, the town of Skalat was to have been declared *Judenfrei*[59] following the mass murder during the "Sobbing

Graves" 'action' in April of 1943. However, since a sufficiently large number had managed to hide, an order came from Tarnopol permitting the surviving Jews to return to the ghetto. Again they were told that they would be permitted to live there peacefully. Most importantly, they were to maintain their strength and sanitation, as they would still be needed as laborers. To encourage them further to believe that they would not be killed, the Tarnopol Gestapo sent down ten Jewish policemen, led by one Aba Tennenbaum, assigned to maintain Law and Order and, at the same time, to serve as tools in the execution of the Germans' plans.

The Jewish police from Tarnopol exerted themselves to instill calm and to persuade the people that as long as *they* were around there would be no new slaughters. This time, however, no one believed them. Every evening, an exodus would begin. As night came on, people sought out lodgings among the Gentiles or crept stealthily into barns and stables to spend the night. At dawn, learning that all was quiet in the town; they would return to the ghetto, only to roam again the next night. Frequently, during those wanderings, the Jews would be robbed and beaten, and the women raped by street toughs and merciless peasant youths.

The ghetto was emptied of many people every night. Those who remained would gasp for breath all night in their underground hideaways, barely surviving until morning, when they would learn that no , 'action' was taking place that day. Then God's creatures would slip back into the ghetto from the fields and other 'secret places' on the other side: their will to live unabated, though their expected life-span was not much longer than a butterfly's. The police searched the empty houses during the nights, taking whatever they liked of the furnishings, and also taking the opportunity to locate and note down suspected hiding places or bunkers.

Generally, the Jewish police from Tarnopol behaved abominably. In addition to maintaining close relations with the officials of the local camp and with the Germans, they engaged in drunken revelry, robbery and rape.

Thus the last of the Skalat Jews lived out the final days of their lives. There is a story from those days of a certain town idiot named Yosele, who had somehow managed to escape the various 'actions.' One day he was seen standing in the empty street sobbing piteously. "Why are you crying, Yosele?" he was asked. "No one throws stones at me. No one chases me. Nobody calls me names," he moaned. Yosele, the idiot, yearned for the 'good old days' when there were Jews alive, when Jewish children would chase him through the streets - their taunts echoing and the stones flying.

[Page 42]

The lives of those miraculously missed during the previous 'actions,' still flickered. But the question remained: how were they to be rescued from the sentence of death?

[Page 43]

18. The Failed Resistance Plan

By May 1943 it was clear that there would be no rescue. The Germans were proceeding with their extermination plans and not a single Jew would be left alive.

In Skalat, the **'actions,'** and pogrom so far had claimed about 6,500 victims, and in the surrounding camps of Borki-Wielkie, Podwolczyska, Romanowka, Stupka and Kamionka several thousand more people suffered behind the barbed wire, plagued by hunger and disease. Even the most determined optimists had lost hope of remaining alive. Life was now reckoned to be a matter of days not weeks. The previous month's **'action,'** the tragedy of the so-called "Sobbing Graves," which had been intended as the final extermination of the local Jews so that the town could be declared *Judenrein*, had not gone entirely according to the German plans. Approximately a thousand Jews had managed to avoid capture. The inventiveness of the Jews in the art of bunker construction had reached a level which made it virtually impossible to discover all the Jewish hideaways and mouse-holes. People strove with their final energies to rescue themselves and stay alive.

The Germans now tried to spread rumors that nothing further would occur. The Red Cross was said to have intervened on behalf of the Jews. America was reported to be exchanging German war prisoners for Jews. Other similar tales were told to create confusion. The real intention of the Germans was to collect and hold together the Jewish remnant so that they could be completely liquidated in the near future. As noted previously, the Germans pretended that they were lightening the Jewish load. "You may live peacefully in your ghetto; we will provide bread and work - just be sure you stay clean and don't get sick so that you can't work..." they would explain to the Jews in a deceitfully friendly tone.

At the same time, a group of brave young people, led by Mechel Glanz, began to prepare for armed resistance against the new **'action.'** Glanz had come from Kopyczince, a strong, dedicated and wise young man of about 26, whose eyes sparkled with bravery and determination. He was soon joined by other young people, including Lonek Pudles, 30, a student of philosophy who had recently come from the Kamionka Camp, Sholem Schechter, 23, Meyer Grinfeld, 35, Bucio Elfenbein, 22, Henek Weinberg, 21, a veterinary student, (the last four from Skalat) and many others. They all attended secret meetings to lay plans for resistance to the next **'action.'** The small group was to have been the core of a broader fighting organization of young people.

In the early days of their activity, Bucio Elfenbein managed to obtain twelve grenades with which the young enthusiasts were as overjoyed as children with new toys. True, the grenades lacked firing pins, but it didn't matter: they began a search for an experienced mechanic to join in their efforts. Mechel Glanz managed to come up with a sum of money to cover the preliminary expenses. Henek Weinberg had established contact with some Gentiles as possible sources for weapons. Meyer

Grinfeld was assigned the task of establishing contact with the remnants of the *Judenrat*, who were still in possession of some communal funds, in order to obtain financial aid. At the outset, the councilmen promised not only funds but active participation. However, nothing ever came of it. Those who had worked for two years in the *Judenrat* could not fathom the lofty idea of resistance. Such people had long since lost their sense of daring, self-respect and honor. How could they now be expected to collaborate in or support an act which, though it could end in death, would be of a great moral achievement? The *Judenrat* members, as expected, did nothing to help in the daring enterprise. On the contrary, they considered it foolhardy: "Your work is doomed to fail before you begin. With whose help do you plan to wage war? With women? With a few broken Jews?"

The brave young people were not discouraged by such talk and continued their work in secret. They now owned some arms which lifted their morale. Meyer Grinfeld had established contact with a few small groups of Jews who had escaped from the ghetto and now lived in the forest. Henek Weinberg had contact with a certain Dymkowski, regarding help from the Poles. However it was soon apparent that Dymkowski was a charlatan and a con-man who merely wanted to cheat them out of their money. Further dealings with him would have certainly led to betrayal and only in the last moment were they able to shake free of him. They continued their search for a non-Jewish underground movement with which they could join to plan a common approach to resistance. It turned out, however, that no such movement was to be found in the Tarnopol area. The Gentiles were not condemned to death, lived under relatively normal conditions and therefore had many opportunities for sabotage. Instead, they fearfully and abjectly danced to the tune of the German oppressors and endured their persecutions.

[Page 44]

Considering the hopeless status of the surviving remnants of the Jews, the mere thought of armed resistance provided solace. Though it would certainly end in death, their suffering would yet make some sense. Such an act, however, required at least a minimum amount of military training, and therefore the resistance group worked feverishly preparing whatever was possible. Unfortunately, the *Kripo* learned of the resistance preparations and it is quite possible that this led the Germans to hasten their plans for the final extermination in Skalat, which took place on 9 June 1943. The carefully woven dream of active resistance was suddenly torn asunder. Being unprepared, with only a pair of pistols and twelve grenades without firing pins, there could be no possibility of armed resistance. Some days before the liquidation **'action'** someone had informed on Lonek Pudles, the escapee from the Kamionka Camp. He was arrested and returned there, where he died in the liquidation of the camp. Thus an important member was missing at the time the resistance might have occurred.

The tragic day of the "Shavuot Action" (to be described in the next chapter) actually led to the liquidation of the ghetto and to the complete extermination of the Jewish community of Skalat. Small remnants escaped to the woods or hid with peasants, who were well paid.

After the town was declared *Judenrein*, only the Skalat Camp remained in existence where some four hundred people worked at the time. Now the idea of resistance took root there, where several young people were working toward that aim. A few weeks later, when the Soviet partisans invaded the town, these people found the ideal opportunity to join up with them. Almost all of the Jews in camp were eager to join the partisans, but the latter refused to take all of them along.

After much effort only a chosen few were allowed to join the partisan force, which proceeded through the Polish forests. Some former initiators of the resistance plan - such as Mechel Glanz, Shechter, Elfenbein, Katz, Miss Hinda Kornweiz, and a few others - had the good fortune to find themselves among the ranks of the heroic fighters under the command of the famous Soviet General, Kolpak.

But more about this in a later chapter.

[Page 45]

19. The Shavuot Action

The decisive final **'action'** was in progress. The "Judenfrei Action" occurred during the holiday of *Shavuot*[60] 9 June 1943 (6 Sivan 5703).

The Germans already knew that the Jews would leave the ghetto at night and return in the early morning when they saw that all was calm. This time, therefore, the Tarnopol SS-men arrived at 9:00 AM and caught all the Jews in the ghetto. The catastrophe arrived unexpectedly. The German wiliness was completely successful and gave them a big advantage. Participating in the **'action'** in addition to the SS-men, the *Schupo*, *Kripo* and the Ukrainian militia, were the Jewish policemen from Tarnopol who even assisted in exposing the bunkers. With great brutality, the bloody job was completed at a rapid pace. By noon some six hundred Jews were assembled in the marketplace. From there they were quickly led to the field, the site of the mass graves of the Pre-Passover **'action.'** There they were forced to undress and then were mowed down by machine gun. From those assembled, the SS-man, Leks, had selected more than twenty younger people and had them transported to the Skalat Camp, along with the clothes of the dead victims. As the Germans drove away from the execution site they sang and shouted: "Long live the town without Jews!"

Now the *shtetl* was completely emptied of Jews. The village peasants descended on the abandoned houses to steal the last domestic items. The Jews who had managed to hide at the last moment, in bunkers or in the fields, were rounded up by the peasants and all of these, some 120 in number, were handed over to the *Schupo*. Since this took place during the Christian celebration of Pentecost, the captives were jailed until after the holiday, then they were taken to the same mass grave site and slaughtered like the earlier victims.

After this "final Jewish extermination," Skalat was officially declared to be *Judenrein*. Thereafter, if a Jew was caught, the *Schupo* shot him on the spot. There were many such cases. Reward posters offered a liter of liquor and 300 *zlotys* for each Jew turned in, dead or alive. Hardly a day went by without some merciless person collecting the prize.

A few days after the liquidation of the ghetto, the Germans also liquidated all the camps surrounding Skalat. Only the Skalat Camp itself was permitted to exist for another couple of weeks.

Yankif Perlmutter, a former prisoner in the Skalat Camp, who witnessed the liquidation of the ghetto Jews and who buried the victims, provides the following testimony:

"The *Judenrat* knew the exact time of the planned **'action,'** therefore they and their families went into hiding. At about 9:00 AM the Tarnopol SS-men, Ukrainians, *Schupo* and *Kripo* surrounded the ghetto. Almost all of the Jews were exposed. The SS-men leaped out of two buses and opened fire. Jews began to dash about in panic, but many were killed. Among the first to die was Aaron Friedman.

I was then a prisoner in the Skalat Camp to which Hermann Muller came and ordered a squad of people to dig a pit in the field. They chose 21 men, myself among them. Frightened, we were marched off by Muller. All along the way he kept repeating the words: 'Do not fear: nothing will happen to you if you work well.'

At the field he indicated a spot, an area ten meters long by five meters wide, and told us to dig a hole three meters deep. Then he left us. He returned a half hour later with Hefner, with whom he was conversing intimately. He called out to us, holding his watch, 'You must be finished in two hours!'

At noon he drove off toward the town. The Germans remaining with us beat us unrelentingly as we worked. Later some fifteen more Jews were brought from town to help in the digging - my brother Mendl among them. The Germans beat the new recruits even more severely. If someone's work didn't please them they would shout: 'Lie down, you!' Then there would be a shot and that person would not rise again.

[Page 46]

Muller returned from the town and, seeing that we were not yet finished, grew very angry but granted us one more hour. Soaked in sweat, we worked with all the strength we had left, while the soldiers shouted wildly and subjected us to brutal torture.

From afar we saw the Jews being led from the town. When the column was thirty meters away, we were ordered out of the pit. The next moments were filled with the terror of impending death. At the last minute, I gave to one of the, captured Jews,

Magus Rothstein, a yellow armband, (camp prisoners who were not yet marked for death wore such armbands) and he quickly joined the group of camp Jews. Earlier my brother had been beaten by the Germans and now refused the yellow band. He thus remained among the doomed ghetto Jews. There was no time for discussions and persuasions, and I was unable to rescue my brother.

The leaders of the slaughter appeared: Muller and Leks, together with many soldiers in SS uniforms, the Ukrainian militia and all the local German civilian officials. We were led about fifteen meters away, ordered to lie face down on the ground, and told not to move under pain of death. None of us expected to leave there alive.

We heard children crying and women shrieking. The Jews were being brutally beaten as they were forced to undress. We felt rather than saw each group as it was led to the edge of the pit, then heard the firing and the sound of the Germans cheering and singing the *Horst Wessel Song*.[61] We heard the sound of laughter and the clinking of glasses as the murderers drank toasts. Cheers were repeated after each round of shots. Terrible shrieks could be heard from the mass grave and we clearly knew that living bodies were still thrashing about.

After finishing their work, which lasted two hours, the murderers ordered us to stand up. Approaching the grave, we saw a terrible scene. We were ordered to layout in rows the chaotically-scattered bodies, many of whom were still alive. The SS-men drove off, leaving only the local police, such as Schneider, Marold, Paul, etc., to supervise our work. We pointed out people who were still alive and gasping for breath. In each instance the Germans administered a *coup de grace*, by firing into the grave.

Before we covered the grave, some sixty additional bodies were brought from town. They were tossed into the grave in their clothes. We buried our brothers and stamped down the mound of earth that was soaked in blood. 'Neatly, elegantly done,' the security policemen proclaimed - 'but the pyramid must be symmetrical!'

While the Germans busied themselves searching the clothing of the dead, I said the Kaddish prayer. Some among us took clothes for ourselves from the pile. I recognized my brother Mendl's clothes.

'Calm down, Jews,' the Germans reassured us, 'the same thing will happen to you soon enough!'

We loaded the clothes onto cars and rode back to camp."

[Page 47]

20. The Origins of the Skalat Camp[62]

Following the "Little Action" of November, 1942, the *Judenrat* realized that it stood on shaky ground. Its members saw that the German murder machine was following a calculated plan. "You will be the last" was the familiar message to those Jews who proved themselves useful in their efforts on behalf of the German extermination project. Sooner or later, it was felt, no one would emerge from the cutthroats' hands.

As ghettos everywhere were being liquidated and cities and towns were being declared *Judenrein,* there was only one place where one could hope to hold on to life a little longer: a concentration or labor camp. This, at least, was the recommendation of the German "friends" to their trusted co-workers. For that reason the *Judenrat* leaders commenced an intensive campaign for the establishment of a camp in Skalat.

In the existing camps around Skalat, such as Borki-Wielkie, Romanowka, Kamionka and Stopki, conditions were unbearable. There, back-breaking work, starvation and death were daily occurrences. The *Judenrat* members strove unceasingly to gain approval for a camp in Skalat, where conditions might be bearable and where they, the leaders, would be rescued when the ghetto was finally liquidated. They bribed German officials from the Otto Heil Co. to intervene in the matter. *Obersturmbannfuhrer* Rebel, then in command of all the camps around Skalat, gave his approval in exchange for a fortune in cash. At a designated time, the Skalat Camp was established as a branch of the Kamionka Camp under Rebel's direction. The *Judenrat,* still officially in office, used all of its influence to carry out the plan as quickly as possible. They called public meetings where *Judenrat* members delivered speeches about the 'vital need , for the enterprise which would allegedly rescue many Jewish lives from the German death sentence. The Jewish populace regarded the matter skeptically, seeing it merely as a precursor to new evil edicts, new troubles.

Only a handful reported voluntarily to the new Skalat Camp, so the *Judenrat* reverted to its old methods of force. The Jewish police were ordered to seize those whom the *Judenrat* had selected for the camp. On the first day they were able to collect approximately seventy younger men. Older people were collected on the following day. People tried to hide in various places and many Jews who wanted to avoid imprisonment in the Skalat Camp sought employment in the surrounding villages, but the *Judenrat* sent its minions there as well. Relatives and/or close friends of the *Judenrat* leadership were spared actual imprisonment in the camp: their names were merely carried on the camp's roster, while they continued to live at home. There were others who still had enough funds to buy their way out or to be replaced by poorer Jews. Young Jewish people tried to hide to avoid the widespread nets of the catchers. They were not always successful since the leadership kept count and knew everyone who would not submit to them.

The former camp inmate Nissen Klein of Mikulince provides the following testimony:

"I was present when Nirler said to one of his police people: 'Eisenstark and Feinstein must be turned in, dead or alive, otherwise bring in their families.'

The policeman drags in Eisenstark's mother and sister. The two women are pale and frightened. Nirler stands, holding his riding crop, staring sharply at them, and asks the mother quietly, but with a tone of command: 'Where have you hidden your son?'

'I don't know,' the old woman replies in a tremulous voice. 'How should I know?'

'Will you turn in your hidden son or not?' She doesn't answer. Nirler approaches her and delivers a resounding slap on the face. The old woman cries out and her eyes redden with tears. Nirler asks again, more forcefully: 'Will you turn in your son or not?'

[Page 48]

The mother chokes back her tears but cannot speak. The savage punches her and the old woman falls to the floor in a faint. Now he begins to shout ferociously: 'Will you turn in your son?!'

He shakes his victim until she revives, stands up and begins to sob: 'Where can I find him? Even if I knew where he was...'

The enraged Nirler assaults her again with his fists and his feet, using the riding crop with sadistic savagery, beating his victim to the floor again. The old woman gathered all her strength, stood up and began to scream: 'You inhuman murderer! You outcast! You're worse than the Germans! You suck the blood from us!...Wait: your living flesh will fall from your bones someday!'

At this, Nirler's savagery reached its peak. She had besmirched his honor. He fell upon her like a wild beast and beat her until she lost consciousness. Bystanders who saw this event trembled with rage: their blood boiling. But no one dared to speak out, fearing the brute - the lord over life and death.

His anger subsided, Nirler calms down somewhat. In the controlled voice of command he calls out: 'Friedlander, come here! Cut off this woman's hair and put her in jail.'

The policeman-cum-barber came in quickly, lifted the unconscious woman onto a chair and carried out the order.

The same procedure was performed on the sister of the fugitive Eisenstark, and both women were put into the cellar, which served as the camp jail. The women were tormented for three days. When it finally became apparent that they really did not know the whereabouts of their son and brother, they were released, bruised and with their heads shaved bare."

*****

The Skalat Camp was opened on 11 November 1942. Within a month it held over three hundred inmates, including about fifty lonely women, most of whom were from outside Skalat: the severed branches of destroyed families. The camp building was the distillery, which included many storage depots and offices. Work scheduling and the establishment of camp routine and discipline went forward at full speed.

Several workshops were set up, all laboring exclusively for the Germans. The *Obersturmbannfuhrer* had assigned a certain Jew, Heniek Zukerman, formerly the *Kommandant* of the Kamionka Camp, to organize the Skalat installation. He was considered a specialist in camp matters and was ordered to set up the Skalat Camp on the model of Kamionka. This talented fellow, based on his previous experiences, was able to establish a truly 'model camp' with a regime that could bear comparison to other camps in the area. To begin, he separated the camp Jews into sections and brigades. Those who were stronger and healthier were assigned to hard labor in the quarry at Nowosiolka, to be used for the benefit of the Otto Heil firm. Some were assigned to other physically demanding jobs. The weakest were assigned to a separate group, which he called the "Shit Brigade." This brigade was made up of the so called *Kalibrakli*[63] - people broken in body and spirit. They were mostly occupied by such maintenance tasks as carrying water, chopping wood, sweeping, hauling garbage, cleaning privies and peeling potatoes in the kitchen. The women worked in the laundry and in the kitchen.

The actual work during the twelve-hour day was not as awful and unbearable as the "camp discipline" and the attitudes of the officials. All inmates were awakened at 4:00 AM for daily roll-call.

[Page 49]

Regardless of rain, cold or frost, all brigades were required to line up and wait for the camp-elder, Zukerman, to emerge in pajamas, carrying his riding crop, to receive the reports of the brigade and group leaders. "*Achtung!*[64]*Achtung!* Hats off" -went the daily refrain in what was called the *Apel Platz,*[65]accompanied by daily scenes of violence against the camp Jews.

Here the orders were given and the slave-workers were sorted for work. Then from here the various labor brigades marched off to their assigned workstations. Although the camp was directed by Jews themselves, all went in a similar fashion as in other concentration camps: conducted with the precision and savagery prevalent in concentration camps.

One specific case at a typical roll-call will serve to show the cruelty with which the camp leaders treated their own brothers. One day the camp leader, Zukerman, chose some of the stronger inmates for the heavy labor at the quarry. Among them was Saul Friedman, the shoemaker, a man of about 56. He asked to be excused because of his age and weakness, begging to be assigned, instead, to the 'Shit Brigade.' "What audacity!" Zukerman shouted in Polish, the official language of the camp, and began to hit the man mercilessly until he fell to the ground in a pool of blood. After the beating, Shol-the-cobbler was truly incapable of heavy labor and was detailed, as a cripple, to peeling potatoes in the kitchen.

Zukerman soon chose as his assistant Bumek Rus, a former law student, and previously a member of the Grzimalow *Judenrat*, whose behavior filled with terror all the Jews who came into contact with him. A month after Zukerman had successfully established the camp, he was ordered by the central camp authorities in Kamionka to organize a similar labor camp in Podwoloczyska, and Rus took over command of the Skalat Camp. *Obersturmbannfuhrer* Rebel, or his aide, Sharfuhrer Maler, would come by every few days to make sure that all was in order. They would conduct careful examinations of the inmates, creating mortal fear among them, and providing them with random beatings for no apparent reason. The Germans would shout insults and curse wildly, while issuing commands which the Jewish *Kommandant*s would accept servilely, intoning the obedient compliance: *"Befehl*[66] *Herr Obersturmbannfuhrer!"*

Camp visits by Germans were usually the occasion for a lavish reception where pastries and beverages were served and where eggnog and wine flowed like water. The Skalat *Schupo* rarely ever missed these celebrations. Often they would go on until late at night, ending with female entertainment provided by the camp management. The Germans would leave, carrying away expensive gifts, cheered in spirit and with favorable opinions of their loyal servants.

The severe (1942) winter weather made life in the camp very difficult, though close contact was maintained with the broken-up families remaining in the ghetto. At that time a relative or friend would help the inmates with some food or warm garments as they passed through the town on their way to work. Soon, however, things became much worse.

[Page 50]

21. The Camp People

Life in the Skalat Camp was moving towards extermination. As in all concentration camps, after several weeks people were hardly recognizable: spiritually broken and physically exhausted, with no will or reason to live. The fetid camp atmosphere eroded one's humanity and people's behavior at times was wild, almost beastly. After their awful experiences: the **'actions,'** the slaughters, the ghetto and the constant fear of death, they were now forced to wear the camp clothes with numbers and yellow badges, while being fed a diet almost totally devoid of nutrition, and to have a decent meal was the dream of every camp Jew. To avoid a beating was to experience a miracle. The camp inmates were in a constant struggle between opposing forces: fear and hope, apathy and strength, powerlessness and a desire for vengeance. They also experienced profound pessimism and a strong desire to survive. All of these contrasts commingled and affected their emotional balance. Often, this inner turmoil resulted in fatalistic approaches toward vital matters, indifference toward one's surroundings and obliviousness toward their common fate. Thoughts and concerns about the future did not go beyond the next day. Further plans were beyond the realm of possibility. The mere thought of what would happen after tomorrow was terrifying. Yet, such evil visions were driven off with all the strength at their command.

At the same time, there was a noteworthy phenomenon among the Jews under German rule, both in general and particularly within the concentration camps, where, despite all their bodily and mental suffering, some sick people actually recovered suddenly. What secret power might have blown the breath of life back into those shriveled limbs? Would it have been possible, under normal circumstances, for bodies and souls to withstand such trials? Typhus victims with raging fevers were known to work and survive. Badly clothed and shod, Jews managed to live through floods and bitter cold. Perhaps someday science will be able to explain the puzzle of this biological anomaly.

Inmates in the camps were not regarded as human. The camp population was considered a sort of imprisoned band of criminal slaves who had been condemned to death. For the sake of a few extra weeks or months of life, they would give up their humanity. The camp people were considered creatures without feelings, without will and without reason. Anyone who wished could beat and belittle them, while they were forbidden even to react. They were forced to endure both spiritual and physical pain with superhuman patience. Camp people regarded their own personal tragedies coldly: their pain had hardened them and left them with obdurate hearts. They could witness bloody and horrible scenes while chewing their bread. They learned of the deaths of close relatives and friends thinking resignedly the *same fate awaits me, too -sooner or later*. Their tear ducts had long since dried up.

In the camps, the population was separated into two groups: the oppressors and the oppressed. The first included the camp leaders, the brigade leaders and other oppressors. In other camps, membership in that 'upper stratum' was the privilege of the Gentiles: either of the SS-men or of Gentile inmates. In the case of the Skalat Camp, the conditions were different. All of the authorities here were Jewish. The SS-men, as indicated, only came to check up every few days. That was sufficient, however, to last until the next visit.

The authorities of the Skalat Camp earned their infamy by the brutality toward their own brothers. Here, most of the people in the upper stratum came from the corrupt *Judenrat*, which the German machine had converted into an institution of demoralization and betrayal. Within the framework of a locked labor camp, they had a fruitful ground for their vile and beastly acts. They became appropriate tools in the hands of the Germans for the execution of their plans and wishes. Robbery, extortion and womanizing made up their days. Usually drunk, or exhausted by their carousing, as well as tense, unruly and violent, they brandished whips over the heads and backs of fellow Jews, while berating and cursing them. The clothing of the camp official gave him the appearance of an underworld dandy or pimp: grey-green riding breeches, shiny black new-looking boots, a brown leather jacket with a stiff collar, like that of a *boulevardier*, smelling of *eau de cologne*, with a cigarette between his lips. The camp people trembled in fear before such 'big shots. 'In their after-hours, they ate and drank the best available. They would stay up to all hours, often until dawn, playing cards and drinking. Money had lost all value to them. They used bank notes to light their cigarettes and the amounts they wagered were staggering. They obtained sexual favors from the women and girls in the camp, who were terrorized into acceding to the slightest whim of these rulers. All the authorities lived in the camp building, together with the inmates, and it was under the same roof that the orgies and festivities took place.

[Page 51]

The administrators and oppressors of the camp were a specific type of person. If everything was lost, then one should savor that which life yet had to offer. Trapped in a diabolic snare, one could live befitting the devil; beyond the corpses, beyond the abyss of sin and crime, beyond filth and self-loathing. They eked out the last bit of life, even at the cost of other lives. "A few Jews will have the right to remain alive under Hitler and I intend to be one of them," *Kommandant* Rus would say - and he did survive.

After the "Sobbing Graves" **'action,'** the entire *Judenrat* fell apart. The main leaders, Nirler, Zimmer, Lempert and Schoenberg, had managed to escape along with their families. All of them were now in the camp, from which they continued to direct the lives of the last remnants of the hopeless Jews who still wandered among the ruins of the ghetto. This handful of Jews knew quite well that the end was near and inevitable. It seemed to them that now the danger of death would be less in the camp, therefore everyone strived to get into the camp. This privilege came at a high price. The camp management explained that the money was needed to bribe the Gestapo. Actually, most of the money disappeared into the deep pockets of the camp officials. The corrupt life of the camp gentry grew ever more expensive. Those Jews who had no money were not accepted into the camp. It was ironic that while previously people had to pay to be saved from the camp, now they had to pay to be admitted.

In this way, the camp population grew by a few dozen, including women and children. These dealings for places in the 'Life Saving Skalat Camp' went on until the final liquidation of the ghetto. With the liquidation of the ghetto, there was no longer a *Judenrat* .

Nirler, having lost his kingdom now became the 'prime minister' to the camp-leader, Rus. Now it was Nirler who, every morning at 5:00, would call the roll of the inmates. He too, like his superior, was dressed in pajamas and carried a riding crop. In so brief a time, he managed to create around himself an aura of fear and 'respect.' All who entered the camp office had to stand and take off their caps If some newcomer failed to follow this custom, even if out of ignorance, he was brutally beaten and confined for several days. Other former leaders of the ghetto (Zimmer, Lempert, Schoenberg, Dr. Brif, etc.) gained infamy by their evil acts. They took charge of the work details and, following the German example, lorded over everyone. Decency and justice simply did not exist for them, even with reference to former friends and acquaintances. The Jewish ghetto police, which had been transferred to the service of the camp authorities, also wrote a bloody page in the painful history of the Skalat Camp.

There were, however, exceptions. As reported earlier, the policeman Shikale-ganif, known in town as a depraved petty thief, when confronted with situations involving life and death showed more humanity and decency in carrying out his orders than the proclaimed intellectuals with diplomas to their credit Shikale-ganif felt the need to give alms to the poor. His thief's conscience would at times awaken as he was carrying out some injustice. He was known to have let dozens of poor people escape certain death by letting them out through a back door, while others of the 'intelligentsia' accepted money to trade the lives of the poor for the rich. The morality of someone like Rus, the camp-leader, or Lempert and others of that ilk, was buried in a far deeper swamp.

In other cases, the common woe cemented a sort of solidarity of spirit among ordinary camp inmates. They huddled together during free time, sharing stories, consoling each other with reports of 'good news' and visualizing images of the future "after this is all over."

[Page 52]

Often, people would share bits of bread while they debated how to accommodate the latest decrees. Jews also conducted trade among themselves and with the world outside, mostly in the form of barter. There was an urgent need to trade, to earn something which could facilitate the path to survival. Widespread commerce was conducted behind the backs of the camp authorities, especially in regard to obtaining bread. In the beginning, the "surplus" from such transactions was earmarked for the camp Jews in Kamionka. This secret operation was led by Nissen Klein of Mikulince, who weekly sent bread to the brothers in the nearby Kamionka extermination camp, where things were much worse.

[Page 53]

22. With Songs on Their Lips

The work brigades, arranged m military forms, would march out early each morning. While passing through the town, especially near the *Schupo* building, they were required to sing marching songs. In content the songs were mostly crude and amateur. The lowbrows among the inmates would think up "dirty" lyrics to fit familiar tunes, and their "naturalistic language" renders them unfit for recording here. The singing was intended to prove to the world that life in the camp made people hale and hearty. The Germans seemed to find a sadistic pleasure in hearing their victims sing.

As is known, orchestras played in all of the large camps, accompanying the work brigades as they marched out through the gates. It was to the sounds of recorded music, blaring from loudspeakers, that millions created in His image met their end in so many extermination camps. In Skalat, as in all other camps, songs were created that depicted camp life in all its sorrow. Typical is the following song, which was written in the Kamionka Camp by an unknown author. The song was sung on various occasions by the inmates of the Skalat Camp.

In nineteen hundred and forty-two,
A new decree to us came through,
Each father his son and daughter must lead,
Like a butcher with cattle, the slaughter feed,

Refrain:

Oh, what can we do and what can we say?

We are caught in the trap the Nazis lay.

Oh, comrades and brothers, in camp we are caught:

How dark our world and our lives are naught.
Friday, oh Friday: on Sabbath eves,
Each Jew sits and each Jew grieves:
With nothing to drink and nothing to eat
A slap in the face is all he receives!

Refrain:

Oh, what can we do and what can we say?.. etc.
On Sabbath, on Sabbath, on the Sabbath at dawn
"Get out and get working until you're worn!"
I want so much to see my home town
But the work order as yet has not come down.

Refrain:

Oh, what can we do and what can we say? ..etc.
Comrade, oh comrade, dear brother of mine,
One mother bore both of us in a distant time.
Today they still call you by your true name
But me they call "Scarecrow!", to my shame.

Refrain:

Oh, what can we do and what can we say? ..etc.

The song, in its simplicity, powerfully reflects the daily life in the camp. The tragedy of the camp people is reflected in both a serious and ironic form. One camp Jew envies another; so alike are they that it could be said that' one mother bore them both. 'Yet, one of them is still healthy enough to work and be regarded as human, hence called by his real name - while the other, ill and exhausted, is considered one of the kalibraki. The administrators are unconcerned whether a person has food or drink, but their supply of beatings is never exhausted. The camp Jew often yearns to see his town, to meet familiar people and perhaps to snatch an extra bit of bread, but the work-column, confined and under guard, has not yet been ordered to march to the workplace.

So sang the camp Jew in Kamionka, and so he sang, too, in Skalat. With a song on his lips he marched through the streets - while silently enduring brutality and pain.

Footnotes:

58 groschen - Pennies, from Polish grosz.

59 Judenfrei - Free of Jews.

60 Shavuot - The Feast of Weeks, a Jewish holiday - celebrated seven after Passover.

61 Horst Wessel Song - A Nazi song.

62 The following four chapters describes the origins and functioning of the Skalat Camp and, therefore, go back in time when the camp and the ghetto co-existed. L. Milch

63 Kalibraki -The "Shit Brigade" in the Skalat Camp (the crippled, aged and sick).

64 "Achtung!" - "Attention!"

65 Apel Platz - Roll call square.

66 Befehl - Command (at your command).

[Page 54]

23. The Passover Seder in Camp

It happened after the Pre-Passover **'action'** in 1943. All the clothes of the victims had been brought to camp for sorting, baling and transporting to Germany. The camp Jews experienced terrible moments in the course of this work. Often someone would recognize his child's dress, or the clothes of a brother, father or dear friend. Although their emotions had long since been dulled, a bloodied garment could have a shocking effect on the strained nerves of an inmate. Who could say whether tomorrow or the next day, some other Jew would be sorting his blood-soaked clothes?

Often American dollars or gold coins would be found sewn into the seams of the clothes. The overseers would watch everyone's hands and the ordinary inmate would wonder: "Whom will these enrich? Obviously some officials. But couldn't we better use the gold to rescue ourselves?" A piece of jewelry would fall from a garment to the floor, it would shine for a moment and then the glow would be darkened by the thoughts of one's own perdition.

A certain part of the camp population sought solace in religion. Hassidic young men, such as Asher Geter, Mechel Klein, Nisan Messing and others, would organize prayer sessions. Marking the *yahrtzeit*[67] and saying the *Kaddish* prayer were the most moving expressions in this sorrowful existence. The daring to be pious under those conditions gave hope to the discouraged and brought dreams of liberation to their souls if not to their bodies. For some, faith and prayer could sometimes cancel out decrees.

It was the first night of Passover. The inmates returned from work, tired to the point of exhaustion. They remembered the Festival of Spring and Freedom. Nature is waking up to life: the skies turning blue, the earth green; first born sons are dying, slaves are becoming free people. The brutal overseers are assailed by various plagues. Pharaohs drown. And homes of the past awake in memories.

They remember a table covered in white, candles flicker in silver candlesticks, the *Pesach*[68] table is prepared, the cups of wine in place. At the head of the table a seat is pillowed for the Master of the *Seder*[69] to eat reclined, as a king. Joy shines all about, encircling wife, children, and friends. Remembering this, eyes start to glisten.

Someone suddenly said: "Jews, let's prepare a *Seder*. Isn't this the first *Seder* night? The *Kommandant*s are carrying on over there - we can take care that they don't catch us. We'll have the *Seder*! "Lookouts were posted at the gate and on the staircase. If anyone were to appear, an agreed-upon signal would be given and everyone would pretend to be asleep on their cots.

The secret quickly spread from ear to ear and soon the very air was filled with it. A table is born. From out of the table grow two burning candles. A bit of matzo lies as a reminder, a tin plate on the table bears *haroset*[70] and *maror*.[71] Three Jews sit on a bench and prepare to repeat the wondrous tale of bondage and freedom. "Today we are still slaves, but next year we shall be free men!" The walls are draped with dark shadows that move surreptitiously with the flames of the flickering candles. Rows of heads look down from the double-decked cots, their frightened glances turn in anticipation to the pale light from the *Seder* table. Hearts tremble, uplifted in ecstasy a shiver rises from the depths of the sleeping shelves, from the corners, from under the table, from beneath the beds, from all of the crowded surroundings. The room is filled with a mass of human heads, resembling frightened ghosts. They want to hear the reading of the *Haggadah*.[72]

[Page 55]

The familiar melodies rise: *Avodim Hoyino* (we were slaves)...times gone by...once there was a conspiracy in B'nai Brak... quiet!...quieter!.. They will hear us! The singing grows softer and softer, the ears, sharpened by fear, bend to the melody but it is hard to catch the living words...quieter! Still more quiet lest we be heard. The path to the heart is open, and the melody is felt even if not heard. From here it is but a short step to the tear ducts. Soon everyone is crying. The very air is transformed into a lake of tears. Everyone remembers the past, yesterday, today...

From the table one can barely hear the intoned words: **Blood...Frogs...Lice...** - and all about one feels the impact of the plagues. Were there camps in Egypt?

The great mystery of faith, though mixed with pain, descends over everyone's spirit and proffers a measure of solace.

Asher Getter chants the *Hallel* (hymn of praise). When the four cups have been filled with tears, Nisan Messing ends with the allegorical song, *Chad Gadyo* (I had a little Kid).

Thus the camp inmates celebrated the night of the first *Seder.*

[Page 56]

24. The Ghostly Promenade

Observing the tragic conditions of the remaining handful of Jews in the ghetto, crammed into thirty huts and, fearing new **'actions,'** spending nights in bunkers or in open fields, the camp Jews felt that for the time being their lives were safer than those of their brothers in the ghetto. The camp Jews had been spared during the recent **'actions,'** and it was said. that in the future the Jews in the camp would be permitted to live. Many unfortunates in the ghetto wished to be accepted into the camp.

Since the ten Jewish policemen had arrived from Tarnopol, the panic in town had reached a point of desperation. One knew that the days of his life were numbered. Truthfully speaking, the Shavuot **'action'** had extinguished the last spark of Jewish hope and illusion. The *shtetl* had been declared *Judenrein.* Then, too, the camp had been spared. Now, however, the last Jews who had managed to hide and to escape the liquidation **'action'** came there begging for admission. Except for a few who succeeded in gaining admission, the camp, with its 400 Jewish inmates, remained a barred enclave. It was one of the few remaining legal Jewish settlements in the area.

By then the ghetto had been destroyed and leveled. Nevertheless a few scores of Jews remained, hidden still in undiscovered underground bunkers. One by one, driven by hunger and thirst, they were forced to leave those hiding places and to find shelter elsewhere. During the night, moving like shadows, these cast-out souls wandered the backroads and streets. At the very edge of the abyss they still sought some way to stay alive. Many fell into the hands of unscrupulous peasants, who first robbed them and then turned them over to the police - to death.

Some of these wanderers slipped into the courtyard of the camp and hid in the piles of furniture and other household goods that had been brought there from the Jewish homes. With almost acrobatic skills they made nests there in crannies, and in the nooks of closets, twisted and huddled together. Some used pocket knives or their own fingernails to scratch out mole-like lairs. These people clung to life with the last remnants of their strength. Their limbs cramped, hungry and dirty, they lay there all day wretchedly, still and afraid to move. But late at night, when all the camp was wrapped in sleep, they would crawl out of their hiding places and soundlessly, on tiptoe, make their way to the garbage dump in the courtyard in order to find some potato peelings or other kitchen waste. These were the provisions that sustained them.

Such was the ghostly promenade that stole through the camp courtyard night after night without anyone's knowledge. At times, rain would wash their skeletal bodies: refreshing them, waking them and cooling their fevered brows, while their parched tongues licked at the raindrops as though they were wine. Although their clothes were rotted and revealed their ribs, and although they were almost devoured by lice, yet they longed to survive: to live!

When the camp Jews discovered the colony of living corpses in their courtyard, they considered themselves luckier despite their own disaster. Some would sneak out of their barracks during the night and, in great secrecy, hand the unfortunates bits of bread and potatoes. This fraternal aid of the camp Jews eased the lives of their rejected brothers.

Who knows how long this "idyllic life" might have continued had the camp administrators not learned of it. "This is impossible!" they shouted, "What will Rebel say if he learns of it? All of the camp Jews will suffer!"

The leadership decided to put an end to the entire affair. One moonlit night, at about 1:00 AM, Nirler, *Kommandant* Rus and Shikale-ganif appeared in the courtyard, rolled up their sleeves and began to remove the piles of furniture and other junk from the yard. Soon they were dragging out, one after another the living beings, who hardly resembled people by now: emaciated, with dark, sunken eyes, they stood, terrified, trembling on shaky twig-like legs. Although to the camp leaders these were familiar people from their own town, it was difficult to recognize them; their faces were pale, their clothes in tatters, as though they had in fact been found in the garbage. Their shoulders twitched with itching, and they gave off a

[Page 57]

nauseating odor. Amid the noisy and constant banging and scraping of moving furniture, this group of some fifty unfortunate souls stood, awaiting further developments. The scene, lit by the moon, was a ghastly horror, as though anticipating a dance of skeletons.

"If you want permission to remain in camp, you must hand over your money, gold, rings, watches and any other valuables. If you don't have them you must leave," announced one of the three pursuers, holding out his hat and indicating with a slight move of his hand where the valuables were to be deposited.

"Oh, dearest Jews, here you are -just let us live!" the Jews responded and each of them gave whatever he had. Those who had nothing were placed to one side.

"Though you have nothing - you will be included as well," one of the three leaders said magnanimously.

The round-up lasted more than two hours. Dawn was about to break and the group of stragglers was allowed to remain alone and unguarded. There was no fear that any of them might escape - for where would they go? Nor did any of them have the strength to run, but now they could breathe fresh air and the hope of being permitted to remain in camp gave them a new strength. They held their aching limbs, rigidly, as though in a trance. Their movements did not appear voluntary but convulsive, as dying people do moments before death.

"But why haven't they admitted us into the camp," someone asked. "We've paid, after all."

"Because we're lice-ridden," someone else replied. "In the morning, when the camp Jews will be gone to work, we will have the chance to wash and they will give us clean clothes and food." Food...a logical observation, everyone agreed - if one could manage to survive until morning.

In the morning, the *Schupo* arrived and led all the unfortunates away. They were taken to the cemetery and shot - putting an end to their suffering and to their lives.

[Page 58]

25. The First Camp-Action

Every event in and around the camp left its mark on the inmates. The camp began to take on the appearance of an insane asylum. Word was spread about the annihilations of all the camps in the surrounding area: Kamionka where there were firing squads, Borki-Wielkie where twelve hundred Jews were burned to death, and Podwolczyska which was wiped out. The feeling grew that the time was nearing for the Skalat Camp as well.

Almost every day, SS-men came on inspection tours. They did not display the beastly savagery of the past. On the contrary, they continually assured everyone that here in Skalat nothing would occur. To emphasize the importance of the Jewish enterprise, they placed large orders for work with the workshops: another sign that these Jews were indispensable. As in the past, the Germans would carouse at parties especially arranged for them. They would get drunk, laugh and play cards.

In time such revelries became orgies, assuming wild and sadistic forms. On a particular night, the drunken *Obersturmbannfuhrer* Rebel commanded all the girls in the camp to appear naked in the assembly hall. Neither pleading nor additional bribes could dissuade him. The girls came, driven by shouts and shooting. The hall was bright and rowdy. The band was playing. Suddenly Rebel stood in the center of the hall and ordered the girls to pass in review, one by one, in a measured tread. He beat them with his whip, shouting wildly: "Bad! Do it again!" The girls were forced to repeat the promenade, in the measured tread, under a hail of whiplashes. Laughter and shouts from the revelers and moaning and sobs from the tortured girls blended with the sounds of music.

Meanwhile, the camp management, understanding the impending danger, bent every effort to establish close contact with whichever Germans they could, in order to secure accurate and swift information about their situation. They succeeded in finding one such person in the *Schupo* member, Marold, whose main motive was, of course, the huge bribes which he received.

On 29 June 1943 this informant came to the camp and whispered a message to Nirler: "The sentence has come down! The liquidation **'action'** will take place early tomorrow morning. You have time to save yourselves," the German said.

Nirler quickly warned everyone: "Hide yourselves wherever you can!" Everyone was shattered by the news. How and where is one to escape? Nirler, Rus and other authorities went off with their families during the night, going outside of town or to villages and well paid for sanctuaries which they had long since arranged for themselves. Many of the inmates, mainly younger people, ran off during the night in various directions. They had no alternative. They ran without planned destinations, wherever their feet carried them. Some 140 people remained in place: the older women and the majority of the 'Shit Brigade' as well as a few lone children, of whom no one took any notice during the general panic. Some of them were ready for whatever might happen so long as it put an end to their torture. Others were dull and apathetic. A small group continued to believe in miracles or that no person should oppose the will of God. However the main reasons for most of those staying behind was the lack of financial resources and having no place to go.

The warning from the *Schupo* member proved accurate. On 30 June 1943 (27 *Sivan* 5703), armed SS-men from Tarnopol, along with the local *Schupo, Kripo* and the Ukrainian police surrounded the Skalat Camp. All remaining inmates were quickly taken to the field outside of town, where the graves of the victims of the previous **'actions,'** were located, and, standing beside prepared pits, they were all shot down. Occasionally peasants brought in newly captured Jews who had been wandering .in the fields, those who had fled the camp the night before, and these Jews, too, were made to stand in front of the machine guns. The total number of victims slaughtered that day is estimated at two hundred (200).

The victims were buried by the Ukrainian Construction Battalions.

[Page 59]

Groups of camp escapees wandered the fields, desperate and starving. Seeing neither a goal nor a way out, some headed off into the woods. Most, however, applied to the Otto Heil firm in the nearby village of Nowosiolka, about the possibility of being re-employed. The reply was unclear because the firm had to consult higher authority. The Otto Heil Company sent a representative to Tarnopol who returned that same day with the "good news" that those who had managed to remain alive could organize themselves in a new locked camp in Skalat.

The next day a truck arrived loaded with foodstuff for a limited period of time. Groups of Jews began to return and a young man named Fogel took over the running of the newly-formed camp. When the former camp administrators learned of this, they left their hiding places and returned to resume their previous "positions." Some two hundred surviving Jews gathered together. The former camp procedures were re-established and the inmates returned to their work in the quarries. The Germans also sent out Jewish labor brigades to other places, since by now they were the only source of Jewish labor.

[Page 60]

26. The Partisans

A few days after the first camp **'action,'** a large group of the surviving Jews was back at work in the quarry at Nowosiolka, near the woods, some two kilometers from Skalat.

It was just about noon when the inmates were permitted to rest from their labor. Suddenly some shepherds ran up and, with bated breath, related the news that Soviet partisans had arrived, that they were now in the woods and had said that before the day was over, they would enter the town. None of the Jews dared to believe the story. From where? How? But the constant sound of gunfire told them that something unexpected was about to happen. By this time no one feared gunfire or exploding bombs: on the contrary, they lightened the spirits and evoked a kind of vengeful glee. By all means! May they thrash the enemy all day and all night, they felt.

Soon squadrons of airplanes appeared in the sky, some flying quite low. Seeing groups of people in the quarry, the planes loosed salvoes of bullets upon the Jews, who, desperate and frightened, tried to run across the fields. They crawled in among the stalks and waited in suspense for the danger to pass.

Meanwhile the news spread like wildfire through the town and neighboring villages. The German and Ukrainian police ran about like poisoned rats, not knowing what to do. The Germans finally managed to organize some groups to offer resistance to the encroaching enemy. Telephone messages went out to the surrounding villages ordering all members of the Ukrainian police to report at once, in full battle gear. Full battle readiness was also ordered for the *Schupo*, the *Kripo* and all other armed forces. Some of the officials and higher ranking members of the German institutions fled into hiding.

At about 5:00 PM. the lead patrol of Soviet partisans appeared in the village of Nowosiolka. The German and Ukrainian defending forces were massed behind the woods near Nowosiolka and, by 7:00 PM, the attack began on the village which the

Soviet partisans soon captured, almost without a struggle. At the woods, a battle developed where the Germans attempted to encircle the much stronger Soviet forces. They were unsuccessful and, after a thirty minute battle, the partisans had wiped out almost three quarters of the German and Ukrainian fighters. A small remnant barely managed to escape with their lives.

Then the partisans, led by the famous General Kolpak, surrounded the abandoned town of Skalat and occupied it. On the battlefield lay some one hundred dead, about sixty of them Ukrainians and the remainder Germans. The Jews in the Skalat Camp were joyful: the Soviet partisans had assumed power and many Jews believed that salvation had truly arrived. Naively, they believed that the Jews of the camp would join the partisans. It did not turn out that way.

The partisans worked all night long in the town. They dynamited the four small bridges leading to the outskirts, blew up the police and military buildings and generally destroyed everything that related to the Germans. The camp Jews were overjoyed with the partisans and spent the night leading them to the enemy institutions. They freed all the prisoners in the jail and blew up the cells. They confiscated all the stored goods and foodstuffs from the Ukrainian cooperative association warehouse. During this time, the local population remained in hiding. When the partisans prepared to leave, almost all of the Jews asked that they be allowed to accompany them, but the partisans refused, explaining that they needed healthy people to be soldiers, not broken camp inmates who could barely drag their feet. The next day, however, when the Soviet partisans left the *shtetl*, they were followed by about thirty of the healthier camp Jews, who, under no circumstances, intended to remain behind and await inevitable death. The partisan soldiers drove them off with sticks, but they continued to run alongside. After much effort and exertion, a few days later they were eventually given weapons and included among the partisan ranks.

The majority of those young people from Skalat perished in the great battle that took place in the Carpathian Mountains. Those who survived that struggle were Mechel Glanz, Nadzio Weinsaft, Buzio Eisenstark, Motek Brik, Bucio Elfenbein and one girl: Hinda Kornweitz. All later joined the Polish Army, which was organized in Russia and participated in battles against the Germans. Among the Jewish heroes from Skalat, who died in those battles, were Sholem Schechter, Yankif Hecht, Moishe Axelrod, Yeshua Katz (and his twelve year old son), Dr. Hadassah Mendelewicz, Yisroel Brik, Avram Rosenzweig, Kuperszmit, along with many others who brought glory to the Jewish People. Honor to their memory!

[Page 61]

*****

[Page 62]

<u>Eyewitness report of the Ex-Partisan from Skalat, Bucio Elfenbein:</u>

"During the last months of the Skalat Camp, a resistance movement began to grow, to which my brother and I belonged. Our primary aim was to obtain arms and to use them against the enemy in the course of the next **'action.'**

Short meetings would take place in the camp courtyard, amid the scattered heaps of furniture which had been brought from the ghetto. Arms had to be purchased and we demanded the necessary funds from everyone, but first of all from our rich 'camp comrades': Zimrner, Lempert, Nirler, etc., - it was to no avail. The 'gentlemen' refused us.

And then, suddenly, the partisans of General Kolpak appeared! What euphoria filled the handful of camp Jews who had been under a death sentence! Moreover, what joy we felt watching the Germans and Ukrainians in their terrified retreat. However, quickly realizing that this was not yet liberation, we experienced bitter disappointment.

The leadership of the partisan brigades, which Mechel Glanz and I contacted, acted purely out of military considerations and would not hear about taking along several hundred people, including women and children. They only allowed thirty people to accompany them, including four women. Mechel and I were both assigned to the Third Company of the Third Battalion. The other Jews were assigned to other battalions (of which there were four).

I remember clearly the first test under fire I underwent, on the day after we left Skalat. It was in the area of Krecilow, where our Third Company was assigned to pin down the Germans who, after their defeat in Skalat, had concentrated quite a large force near the highway. We proceeded in a long line from the partisan camp to the site of our assignment. I marched with special pride since, for the first time, I had an opportunity to take part in a real battle and would finally be able to take vengeance for the murder of my mother and for all our suffering! At our leave-taking, my comrades and those who knew me from Skalat could see the joy of battle-readiness on my face! At that point I could think of nothing else.

The battle ended in a great rout of the Germans and our partisans had almost a clear road all the way to the Dniester River (approx. 22 km away). We did engage in several skirmishes along the way. Between the Dniester crossing and the Carpathians we were in major battles. The Germans sent tanks against us and strafed us daily from airplanes. Hunger and exertion had weakened me to the point of exhaustion. Loss of blood from a wound in my wrist weakened me still further. But I did not lose hope and managed to climb to the highest peaks of the Carpathians.

And there is another episode of those days I cannot forget. Our brigade was located in the hilly region between Delatyn and Mikuliczyn. We were seated in a field, engrossed in a radio communique being read by the aide to the company leader and we heard the news that Mussolini had been driven from power. (I didn't know the date, since by then I had lost all sense of time.) Indescribable joy! We all believed that the war was finally at an end! I searched for Mechel Glanz, hoping to share the overwhelming news, but could not find him.

I was called to headquarters and learned that I had guard duty that night. My post was on a hilly forest path. It was a beautiful clear, moonlit night. I came to a post that once held a directional sign. By the light of the moon I made out the Hebrew letters carved into the wood: the first and last names of the *chalutzim*[73] from Lodz, Warsaw, Lwow, etc. They had been here in 1938 for pre-emigration training. Below one family name and the date, they had carved: *L'shana haba'a b'Yerushalayim.*[74] I wondered: were their dreams realized? Were any of them alive?

Only six of our thirty Skalat partisans survived. Some were wounded, as, for example, Hinda Kornweitz who was hurt in the leg. The others perished in battles and bombardments."

[Page 63]

27. The Last Act of the Tragedy

Skalat remained ungoverned for three days after the partisans departed. Understandably, the Jews expected severe reprisals. When the Germans did return, the local Gentile population informed them about the Jewish behavior and that many Jews had left with the partisans. The Germans, on their part, did little about this information at first: they wanted to avoid alarming the camp Jews and to keep them firmly in their grasp.

Such tactics had always served to deceive the Jews before, enabling the Germans, subsequently, to send the Jews to their deaths. In fact, many Jews emerged from hiding and returned to the camp after learning that all was quiet there. By this time there were some one hundred fifty Jews in the camp, working in the quarries outside of Skalat.

The *shtetl* was officially considered *Judenrein*. During this period, there were many incidents in which peasants who had been sheltering Jews murdered them themselves or turned them over to the police. Lonek Kleiner and Beryl Pikholz were among those who met their deaths that way. They were bound with barbed wire and then stabbed to death. When old clothes were brought to the camp for sorting and shipment, the inmates could tell at once how many more Jews had been murdered. Often they even recognized the clothes which belonged to friends and relatives.

The administration of the camp no longer indulged in orgies or other weird behavior. People faced life in the re-established camp with ever increasing doubt and concern. They faced the next day's survival with the special awareness of a Jew. They lived with the constant sense of the executioner's presence and in a state of stupor.

Their minds were dulled as if under an anesthetic, inhibiting the drive toward self-preservation. If someone did manage to focus, somehow, on the future it was only under the sway of morbid or mystical ponderings, which at that time shaped the imagination. Thoughts of family would weave in and out.

There, in the mass graves outside of the town, lay buried parents, children, the closest relatives and friends. In what way is one better than the rest? Even if rescue were managed - although that was impossible to believe because there were no miracles -what would life be like then? People are no more than beasts: all is destruction. Life is a vale of tears. The world is drowning in blood and fire. And what good things can be expected from anyone? God, the World to Come and Death - these are eternal. Perhaps self sacrifice and sacred death is really the highest achievement one can attain. Why, then, separate oneself from the whole?

But this does not last long. While these gruesome thoughts raced through the mind, suddenly, with a jolt, one would awaken to the prosaic matters: to life at the moment and to the feeling of hunger and pain. One is instantly sobered by the body's demands and the stomach's need for food. The work was oppressive. Days dragged on and the nights were passed in sleepless fear.

The area where the Jews of Skalat still were was called a camp, but everyone knew it was really a lion's den: a trap leading eventually to death. The *Schupo* remained in constant contact with the camp. Noting the chronic unrest among the inmates, some of the Security Police tried to calm and console them: demonstrating ostensible understanding and sympathy for the tragic plight of the Jews.

One evening in late July of 1943, the *Schupo Kommandant*, Schneider, came into the camp in a very good mood. He showed interest in every detail of camp life and spoke with the Jews in an "Oh, so friendly" and jolly manner. It almost seemed that a change for the better was about to occur. He even cheered the crowd somewhat by telling hearty jokes and the Jews did try to forget their sorrows for the moment.

Seeing Schneider's open-heartedness and good mood, some Jews dared to ask him about various things, but mostly about what concerned them most: what were the prospects for the Skalat Camp and what would become of the tiny remnant of the Jews? Schneider stared in disbelief at the Jews and their fears. "Nothing will happen to you," he declared. In his great enthusiasm, Nirler presented him with his own gold fountain pen, and Schneider responded with his sacred word of honor that the Jews could remain calm. He guaranteed that there would be no **'actions,'** in the Skalat Camp for a few months at the very least. The Jews must just work faithfully and, most important, keep themselves clean. After such assurances, the camp Jews went to sleep with a degree of calmness.

[Page 64]

At about 11 :00 PM. when the camp was wrapped in slumber, they were all awakened. The Night Watch reported that someone was approaching. For some time now, almost all of them had slept in their clothes out of constant fear and now, in one minute, the entire camp was on its feet -fearfully awaiting what was to transpire. Suddenly the *Schupo*-member Marold appeared at the entrance breathing heavily. Hurriedly he said: "Run quickly -there's danger!" and then quickly disappeared.

The German Marold apparently had his own personal score to settle with the SS-men and was determined to see their murderous efforts fail. In addition, as noted before, he had been well bribed by the Jews and had promised to warn them in the event of danger.

The Jews began to run in panic, not knowing where to go. Soon most of them, including Nirler and Rus, had vanished somewhere in the darkness of the night. This time, again, there remained behind the old people of the "Shit Brigade," some women and children, and those bereft of all will to live: some sixty to seventy people in all.

At dawn on 28 July 1943 (25 Tammuz 5703), a group of SS-men arrived from Tarnopol. *Obersturmbannfuhrer* Rebel was among them, of course. They surrounded the camp building and then dragged all of the Jews they found to the field: to that same mass grave of the previous slaughters. There, with a machine gun, they shot down every one of them.

While the Ukrainian Construction Battalion was burying the bodies, peasants brought them a group of twenty more Jews whom they had caught in the fields. These, too, were shot on the spot and buried in the same grave as the others. It is said that when the captives were led through the town, they were savagely beaten by the village peasants and street toughs who stuck feathers in them and spat in their faces, while bystanders laughed loudly in amusement. It was the closing act in the bloody drama of the Skalat Camp. This final mass murder put an end to Jewish life in Skalat. The town was now truly *Judenrein*.

Some individual Jews remained hidden with peasants in the surrounding villages. Their situation, however, grew worse from day to day and the toll of victims among them grew steadily. Mordechai Parnes, one of the most honorable members of the former *Judenrat*, had lost his entire family. He was hiding in Mantiawa. It seems that the peasant there ordered him out and, since he could find no other place to hide, he decided to put an end to his life. In October of 1943 he turned himself in to the *Schupo* and asked to be shot. The gentleman obliged him. At about the same time, Shimen Chassid also reported to the *Schupo*. He had been intercepted by peasants, who tried to dissuade him from turning himself in. They even fed him. But he had no alternative, because there was no possibility for him to survive.

The last Jews escaping from Skalat now turned to the nearby forests. They were turning toward life.

[Page 65]

28. In the Forests

The Tarnopol Gestapo announced officially on 30 July 1943 that all of the Tarnopol region had been cleared of Jews. "However," the announcement continued, "since there are still some Jewish individuals hiding in the forests or sheltering with irresponsible private persons, such persons are warned that if a Jew were found hiding with an Aryan, the Aryan's entire family would be shot and his property confiscated."

The posters also declared that there would be a reward for every Jew turned over to the police dead or alive - in the form of one liter of whiskey, one kilogram of sugar and three hundred *zlotys* in cash.

As long as the fields had not been harvested, many Jews were able to hide among the stalks. Whole armies of unscrupulous peasants spent their days and nights searching the fields for wandering Jews, robbing them first then killing them. If the victims did not have any money, they were promptly turned over to the police or to the village elder, who paid the announced reward per head. Not a day went by without one or more captured Jews being delivered to be shot on the spot or at the cemetery. There were Jew-catching experts who had dozens of Jewish lives on their conscience. In addition, the *Kripo*, tipped off by informers, would often drag scores of Jewish victims from their paid-for sanctuaries among the peasants. In many places, dead bodies were found: discarded to avoid suspicion of the identities of the robbers and murderers. At that time, there were some three hundred Jews alive around Skalat, most of whom found shelter in the forests.

The forest hiding places had been prepared earlier. The first people went there back in October of 1942. These were: the Crakow tailor, Froszgang, his four-year-old son, and the Wasserman family. Very few people joined them during that winter. But following the Pre-Passover "Sobbing Graves Action," a score of Jews joined the group. After the *Judenrein*, or "Shavuot Action," the number of Jews in the forest reached one hundred. The total grew to two hundred fifty after the liquidation of the camps in and around Skalat. People began to spread out into the adjoining forests of Ostra-Mogila, Chmieliska, Okno, Malinik, Hory, Krecilow, etc. In view of the constant movement from one place to another, it is difficult to cite accurate numbers of people in each forest, but the overall total is accurate.

Approximately 32 Jews lived in the Ostra-Mogila Forest. At the edge of the wood was a tiny village with thirteen huts. As soon as night fell, one of the peasants who was trusted would signal with a light to indicate that no Germans were around and then the Jews would sneak into the village to obtain food, returning quickly to their hiding places in the forest. The people in this village were friendly to the Jews and provided them with whatever they could. When the Germans or the Ukrainian police arrived, the villagers would promptly alert the Jews who would withdraw to another part of the forest. Nevertheless, there were three incidents of robbery/murders there, carried out by unknown criminals. Twenty-nine Jews survived in Ostra-Mogila.

Fifty-two Jews lived in the Chmieliska Forest where various raids took forty-two lives, and four died there of hunger and cold. Only six people emerged alive.

In the Malinik Forest, out of forty people eleven remained alive. Twenty-four were murdered in raids and five died of hunger and cold.

The largest Jewish group was in the Hory Forest. Of the original seventy-five, fifty survived. Starvation and cold took nine lives and the Germans murdered nineteen people.

Fourteen people lived in the Krecilow Forest. A raid by the *Bulbowcy*[75] resulted in three Jewish fatalities including among them Zimmer". One of the former leaders of the Skalat *Judenrat.*

[Page 66]

The Okno Forest sheltered primarily the famous group of Hershke's band, described in the following chapter. Two of Hershke's people died of natural causes and three were killed by the *Banderowcy*[76]. Thirty-three remained alive.

*****

Following is a description by engineer Joseph Kofler of his life in the forest between 3 June 1943 and 23 March 1944.

"We, a group of five, fled Skalat on the night of 2 June 1943. In addition to myself, the group included my wife Ida, Henek Weinberg, David Landesman, and his sister. We made it to the forest known as Hory near the hamlet where a family by the name of Krupa lived. We remained there until the end of July. We were able to purchase our food in that hamlet. As long as the Skalat Camp existed, we could return to town at night, from time to time, entering the camp where we would spend the following day, taking care of various matters and also buying food. At night we would return to the forest.

In the beginning we lived under the open skies. For reasons of security we did not want to dig any hiding places, and almost every other day we would change locations since frequent walking in the same area would trample the grass leaving a clear clue as to our whereabouts for passing peasants. Of this, we were terrified. Originally, in addition to us, there were about fifteen other Jews in the forest. More people arrived after the liquidation of the ghetto and still more after the first camp **'action.'**

Following the passage of the Soviet partisan brigade, at the beginning of July 1943, the Skalat *Schupo*, with the help of five hundred peasants from the surrounding villages, organized raids in the woods. They also used this occasion to find the bodies of the Germans who had fallen in recent battles with the partisans. During these raids they caught three Jews who had been hiding in the woods. But thanks to the intervention of *Kommandant* Fishbacher, those three Jews were not killed but turned over to the Skalat Camp (which was then still in existence). The three were two escapees from the Kamionka Camp and Blumenstein, from Skalat. Fortunately none of our group was caught because we were in a different part of the forest where they were not searching.

Following the "Second Camp Action" in Skalat (28 July 1943), when the forest became populated by escapees from the camp, we were forced to seek new places to hide. We had to do so because the influx of more people made it evident throughout the area that there were many Jews hiding in the forest, which we feared could lead to new raids. In addition, the supply of food became even more critical, as the nearby hamlet consisted of no more than four households and could not sustain more than a score of people.

At the suggestion of a peasant by the name of Wyszkowski, we moved to the Ostapie Forest, near the small town of Ostra-Mogila. By then our group had grown to eleven people. We encountered two larger groups of Jews in various locations in the new forest. One was the so-called Hershke's group, from Grzymalow, which consisted of more than twenty people who had been living in the woods for several months. Another group, the so-called Elfenbein group, had only been in the forest for one day. These were Jews who had fled the night before the liquidation of the Skalat Camp.

[Page 67]

At first life in the woods was not bad. We were able to breathe more freely after our tragic experiences in town. We bought our food in the village and because the forest was rarely visited, very few knew of our presence and we felt relatively secure there.

After about a month, the decimated remnants of a Soviet partisan brigade from the Carpathians began coming through the forest on their way back to the Soviet front. They spent some days in our woods, resting up, and we met one such group of five men. To obtain provisions, our group joined them and, together with Hershke's group, we undertook an attack on the Turowka estate. Our group came away from there with many provisions. We even captured a live cow, which we slaughtered in the forest. We had enough to eat for two days in a row.

After the attack on the estate, the Germans staged a raid on the partisans and the Jews. A peasant pointed out our location and though we scattered, they managed to capture   one   of   our   comrades: Dolko   Tennenbaum. The partisans left us after the raid and we moved to the neighboring woods near the village of Okno. We spent more than a month there, alongside Hershke's group. Then one day in September 1943, the Germans staged another raid in that forest. Several victims fell into their hands.

We became convinced that Hershke's actions were antagonizing the peasants of the area, so we returned to the Ostra-Mogila woods. In early October we dug underground bunkers deep in the forest. But soon thereafter we experienced great panic: in mid-November some peasants murdered and robbed our comrade, Blank. We buried him in the forest and his father said Kaddish for him. Munio Rosenzweig, son of Solomon Leib Rosenzweig, was similarly murdered a month later.

In December, we moved to the Malinik woods under the impression that there it would be less dangerous. We remained there until the beginning of January 1944. When the German retreat from the Eastern front drew closer to us, we returned again to the Ostra-Mogila Forest and remained there until our liberation on 23 March 1944."

*****

Another Jew from Skalat, Yankif Perlmuter, tells the following about his experiences in the forest.

"During the night before the total liquidation of the Skalat Camp, four of us sat together, waiting for news about the fate of the camp: Mordechai Nusen Ginzberg, Gritz, Megus Rothstein and myself. Around 10:30 PM we were told by the Jewish police and by the *Schupo Kommandant*, Schneider, that all would be calm that night. We all went to sleep. My fourteen year old son undressed. I, however, slept in my clothes out of fear of any unexpected events. At about 1:00 AM, I was roused from sleep by an instinctive indescribable terror. What had happened? None of my bunk-mates were in bed. Looking through a glass door I saw some camp Jews wandering about with lighted candles and I could tell that they were gripped by fear. They told me that all of the police and camp leaders had left the camp. I quickly awakened my son and helped him to dress.

Upon entering the courtyard we met many despairing Jews who did not know what to do next. In panic, some decided to head into town and try to hide among the ruins or perhaps under the Bath house. Others thought about escaping into the fields.

People darted off in groups but no one wanted to include me in his group because I was suffering from a wounded leg. My son and I wandered about the courtyard until 3:30 in the morning. Then, consigning our lives into the hands of God, we left the camp and turned down the street. Directly across from Benjamin Brik's little house we came face-to-face with a German, gun on his shoulder and helmet on his head. It was a miracle! In great fear, heart pounding, I somehow felt a Higher Power had turned me back toward the camp.

[Page 68]

At the barbed-wire fence of the courtyard, we suddenly met with two groups of camp Jews who were debating which way to go. 'We are surrounded by Germans and we are lost!' I told them.

In resignation and overcome by indifference, one group chose to remain in camp, saying "There is nowhere to go."

The other group climbed quickly over the wire and disappeared into the dark. My son and I did the same. We headed in the direction of the peasants' huts and gardens. Around fifty or sixty people remained behind in camp: older men, women with

children,   and   the   exhausted,   who   had   resigned   from   life.
As we dragged ourselves among the gardens, we heard constant gunfire which
confirmed that the slaughter had begun. We wandered around the rest of that night
and hid among the stalks the next day. We straggled in the dreary dawn across
gardens and fields, wet with rain and cold. We managed to drag ourselves to the
village of Polupanowka. Thirsty and hungry, we found a peasant who gave us food and
drink. But fearing for his own life, he would not agree to keep us hidden. He showed
us, however, the path into the forest, where we met two other brothers in woe: Itamat
and Yisroel Werber, from Chmieliska.

During the, first ten days there, we were joined by ten more Jews. The Werber
brothers, together with my son and myself quickly moved to another part of the forest.
There we met three girls and two orphaned children. A few days later we saw two large
dogs running past us. We became alarmed because this meant that there were
Germans nearby on a hunting expedition. We could hardly wait until nightfall when
we could alert the other Jews in the forest.

We decided to leave this dangerous part of the woods and to move several
kilometers deeper into the forest. By then there were nineteen of us. We were able to
make tents out of boughs in the new location, but we had great difficulty in obtaining
food. During the nights, some of us would sneak into the villages to buy foodstuffs
from peasants whom we knew. The nearest stream was a long way off. After two
weeks, a shepherd discovered us. Although he promised that he would never reveal
the secret to anyone, we decided, nevertheless, to move to the other side of the forest:
closer to the village of Chmieliska. There we met a group of eleven fugitive Jews. Now
our group amounted to thirty people.

We spent a couple of weeks in that place. Autumn was approaching. The weather
grew cold, the rains came down and we started, therefore, to build a bunker. During
this time, there were raids taking place against Jews hidden in Chmieliska. We
learned that many had been caught and that the Germans were planning an attack on
the forest encampment so we abandoned the uncompleted bunker and moved again to
another location, in the Malinik woods.

There we met another twelve Jews. As it was the eve of *Yom Kippur*,[77] we preceded
the fast with roasted potatoes, and Moishe Leib Hecht recited the *Kol-Nidre*[78] prayer
from memory .The next morning, Tune Schwartz prayed and we joined in the
sorrowful chants.

[Page 69]

Fall came. We built lean-tos with boughs. Despairing, wet, cold and in fear, we
managed to live there until the end of November 1943. One morning, the peasant
Ziemba, carrying a gun, stopped my son who was on his way to obtain water. He
questioned him about how many Jews were in the forest and whether we were armed.
Ziemba then commanded that the Jews bring him all their gold and other valuables

within a half hour or he would call out for many more of his armed buddies and they would slaughter all of us. My son came running, breathless, and told us what had happened. We ran off quickly to another part of the forest.

Ziemba waited the half hour and became impatient. He then started to search the forest and came upon the tents of other Jews. He happened to find Rysia Katz whom he robbed of her entire fortune, which amounted to a handful of *zlotys*. All the other Jews scattered.

When he came searching for us in other parts of the woods, he was met by a well known ex-boxer from Lodz named Schwartz, who, after a brief struggle, managed to take the bandit's gun and cap.

We realized that we could not remain together any longer, and therefore decided to split into smaller groups and travel separately to other forests. My group went to the Hory Forest, some four kilometers away. It was a very difficult journey. A blizzard was howling and for some hours we lay, covered with snow, not knowing the way. Starved and half frozen we finally arrived at our destination before dawn. We began to dig a bunker for eighteen people. Meyer Grinfeld was very helpful - just as he was generally helpful to other Jews in the woods. He was the contact man among all the forest Jews.

Before we managed to finish the bunker, we were attacked by three Polish peasants, whom we knew: Krupa, Benzer and Wyszkowski. Claiming that they were searching for arms, their real intention was to rob us. They beat us, destroyed our bunker and iron cookstove and committed foul deeds, such as rape. After that incident, the peasants never returned. We later learned that they had received warning letters from some sort of "Polish Committee" which appealed to their sense of national identity and urged them not to besmirch the honor of the Polish People.

We became accustomed to the hardships of forest life and finished digging the bunker, which measured 3 meters in width and 1.7 meters in length. Everyone had an assigned place to sleep.

I formed a collective among our people in the bunker and divided the work among us. There were separate groups for cooking, chopping firewood, securing food and managing the money. We washed our clothes in the snow but we were tormented by lice. During our free time, we would tell each other stories. At times we obtained newspapers from the village and would read every word intently. Sometimes we would sing Yiddish folk songs or *nigunim*.[79] We marked death anniversaries and on calm days we would gather a minyan[80] for prayer. All of us said the Kaddish prayer, since there was no one among us who had not lost family members. We had debates and consoled ourselves with good news and hopes for our future liberation.

[Page 70]

Every couple of days a new terror would rise among us. It was said that January was the month for hunting in the woods, during which time ferocious dogs would come upon our tracks. Although compassionate peasants warned us of raids which the Ukrainians and Germans were planning, there were always reasons to be deprived of rest and sleep.

Some forty to fifty Skalat Jews lived in the same forest under conditions similar to ours. From time to time, small groups would separate and wander off to other forests. The constant threat of death tormented our minds. During the night we stumbled about like shadows, seeking greater protection and security. Some groups would leave but, after wandering about and not finding a hiding place, would return to the place which they had left. One group of seven people even went back to the town where they carved out a hiding place in a boulder outside the *shtetl*. During such wanderings, a German bullet took the life of the son of Weistaub, the surveyor.

Around the middle of February 1944, almost all of the people who had wandered off and survived had returned. We lived calmly for a couple of weeks before the resumption of the attacks, now by the *Volksdeutsche*[81] who were rewarded for each Jew they turned in. Those days were very dangerous for us and we suffered two special losses: Leib from Tarnopol and Magus Rothstein (grandson of David Rothstein) of Skalat. One day, the forest rang with shots and we were surrounded. We scattered in chaos throughout its length and breadth. Those who survived, as though by miracle, once again sought new hiding places: some went off to other forests and others hid with peasants.

Seven of us, who had nowhere to go, remained behind. After some hesitation, we decided to go to the Malinik Forest although there had been many victims there in a recent attack. We found a bunker that had been abandoned and wrecked, and we spent some time there under the most difficult conditions. We suffered because we had no fire and therefore we were freezing. By this time, we also had nothing to eat and were on the verge of starvation. We managed to stay alive by eating snow and frozen sugar beets left behind by the murdered Jews. A couple of days later we encountered a group of seven Jews in another destroyed bunker.

On the thirteenth day, we had a visit from two Germans elegantly dressed in civilian clothes. Standing at the edge of the ruin, they called on us to emerge from the bunker. Some of us crept out, hoping that we might get a piece of bread. The Germans saw before them living corpses: barefoot, in tatters, swollen and sick. They said that they would return. Each of us interpreted the encounter differently. By now we were indifferent to life. But the Germans did not return.

Our collapsed bunker had two sections. One of them was occupied by Froszgang (the first settler in the woods) and his son. A hunchbacked young man from Grzymalow named Schwartz, and two boys from Skalat (grandsons of Pesach Yosif, the sexton) were also there. All of them were swollen, sick, and covered with lice. It was frightening to look at them.

It was impossible to obtain food because of the severe cold and drifting snow. Some tried to go foraging but quickly returned. Considering how hopeless it was to remain there, we decided to return to our exposed bunker in the Hory Forest. 'It is better to die by the sword than by hunger,' I said in Hebrew as we set out.

[Page 71]

A few kilometers along our way we came upon a large forest tire. Hundreds of trees were burning. We warmed ourselves at the flames and were also able to heat water from melting snow. Appeasing our hunger and thirst with hot water, we rested before continuing on. Only nine of us returned because the other five did not survive the trip. They died a few days later of starvation and exposure. We spent another three weeks in our old bunker in the Hory Forest. The Soviet forces were advancing towards us and we heard cannonades. German 'Tiger Tanks' rolled around, shelling our woods - but the Soviets were the victors. When the Soviet soldiers learned of our presence, they sent us a doctor and evacuated us to the rear. Ephraim Liblich died unexpectedly during that evacuation.

Our tiny group of survivors from the forests gathered together in the ruins of Skalat. Eventually we all fled from our former home to rebuild our lives elsewhere. In Skalat we left our graves."

Footnotes:

67 yahrtzeit - Anniversary of the death of a family member.

68 Pesach - Passover.

69 Seder - Ritual meal and service of Passover.

70 haroset - Mixture of fruit, nuts and wine, symbolizing mortar (used during the Passover meal).

71 maror - Bitter herbs symbolizing the bitterness of Jewish slavery in Egypt (used during the Passover meal).

72 Haggadah - The story of the Exodus, read during the Passover Seder.

73 chalutzim - Zionist pioneers.

74 l'shana haba'a b'Yerushalayim - Next year may we meet in Jerusalem.

75 Bulbowcy - Members of a Ukrainian Fascist gang.

76 Banderowcy - Members of another Ukrainian Fascist gang.

77 Yom Kippur - Day of Atonement, holiest day in the Jewish calendar, devoted to fasting and prayer.

78 Kol Nidre - A prayer sung on the eve of the Day of Atonement

79 nigunim - Cantorial melodies (Hebrew).

80 minyan - Ten men (a quorum required for praying).

81 Volksdeutsche - Polish born Germans.

[Page 72]

29. My Own Experiences in the Forest
(A. Weissbrod's Account)

An unknown criminal murdered a Jew in the Ostra-Mogila Forest on the same day that my mother and I arrived there. The dead body lay at the edge of the wood. The peasants had placed it there so that the Jews could bury him themselves. No one, not even the victim's father, gave thought to burying him because we were expecting a raid. About a score of frightened Jews crept out of their bunkers and quickly formed into groups, scattering in every direction throughout the forest.

No one wanted to bother with us, the most recent arrivals. We remained where we were, desperate and helpless. How could we flee, not knowing the forest?

Suddenly, out of nowhere, Meyer Grinfeld and Mrs. Chrein appeared. They, too, had been wandering all night in Bortnik's woods, just as we had, and had barely managed to make it here. Meeting a friend from my youth at such a difficult moment, and under those conditions, was an unexpected and wondrous event for me. We hugged each other, cried and for the moment forgot the sadness and danger hovering over us. "Come with me! I know all the paths and byways!" Grinfeld said.

Together we followed twisting trails for many kilometers and for hours on end moved along thick overgrown paths, leading us to another forest. There we pushed our way into a thicket and rested. Quietly we told each other of our recent experiences and made plans for our dubious future.

Late that evening we returned to the Ostra-Mogila Forest. We met other Jews whose fears of a raid had proved unfounded. The Ukrainian police had examined the deceased and, determining that he was a Jew, merely wrote up a report and continued on their way. We spent the night in the bunker of the Blank family and the next morning all of us took spades and axes to bury the body. The late Autumn morning was foggy and dreary. After completing the work we all stood around the new grave, heads bowed in silence. The wind whistled and trees rustled as if they were reciting the *Kaddish* prayer. At the edge of the woods, near a path, among tall trees with naked limbs like outstretched arms, was the grave of a young Jew whose suffering was finally over. We covered the mound with yellow leaves that fluttered in the breeze and Bucio Elfenbein, with a penknife, carved into the bark of a tree the initials of the murdered victim: G.B. "Let this be his tombstone," he said. Then we returned to our dwellings in the forest.

We gathered dried branches. A fire burned between two stones, over which a large kettle of soup was cooking. The Jews in the forest were not pleased to see us. They were afraid because the peasants considered us to be rich. "This can bring on a catastrophe, " they said. "Make yourselves a bunker in another part of the forest."

In truth there actually were peasants on our trail. We decided to leave as soon as we could, feeling danger at every turn. That night Grinfeld went off to look for a hiding place with a peasant and, after having spent twelve days in the Ostra-Mogila Forest, we set out on a snowy night.

Late that night we passed the mass graves in the fields outside of Skalat. The mounds were covered with snow and nearby twelve tall poplars stood out against the white background like tombstones stretching ever higher and nearer to Heaven. Our feet on the snow were the first to engrave a bouquet of human footprints: the first steps of mourners at the graves of our fathers. My father had met his death here along with all the other martyrs. I managed to say the first few words of *Kaddish* but tears choked off the rest. We quickly fled from that blood-soaked place.

With luck, we arrived at the home of our peasant-benefactor. In a lonely cottage in the middle of a field we concluded a deal with our "gracious host" who was a clever peasant - a businessman, and a Ukrainian as well. A meal, some warmth and a bed restored our tired limbs. Grinfeld wanted to leave us, but we would not allow it. Although he was drawn back to the forest, he stayed. All in all, we felt very fortunate in our new hiding place.

[Page 73]

Weeks passed. At night, Grinfeld would sneak out into the forests to check on the condition of the Jews there, but our peasant was not happy about these excursions. He felt they could arouse suspicion and do us all in. At about this time our money ran out and Grinfeld undertook to go to our house in town, now occupied by Gentiles, where we had some money buried. He succeeded in what was surely a heroic act, since by wandering about at night he put himself in mortal danger. Grinfeld could accomplish what no others could. He had great courage. He often dared hair-raising undertakings and his luck always held.

According to the latest reports on life in the forest, many Jews were ill with scabies and the cold and hunger made further survival almost impossible. We felt impelled, therefore, to think of ways to provide practical help to the forest Jews. Grinfeld went to see some Gentiles whom he knew and got them to exchange $110.00 U.S. Dollars for 9,000 *zlotys*. The money was distributed that same night among the forest Jews in the Hory and Ostra-Mogila woods. "The Polish Committee has sent this to you," Grinfeld told them.

"If such miracles can happen in these times, it is a sign that we will survive the war!" said Magus Rothstein one of the recipients. Unfortunately, he did not survive. *Volksdeutsche* shot him. Naively, everyone believed that such a generous act was possible.

Grinfeld returned from the forest with a list of signatures attesting to the receipt of the distributed funds. His act had endowed the forest Jews with a new lease on life. They could hope for a better future: "Just think! A Polish Committee that helps Jews!" We told the same story to our peasant-benefactor, who was moved to tears. He pulled out 250 *zlotys* from his pocket and said: "Here is my contribution. Enroll me in the Polish Aid Committee - even though I'm Ukrainian."

We, of course, took advantage of that opportunity to broaden our relief work for the forest Jews. A few days later we obtained medications for the sick and we also gathered some clothes that were taken into the woods late at night. Under our direction and with the help of our peasant, letters were written in the name of the Polish Aid Committee to the Polish bandits Wyszkowski and Benzer, stating that it was not fitting for Poles to commit such shameful acts against Jews. This helped to keep the bandits from re-entering the forests.

We had also prepared a significant quantity of foods - potatoes, oil and grains, which were to be carried by the peasant's horse and left at a pre-determined place in the woods. This project did not come to fruition because suddenly some Volksdeutsche were billeted in the peasant's house and their horses were quartered in the barn under guard around the clock. We clambered hastily up into the attic, where a well hidden hole led to a narrow hiding place between two brick walls. We found ourselves under one roof with the Germans, separated from them only by a wall. Thus, our contact with the forests was severed.

We were joined by another Jew, named Asher Kleiner, also from Skalat, whom the peasant had been hiding in the barn without our knowledge. He had been kept hidden and fed in exchange for his carpentry services.

We passed difficult days between those brick walls and envied the Jews living freely in the forest. For us every minute was fraught with danger because the Germans kept moving about and could come across our hiding place. Our peasant was very nervous as well -and with good reason - but continuous bribes of money helped to soften our benefactor's heart. Even if we had chosen to leave, the constant guard in the barn made it impossible to do so. Thus, there was no alternative but to stay.

The peasant told us that the very soldiers billeted in his home were the ones who were raiding the forests and that they had already captured many Jews. For these heroic deeds the police would reward them with whiskey and sugar. When they held revels, we heard them through the thin wall and those revels would also tell us that more Jewish lives had ended at their hands.

When the Soviet front drew closer, we began to hear loud artillery bombardments and we knew that liberation was near. Our benefactor told us nothing about this, begrudging us a reason for joy, since he, himself, feared the Soviets more than the Germans. One night we listened through the wall as our peasant's entire household prayed, and tearfully intoned: "May the Lord have mercy and keep out the Bolsheviks, lest they destroy our cattle and our fields! " Our prayers, however, were the very opposite.

[Page 74]

The next day there were Soviet soldiers under our roof and battle operations had been transferred to our front yard. We found ourselves in the midst of the battle and that night the peasant evicted us from our hiding place. "Go back to the woods! If you don't, we are all lost; the Soviets have retreated and the Germans will soon be back, " he said.

Under a hail of bullets and by the light of rockets, we managed to crawl out and to reach the woods. The Soviets were there. At their suggestion, almost all of the Jews passed through the front lines to the rear - to the village of Molczanowka, where three Jews died in a German air raid. We later learned that two hours after we left, the cottage in which we had been hidden was hit by a bomb and totally destroyed. As it turned out, the eviction by the peasant saved our lives.

After twelve days of siege and battle, the forest settlement liquidated itself. Skalat was liberated. The tiny remnants returned from the forest -the remaining few from the thousands of the Jewish community of Skalat. They returned: bereaved, exhausted, broken and sick.

[Page 75]

30. Hershke and His Band

During the period when the Jews were hiding in the forest, there were bands of robbers operating in all the areas around Skalat. Not a night passed without some raid on a village. The youngest peasant boys were already engaged in theft and violence and some of their elders led double lives: posing as peaceful citizens by day, and robbing at night. There were frequent attacks and robbery motivated murders of defenseless Jews who wandered the fields in fear of impending **'actions.'** What could be expected from the mob when government laws advocated the robbing and killing of Jews?

Then rumors started to spread through the town of Skalat that Jewish robbers were staging nighttime attacks on the villages. In a short time all thefts and criminal attacks were attributed to the Jews. In fact, by that time Jews in the forests were stealing food from peasant storage places in order to stay alive.

On a much grander scale, the exploits of Hershke's band later became legendary as a result of their daring raids which threw a pall over the entire area. Hershke and his people, however, could not be judged as mere common robber bands. There were not the usual depraved traits which led to the formation of this band. The driving force of these people was a reaction to the savage times, and the result of enforced human deprivation. At the brink of the abyss, surrounded by enemies and seeing death before their eyes, with no hope or escape in sight, the forest Jews were forced to become what they became.

We do not know why more Jews didn't escape to the forests and why so many allowed themselves to be slaughtered like sheep. But we do know that the Germans and their deceitful methods managed to dull the senses of many Jews, including their senses of self-defense.

Yet there were also individuals with particularly strong character traits who faced reality with open eyes and, in times of great peril, sought and found different paths. They ran off to the forests! These small groups tried a different way of survival and lived in another world, even though their new situation was also fraught with danger. There, too, one was in constant fear, but living under the sky, surrounded by nature among trees and wild life, gave them a sense of freedom and seemed to straighten their backs and restore their spirit.

Some Jews began to arrive in the forest when the situation in Skalat first seemed hopeless, following the so-called "Little Action" of November 1942. By then the destruction of homes had begun, loved ones had been dragged off and killed, and most of the bunkers in the ghetto had been exposed. Very few had enough money to buy off the greedy peasants, the so called benefactors who, in exchange for gold provided hiding places that were at best doubtful and insecure. The benefactors themselves often delivered the Jews into the hands of the *Schupo* or *Kripo*.

The Skalat *Judenrat* spent great sums of money in order to convince *Obersturmbannfuhrer* Rebel to establish labor locations in many of the surrounding villages and towns as branches of the Skalat Camp. Groups of twenty to forty Jews, a hundred fifty in all, were accepted into the newly created workplaces in Podwoloczyska, Grzymalow, Tarnoruda, Kaczanowka, Okno, Ostapie and Polupanowka. The Jews there worked as farmhands, in the quarries, or at collecting rags and feathers. They had to live under the guard of the Jewish security forces, for which the Skalat Camp was responsible. They were relatively content with this arrangement. Since it was possible to move about more freely in the villages, fear was not as pervasive as in the town and food supplies were better.

The labor locations at those outposts did not last long, however: the Germans began to liquidate them after three months. Heggner, the *Kommandant* of the Border Security Guard, reported that the Jews in Kaczanowka were hardly working. Instead they were eating and drinking and buying up all the chickens and other food from the peasants, causing unhappiness among the local Gentile population.

In early March, 1943, a liquidation squad arrived from the Tarnopol SS to "take care" of the Jews. The squad surrounded the segregated dwelling of the Jews at dawn, dragged them out into a field, ordered them to strip and to lie face-down on the ground, then shot each of them in the back of his head. Some people in Kaczanowka had, by chance, left the dwelling that day and therefore managed to escape. One girl, Tynka Rosenzweig, was wounded in the head. She saved herself by feigning death.

[Page 76]

Leaving the bloody row of fifteen corpses in the field, the assassins quickly drove off to the village of Tarnoruda and, using the same methods, wiped out all thirty Jews in that labor location.

That same day, the administration of the Skalat Camp was ordered to recall the rest of its people from all of the labor locations and to keep them in camp, temporarily. The Okno labor location employed people mostly from Grzymalow, as well as some from the village itself. Henek Weinberg was one of the Skalat people working there. No one there wanted to return to Skalat, since returning to town meant certain death, they said. Two large families, named Birnbaum and Pikholtz, had lived in Okno for many years. They, along with Weinberg, had prepared a bunker in the forest to be available as a hiding place when the time came. The Okno Forest became the area where a famous group of Jews kept the entire district in fear for over a year.

The founder and leader of the band was Hershke Birnbaum. He was a bachelor of about 30, small of stature but with an athlete's strength. He was dark with blue eyes, and had a small black mustache. He looked like a typical peasant. The clothes he wore, his fluency in Ukrainian and the characteristically peasant manners all seemed to be natural to him. A stranger would never have imagined that he was Jewish. He was a blacksmith by trade and though the peasants feared his strength, they also respected and liked him.

He was a capable young man and, though a blacksmith, there was hardly a trade he didn't know: he was also a locksmith, a carpenter, a mechanic and, if need be, a musician, an actor and a wit. He knew by heart all the peasant folk-songs and customs. Seemingly always in good humor and full of fun and laughter, he would often trick the hens at night by crowing long before dawn so that the hens would flap their wings and join in the crowing, in turn causing the peasants to arise hours too early. He was also adept at imitating other birds and beasts.

His intelligence was not acquired but innate. He had a strong sense of direction and an eye for detail. His agility helped him out of many difficult situations. "Hershke won't perish, even in a fire." If he wants to, he can turn himself into a bird," the peasants said of him, paraphrasing a folksaying.

He was a constant counselor to the peasants. On Sundays he would pretend to preach from the Scriptures and the crowd around him would roar with laughter. He always seemed to know what the priest had said in church and he also knew all the secrets of the village organizations. During the German occupation, while three-quarters of the Jews in Galicia were eliminated, the peasants among whom he lived promised that he would be safe from harm

Hershke, however, did not bet his life on their assurances. Back when groups of Jews were laboring on the farms, Hershke Birnbaum, Henek Weinberg, Mates Goldstein, Leibke Seigel and David Schwartz would sneak out of the houses at night and go into the forest where among; the trees and bushes they built a large bunker with a three meter long tunnel. When the order came to return to the Skalat Camp, Hershke dug up his rust-covered weapon, then cleaned and repaired it. He gathered up his family and the rest of the Jews in Okno -twenty-one in all, including four children between the ages of four and twelve - and led them directly to the forest.

*****

Thus began the glorious activities of Hershke and his band. Only four of that whole group were healthy enough to work: the rest consisted of some ailing couples and their children. "My hospital!" Hershke would say. "Look whom I'm taking with me into battle...but never mind: God will help."

[Page 77]

In the early days there was no money, food supplies were soon exhausted and his people had to eat. Each night, therefore, Hershke would take a gun, and with two companions go to the villages in search of sustenance. Hershke knew every nook of the villages and which peasants had the fullest pantries, which roosts the best chickens and where the honey was stored. Hershke and Leibke showed real virtuosity in carrying out a theft. Once they stole all the bread, still hot and fresh, right out of an oven. They seemed to know by instinct when the dogs were asleep. The peasants saw that the. thefts were continuing unabated but they hadn't the least idea of their origin!

Hershke's work went on steadily, according to plan. Soon he set up an "Intelligence Service" - a group of trustworthy peasants, all good buddies of old, who brought all kinds of news from town including reports of the constant slaughters. Almost every day he would meet the peasants at an appointed time and place to discuss necessary matters. At one time, the "Intelligence Service" warned him to take precautions because in a few days the Forest Administration was going to start clearing the underbrush. On such occasions, great crowds of peasants would spread over the length and breadth of the forest, and the work could go on for several weeks. Hershke's band had to wander the woods from one place to another for three weeks. Every night they returned to the bunker to sleep and at dawn they went to another part of the forest, five or six kilometers away.

Upon their return, the forest Jews found their bunker exposed and plundered. They later learned from the friendly peasants with whom they maintained contact, that it was the people in the brush-clearing project who discovered the Jewish hiding place. According to the peasants, they ran off to Skalat to report their find to the *Schupo*, who came immediately, in large numbers and with bloodhounds. Fortunately they did not encounter any of the Jews. They took everything they could find in the bunker and then blew it up with a grenade. For good measure they fired a score of rounds into the trees before driving off. From then on the whole district knew that there were Jews hiding in the woods and that all the thefts were their doing.

Legends began to circulate about the Jewish robbers in the forests. It was said of Hershke and his "band of Yids" that their number ran into the hundreds: practically an army, manned to the teeth and led by the invincible Hershke. It was no laughing matter! Fear spread throughout the district and grew into a panic. At night the peasants would deploy a watch of ten men to guard each village. When they went into the forest to chop wood or gather mushrooms and would suddenly meet up with a Jew, they would flee in great fear and return home thanking God for having saved their lives. "Oh, Holy Mother!" they would exclaim, crossing themselves, whenever they recalled the encounter. Their neighbors would listen and relate the story to other neighbors. Out of fear, peasants would no longer go into the forest alone.

The Jews saw danger to themselves in this notoriety. Cautiously they began to move from one place to another - never spending more than a few nights and days in the same spot. They built bunkers in different woods and in dense thickets built lean-tos of boughs and sackcloth. They were forced to change locations almost every week.

The sojourn of the Soviet partisan detachment in the Skalat forests in early July of 1943 left Hershke and his staff with ambivalent feelings. On the one hand they wanted to join the partisans and go off to battle, but, on the other, they could not leave the old people, the women and children, to the mercy of God. Who would feed them?

They rejoiced with the partisans and swapped stories with them. The Red Fighters marveled at how such a band could exist in a forest under these conditions. "Just hang on! It won't be long now before we liberate you!" they reassured the Jews - and then set off on their way.

Hershke realized that things could not go on this way and the partisans' visit inspired him to become even more daring. He began to aspire to a more meaningful purpose to his acts. "After all, we are not a gang of thieves and robbers," he explained to his comrades. "We are Jews seeking to rescue ourselves from murderers. We must be able to defend ourselves from a German attack. But with what? With one gun? We must think about getting arms. We do not rob for the sake of robbing. We won't attack innocent peasants, who themselves are appalled by the bloody German acts and who suffer in their own way. We will take revenge on our enemies: mainly on the

Ukrainians who participate in the slaughters. And we must also punish all those who have grown rich on the Jewish disaster."

[Page 78]

Following this discussion among Hershke and his comrades, they determined: 1) to obtain arms at any price; 2) to avoid harming innocent peasants and where possible even to help them; and 3) that every act and every attack be directed toward vengeance against those whose hands were stained with Jewish blood.

Since constant wanderings among the villages were risky, it was also decided that in the future their attacks would be less frequent but on a larger scale, so as to obtain a bigger supply of food. Hershke and his people were now to be known as partisans and fighters. He began to give his peasants new instructions. These devoted peasants, his suppliers, actually worked with him in an exemplary fashion, although their efforts were not completely without profit for them.

On 25 July 1943, at midnight, four partisans marched out of the forest: Hershke with his rifle, Leibke with a realistic looking toy revolver, and Schwartz and Weinberg with wooden "rifles" - heading for a raid.

In the Zielona woods there had worked for years a forest ranger named Zabawczuk. He was a Ukrainian nationalist and a mean Jew-hater. It was widely known that he had participated in the pogroms and slaughters of Jews. He also possessed much booty, stolen from Jewish victims. Hershke knew that Zabawczuk had weapons. At 1:00 AM the group arrived at the cottage, located at the very edge of the woods. Weinberg and Schwartz were posted as guards in the yard while Hershke and Leibke broke into the cottage. In fear, Zabawczuk leaped from his bed shouting "Who's there?!" Hershke put the barrel of the gun to his temple and, in Russian, ordered him to turn over his arms immediately or he would be shot at once. Zabawczuk's two grown sons became hysterical and fell to the floor. His wife also fell down in a faint. When Zabawczuk regained his wits, he categorically denied that he had any weapons: "You can shoot me, but I can't produce what isn't here."

Neither threats nor blows were of any use. The peasant attempted an escape but drew back when he saw the armed guards outside his window. He was beaten soundly, until be begged for mercy: "Take what you want - but don't kill us!" In the middle of the wrangling, the peasant's wife revived. She quickly went to the cupboard, took out a rifle and, trembling, handed it over to the partisans. "Here you are," she said. "Take whatever you want, but let us live!"

Then the men set to work. A small barrel of honey, half a hog, whiskey and other provisions were stuffed into sacks and then the partisans headed for home. "If any of you breathe so much as a word about our visit, your lives won't be worth a cent and your house will go up in flames!" Hershke warned the forest ranger and his family before leaving the cottage. The ranger, who knew Hershke quite well from the past, was simply too frightened to tell anyone the details of the attack. He just said that he had been robbed. Two weeks later he and his family moved to a more populated settlement in the village of Pajowka.

The success of that raid and its larger scope encouraged the band and produced a desire for more action. During the month of August, the nearby villages complained of thefts of cows, pigs and other foods. The work went on efficiently, boldly and with agility, while fear among the peasants grew. Delegations of villagers arrived in town daily to implore the Germans to put an end to the Jewish activities, and to the partisans who were roaming the woods. But the Germans, remembering well their defeat at the hands of the partisans, were now in deathly fear of the forest. They put off the peasants with words of advice: "Go into the woods in groups. Spread out and catch them. Bring them here and we will take care of them for good! "

Seeing that their protests were of no avail, the peasants began to send petitions to the District Chief in Tarnopol as well as to Hefner, the agricultural official in Skalat. At first they were promised that everything possible would be done - but nothing ever came of it. When the woodsmen were ordered to provide larger quotas of firewood to the military, they categorically refused. "We are afraid," they pleaded. They agreed to enter the woods only if they were guarded by a strong force of soldiers and Ukrainian police.

[Page 79]

*****

When the ghetto and camp in Skalat had been liquidated, the small remnant of surviving Jews wandered alone through the fields and forests. At that same time, Jewish settlements began to be founded in almost all the woods around Skalat. Hershke's band grew to thirty-two people, among whom eight were able-bodied men. Though life was bearable and there was enough to eat and drink, Hershke himself would often become depressed. "There is no end to it and how long can one go on living like this?" the people would ask.

The peasant suppliers brought alarming reports about the German plans to raid the forests. Only one overriding concern gnawed at the Jews, day and night: how to avoid the murderers. The life of constant wandering exhausted the older people and made the women and children barely able to drag themselves about. The group moved whenever it was felt that danger loomed - even if the feeling was baseless.

This was how they lived for a long time and, having no other choice, they got used to the wandering. As soon as darkness approached, the group would head off like a row of ducks, through fields and forests, carrying their belongings on their backs. Leibke was always the leader and guide through the winding paths. Between the flights they carried on successful raids on villages and managed to have enough food and clothing. They succeeded in obtaining weapons during a raid on the village of Kopyczince and the Jews now had at their disposal three rifles, one double-barreled shotgun and a pistol. They even began to dream of obtaining a machine gun and

Hershke established military discipline. Sanitation and order were of high priority and everyone had assigned tasks.

These arrangements were hardly normal but they were well suited to the situation in which they lived. Nine men were the fighters, while the rest, the so called 'hospital,' had specific jobs to perform such as cooking, washing clothes, securing water, guard duty, gathering dry wood, etc. When the peasants brought good news heard on the radio, such as bulletins that the Germans were being beaten they would rejoice, hanging on to every word. Once Hershke turned to his band and said: "Why don't we think about getting our own radio so we can know when rescue is close at hand?" No sooner said than done. At the end of August, Hershke and his band did a 'job' in the village of Ostapie at the home of the Jew-hating Ukrainian priest. In addition to many other useful things, they also managed to get a four-tube portable radio. Hershke set it up so that everyone could hear the news of the world - especially communiques from the war fronts. Unfortunately the batteries lasted only two weeks and it was difficult to obtain replacements.

During that period, Hershke's band grew to thirty-eight members. Six Jewish partisans (all of them natives of Wolin), who were among the returning remnants of a partisan army, joined Hershke. Among them were Yeruchem Guz, Sioma Gorzanski, Velvel Waks and David Kleinman. With this added manpower Hershke's band now felt itself to be much stronger and they began to use different tactics in, their raids.

In the month of September they carried out a daring raid on an estate in the village of Turowka. The German manager there, named Johann, was believed to have weapons. The entire fighting group took part in the raid. At the last minute, however, one of the workers on the estate spread the alarm that partisans were approaching so the Ukrainian policeman and the German manager ran off in terror. The raid took place around 9:00 PM. At first the Jews encircled the estate and ripped out the telephone wires.

[Page 80]

Then they took over the farm property as if they were the owners. The farmhands and servants trembled in fear and obeyed all the commands that were boldly delivered in Russian. Meanwhile the Polish cooks and the governess prepared a festive dinner for their 'honored guests.' The so-called partisan band feasted at cloth-covered tables. At about midnight they ordered a horse and wagon to be loaded with a sack of flour, a hog, a crate of eggs, butter, cheese and grain. They also selected the best looking cow and tied her to the heavily laden wagon.

Hershke ordered: "Move out!" - and the whole group set off on its way. As they passed through the village, other peasants presented them with loaves of bread and bottles of whiskey. They praised and thanked God that the village hadn't suffered.

The Ukrainian policeman and the German did not return for two days. The horses were returned, having been set free by the Jews in the forest, since Hershke knew that retaining the horses would interfere with the band's mobility. After the peasants' fears had been somewhat allayed, they suggested that some of the 'partisans' had looked like Jews, so that it became apparent that the raiders were none other than Hershke and his "gang!" Exaggerated reports of the event spread like lightning through all the surrounding villages and the peasants increased their night guards.

A week later the village of Sadzawka was the focus of a new surprise. Hershke had learned that the Ukrainian cooperative there had merchandise and, above all, footwear. Since winter was approaching and feet had to be covered, the footwear was much needed. On 2 October 1943 at 9:00 PM Hershke and his band paid a visit to the mayor of Sadzawka. Using threat they forced him to hand over the keys to the cooperative's treasury. With trembling hands, the mayor turned over all of the cash - more than 10,000 *zlotys*. Further, he was forced to provide the 'partisans' with carriages and to help them load crates of eggs, sacks of sugar, bundles of shoes and cases of whiskey. These goods had been allocated by the Germans as rewards for those peasants who delivered their grain quotas on time.

When all the wares were loaded, Hershke gave the order to withdraw. He placed the mayor himself on one of the carriages and the entire village saw the 'partisans' departing with their prisoner. Although some of the peasants had weapons, none dared to resist. Their fear of the partisans was so great that they lost their nerve. On such occasions it was usually the Ukrainian police who fled first, abandoning the village. In some cases, the Germans also revealed their cowardice. Throughout the villages the legend persisted that there were thousands of Jewish partisans.

That night the partisans plied the mayor with liquor and food as a reward for his good behavior and then: a few kilometers down the road, they tossed the now dead-drunk mayor off the carriage. The entire village had been buzzing over the event and mourning the mayor as a martyr. But at dawn the still tipsy mayor returned, hard put to decide what story to tell. Later the Germans pulled the mayor to testify, to fill out reports, and, for good measure, gave him a sound beating for his thoughtlessness and cowardice. "If our police ran off with their rifles, what was someone like me to do?" he said in his defense.

The villages in the area continued to demand that the German authorities do something about the partisans. In early October, an entire battalion of German SS and Ukrainian police, accompanied by a few hundred peasants carried out a series of raids in the surrounding forests. Unfortunately, quite a few Jews fell into their hands during the course of these raids. They were Jews who lacked the advantages of Hershke and his band. They were starved and broken, without money or clothes and, above all, unarmed. In the Ostapie Forest alone twelve Jews were caught, women and children among them. Hershke and his, band, however, were not caught; his spy contact brought him regular reports about the planned raids. Everyday he and his people moved to a different spot - fifteen to twenty kilometers away from the danger.

At that time many non-Jewish bands of various types ran rampant through the forests. Some of them had taken on political characteristics, such as the *Banderowcy* and *Bulbowcy*, Ukrainian Fascist gangs, while others were merely robbers. The Skalat area was overrun by thugs and in the grip of widespread banditry. The town and village population was demoralized, frightened and helpless, all of which

[Page 81]

undermined the German authorities, who were unable to control the situation. It also hampered their ability to collect the assigned quotas of produce from the rural populace. Rumor and fear were widespread and one hardly dared to approach the forests. When the Germans had to drive through them they did so firing their weapons, to scare off the forest dwellers, and speeding as though fleeing from a great danger.

The successful raids and the general disorder strengthened Hershke's will to obtain more weapons at any price. In addition, he itched to expand his raids. At the end of October 1943, Hershke and his gang attacked the Ukrainian *Maslo-Soyuz*[82] in the village of Okno and came away with two new pistols and 150 kg. of butter and other foods. They also demolished the meeting halls and took a horse, a wagon and a peasant. As he did before, Hershke got the peasant drunk and sent him home, while the horse returned on his own.

More severe Autumn weather was coming. The rain and wind depressed them and they pondered over their daily misery and sorrows. What could be the outcome of such a life, they wondered. How tiresome this terrible adventure had become for everyone, and how they yearned for a home, for rest and for normal lives.

They were busy preparing for the winter. Deep, wide bunkers were dug in the forest. Some areas were set aside as storehouses for food and clothing. They planned to take a long break in activity over the winter. For the time being there, was enough food to live on, and further raids would be dangerous' "So, enough!" they said. Perhaps Hitler's quick defeat would put an end to this enforced, rotten life. Good news was reaching them from the war fronts. The peasants assured them help was near - just a matter of days.

Hershke's informers (mostly anti-Ukrainian Poles) came one Autumn day and told him that the beekeepers in Ostapie were preparing to go to Skalat to pick up a large quantity of sugar to feed their bees over the winter months. Hershke couldn't pass up an opportunity like that and, with the help of the Poles, worked out a plan for a new raid. One early November night, around 8:00, a peasant arrived in Ostapie with eight sacks of sugar. He began to unload the sacks and to unharness the horses. Suddenly Hershke appeared with eight companions. They surrounded the cottage. The peasant was ordered to reload the sugar and to re-harness the horses. A chest full of belongings was taken from the cottage and loaded onto the wagon.

When the peasant was ordered to climb aboard, he resisted. They were welcome to the sugar, he argued, but he did not want to give them the horses. Hershke's men fired into the air and gave the peasant something to remember them by, thus forcing him to come along. This time, again, the Ukrainian police fled in great panic, leaving the village to the mercy of God. The attackers rode through the village and no one dared to say a word. They sent the peasant back, but kept the horses. They disassembled the wagon and presented its parts as gifts to their peasant helpers.

Once, at mid-day, the Jews were sitting among the trees, eating their meal, while the horses grazed nearby. Suddenly they heard shouts and loud noises, drawing nearer and nearer. The people grew frightened sensing an army advancing through the trees. They saw the peasant of the sugar and the mayor of Ostapie along with many armed Germans and Ukrainians. Hershke kept his wits and, by hand-signals, issued commands. Suddenly they heard the peasant shouting: "I have a feeling my horses are somewhere nearby!" The danger grew that the horses, sensing their master's presence, might begin to neigh. Hershke was ready to do battle, but recognized that the terrain was strategically unsuitable. He therefore avoided an attack, knowing that the outcome would be tragic. They waited, instead, and a near miracle occurred. The enemy did not spot the Jews. They continued deeper into the forest, searching for the horses, while the Jews remained silently where they were. To have survived this close a brush with death appeared to the people .in the woods an incredible miracle and, like a blessing, had brightened their somber lives.

[Page 82]

Hershke's 'hospital' with its women, aged parents and children, breathed a sigh of relief, as they lifted their eyes to Heaven with thanks.

Now they had to move to another part of the forest. Hershke wrote on a piece of paper the words: "A FOOLISH PEASANT HAS MORE LUCK THAN BRAINS," and signed it "PALIWO."[83] He then tied the paper to a horse's tail and turned the horses loose to find their master.

There was no end to the wanderings of Hershke's band as the mean-spirited peasants continued to spy on them, hoping to pay them back for their attacks. Winter had arrived. Snows had whitewashed the distant fields and deep woods. Human footprints left evidence of passersby on the roads and they became road-signs to the secret places where the Jews hid.

On the evening of 31 December 1943, peasants led by the *Banderowcy* set off for the Turkow Forest to find and wipe out the Jews there. "They approached as close as 100 meters," relates Yeruchem Guz, a former partisan and a member of Hershke's band. "We were ready for them weapons in hand, awaiting the orders of our leader. The peasants opened fire on us from two sides. They fired more than one hundred rounds and the battle cries grew louder, as they were preparing to storm our positions. We had taken up defensive positions, looking for an opening allowing us clear aim before shooting, in accordance with the basic strategic rule that soldiers do not shoot blindly. We lay on the ground, heads partly raised, trigger fingers trembling nervously, and eyes peering sharply forward. We were surrounded, but we waited. Suddenly we saw bullets hitting around us and we began to fire back. We heard nearby cries and threw grenades.

Suddenly the firing ceased. Hershke shouted the command: 'Forward!' - and we crawled ahead on all fours. It became quiet. We waited with baited breath and soon we heard retreating steps. We ran forward. Our victorious 'army' then consisted of twelve men. The remaining 'fighters' of the so-called hospital were in the bunkers, saying prayers. Regrettably, three aged Jews, who were unable to run, fell into the murderers' hands."

The next day, when Hershke and a small group returned to the bunkers, they caught a group of peasants in the act of robbery. They shot one of them. Hershke and his band then relocated in the Okno Forest, where they had earlier built their bunkers. One day, trusted Poles delivered a machine gun. The members of the band were overjoyed to have it. Hershke overhauled and cleaned the gun, polished it and hung belts of ammunition on it. "Now if even a whole regiment of SS-men move against me, they'll get a taste of my fighting."

Hershke and his group still had an important job to finish. There was an infamous man in Skalat named Kolcun, who had more than four hundred Jewish lives on his conscience. Hershke wanted to wipe him off the face of the earth and sent spies to track him down every day. One day even Hershke himself, dressed as a beggar, went to town to find him, but he did not succeed. The murderer, realizing that he was being hunted, hid in various villages and later joined other Ukrainian pogrom instigators who fled deep into Germany and eventually settled in the American occupation zone as displaced persons.

Things were going badly for the Germans on the war fronts. Kiev, Berdiczew, Proskurow and Kamienic-Podolski were, by now, back in Soviet hands. The Germans and their Ukrainian collaborators scurried about in fear. They were no longer concerned with the Jews but with their own escape. Joy reigned in the forest. Help was near and Yosele Birnbaum, a former coachman, now twisted and sick, but still a great wit, spent days rehearsing a speech to welcome the Red Army when it arrived.

Then it was February of 1944. In the forests one could hear the sounds of artillery and exploding bombs emanating from the advancing forces. The hearts of the forest Jews were stirred with yearnings for freedom and peaceful lives. Finally on 23 March 1944, after a heavy battle, the Soviets arrived and liberated Skalat. The forest-Jews had survived the German occupation.

[Page 83]

All thirty-three surviving Jews returned to Skalat. They did not find any of their family nor their relatives alive but they did find their ruined homes. Some joined the army to continue the battle against the enemy, while others returned to their daily labors. The Jewish band dissolved and none of them remained a bandit. Every one of them wondered at the source of his strength and the courage which had enabled him to endure such an ordeal.

Hershke and his band left behind a legend of those times. Stories about them are told in various versions. The peasants of the Skalat area spoke for a long time of the Jewish bandits who had the nerve to want to live - and still don't believe that they survived.

After the liberation, some of the surviving Jews were conscripted into the Red Army. Others were still sick. A Jewish *Kehile*[84] was established in Skalat, registering seventy-nine souls. The Soviet administration appointed Fishl Gelbtuch as representative of the *Kehile*. Since the *shul* was half-destroyed and defiled, the Jews gathered for prayers at the home of Moishe Gelbtuch. They baked *matzos* for Passover and, among themselves, collected 6,000 rubles to repair the *shul* and to fence in the cemetery and the mass graves in the field.

In May of 1944 a Medical-Judicial Commission inspected the mass graves in Skalat. In addition to the representatives of the Soviet regime, the commission included local doctors, judges, priests and representatives of the surviving Jews. All the Jews in Skalat attended the commission hearings. It was determined that there were nine mass graves. Some of the graves were opened and ten corpses were exhumed. The Jews could only identify Getzel Streicher and his wife, Nechame *(nee'* Hecht). The doctors determined that two of the children had been buried alive as they found no evidence of gunshot wounds. They took photographs. Those present reacted emotionally. All of the participants sobbed.

A few days later, the Jews strung wire fences around posts and planted 450 seedlings around the graves. Every Sunday was devoted to tending the gravesites. Tablets were erected over them reading, in Hebrew, - *Here were murdered thousands of our brothers, sons of Israel, may their names be sanctified; who were cut down by the Sword of Hitler, may his name be expunged.*

The Jews also cleared and fenced in the devastated cemetery. Ritual burial was accorded the half-burned *Torahs* which some Jews had collected. The bodies of individual Jews buried in various nearby locations were also given a Jewish ritual burial.

Most of the Jews in town worked. A year passed. The war ended and Eastern Galicia remained part of the Ukraine, under Soviet control. The Soviets announced that prewar Polish citizens wishing to resettle in Polish territory had to register. All the Jewish survivors decided to leave their home town. In July 1945, all of the Jews gathered at the mass graves to bid farewell to the dead. They said Kaddish and the memorial prayers. The entire assembly walked around the graves three times and asked forgiveness from the dead for leaving them.

"No Jew will ever again set foot on this accursed earth," said Yankif Perlmuter, one of the speakers. Moishe Shechter and Fishl Gelbtuch also spoke. There were tears, and little children threw flowers onto the graves. Then the same sad leave-taking, and asking forgiveness of the departed, was repeated at the cemetery.

Not a single Jew remained in his old home town. They fled to Poland from where they resumed their wanderings across the world.

[Page 84]

Afterword

Thus died a *shtetl*.

A Jewish settlement was uprooted - one among thousands.

There was once a *shtetl*, a home; people, hope and faith...And then we suddenly found ourselves in a wilderness: stripped of all values, rejected and pursued. We are still affected by the deathly terror of yesterday and our tomorrow is clouded. There is no foundation on which to build our lives.

The greatest horror of all times emerged on German soil under the mantle of European culture and civilization. This unleashed evil brought on a great destructive force against the noblest achievements of the human spirit with Satanic power. Jews and Jewishness were its main victims. German madmen managed to mobilize a broad circle of international killers, even among the oppressed peoples. Among the Poles, Ukrainians, Lithuanians and Latvians, there were significant segments of debased elements who lent a hand to the oppression of those still weaker: the Jews.

The extermination machine functioned according to plan. Millions perished. *Shtetl*s died.

Somewhere the town of Skalat goes on living. New houses are being built, trees grow, gardens flourish. Only one thing is missing - the Jewish community. It will never return. because it was torn up by its roots. And we, the escapees from those corpse-filled towns, will certainly never return.

For us the *shtetl* has died; Jewish Skalat is no more.

Somewhere in the world, far from one's native town, miraculously rescued survivors wander about in search of a home and a faith. After much wandering we may yet find a home, but faith - faith itself?

Footnotes:

82 Maslo-Soyuz - Butter cooperative (Russian). L. Milch

83 PALIWO - Fuel, here indicating danger. J. Kofler

84 Kehile - Community organization.

[Page 85]

APPENDIX I
List of Jews on "Aryan Papers"
M. Grinfeld

"To my knowledge, people who survived through my documents include:

Mrs. Fay and her two daughters born in Auschwitz (recently in Cracow).

Dr. Cyla Rathauser and her daughter Pola from Grzymalow (lately in Germany).

Sydzia Brust, granddaughter of Munio Tennenbaum (recently in Gliwice).

A daughter of the pharmacist Schor from Podwolczyska (recently in Rzeszow).

Mita Schoenberg (recently in Warsaw).

Bumek Russ (recently in Wroclaw).

Dr. Frederyk Sass (recently in Lignice).

Kamila, the young daughter of Nirler (recently in Szczecin).

Miss Wasserman and the Monias family (now in America).

Wladzio Jawer, Moshe Safir and many others of whom I have heard, but whose present whereabouts I do not know.

Sadly, my own wife, Rozia (nee Glassner), from Grzyrnalow, was not saved by her "Aryan Papers," nor was her cousin Genia Schifman from Budzanow. Both of them left Skalat on 28 October 1942 and perished near Zolkiew in June 1944, just before the liberation.

Others who died include Siunio Kanarek, the son of Zusse; Feige Kaczor and many others whose names I do not remember."

[Page 86]

APPENDIX II
List of Witnesses
Interviewed by A. Weissbrod
1945-1947

Below is a partial list of authoritative witnesses who made major contributions to the completion of my work:

Munia Bernhaut	Abraham Schapiro
Ester Fischbach	Abraham Sommerstein
Meyer Grinfeld	Hadassah Sommerstein
Nisen Klein	Mordechai Spiegel
Josef Kofler	Henek Weinberg
Max Monias	Amalia Weissbrod
Yankif Perlmuter	Josef Weksler

Among the non-Jews (Poles and Ukrainians):

Josef Bernacki
I. Kowalewski
Piotr Kuzdeba
Josef Neimauer
Michal Olejnik

[Page 87]

APPENDIX III
Dates and Count of Skalat
Victims and Survivors

Jewish population of Skalat, 1941	4,600
Driven to Skalat from surrounding areas, 1942	3,900

Total Jewish population of the area: **8,500**

Victims of pogroms, actions and deportations:

1. First pogrom (11 Tammuz 5701) 6 July 1941	560
2. Live Contingent (11-18 Elul 5702) 30-31 August 1942	560
3. "Wild Action" (10-11 Heshvan 5703) 21-22 October 1942	3,153
4. "Little Action" (29 Heshvan 5103) 9 November 1942	1,100
5. "Sobbing Graves" (2 Nissan 5103) 1 April 1943	760
6. "Shavuot Action" (6 Sivan 5703) 9 June 1943	660
7. From the camp courtyard (13 Sivan 5703) 16 June 1943	50
8. 'First Camp Action" (21 Sivan 5793) 30 June 1943	200
9. 'Second Camp Action" (35 Tammuz 5703) 28 July 1943	130
10. In the various forests	144
11. At the hands of peasants	43
12. Various other slaughters	47
13. Skalat Jews killed at other camps	900

Total Jewish Victims   **8,307**

The Final Count of the Survivors in the Woods

	Originally	Survived
1. Ostra-Mogila Forest	32	29
2. Chmieliska Forest	52	6
3. Okna Forest (Hershke's Band)	38	33
4. Malinik Forest	40	11

5. Hory Forest	78	50
6. Krecilow Forest	14	11
7. With various peasants	90	46
8. Skalat Jews with partisans	36	7
TOTALS	**380**	**193**

Jewish survivors from Skalat (proper)	160
Survivors from Hershke's band (mainly from Grzymalow)	33

| **Total Number of Jewish Survivors** | **193** |

NOTE: According to some sources, out of 2,200 Jews living in Grzymalow in 1941, 60 Jews survived in that town, and about the same number survived in Podwolczyska. Of the more than 8,000 Victims from Skalat, about 3,000 are buried in the cemetery, in the mass graves and in the fields around Skalat. The rest perished in the extermination camp Belzec.

[Page 88]

APPENDIX IV

Testimonies of Witnesses,
Obtained by Lusia Milch
1992-1995

[Page 89]

The Day I Survived the Pogrom in the Bashtis

I was born on December 9, 1922 in Skalat, Poland. My name at that time was Isaac Birnbaum On February 1, 1949 I migrated to the United States and changed my name to Isidor Butel.

In Skalat, I lived with my mother, Sarah Birnbaum (nee Parnes), my father, Simon Birnbaum, my sisters Bleema and Laya and my brothers Moishe, Kuni, Yossel and Aley. My sister Bleema married Mailach Kornweitz and they had two young daughters named Goldie and Pepe. My brother Moishe married a woman named Laya and they had one little boy. In 1940, my brothers Moishe, Yossel, Kuni and Aley and my brother-in-law Mailach were active in military service. I remained in Skalat with the rest of my family.

On July 6, 1941, I was 19 years old. I was in my house with my mother, my father, my sisters Bleema and Laya and my two nieces. Out of fear, we were all confined to the house. I seem to recall that this day was not the Sabbath, since no one went to the synagogue and on the previous evening my mother did not light the Sabbath candles. On that day which I believe was a Sunday, I recall seeing Gentile teenagers walking around with German soldiers, pointing out Jewish houses, and among them ours. In the morning, though I do not recall the exact time, approximately six teenagers, either Ukrainians or Poles, walked into our house. Since the doors were unlocked, they entered our house freely. Once in the house, the Germans ordered me and my father out of the house. In German they told us to "Come out, come, come" as they waved their hands summoning us to follow them outside. They did not hit us and they did not shout. They spoke firmly, with authority, expecting submission and compliance.

My father and I offered no resistance to their command. We stepped out of the house and proceeded to walk with the soldiers, stopping at a neighbor's house. Then we waited outside while the Germans entered a neighbor's house and brought out two teenage brothers by the names of Aley and Dovid. The Jewish teenagers joined us and then, accompanied by the German soldiers, we all walked as a group a distance of approximately one mile outside of town. The Germans led us to an empty lot where we saw a group of about thirty Jewish men. Among them were both young and older Jews. All of these people were from my home town.

When we arrived where the group of Jews were assembled, my father and I were separated. I watched as the German soldiers led my father away. I didn't know where the Germans were taking him and I didn't know what was going to happen to him. I did not have an opportunity to say anything to my father. I looked at him and those next to him. When they took my father away, my mind went blank. I kept on looking at my father and he looked back at me as he left. He too didn't say anything. He just went with them and that was the last time I ever saw my father.

After my father was taken away, I remained standing in a group with about fourteen other teenage Jewish boys from Skalat. Several German soldiers led us all a distance of approximately one-half mile from this location. We were led to a p ace where there were trees, more German soldiers, and military trucks. The Germans gave us axes and ordered us to chop down the trees, chop the branches off the trees, and then camouflage the trucks with the branches. While I chopped the trees, the Germans did not hit me. I did not think of trying to escape though I wanted very much to go home. As I chopped the trees with the other teenage boys, we did not speak to each other. No one said a word or expressed any emotion. We were all like stones.

We continued to work for hours, until it became dark. Then, the Germans took us to the "bashtis" (towers), which were about one and one-half mile or so from the place where we were chopping the trees. The "bashtis" were located in the center of our town and were used by soldiers during World War I. I was familiar with the "bashtis" and had seen them from the outside many times in the past. The Germans ordered us to run into the "bashtis." At their command, we all ran inside where it was completely dark. Suddenly, the Germans started shooting their machine guns from the outside into the "bashtis." I heard the bullets being fired inside but I heard no screams or cries from any of the other Jewish boys who were there with me. While the Germans were shooting, I fell, pressing my face and body against the floor. Then, when the shooting ceased, some German soldiers came inside the "bashtis." Though I could not see them, I could hear them checking the bodies to see if anyone was still alive. I don't know how many soldiers came inside because it was dark, but I could hear them moving bodies around. One soldier kicked me with his foot to see if I was alive. I was lying motionless, face down and pretended that I was dead. As the Germans checked the bodies, they did not speak and they did not shine any flashlights. I remained on the floor in the same position. Some time passed and I no longer heard any sounds from inside or outside of the "bashtis." I believed, therefore, that the Germans had left. More time passed. After a while I stood up in the dark and made my way to the entrance.

[Page 90]

I looked outside and saw that no one was there and that the Germans were gone. It was approximately 11:00 p.m. I walked out of the "bashtis," leaving from the same entrance through which I was driven in by the Germans. The doors at the entrance of the "bashtis" had been removed and I was able to walk around the back and into a square. This square was a place where people used to play tennis, but at this hour it was deserted. I quickly left the "bashtis" and ran home. In the dark, I crossed over puddles and running water, and made my way back to my neighborhood. I did not go straight to my house. Instead, I went into a stable owned by a neighbor, Yoini Drat, which was located across the street from my house. I then stood at the door of the stable and waited to see someone from my town. When it became light, I saw a teenage girl, Chajka Sass, pass by. I opened the door and called her over. She was the first person who saw me after my escape from the "bashtis." I asked her to go to my house and tell my mother and my family that I was alive and that I was in the stable. A little later, I went home and related to my mother and my sisters what had happened to me, and that my father and I were separated. My mother asked me where my father was and I told her that I did not know where the Germans had taken him nor what had happened to him,

When I was in the "bashtis," I was grazed by bullets in three places: at the bridge of my nose, on the inside crease of my left elbow and near the ankle of my right foot. During my ordeal of being shot at I was like a stone and did not feel any pain. It was much later, the next morning, that I remember feeling pain. It was also later, either in the stable or in my house, when I realized that I had been shot and observed blood from the bullet wounds on my clothes.

I am the only person who came out alive from the "bashtis" on that day.

When all of these things were happening, I was not fearful or nervous. I had ho feelings about anything; I didn't cry .The only thoughts I had were about my father. I thought, if he were alive, he would have come back too. But he didn't. Nor did Aley or Dovid or the other Jewish souls who were driven into the "bashtis." I was the only one to come out of the "bashtis," as well as the only survivor of those who were caught in this pogrom.

My thanks to my daughter, Linda Butel Kish, for setting forth this event in writing.

Isidor Butel (Isaac Birnbaum)
Brooklyn, New York 1994

[Page 91]

A Childhood Denied

A child's crying out but his voice can't be heard
the anguish repressed as he hides
a shield against danger is stillness he learned
and silence, a savior of lives.

Feelings are secrets to friends and to strangers
with caution perceive them in kind
lingering lessons, like undying embers
once urgently seared in his mind.

Trust is a perilous, hazardous journey
beware of the sudden surprise
truth into lies can be instantly turning,
betrayal as promise disguised.

With endless suspicion and cunning pretenses
life was upheld like a crown
laden with memories imprisoned by fences
and walls that refuse to come down.

How mighty the price survival commands:
a childhood forever denied,
a soul left in shambles no one understands,
a child who within me still hides.

By Dunio Bernhaut
River Edge, New Jersey 1992

[Page 92]

Unanswered... ?

Will I always remember?
Can I ever forget
or is the sentence perpetual and conclusively set?

Will the memories dwindle?
Can the torment subside
or is the cycle relentless as the flow of the tide?

Will sadness release me?
Can I ever know joy
or is fate still unfolding some merciless ploy?

Will somebody know me?
Can I be seen through the haze
or is the image evasive in an intricate maze?

Will my past serve a purpose?
Was it craftily planned
is destiny just adding one more granule of sand?

Like shadowy visions concealing in fear
most answers elusive, opaque and unclear
but these so translucent through a shroud of regret:
yes, I will always remember; no, I can never forget.....

By Dunio Bernhaut
River Edge, New Jersey 1993

[Page 93]

Testimony of Munia Bernhaut

In June 1943 when Skalat was, declared Judenfrei, by the Germans, I, Munia Bernhaut, my son Dunio, aged three, and my daughter Nusia, aged five, had miraculously been spared the fate of our brothers and sisters. By then, thousands of Jews from Skalat had already perished by torture, starvation or disease. The majority were murdered and buried in mass graves, or captured in '**actions**,' and shipped to the extermination camp of Belzec.

After every '**action**' hundreds disappeared, and those who remained surfaced from hiding places stunned and bewildered. Everyone who saw me with my two young children hanging on to me shook their heads in disbelief. Very few children remained among the living in the Skalat Ghetto.

After the first '**action**' was unleashed on the ghetto, I and my friends Sima and Joseph Kofler began to build a bunker under our house. We sealed off part of the cellar with bricks and other building materials, which we smuggled in at night. A trap door hidden underneath a bed and covered with carpet lead into the bunker and the descent to our hiding place was by means of a wooden ladder. By sheer luck our bunker was never discovered during all the '**actions**,' even after thorough searches of the house and its surroundings. We remained hidden in that bunker during every one of the '**actions**,' in our town. It was there, after the final '**action**' , that we learned that Skalat had been declared Judenfrei and Jews were no longer allowed to exist, not even under the horrendous conditions of the ghetto.

The few who survived the last '**action**' in our bunker began under cover of night to flee wherever they could. In spite of my pleas no one considered including me in their plans. For me, it would have been suicidal to attempt such an escape with two small children. As we were left all alone, I had weighed my alternatives: stay and perish in the bunker, give up and go out to be shot on the spot, or attempt an escape on my own, I decided to flee although I had no idea where or how to do it.

A day after the final '**action**' the streets of the ghetto were deserted. Trucks driven by inmates of the Skalat Camp began rolling in to pick up whatever was left of the household belongings from the empty Jewish homes. By sheer luck, the assigned driver to one of these trucks was my cousin Isaac Gritz. After careful planning, he managed to stop by our house on his last round of the day, hoping to finding his mother who had been in our bunker. When he quietly signaled his presence in the house, I knew this was my only chance. I pleaded and implored his help to smuggle us out of the ghetto. He agreed, though with great trepidation and fear, to drop us at the edge of town on his way back to the camp. One by one he carried us out hidden underneath feather bedding and placed us on his truck. When he approached the outskirts of our town, he slowed down. I quickly threw my daughter out of the truck and then jumped out after her with my son in my arms. As he drove away, hidden by the darkness, we crawled into the surrounding fields.

My hope was to reach the forest where I knew there were groups of Jews and partisans in hiding. So began our long wandering through the fields and woods. I walked day and night carrying my son in my arms or on my back and holding my little girl close to me. We ate whatever we found, kernels of wheat from the fields, raw potatoes, beets and anything else I could dig up. Thus, we wandered hungry and thirsty; our clothes, dirty and wet from mud and rain. In despair, I took a chance and knocked at the door of the solitary farmhouses we occasionally encountered. I begged for food and shelter, but the pitiless peasants would only unleash their dogs on us and threaten to turn us in if we didn't leave immediately. A few times, in return for a little money which I still had on me, the peasants sold us bread and milk and allowed us to hide in the barn or the hayloft for a couple of nights. Harboring Jews put them at risk for had we been discovered, they too would have been shot. Therefore, our stay was always cut short with a demand that we leave by nightfall. One peasant woman was willing to keep us in return for all the money I had left and a promise to give her more when the war ended. When I gratefully agreed, she insisted on another condition. She demanded that I leave my little boy in the forest because his presence posed too great a danger of discovery. A three year old child, she said, could not be counted on to remain silent. That had been suggested to me before, but abandoning one of my children was out of the question. I was determined that we would either survive together or die together, and once again we took to the road.

[Page 94]

Weeks passed and as the weather turned colder, we often found shelter inside haystacks still standing in the fields or in an abandoned cave where we would spend a few nights sheltered from the winds and the rain. .At times when my children had nothing to eat for days, I summoned the courage to stop farmers on their way to the market and to beg for food. On one such occasion, they began throwing stones and hitting us with sticks while calling us dirty Jews. Fortunately, the attack was thwarted by an old man who suddenly appeared on the road and began shouting at the peasants that some day they would be punished for such inhumane treatment of a woman with small children. I felt very lucky to escape and continued my wanderings.

I still could not find the hiding place in the woods. The weather was getting worse and I was losing strength. Despondent, I began thinking of going back into town where I knew that I and my children would be killed. At the end of one such desperate day, we were approached in the cave where we were hiding, by a farmer who had spotted us while working in the fields. He waited for the others to leave and assured me that he meant no harm. He offered to take us to his farmhouse where we could hide in .the barn until the end of the war.

I could not believe my good fortune. The farmer and his wife shared with us the meager food they had while I mended and sewed clothes for their children. We spent several weeks there. One day, with tears in their eyes, the farmer and his wife told us that we had to leave immediately. The Germans had begun checking the farms to make sure that no one was hoarding products which the peasants had been ordered to deliver to the German army. The farmer took us to the side of the forest and prayed that we would find Jews to help us.

The next afternoon, as we were walking through the woods, I heard someone approaching on horseback. We barely had time to duck behind a tree when a command came loud and clear: "Juden raus" or we'll shoot. I came out with my children to face rifles pointing at us. I instantly recognized Hefner, a local German administrator in charge of agriculture, accompanied by two SS officers. They were amused when I said that they might as well shoot us and get us out of our misery. Hefner remarked' to his companions that it was the first time he heard a Jew asking to be killed. Then, turning to me, he admired my blonde children and announced that he had no intention of shooting us. He advised me to follow the path in front of us which would lead us to Jews hidden deep in the forest. I was sure that they would kill us as soon as we turned our backs. I started to walk clutching my children tightly. I told them not to be afraid and that at any moment now, we would be in heaven together with the rest of the family. As we were walking, I heard the Germans behind me riding away. For us, another miracle had taken place!

Many years later, at a wedding in New York City, I met a woman who had survived on "Aryan Papers" and worked as a maid for Hefner during his stay in Skalat. As we talked about the Holocaust, she recounted that when Hefner returned from the woods that day he announced to his wife at dinner that he had just spared the life of a young Jewish woman with two beautiful children. He then added, "If I didn't shoot them, they will surely survive this war." And indeed we survived.

Eventually, I did reach a bunker where a small group of Jews from Skalat was hiding. During my desperate wanderings, I was often fortified by the hope of being welcomed with open arms by my own people. That, however, was not the case. The head of the bunker demanded that I leave immediately because he was afraid that my small children would expose all of them to danger. I cried and implored for compassion. Finally the majority of the group overruled his decision and allowed me to stay. I promised to pull my own weight and contribute to the search for food and water.

[Page 95]

My children and I were among the very few who survived the bitter winter, the starvation, the diseases, the encounters with hostile Ukrainian woodsmen, and the periodic ambushes by the Germans. We were liberated in the forest by the advancing Soviet army and returned to our devastated hometown. There we were ultimately reunited with the only other surviving member of our family, my husband Joseph Bernhaut, the father of my children.

I close my eyes sometimes and imagine that the Nazi occupation was just a nightmare. I awake and realize that it really happened. Our families, our homes, our communities are gone. Nothing is left, just memories of home and family.

Munia Bernhaut nee' Somerstein
North Miami, Florida 1995

[Page 96]

Testimony of Yoel Ben-Porat

I, Yoel Ben-Porat, whose name before the war was Julek Weinraub, am the son of Joseph and Malka Weinraub (nee' Bauer) and the grandson of Yechiel Weinraub. I come from the town of Skalat where my family lived for many years.

Our house was located at number 10, May the 3rd Street and we lived there until the fall of 1942 when the Skalat Ghetto was established. Then we were forced to leave our house and to move into an apartment beyond the synagogue. It was an area of some old, dilapidated houses in a poor Jewish section known in our town by the Yiddish phrase "inter da bud" (below the public bath house). We shared the tiny crowded apartment with two more families. The name of one was Kiwetz and the name of the other, I do not recall.

I spent the Nazi occupation in the town of Skalat, where the lives of the Jews were in danger at all times and I wish to relate here one of my experiences during this period. It was October 21, 1942, the first day of the "Wild Action" in Skalat. I remember that on that day, at dawn, someone had knocked on our window and tried to awaken my father. A man's voice said in Ukrainian, "Yosio, vstavaity!" (Joseph, wake up). When I heard the message, I was the first to jump to my feet and to run outside in order to see who was there. I looked around, but I saw no one. Till today I do not know, for sure, who came to warn us. My family thought that it probably was a Ukrainian peasant, named Masnej, who was very fond of my father and in whose Mantiawa orchards, on the outskirts of town, we kept our bee hives.

Not being sure that the knock on the window was a warning, my father told me to walk over to the Judenrat area of our town, only a few minutes walk from our house, to see what was happening. Under the Nazi occupation I used to accompany my father during his deliveries of newspapers to German and Ukrainian institutions such as the *Schupo* and *Kripo* , and I was acutely aware of our dangerous situation. Therefore, though I was only eleven years old, my father considered me reliable to bring back some news of what was going on. Arriving at the *Judenrat* I saw nothing unusual, and since everything was quiet, I decided to go back home.

When I reached the street near the synagogue, suddenly the town exploded with noise. The shooting and shouting was of such intensity that it exerted the intended shock effect on the Jews. The Germans and the Ukrainian police, who were all around, fell upon us and I was among the very first twenty or thirty Jews caught. We were immediately led to the synagogue. There we were stopped in front of the large, iron door which was shut tight. I remember a German soldier with a grenade in his hand, walking up to the heavy door and hanging the grenade on the door handle. Then he moved to the side of the building, detonated the grenade by pulling a string and thus blew the door open. By then, more people had joined us in front of the synagogue and we were the first group of about forty or fifty Jews to be chased inside.

The sanctuary was huge and empty when we were driven in. But every few minutes more people were brought in and within an hour, hundreds of victims filled the synagogue. Since I was caught alone, I decided to stand near the front entrance in order to see whether my parents would be brought in. Even at that young age I realized that it would be better for them not to be caught. Yet, I thought, just in case they were brought in, at least I would be with them and not alone. I remained standing at the entrance all the time, seeing tens of people being chased in every couple of minutes. Some of them were wounded and all were in a state of panic. We didn't know exactly what was going to happen to us, but we knew that from here we would be brought to some terrible place. Inside, the atmosphere was one of shock and terror. The air was permeated with moans and screams of the wounded, and the cries and prayers of the trapped victims. After a few hours when the sanctuary was half filled, Obersturmbannfuhrer Muller appeared. I recognized him from his frequent visits to the Skalat Schupo. He came inside, took his pistol and shot at random into the crowd. This caused the people to retreat deeper into the sanctuary, enabling Muller to see how much space was left for additional victims to be brought in.

[Page 97]

I stood a few more hours at the entrance. Suddenly I saw my Aunt Esther Zimmer, my mother's sister, her sixteen year old daughter, Betka, and ten year old son, Yitzchak, the family of Shaye Zimmer , being brought into the synagogue. Shaye Zimmer was the second in command of the Skalat Judenrat, therefore, I realized that his family was caught by mistake and would probably be released. I was right. I decided to attach myself to them and not let go. I don't remember how long we waited, perhaps a half an hour or an hour, when an SS officer came in with a list and started to call the names of families of the Jewish police and the Judenrat members who were caught. Among them he called the names of my aunt and two cousins.

By that time the synagogue was almost full and everybody was pushing. We too pushed, trying to get out when the Zimmer names were called. When we came outside and my uncle spotted me together with his wife and children, he became pale. An SS officer approached him and asked my uncle "Is this your family?"

He answered "Yes."

"All of them, the wife and three children?"

Again, my uncle said "Yes."

"But you told me that you have a wife and two children," the SS-man hissed.

"No, my Sturmfuhrer, I said a wife and three children."

"Don't you lie, you dog you! You said a wife and two children."

I looked at my uncle and our eyes met. My life was hanging on the thread of his next answer. He would either panic and say it was a mistake and deny that I was his son, or at the risk of the lives of his wife and children, claim me as his son and thus save me. My uncle repeated almost in a shouting voice, "I said a wife and three children." An exchange of shouting between my uncle and the SS-man took another turn, but finally I, together with my aunt and two cousins, were motioned to be released. We were taken to the *Judenrat* where we were kept for the duration of the '**action**' - two nights and one and a half days.

After the '**action**,' I found out that my father was also caught and was killed near the well of the Skalat marketplace, from where he tried to escape. My mother and her three brothers, Israel, Chaim, and Yoel Bauer; were all caught. My mother jumped from the train, but was shot and killed near Borki-Wielkie. All three brothers also jumped from the train; two of them were killed after they jumped and only one, Israel, survived.

I survived the "Wild Action" alone. This '**action**' claimed the greatest number of victims from Skalat, as well as Jews from the towns of Grzymalow and Podwoloczyska, who were brought to our town. With this slaughter, the systematic mass murder of the Jews in Skalat was begun.

Taped testimony as given to Lusia Milch
by Yoel Ben-Porat, November 1995

[Page 98]

Nine Months in Hiding

In 1943 when Skalat was declared Judenfrei, I was ten years old. Our family consisted of my parents, four sisters, and two brothers. Before the war my home town had been a vibrant Jewish community .My father owned a leather tannery and I can still see his face with a red, neatly trimmed beard.

My brother, #testimoniesripted into the army. My older brother, Yitzchok. had aspired to take over the family business and he had worked hard under father's stern supervision. All our hopes and dreams were shattered, however, when the Nazis occupied Skalat. My father and two sisters were killed. My mother, remaining sister, brother and I began our struggle to survive.

In 1942 when the Skalat Ghetto was formed, we moved in with the Sass family, Together we were reduced to the same deplorable living conditions and shared what meager food the circumstances provided.

Through pre-war trading connections, the Sass family knew many people in the villages. It was through these contacts that the Marko family had agreed to hide us. They were poor but exceptionally good people who lived in the village of Poplawe. This family risked their lives for us. They gave us what they could; a small attic room with a little ventilation and some light, and what food they could spare. Although, the nine of us were hiding in such tight quarters that we practically shared the same breaths and our bellies groaned constantly, I will always be grateful to the Marko family for their incredible sacrifice.

We remained at their home for three months. Then we had to leave. I can never forget the worried looks on their faces and the sadness that dwelt in their eyes. They had no choice but to send us away. In those days people watched each other. They counted things. A few more potatoes in a pot could mean Jews were being hidden. Most of their neighbors were not as good as the Marko family and many of them would have gladly handed us over to the Nazis.

We had to form a new plan quickly. My brother, Yitzchok. and two of the Sass boys, Motl and Szajko, had decided to hike ten miles to the woods of Stary (old) Skalat in order to find out whether Jews were hiding there. Meanwhile, the Markos led us to some potato fields, a couple of miles from their house. There my mother, sister, the three Sass women and I laid down in the trenches between the potato fields and waited for the boys to return.

We waited for 24 hours. Our bodies ached with cramps from remaining still for such a long time, but we did not dare to move. We had to be vigilant of the Nazis, the Ukrainian police, and the peasants. I was not yet eleven years old and already had so many enemies.

This ordeal affected my mother worst of all. The murders of my father and sisters had taken away her will to survive. For three months while we were hiding in the Marko's attic, mother lay curled up in a dim corner. She could not bring herself to eat what little food was offered. Occasionally, she would sigh. More often, she would whimper. Though she seemed to look. her eyes refused to see. Then she no longer looked at us. Once a beautifully groomed women, she no longer brushed her hair or attended to her own hygiene. Fayga Epstein, my mother, died in the potato field as we lay waiting. We left mother unburied in the field where she died. While hiding in the woods, we learned that the Marko family buried her not far from where she died.

When our brothers returned, we left quietly for the woods. We walked in silence and the only sound that we made was the dirt crackling under our shoes. Our breaths combined with the cool night air, and though I was tired to exhaustion, I didn't dare to complain.

In general, I barely spoke from the time we escaped from a cellar in the Skalat Ghetto a few months earlier. At that time a baby's cry brought the Nazis down to our cellar, and that led to the shooting of my father. I learned then that children did best to remain silent.

Deep in the forest of Stary Skalat, the boys dug a large foxhole and there we spent three months. With the onset of the cold, damp weather the insects, snakes and other creatures were asleep. I was relieved in that dark hole - dirt permanently embedded into my body - not to be tormented by those crawling and slithering creatures. It rained nearly all the time. The cold and dampness seeped into my bones. It seemed as if I would never feel warm again.

[Page 99]

The boys spent their nights foraging for food, mostly in the fields and gardens of local farmers. They would return in the morning with vegetables which we cooked into a soup using water from a stream and cooking in a bucket on a small campfire. We sat together on a dirt floor, under a roof of bare trees and gray sky. Then the snows descended.

By December of 1943 the ground was covered with a smooth white blanket. This presented a new problem. How do we walk without creating footprints? These would certainly lead the Nazis and the Ukrainian militia to our hiding place. We had to find a new hiding place and once again we needed to rely on Gentile people. But who would be willing to risk their lives for us? Motl Sass had an idea, though it was risky.

There was a family named Szewchuk living in the village of Chopcianki. The father was a member of the Bandera gang - a militant Ukrainian group - which sought to murder Jews. No one would suspect Jews to be hidden among these people. Motl arranged a place for us in this family's stable. This is where Mrs. Sass, her two daughters, Chajka and Nechama, my sister Bronia and I survived the last few months of the war. Before Motl left he gave Mr. Szewchuk a firm warning, "One of us from the Sass or Epstein families is sure to survive and we will hunt and kill you should as much as a hair from these women's heads be harmed."

Mr. Szewchuk must have held Motl's words in earnest because every night we watched him leave in a Nazi uniform. We knew he was hunting for Jews, yet he and his family were hiding us. His wife brought us a small portion of potatoes and some cereal each day. If we were thirsty, we drank water from the horse's trough.

In March 1944 we were informed by the Szewchuks that the Russians liberated Skalat. Jews were slowly returning to the little town. Shortly thereafter, Motl returned to bring us home.

Ruth Ellenberg Eisenberg nee Epstein
Lakewood, New Jersey 1995

[Page 100]

Testimony of Nusia Frankel

It is late afternoon in a forest outside of Skalat. The Germans are sweeping through the forest, hunting for the small number of Jews who survived the **'actions,'** escaped the ghetto, and are now hiding in the forest.

I'm six year's old and running for my life. The Jews are running towards another hiding place in the forest and I know I must not lose sight of them. I'm the link between them and my mother who lags behind, slowed down by the weight of my little brother whom she is carrying. My eyes are darting in every direction as I try to keep up with the group without losing sight of my mother. Gunfire breaks out around us and shots echo ominously through the woods. Panic drives me to run much faster than my short, skinny legs are normally capable of.

Everyone scatters. The woman ahead of me has been shot and falls to the ground. She's dead. Intuitively, I throw myself on the ground and lie motionless holding my breath. I hear screams, more shots, and the cracking of twigs under heavy German boots. Suddenly there is silence, complete and utter silence.

I am terrified to open my eyes or get up. Hours pass and night falls. Not a human sound. is heard anywhere around me. I am all alone. Slowly I get up, whimpering silently. I have long ago learned not to cry. I begin to look for a familiar landmark, but all the trees and bushes look alike. Which direction should I take? Will I find my mother and brother? Is everyone dead?

Cautiously, I move through the woods. Suddenly, a human shape is walking towards me. I stop, frozen in my tracks. I see a woman approaching and I begin to tremble uncontrollably. A sigh of relief. She is one of the women from our bunker. She tries to console me, although she seems as terrified as I am. The Germans have left she says, and assures me that my mother is looking for me and will probably find us by morning. It is too dark to proceed so we hide under bushes huddling together to keep warm. Exhaustion and the reassuring presence of an adult watching over me allow me to drift into sleep.

I awake at dawn. The woman is convinced that our people are looking for us and insists that we stay where we are. I urge her to start walking so as to try and find our way back. I think I would recognize the trail leading to a brook, from which my mother and I fetch water. I would also recognize another trail which we use at night to go into the fields to forage for food.

We begin to move tentatively through the underbrush trying to avoid the clearings. After walking for hours, we come to a path which I think is the one leading to the brook. We are too weak and exhausted to continue. We hide at the edge of the path hoping that sooner or later some of our people will come for water.. It is dusk and another night without food or shelter looms ahead.

Listen! What? Listen carefully! The faint sound of steps on the trail. Steps and whispers. Yes, someone is approaching. They are Jews from our bunker and they lead us back.

In the bunker the atmosphere is full of gloom. Not everyone has made it back. My mother is mourning. She is sure that I was either captured or killed. Yet she clings to a faint hope. She knows that at the age of six I have already acquired the skills of a survivor. Tears of joy, hugs, kisses, and prayers of thanks surround me. For us, another miracle had taken place! The three of us are alive and once again together.

Nusia Frankel nee' Bernhaut
North Miami, Florida 1995

[Page 101]

Testimony of Dzidzia Gelbtuch

Before World War II, I, Dzidzia Gelbtuch nee' Dlugacz, lived in Skalat with my parents and younger brother. From my immediate family my father, David, and I survived, but my mother, Sarah, and my brother, Benjamin, were killed. When the Germans occupied Skalat, I was subjected to deprivation. suffering and forced labor. I was hunted during the **'actions.'** I was beaten and stabbed by German SS men and till today carry on my back the scars of their bayonets.

From the first day when the Germans entered Skalat, I was witness to scenes of terrible brutality and inhumanity. During the pogrom of 6 June 1941, I was hiding in the attic of our house. Through a small. opening I saw Ukrainians pulling, pushing, and kicking helpless Jews, both young and old, while stabbing them with knives. I saw a bearded, dead Jew wrapped in a talis, laying on the ground in the market square. This scene and others, as well as my two escapes from certain death, took place in Skalat a long time ago, but they shall always be part of my terrible memories.

During the **'actions,'** Jews were rounded-up for killing. Of those who were caught almost no one returned. Since I was caught in two **'actions,'** and came back. it was as if l had returned from the dead not once, but twice. When I jumped off the train and finally reached the Tarnopol Ghetto, the Jews there called me "uciekinierka" (a fugitive) and looked at me in disbelief.

On 21-22 October 1942 when the "Wild Action" took place in Skalat, I and my family were still living in our own house. Our house had a deep cellar, which led to a long, narrow tunnel where one could only crawl. It was said that the tunnels ran under the market and extended to the towers. Fear of getting trapped and lost in them, stopped us from hiding there.

When the **'action'** had started, about ten people living in our house ran down the cellar where we huddled together in a dark corner. There we stayed for some time until two German soldiers with very powerful flashlights came down into our cellar. With them were two or three policemen, though I don't remember whether they were

Ukrainians or Jews. They spotted us immediately and we started to yell "Wier arbeiten" (we're working), meaning we're willing to work. to which the Germans answered with cruel irony, "Wir arbeiten auch" (we too are working)!

Then they took us out one by one from the cellar and led us to the marketplace. When we arrived, we saw small groups of terrified Jews standing in different places of the square. I saw a German. drag a crying boy of about four or five, slam him against a wall and then shoot him with his pistol. More Jews were caught. Then we were led to the synagogue where our relatives, friends, and many neighbors were already assembled.

We were being pushed into the synagogue and as I was passing through the vestibule, I spotted an exit door on the left side. Luckily, no one noticed me as I opened the door and entered a small room cluttered with boards and broken benches. Behind the door was a chimney with an opening. I quickly climbed inside and stepped on some debris and protruding stones in the chimney wall. There I stayed the rest of the day and though I could not see the Jews inside the sanctuary, I could hear their terrible screams. Night came, the screams stopped and it became quiet. The victims had all been taken away. Fearing that the synagogue may still be guarded, I remained standing in the chimney during the entire night. In the morning, after the **'action,'** I came out and went home. There I found my father who had somehow survived this **'action'** as well.

On 9 November 1942, the "Little Action" took place in Skalat. We were no longer living in our house but with the Wilners, inside the ghetto. The house was not familiar to me and I knew of no hiding place or bunker there. At dawn the SS-men and the Ukrainian policemen surrounded the ghetto and closed off all the roads leading outside. Though I realized that there was little chance to leave the ghetto, I, nevertheless, walked out through the back door of the building, in hope of escaping. Near the Ukrainian church, a few yards away, I saw a construction site next to the Cooperative store. I ran across and fell into a covered, deep hole excavated for a foundation. On one side of the excavation was a door leading to the cellar of the Cooperative. I opened it, went inside, and stood in the corner of a dark hall. Within twenty minutes the SS-man Muller (whose face, with a few gold teeth in the front of his mouth and whose coat with a fur-covered collar, were familiar to me) stood in front of me holding a lit candle. He ordered me to tell him whether the Ukranian supervisor of the Cooperative provided me with a hiding place. I answered honestly "No." He then asked me to show him how I got in. I simply told him that I fell into the hole. He was surprised, but did not question me further. He then handed me over to another SS-man who led me to the synagogue.

[Page 102]

When we approached the synagogue, and as in the previous 'action,' I heard horrifying sounds coming out of the inside. The sanctuary was filled with people, wailing and praying. When I entered I was overcome by the stench and lack of air. There I stayed for some time. Suddenly, the doors were opened and the loading onto the trucks was begun. During the loading, the SS-men subjected us to merciless kicking and beatings. With me in the truck was my future brother-in-law and his family. When we reached the out of town area, he tried to escape by jumping off the truck, but he was shot in front of my eyes.

We arrived at the Tarnopol railroad station, where under constant blows to the head with rifle butts, we were forced into cattle cars and packed like herring in a barrel. Then the doors were sealed.

In the train car there were no windows, toilets or water to drink. There was one small opening covered with barbed wire. As in the synagogue, we suffered from lack of air and a terrible stench. Our situation was unbearable and some people attempted to escape.

Mr. Ratzenstein pulled the barbed wire from the opening and a man, whose name I do not remember, was the first to jump. He fell on the railroad track and was killed. I was next in line to jump. Someone pushed me through the opening and I fell near the tracks. Not far away, I saw the crushed body of the man who had jumped before me. A German riding on a motorcycle along the moving train caught me and two more people and led us to a tool shed filled with shovels, pitchforks, and hammers. He ordered us to go inside and then he locked the door.

It was a cold, drizzly fall evening and the ground was frozen. I spent the night in the shed dressed in a thin jacket and one shoe, having lost the other one during my jump.

Dawn arrived. A German came, unlocked the shed and told us "laufen, schnell laufen," (run, run fast). I thought he was going to shoot us, but he did not. The three of us ran in different directions. Exhausted, cold and half conscious, I continued to run till I fell into a ditch. A peasant on his way to a flour mill helped me out of the ditch and told me that I was not far from Tarnopol. Jewish road-repair brigades were working on this road and again I started to walk in hope of finding Jews. I walked till I reached Tarnopol. When I reached the ghetto, the Jews there looked at the few escapees in wonder, but with the full awareness that our attempts at saving ourselves were futile.

On Tuesdays, members of the Skalat Jewish Council would come to Tarnopol on 'business.' Mostly, they came to bribe the Gestapo and try desperately to get "news for the Jews." Tuesday evening they took me back to Skalat.

As told by Dzidzia Gelbtuch nee' Dlugacz to Lusia Milch
New York, New York 1995

[Page 103]

Testimony of Chajka Kawer

On Sunday, July 6, 1941, the day of the pogrom in Skalat, our town was in a state of upheaval. Germans, but mostly Ukrainians and some Poles unleashed a barrage of beatings, torture and killings which dazed us with its suddenness and brutality. When the Germans entered we did not know what to expect, but no one in our town could have ever imagined the slaughter which took place.

Early in the morning on that day, our family, my parents, Fayga and David Sass; my three brothers, Motl, Jacob, and Szajko; my sister, Nechama; and I were at home. When rumors spread that Germans and Ukrainians were looking for Jewish men to be taken to work, panic swept through the neighborhood. My oldest brother, Motl, decided to leave the house and walk over to a Ukrainian acquaintance named Michael Datsky, who lived in a Ukrainian part of town in the direction of the Krzywy village.

Soon thereafter Germans accompanied by Ukrainians began to enter Jewish houses and to drag out all the men that they could find. The Ukrainians, some of them only young boys, pointed out Jewish houses and yelled, Jude! - Jude! Confused and not knowing what was going on, I looked outside. There, I saw a Polish teenager, one named , walking down the street and pointing at Jewish houses, including ours. I knew Ryszlewski well since his sister was a classmate of mine. Soon after, soldiers entered our house, took my father and my brother Jacob, and led them to the market square.

Seeing what was happening, I ran out and tried to reach the Datsky house in order to warn my brother not to come home. As I walked through the back streets and alleys in order not to attract attention, suddenly I came face to face with three Ukrainians, each holding a huge knife. Though I don't recall their names now, they were all grown men from our town and I knew each one of them. They asked me in Ukrainian "Where are you going?" Petrified, I stammered out truthfully that I was looking for my brother. One of them asked me then what was my brother's name, and again I answered truthfully "Sass."

"Oh, " they said, "then he's already dead. Go behind the bathhouse and you'll find him there. " I proceeded to walk towards the bathhouse and when I got there, I saw a sight which I always carry in my memory. Three Jewish men, Berl Sass, my cousin, Moishe Bernstein, in whose house my cousin lived; and Dr. Fried, wearing a gray suit, lay on the ground with their heads cut off. The blood was still oozing from their decapitated bodies. In a state of horror because of the scene in front of me, and realizing that the murderers mistook my cousin for my brother, I quickly turned around and headed for home.

Late in the afternoon my father, whose beard was cruelly cut off, and my brother Jacob returned home. They had managed to run away from the market square during a brief bombardment from a Russian plane which interrupted the pogrom in Skalat. Though they escaped being shot on that day, they were nevertheless, killed later on.

As told by Chajka Kawer nee' Sass to Lusia Milch

Lakewood, New Jersey 1995

[Page 104]

Testimony of Joseph Kofler

My name is Joseph Kofler. I was born and raised in a *shtetl*, Medenice, near the town of Drohobycz. I attended high school in Stryj and the Politechnik University in Lwow. This area was in Eastern Poland and was occupied by the Soviets in 1939, and by the Germans in 1941. My family, at that time, consisted of my parents, 4 brothers, 3 sisters, their spouses and children. They lived in Medenice, and the nearby towns of Drohobycz, Boryslaw and Stryj.

They all perished. I am the only survivor. I learned after the war that most of the Jews in that area were rounded up and taken to Belzec, an extermination camp in Eastern Poland.

I was living with my wife, Sima, in Lwow when the Germans invaded the Soviet Union in June 1941. In August 1941 my wife and I made our way on foot and by hitchhiking to the town of Skalat where my wife's family lived. We settled in the ghetto where I worked with a group of Jewish men assigned to forced labor on the highway, breaking up stones for paving. We worked there until the **'actions,'** began in August 1942.

At dawn on November 9, 1942, the Skalat Ghetto was surrounded by German SS-men and the Ukrainian police. Early in the morning they started entering Jewish homes and dragging out people. We could hear the shouting of the Germans and the screaming of the victims.

I managed to hide our family in a prepared hiding place in the attic, but I had to stay outside to cover and camouflage the entrance. My intention was to hide in a different place. As I stepped out of the house, however, I was grabbed by a German, who was already holding an acquaintance, Munio Pudles, whom he had caught a few minutes earlier. We were both led to the assembly point at the synagogue.

At the synagogue were assembled many men, women and children who were wailing and screaming. Every few minutes the Germans and Ukrainians were bringing in more victims. At about noon the commanding SS-man stopped the round-up and ordered the transport to begin. Trucks normally used to carry rocks were brought from the Nowosiolka quarry. The people were herded from the synagogue and the Germans, using whips and delivering blows with rifle butts, made us climb the lorries at a fast pace. The Germans forced their victims to squeeze together so more people could be loaded on a truck.

When the loading was completed, but before the trucks started to move, a Judenrat official by the name of Lempert, arrived and asked the SS-man to release an employee of the Judenrat and a friend of Nirler (the head of the Judenrat). The SS-man agreed and called out the name of the woman who was on the truck with her 10 year old son. The German, however, would not release her child and gave the woman one minute to decide whether to leave alone or stay with her son. She decided to get off and her son continued alone with the transport.

The trucks transported us from Skalat to the railroad station in Tarnopol. There, the Germans made us once again leave the trucks at a fast pace, under a hail of severe beatings and with shouts or "Judenschwein."

After the unloading, we were ordered to sit on the ground in complete silence along with other Jews from Zbaraz, Trembowla, and Kopyczynce. Round-ups of Jews were carried out in those towns the same day as in Skalat. It was a cold day, the temperature was below freezing and the frozen ground was covered with snow.

People were shivering because they had been driven out of their homes in their night clothes, and therefore unprepared for the cold. The children suffered the most. They were crying and their mothers were wailing. The Germans ordered the crowd to be quiet, but the children continued to cry. One SS-man became so enraged by the noise that he picked up a few screaming children, took them behind a wall and shot them. This subdued the crowd and the other children stopped crying as well.

Towards evening a freight train arrived and the Germans and Ukrainians herded the crowd towards the cattle cars. At the same time they selected able-bodied men for assignment to forced labor camps.

[Page 105]

This selection involved separating the men from their families and resulted in tragic scenes and the crying and wailing of women and children. Some men resisted being torn away from their loved ones but the Germans cut the scene short with their usual method of terror, and with the help of whips and rifle butts. The old men, women and children were pushed into the cattle cars, the doors were shut and the victims were dispatched to their destination - the gas chambers.

The men selected for forced labor were assembled in columns and assigned to various camps, Hluboczek, Zbaraz, Zloczow, Zborow and Kazimirowka. I was assigned to Kamizirowka. After the train left the station, our column was ordered to march at a fast pace along the highway towards Zborow, which was about 40 km from Tarnopol. We were guarded by many Ukrainian policemen on foot and by two Germans in a car, driven slowly behind the marching column, with the headlights directed on the marchers. After marching a few hours, trucks arrived to pick us up in order to speed up the transport to the camp.

Around midnight, we arrived at the Zborow camp. There we stayed overnight without food and slept on the floor because all the sleeping bunks were fully occupied.

We were awakened before dawn and given breakfast consisting of black water, which was the camp version of coffee, two slices of bread and a stick of margarine. At five o'clock we were marched under Ukrainian guards to Kazimirowka.

Conditions in the Kazimirowka camp were horrendous. We were housed in wooden barracks , which had been converted from a horse barn by installing three tiers of sleeping bunks. In an area which was built for twenty horses, the Germans crowded in 250 inmates. The bunks had only enough room to slide in. One could not sit up. We were packed so tightly that when all the inmates were in place, it was hardly possible to turn around. A hole in the ground behind the barracks served as a latrine. The hole was small and people had to wait in line to use it. At night many inmates were so tired and weak that they were unable to wriggle out of their bunks. This resulted in inmates urinating in their bunks, wetting those who were sleeping below.

The camp grounds were surrounded by a fence of barbed-wire and one watch tower. The Kommandant of the camp was a German named Riesberg, who was assisted by about 15 Ukrainian policemen. We were awakened every day about 4:00 a.m., except on Sunday, and served breakfast which consisted of ersatz (imitation) coffee and two slices of half-baked, black bread. Within 30 minutes after wake-up call we had to attend the line-up. The Kommandant reviewed the column and then we marched to work at a rock quarry a few kilometers away.

A German named Schelhorn was in charge of the quarry. During work the quarry was surrounded by Ukrainian policemen in order to prevent escape attempts.

There was no hospital or clinic. There was a sick room with one doctor who did not have any drugs or instruments. Once, while at work, I was hit with a shovel over the head by a German and I was bleeding heavily. All the doctor could do was wash the wound with water and apply a clean rag torn from an old shirt.

In the shower room, which was open only on Sundays, there were three shower heads. Only a fraction of the camp population was able to use the shower. Most of the inmates were infested with lice, resulting in the spread of typhus and causing the death of many inmates.

A sick inmate was not allowed to stay in the barracks during work hours. He was carried on a stretcher to the quarry and left there all day in the cold. Most of the time the patient died. Otherwise, he was carried back to the barracks and the same procedure was repeated the next day. In order to stay in the barracks a sick inmate had to bribe the Kapo who would hide him during inspection.

This camp was small compared to the notorious concentration camps equipped with gas chambers and crematoria. There were hundreds of similar small camps in Eastern Poland, the names of which are forgotten. They were established to supply slave labor for the local economy and also to hasten the elimination of the sick and weak Jews without having to build expensive killing installations. No bullets were needed to kill inmates except in escape attempts. Since bullets were in short supply and were needed for the battle front, they were used sparingly. The Jews had to die without them. The bodies were dumped in a nearby ravine and covered with the soil stripped from the rock quarry.

[Page 106]

The work at the quarry consisted of breaking up large stones into gravel using heavy sledgehammers. We worked from 5:00 in the morning till about 5:00 in the evening, when it became dark. There was a one hour noon break, when we were given a hot lunch brought from the camp kitchen. The lunch consisted of watery soup and two slices of bread. Sometimes on a Sunday, the *Kommandant* would present to the camp kitchen a few dogs or cats which he shot during a hunting trip to a nearby village. Inmates were then treated to soup made from this meat.

A few days after our arrival a 14 year old boy was caught at night, trying to escape. The next morning all the inmates were assembled at the line-up to watch the punishment. The 14 year old prisoner was brought to the gallows and his teenage friend was summoned and ordered to place the noose on his friend's neck. When he refused to do so, a German beat him severely with a whip over his face and then shot him. A Ukrainian policeman then placed the noose and the boy was hanged. After that episode there were no other attempts to escape.

The remaining Jews of Skalat who avoided the round-up, came out from their hiding places and tried to go on with their precarious lives in the reduced ghetto.

My wife, who luckily avoided capture, learned after a few weeks that a number of men from Skalat were confined in the Kazimirowka camp, and that I was among them. With me from the town of Skalat were: Gelbtuch, Wilner, Sharf, Sass, Kiwetz and a few others, whose names I do not remember. She managed to make contact with the Judenrat in the town of Zborow, which is located near Kazimirowka. They indicated that it was possible to get an inmate released for a ransom. They were especially interested in jewelry.

As the negotiations were going on concerning a ransom, I contracted typhus and developed a high fever. A friend, David Gelbtuch, bribed the Kapo, who managed to hide me from the Kommandant and shielded me from being carried to the quarry .My wife delivered the ransom and I was released unconscious and with a high fever. I was taken to a so-called hospital in the Zborow Ghetto. It was a small, crowded place where two or sometimes three patients shared a bed. Two doctors and three nurses cared for about two dozen patients. After ten days, without drugs or proper treatment, I miraculously recovered. My wife managed to find transportation and we made our way back to Skalat.

NOTE:

As I found out after the liberation, all of these small camps were liquidated by the Germans in the Spring of 1944 as the Soviet Army was approaching. The following method of liquidation was used. The inmates were assembled inside the barracks, which were surrounded by German and Ukrainian guards with machine guns. The doors were shut, the buildings were then doused with gasoline and set on fire. The inmates were burned alive, and only a few escaped to tell the tragic story.

Joseph Kofler
Santa Monica, California 1993

[Page 107]

The Day My Father Cried

Among the many joyful memories of my childhood, were the Shabbos visits to my grandmother's house. Everyone in Skalat knew my grandma, Sura Elfenbein. As a child, I never identified myself by my name, Fancia Niessenbaum, instead I would say "I am Sura Elfenbein's granddaughter," that was sufficient as an introduction.

Sura Elfenbein was a hotel owner, saloon keeper, restaurateur, and the best cook in town. Molly Picon and a cast of actors stayed at her hotel when they performed in Skalat. Once, even the President of Poland whose name I believe was Moscicki, stayed in her hotel. This was a proud event for grandmother and each time a new guest registered, grandma would leaf through pages of her guest book until she came upon the President's signature.

I had loving grandparents. Grandma was strict, a disciplinarian, and she demanded respect from us, as well as from her children. She often used the word *mitzva* and one day I learned its meaning. My sister, Rozia, and I were entrusted to deliver food to a poor lady with a large family. When we arrived at her house and I saw the happiness on the woman's face at the sight of the food, I understood the word *mitzva*. In addition, every Friday and Saturday there was always a stranger eating with the family, and my sister and I would call that person the "mitzva guest."

Grandpa Yisrul Elfenbein, on the other hand, was the complete opposite of grandma. I do not recall grandpa working as much in the business as grandmother because he prayed a lot. He was fun to be with. He would let me snuff tobacco from his little silver box and on Shabbos he would dip some sponge cake in the wine and each grandchild would be given a taste of the sweet wine. Grandma scolded grandpa for this, because she feared that we would get tipsy.

Besides my caring grandparents and loving mother Hania Niessenbaum nee' Elfenbein, the most important person in my life, was my father Wiktor Niessenbaum. He was always there to protect me, to console me when I had bad dreams, and to buy me things. Though he threatened to spank me, he never laid a hand on me. To me he was the smartest person, who knew all the answers to my questions. Physically he was strong, with beautiful, big, blue eyes, and a shiny bald head. He was truly a pillar of strength to the entire family.

I used to look forward to Shabbos, which was the best day of the week because my father and grandpa would go to *shul*, and let me tag along with them. I helped grandpa carry his talis in the velvet bag. I felt very important when I carried grandpa's velvet bag because I knew that the talis in the bag meant a lot to him. Once I dropped it on the floor by accident and grandpa got upset; he picked it up and kissed it.

Life was wonderful in Skalat, especially to a little girl who was surrounded by many aunts and uncles, sister, grandparents, and parents. During my childhood, Skalat was a lively and vibrant town, where moral, ethical and Jewish values were instilled in us.

Unfortunately, all of it ended on a beautiful, sunny Saturday on July 5, 1941. That day, grandpa, papa and I were on our way to the shul, and suddenly our town was invaded by many soldiers in weird black uniforms wearing shiny black boots. Their hats were adorned with silver skull heads, and the same insignia adorned the rings on their hands. On their arms they wore the white sign of the swastika. They entered Skalat riding shiny motorcycles, trucks, and tanks.

The festive and happy mood on the street changed to bewilderment and fear. I heard the words Germans and war many times before, but I had never really known their meaning. Looking at grandpa, my father, and the people around us, I realized that something horrible was about to happen.

All three of us ran quickly to the shul and even before the men started praying, the soldiers in the black uniforms entered the shul and started shouting in German. As soon as they entered, they began to whip the Jews and gathered all the men, among them grandpa and father. There was chaos, fear, and confusion. I ran quickly to grandma's house to tell her what had happened. Then I sat down in the corner frightened and in a state of shock.

[Page 108]

In the late afternoon my father came back without grandpa. He was a changed man and did not look like my strong, handsome father. His Saturday suit was gone, his clothes having been ripped off him, and his whole body was pierced; blood gushing from each hole. His back was marked with red stripes, from whip lashings that he had received. My mother was trying to stop the bleeding, but each time she touched him, he screamed. After a while, he began telling us what had happened.

The Germans had gathered the Jews and made them wash their cars and motorcycles in the marketplace. Some of the captured Jews were shot there and then. One German soldier did not like grandpa's peyes (sidelocks), so he pulled his hair out one by one and then shot him.

A soldier approached my father while he was washing cars, and kept hitting him and piercing him with his bayonet. When my father asked the soldier, in fluent German, why he was torturing him, it was then that the soldier decided to let him go. It was a miracle because most of the men who were caught that day were killed.

This was the first pogrom in Skalat, and the start of the tragedy. As my father was telling us all that had happened to him and the others, he cried like a baby. It was the first time I ever saw my father cry and I never forgot it! That day our roles were reversed. My father sat and cried like a child while I grew up there and then. Saturday outings to the shul never happened again.

Phyllis Linell nee Niessenbaum
New York, 1995

[Page 109]

My Remembrances of Skalat During the German Occupation

These are the remembrances of Lola Margulies, nee' Elfenbein; of how I, my father Arthur my mother, Erna, and my brother, Michael survived the Holocaust; specifically during the years 1942-44 in the town of Skalat. It is above all the story of the superhuman courage, self sacrifice and resourcefulness of one man, my father, to whom this tale is dedicated.

Neither this narrative, nor any account, can do justice in describing the brutality and inhumanity of the systematic extermination of millions of Jews by Hitler and his enthusiastic followers. But my experiences In the town of Skalat may mirror the horrors associated with the liquidation of a ghetto and making a town inhabited by thousands of Jews Judenfrei.

The systematic massacre of Jews confined to the ghetto began with the **'actions.'** During these surprise attacks the SS-men would storm into the ghetto in the middle of the night, round up Jews, and drive them like cattle into trucks. The victims would then be delivered to trains heading for concentration camps and extermination. The first of these ' actions' in the fall of 1942 lingers in my memory. It is the memory of a twelve year old crushed by the fear of death that would become a reoccurring nightmarish reality. Helpless, hopeless, overcrowded and undernourished we waited for the massacre. We, other members of my father's family and neighbors, survived the first **'action'** and the subsequent ones in a miraculous fashion. This miracle was engineered virtually single-handedly by my self-sacrificing father. To hide us he used a large cellar which had a trap door in the floor of the courtyard. The cellar was not equipped in any way as a hiding place prior to the surprise attack of the first **'action.'**

When we were awakened in the middle of the night by the shouts of truckloads of SS-men demanding "Juden" to fulfill their quota, my father rounded up everyone and rushed us into the cellar. As my mother and I searched in the dim candlelight, our hearts sank as we became aware that my father was not among us and that he undertook to save all of us at the risk of losing his own life. Within minutes of the stormy arrival of the SS-men, my father staged the scenario that succeeded in confusing and outwitting our assassins. He covered up the trap door leading to the cellar with many bulky articles that both masked the entrance and muted the sound which could have emanated from the cellar. Ingeniously, he left numerous bottles of vodka, a remnant of his parents' tavern business, on display in the most conspicuous places in the rooms above the cellar. He then hid himself under the staircase leading to the attic, becoming an obvious target for the Germans and the journey to the death camp.

As we sat almost lifeless in the cellar, we heard the footsteps and voices of the Germans above us. Suddenly, a thirst cry rang out from my three year old cousin, Kamila Nirler, which would have given us away. Worse, since the cellar was not equipped with any beverage, all our desperate attempts to quiet down the frightened and thirsty child failed. Many panicked and insisted that the mother Cover up the child's mouth. Choking the child would have been the sacrifice to save the rest. The desperate mother collected some of her own urine and gave it to the child to drink! Death was staring us in the face and we were sure that all was lost. But my father's miracle worked! In spite of the flimsy and hasty camouflage of the cellar entrance, the child's crying and my father's conspicuous hiding place, the Germans failed to find us. We heard their merry laughter upstairs as they were consuming the vodka which father so generously provided.

Our existence until the town of Skalat became Judenfrei was worse than hell on earth. The repeated assaults, the dread of the nights, lest the **'actions,'** catch us unaware, drained us of hope and strength as the inevitability of death drew closer and closer. We endured nevertheless and survived the winter of 1942-43 while father made the cellar into a highly effective hiding place. The worst was still to come, however: the brutal liquidation of the Skalat ghetto and camp. Again, there was only one person among us who never lost hope and presence of mind, and who devoted all his mental acuity, resourcefulness and energy to the virtually impossible task of saving his family.

[Page 110]

Father began to search for a way to save our lives outside of the ghetto. He first focused on saving the women of our family, my mother and me. Father's plan was to find a Polish peasant who would be willing to hide Jews if the reward, such as money or jewelry, was high enough. But I, aged 13, became extremely disturbed by my father's insistence that we split up the family. I pleaded with my father to disclose his secret plan. In what miraculous fashion did he hope to save himself and my 15 year old brother if they did not go into hiding with us, I wondered? If we must perish, we shall die together, I insisted. All in vain! Did I not realize that he was a survivor, he said with a smile. It was all part of his master plan, never disclosed. I knew that my father believed in miracles and above all in God. His deep religious beliefs and the recollection of numerous stories father narrated from the Bible did not make me believe in miracles. Yet they did occur during the Holocaust for a few lucky ones!

There were three ways to try to save ourselves - all measures of desperation, rather than realistically hopeful approaches. Find a Polish peasant, poor enough to hide Jews for money, surely not for any altruistic reasons! Alternatively, acquire forged papers, move to a big city and pass as a Pole. As a last resort, hide in the icy woods without any shelter or food. Father chose the first option for me and my mother.

One evening a Polish peasant appeared with a horse and wagon already carrying some other desperate Jews. He was going to save us all. I went into hysteria. I refused to try to save my life without my father and brother. We all go or we all die, I lament! My father is devastated as the wagon departs without us, and swears no forgiveness for my childish and irresponsible behavior until the next day's news reached us. The "angel" Pole turned the wagon full of Jews over to the German town police and they were all killed. My mother was convinced that it was a young girl's premonition.

As Hitler's promised Judenfrei approached, another episode of hysteria occurred. I again refused to leave without my father when he arranged for another Polish peasant to take us into hiding. That very evening the German police intercepted and searched the peasant's wagon. Thanks to God and to my hysteria the wagon was empty. My mother claimed I had a special uncanny gift, nothing short of clairvoyance. But why did we consider ourselves so lucky? We were not apprehended the night before, but here we were, just waiting for death or it seemed hopelessly buying time.

My father's two sisters, young and pretty (one, the mother of three year old Kamila, who was given away for adoption and survived), took a fifteen year old niece with them and left for Lvov. Alas, we never saw them again! They perished, as one of many Polish collaborators recognized my younger aunt and denounced them to the Gestapo. The natives rejoiced as they helped in the extermination of the unwanted millions who, they always felt, were "outsiders" in their country and exploited them. Hitler was a messiah sent to carry out the good deed which they always wanted to do themselves.

Another desperate attempt of a few of my cousins to save their lives occurred during the penultimate **'action'** on the town ghetto which was supposed to have rendered the town of Skalat Judenfrei. Three of them ran to the woods. A few months later, on a bitter cold night, one of them, a thirteen year old girl, froze to death.

During the first Skalat camp **'action'** my father was recovering from typhoid and could hardly walk. He and all the remaining Jews were taken from the camp to the graves dug outside of town which were prepared for their slaughter. With him was his brother-in-law and sister-in-law. At this time my mother and I were already in hiding. I finally did agree to be taken into a bunker by the peasant with whom I refused to leave the first time. This time my father promised that he and my brother would follow shortly. Why did I believe his story? There was no such arrangement. It turned out that there was no room in the bunker which was dug out thirteen feet underneath a peasant's chicken coop near the end of the woods. This grave for the living could only accommodate eleven people which did not include my father and brother. Father paid the Wassermans, a family of six, to hide five women from our family: his mother, Sarah Elfenbein, his sister and. her daughter, Anna and Phyllis Nissenbaum, as well as my mother and me. In fact, the peasant never disclosed to my father where our hiding place was. This was the absolute condition that the peasant insisted on. What if my father was caught, tortured and disclosed our whereabouts? The Polish peasant might then get the death penalty for hiding Jews.

[Page 111]

One evening the peasant as usual descended to our bunker carrying potato soup and some pieces of bread, the daily diet that got thinner and smaller during the nine months we spent in that grave. He also brought the dreadful news! The remainder of the Jews in the camp were exterminated. They were shot and some were still alive when they were buried in the prepared graves. We shudder, wail and grieve as we realize that our loved ones must have been among the dead! My cousin, whose father was also at the camp, and I are convinced that we are orphans. But miracles do happen. A few days later, the chicken coop door opens unexpectedly and lo and behold my father and brother descend on the ladder. Were they buried alive and rose from the graves? And how did they find us? Here is the story my father narrated. It was a horror story that would be imprinted in the memory of his children, grandchildren and hopefully his great-grandchildren. Father lived to the age of ninety one to describe the miracle.

The Jews were standing in front of the graves waiting to be shot. Suddenly, the voice of the head SS-man resounds loudly: "If there are any artisans among you: tailors, barbers and shoemakers, step out of the line and go across the narrow dirt road." My father who was none of the above, but did bake bread in the camp, says "I am the camp baker." The SS-man who was busy with other matters, may not have even heard him and did not react. My father, taking advantage of the situation, begins to move away from the grave and tugs on the clothing of his brother-in-law, Wiktor, motioning him to join him. Wiktor is alive, but paralyzed with fear, as though he were a living corpse. He refuses to move and as father goes across the road, Wiktor is shot in front of my father's eyes. Father is then put on a truck with a handful of other Jews whom the Germans needed for a few more weeks until the camp was totally liquidated.

This time, my father did not wait to be shot. Joined by my brother who fled from the camp at the time of the **'action,'** they escaped from the camp that very evening and were not apprehended as they headed for the woods. My father said without hesitation that they were going to find me and my mother. "But we have no idea where they are," my brother exclaims. Father, as sure as he was that he could rise from the grave had only one answer. "I'll find them! Watch me outsmart the Polish peasant!

Unwittingly, he gave me a hint or two as to the whereabouts of the hiding place. I know the woods pretty well from the time I used to smuggle vodka when I was about your age." The peasant gave away two hints: the bunker was located in the beginning of the deep part of the woods and there were three farmhouses nearby.

It was late in the evening, July 1943. They entered a poor peasant's little house just skirting the woods. Moments earlier, father disclosed to my brother another piece of disturbing information, namely that the peasant who engineered the hiding place was a clever cousin of the very poor peasant who was hiding us, and that father had never seen the owner of the house which they were seeking.

As they entered the house and begged for bread, father had the strong feeling that this was the peasant who was hiding his family. He did not hesitate: "My wife and daughter are here, please let me and my son join them," he pleads. The peasant and his wife strongly deny any knowledge of our whereabouts. But, from their reaction my father becomes convinced that they are not telling the truth. He pleads to be let into the bunker, but to no avail. At this moment by brother reacts instinctively. He falls to his knees at the feet of the peasant's wife who is cleaning the lice out of her eight year old daughter's hair. " Imagine," he says with tears in his eyes, "that your daughter is separated from you and that the only way her mother could be saved is by joining her. How would you feel if you could not be reunited with your daughter?" Filled with pity, the peasant woman breaks into tears and commands her husband. "Let them in!"

And so we were finally reunited. Within a few hours, however, our joy was transformed into panic as we all began to choke. There was not enough oxygen in the bunker for thirteen people! At the risk of being apprehended, we spent a few evenings in the barn, while father took charge of enlarging the bunker and making one more small opening to the outside to allow air to enter. Periodically we were threatened if we did not come up with more money or jewelry. Thus starved and frightened, without ever seeing daylight, the thirteen of us spent nine months in our grave. During this time we witnessed my mother's self-sacrifice. She gave away the meager portions of her food to her growing son in fear that he would become a victim of tuberculosis. The forty two year old woman became completely gray and emaciated, a mere ghost of her former self.

[Page 112]

Finally we were liberated by the advancing Russian army in March of 1944. Earlier, father had prophesied that if we could survive for nine months we would be saved. Almost to the day, we hear shooting. The peasant insists that these are local partisans fighting with the Germans. He refuses to tell us the truth and let us out, for fear of being shot by the Germans as a Jew rescuer. Father again takes charge. Convinced that this is the advancing front of the Russian army, he declares that we are leaving the bunker immediately. We walked out practically barefooted on the white March snow, amidst the fighting front. Our bunker collapsed shortly after we left.

Were it not for my father's speedy decision, we would have been buried alive. We were all emotionally drained and sapped of physical strength but my mother could not walk by herself. As we were carrying her, the liberating Russian soldiers took even more pity on us. Referring to my mother as the sick "babushka," an old woman, they left their line of fire and hastily put us on a truck heading towards the Eastern Ukraine in the Soviet Union.

How does one survive such torture and confinement and retain one's sanity? Though we were by far the exception and survived as a family, the psyche of a Holocaust survivor bears a permanent scar. The threshold for suffering steadily declines during life's ordinary trials and tribulations. The nightmares persist and the hysteria manifested during the war lingers on.

Lola Margulies nee' Elfenbein
New York 1995

[Page 113]

The Day Skalat Was Declared Judenfrei

It was the end of the second year of the German occupation.

The Skalat Ghetto was again made smaller and once more we were forced to move. The remaining Jews were now confined to a few narrow back streets of our town and this time the Rosenblats took us in. We shared two small rooms and a kitchen with several families. The house was crowded and each family confined itself to a bed.. There we slept, ate, agonized over our inability to find a hiding place, and spent anxious hours awaiting inevitable death. The nights terrified us and everyone with whom we shared the house was exhausted and on edge from tension and lack of sleep. Another day had started without an **'action,'** nevertheless we knew that our days in the Skalat Ghetto were coming to an end.

Someone opened the door and we saw Jews appearing in the street. Was it safe after all we wondered? Inside the house people moved about mechanically, but our minds were alert to the danger all around us. No one spoke very much and even the complaints, which at times would arise from living; together in tight quarters, had stopped. About our common obsession of finding a hiding place, we were all secretive.

We spent the night awake and as had been our habit for a long time now, we kept our clothes on. As I was getting up, I felt over-dressed and uncomfortable. My mother, sitting on the edge of a narrow bed, which she shared with me and my five year old sister, stood up. She placed a black shawl on her shoulders and went outside. Assured that the streets were safe, she returned, took my sister and me by the hands, and without saying a word, led us out of the house.

Outside, some Jews were returning to the ghetto from a night spent on the safe " Aryan" side. We did not speak to them nor did they make any inquiries. Because it was safer, we were walking through back streets and alleys, staying close to the doorways wherever possible, in case of a sudden need to hide. Since the Skalat Ghetto had no physical barriers, no one stopped us as we made our way outside the designated ghetto section.

Making sure that no one could hear us, my mother started to speak. She explained that we were going to a Gentile family to whom she had given all our remaining possessions and who, in turn, had promised to hide us when the time came. The family lived off the marketplace in a formerly Jewish-owned house and very near our own home. I knew every corner of that house, where, before the German occupation, I used to play with my cousins and friends. It was getting late in the morning. As we passed the Prayer House where our family worshipped, my mother recalled how, before the war, on holiday mornings such as this, my father, grandfather, uncles and cousins would already be gathered here for prayers. She was quickly jolted out of her reminiscences by the appearance, here and there, of local Gentiles, who knew us. It was, therefore, becoming dangerous for us to be on those streets.

We were approaching the house. Suddenly we heard awful shouts and cries. The terrifying sounds of shooting coming from the direction of the ghetto which we had just left convinced us that an **'action,'** had started. Since all previous **'actions,'** in Skalat had started at dawn, this sudden, unexpected attack caught us off guard. In the grip of panic, we became dazed, and didn't know which way to turn. Within moments we heard shots coming from many directions and heard the Germans and the Ukrainian policemen, accompanied by barking dogs, running down the narrow streets and alleys. Bellowing commands and insults, they were inflicting merciless blows on the trapped Jews. The round-up was taking place with a deliberate frenzy: it was fast, loud and full of painful screams and death. People everywhere were running and we too started to run as fast as we could. We reached the street and saw the house where we would be saved! We ran faster and finally made it to the Gentile family.

As we pushed our way inside, we found ourselves standing in front of a man, his wife, and two small children. The man stared at us in disbelief and told his wife to take the children to the back room.

[Page 114]

He then turned to my mother and in a loud and angry voice shouted "What are you doing here? You must get out immediately!"

We can't leave, an **'action'** has started and you promised to hide us" my mother said. "I have no hiding place and I want you out of here, right now! " He started to push us out of the room as my mother continued to plead.

Have mercy on my children, the streets are full of Germans" she sobbed "and if we go out, we'll be killed!" The man's wife returned and, confronting her husband, demanded that he throw us out immediately. In the ensuing commotion, my mother turned her head quickly and looked at me. On her face I caught a glimpse of unspeakable desperation. She was afraid to speak, but her gaze was totally fixed on me. With all the strength left in her she wanted to say something, but her lips remained closed. Suddenly she opened her eyes wide and shot me a glance wild with urgency. Then, with an instant wink she willed me to move. She was telling me to get away now, to run, to save myself! As I stepped back, my mother turned from me and I never saw her face again.

I moved back into a small vestibule, through which only moments before we had entered the man's house. There were several doors and, since I knew the house well, I opened the one leading to a pantry. When my eyes adjusted to the dark, I noticed some firewood on the floor and sacks half-filled with grain and other items. In the corner of the ceiling was an opening leading to the attic. Although there was no ladder and the ceiling was high, I was drawn to the attic with indescribable willpower. With a sudden strength and agility far beyond my years and expectations, I lifted a heavy sack and placed it on top of another one. Then, I climbed on top of the sack and stepped from it onto a door handle. Digging my nails into the wooden door, I grabbed a hinge and hoisted myself up onto the attic. I could not believe it! I had just managed to climb up a straight wall, but this was no time to stop and reflect.

Once in the attic, the only thought racing through my mind was to hide quickly. I took in my surroundings with a glance. The attic was dusty, the floor covered with straw, but otherwise it was empty and there was no place to hide. I thought of climbing out and clinging to the roof, but I feared that I would be spotted from the street. I also thought of breaking through the wooden partition of a neighbor's attic in hope of finding a hiding place there, but I knew that to do so would take too long and would be dangerously noisy. Other ideas rushed through my mind while precious. minutes ticked away. I was desperate and so frightened that my legs became shaky and I sank to the floor.

It was incredible, for as soon as I sat down, my hiding place stared me in the face. In a broken spot of the attic floor, I noticed a small space between two beams and I knew that somehow I had to get in there. From years of surviving 'actions,' in the ghetto, I also knew the importance of not leaving a trace behind me. I, therefore, got up quickly, removed all my excess clothing, folded it into a bundle and pushed it through a small trap door inside a chimney. Then, feet first, I slid on my stomach into the narrow space disturbing the straw, in order not to leave a trail and covering the opening by pulling down some straw. In front of my face I left a tiny slit for air and vision. I was finally hidden.

As I lay, I became aware once again of the horror taking place outside. My mind drifted back to my mother and sister. Did the man have pity? Did he hide them? The frightening sounds outside were now on the street where I was hidden and the Germans were running up and down in front of the house.

Within ten or fifteen minutes, I heard the front door burst open and Germans accompanied by a barking dog were shouting "Juden raus!" They were searching the house. Now they were coming up to the attic and once again that morning I was overwhelmed by an indescribable fear. I started to shake uncontrollably and had to push my tongue between my lips to stop the noise of my chattering teeth. The Germans were in the attic. Through the opening in the straw, I could see the bottoms of the soldiers' boots and the legs of the dog. I held my breath as they passed only inches from my face. Then I saw the beam of a flashlight. In minutes the search was over and the Germans left. My brush with death was over, but I have lived with it all my life.

[Page 115]

With my head turned to one side and unable to move, I lay for hours, squeezed between two beams. I felt no hunger, or thirst, only pain from the twisted position of my neck and head. I drifted into merciful sleep, only to awaken frightened and angry for allowing myself to slip away from vigilance. I was all alone and again fear assaulted me. What should I do, I thought? Who will help me? Words of my mother's inordinate effort to save me came back to me.

Leave me and try to save yourself," she would say over and over again when we were in the ghetto. "You must go far away from Skalat" she warned, "so no one would recognize you. Forget that you're Jewish you are small, you don't need papers and you have a chance to survive as a peasant girl." At such times, tears would well up, as I begged her not to make me leave her. Lying alone in the dark attic I cried silently because I still did not know where to go nor how to save myself.

As daylight waned, the streets became quiet and then it got pitch-dark. I fell asleep again and when I woke up, I was aware that I was wet. I could no longer sleep. Dawn was breaking. How long was I hiding? I lost track of time.

Early in the morning I heard someone coming up onto the attic. It was the man and he was alone. He was walking around and calling on whoever was there to come out. I had no choice. Weak and stiff, I crawled out of the hole. I had wet his ceiling he said and therefore he knew that someone was there. When he saw me he could not believe that I was in his house while the Germans were searching it. He demanded that I leave his house immediately. "Is the **'action'** over? Is it safe to go back to the ghetto?" I asked. "And where are my mother and sister?" He told me that there were no more Jews left in Skalat and that my mother and sister had been killed. Where was I to go then? He didn't care. I begged him to let me stay until evening because if I were to go out in the daytime, I said I would be immediately recognized and shot. They might question where I had hidden and then both of us would be in peril, I reasoned. He agreed reluctantly and as he left, he warned that he would be back as soon as it got dark. When the man left, I retrieved my clothing from the chimney and remained in the open attic for the rest of the day.

It was exactly twenty-four hours earlier on June the 9th 1943 on the second day of Shavuot that the last **'action'** in Skalat took place and the town was declared Judenfrei. On that day the Jewish community which existed there for hundreds of years came to an end, and with it the lives of my mother, Necha Rosenzweig-Goldberg, nee' Rubin, and my sister, Ginia Goldberg. My stepfather, Jacob Goldberg, was confined to the Skalat Camp and was later burned alive in the Kamionka Camp. That evening as I walked out into the unsafe streets of my native town, I was twelve years old, all alone and in mortal danger. Little did I know what was yet in store for me in the months ahead during my struggle to survive.

Lusia Milch nee' Rosenzweig
New York, 1993

[Page 116]

How I Survived

It is fifty years since those awful days of the round-up of Jews in Skalat, during the "Wild Action" of October 21-22, 1942.

Over 3,000 Jews - young, old, men, women and children were dragged from their homes and driven to the assembly point of the main synagogue of our town. Among them were my parents, my two sisters and I.

Though fifty years have passed, I still have before my eyes the horrible scene in the synagogue where people stood weeping and children were screaming. A man stood wrapped in a prayer shawl, praying loudly and hoping that God will hear and help. After twelve hours in the synagogue, the Germans and Ukrainian police forced us to walk toward the railroad station. Along the way the local population were lining the streets and enjoying the spectacle of Jews being driven to their death.

At the station the train was waiting for us. All the windows in the cars were boarded up, to insure that no one would escape. With kicks and blows of rifle butts, people were driven at a running pace into the cars and then the doors were shut. In the cars we were pressed together like sardines, without water and without any sanitary facilities.

I knew that we were all going to die. Since we had nothing to lose, I and a few other young men decided to escape. We managed to pry open a board in the window and I told my parents that I was going to jump from the train. My mother told me that if I were to survive the slaughter, I should go to Palestine, and there join my sister Rivka.

After taking leave of my family, I was helped by others to slide through the opening in the window. I jumped from the running train and fell near the track. Immediately the Ukrainian train guards began to shoot. The bullets were falling all around me as the train was moving away, but I was not hit. Noticing a wooded area nearby, I started to run in that direction in hope of finding shelter there.

It was a chilly, fall day and it was raining. When I reached the wooded area, I was wet, very cold and so exhausted that I fell asleep. In a dream my grandfather appeared before me draped in a "talis" (prayer shawl) and a "kitel" (white robe), as if he were dressed for Yom Kippur (the Day of Atonement). In his hand he held a sword and he ordered me to follow him. When I awakened, I started to walk. After a while I arrived at an intersection where the road branched out in several directions. I stood there confused and not knowing which way to proceed. Then the shadow of my grandfather appeared and pointed the way. That was how I arrived in Skalat, from where we had departed only hours before.

I realize that it is hard to believe what I have just related, therefore, I have never told it to anyone, until now. When I arrived back in my town, people looked at me as if I were resurrected from the dead. After a short time, I was interred in the Skalat Camp and there I joined the brigade which worked in the rock quarry of Nowosiolka. When the situation in camp became dangerous, I decided to escape. I left the camp at night and managed to reach the forest near Ostra Mogila. There I found a group of Jews from Skalat. Among them were the Koflers, Weinberg and others. We hid in the forests until we were liberated by the Russians in 1944.

After the liberation, I returned to Skalat and joined the Soviet Army. In 1945, at the end of the war, I was demobilized. Then I traveled to Germany, Belgium, France, and in 1946 I arrived in Israel, which at that time was still under the control of the British Mandate.

Translated from Yiddish by Joseph Kofler
Gershon Ratzenstein
Israel, 199

[Page 117]

The Roundup at the Ostra Mogila Forest

In July of 1943, the well-known partisan group under the command of General Kolpak was surrounded and crushed in the vicinity of Delatyn in the Carpathian Mountains.

Under the orders of the Soviet command, their remnants, divided into small units, began to track back to their initial bases deep in Russia. By the end of July, several of these partisans stopped by in the Ostra Mogila Forest. They participated with us in the raid on an estate in the village of Torowka. Afterward, the Germans organized a roundup in the forest. Toward evening, we heard the sound of a trumpet and immediately realized that we were surrounded. We found ourselves in a young, but dense wood which gave us good protection. The Koflers, a husband and wife, two partisans and I hid behind a boulder which protected us from the bullets, at least from one direction. We were ambushed, fun of fear, and we saw death before our eyes. Our only wish was not to be caught alive but to die from the bullets.

Voices of the Germans calling to one another became clearer and clearer. Suddenly, a hatless SS officer, with his revolver in hand, ran behind us but did not notice us. In front of us, two silhouettes of policemen appeared. The partisans loaded their guns. We waited, tense and fearful, aware of the fact that these were the last moments of our lives. The two policemen, to see better through the dense trees, strained their heads through the growth. Both partisans shot at them and we saw the policemen fall to the ground. Wild shooting erupted all around us. But after a while, the shooting stopped. It became dark and quiet. We were sure that the Germans would put guards around this part of the forest and in the morning would begin the roundup again. Trying to save our lives, we decided to run to another part of the forest. When it became completely dark and quiet, we formed a single-file to get to the road. To avoid the crackling of the dry leaves and branches, each step that we took had to be careful and well executed. It seemed like an eternity before we reached the road across from where the taller trees grew. We did not see or hear anyone. One behind another, we ran into the older forest.

It turned out that the Germans caught only one of us, Dolek Tennenbaum, while they themselves suffered two casualties - one killed and one wounded. They returned to Skalat the same day. Next day, they publicly hanged Dolek and buried the dead policeman.

Translated from Polish by Adam Kanarek
Hillel (Henek) Weinberg
Israel, 1992

[Page 118]

Testimony of Bernard Weinsaft

I, Bernard (Nadzio) Weinsaft, lived through the three years of German occupation with a lot of terrifying incidents occurring during that period. But there were two particular episodes that stand out, where my life hung in the balance, and these are deeply etched in my memory.

The first incident occurred right after the Germans entered our little town of Skalat. Jewish refugees from Germany had told us that front-line soldiers resented the Jews for coming out of their homes to watch the soldiers entering a town. My mother, father and I, therefore, locked all the doors and barricaded ourselves in the house.

The Germans marched into town on Friday, July 4th, at night. We spent the whole day of Saturday, July 5th, peeking out of the windows. We saw our Gentile neighbors running amok through the streets and trying to break into the Jewish homes. They tried to break into our house but did not succeed. Perhaps they looked for easier prey.

We weren't as lucky the next day, Sunday, July 6th. This time, the German soldiers were roaming the streets, led by our Gentile neighbors who were pointing out the Jewish homes. The Germans were more vicious. They broke through our front door as we made our way down to the cellar from an entrance within the house.

The safety in our cellar didn't last very long. We heard the Germans threaten to lob grenades down the cellar unless we came out. My parents decided to come out the front entrance from the cellar, where we were met by German soldiers. My father was taken away to work and my mother was left alone. In all that confusion, I darted away, soldiers in pursuit. I zigzagged through the narrow streets, and escaped to my grandparents' house, where I ran down to their cellar and hid in a chicken cage.

I spent the whole day in hiding, and the only thing which saved me was the fact that the entrance to the cellar was flooded, and the German soldiers did not wish to get their boots wet. In the evening, I came out of my hiding place. On this occasion my father was fortunate to be released by the soldiers. A lot of others were not as fortunate. I spent the next day in the cellar.

Once the front-line soldiers left, we settled in for the long three years of occupation that followed.

It had been rumored that there was going to be an **'action'** in the Skalat Camp. Everybody expected it. Not having anywhere to go, I remained in the camp, but I was up the whole night. I was restless and frightened, and had a strange feeling that if I could only hide out for one more day, I would somehow be able to go on for a while longer.

At dawn on June 30, 1943, the Jewish policemen were away from their posts, and I was able to walk out of the camp. I walked over to a Gentile's house, lay down in the backyard, and overcome with exhaustion, fell asleep. I was awakened by the Ukrainian police and taken back to the camp. There, I found other Jews sitting on the ground. I was searched, told to sit and keep my arms above my head. Later, we were loaded onto flat trucks that had very low sides. We were ordered to lie down on our backs and other people were piled on top of us. This was probably done to prevent people from escaping.

We were taken to pre-dug graves outside of our town. While we were walking from the road to the graves, one of the German officers decided to pick twenty young men and bring them to the camp so as to lure the remaining Jews back to camp for a final **'action'** at a later date. I was one of the lucky ones who was picked and given a new lease on life. A few weeks later, the Russian partisans appeared in Skalat. I joined them to fight the Germans, and that's how I survived.

Bernard (Nadzio) Weinsaft
New York 1995

[Page 119]

How I Survived the First Camp Action

The events which I am about to relate took place on June 30, 1943 during the First Camp Action in Skalat.

Early in the morning, the Germans came and surrounded our camp. Since we were warned that an **'action'** was coming, many inmates decided to run away. Among those who ran were my two sisters, Nusia and Yochevet, who were kept in the women's section of the camp. We agreed among ourselves that if we were separated, we would meet near the Bath section of our town. There, in the fields, tall hemp grew and, therefore, the area provided a place to hide. I tried to persuade my father to leave the camp with me, but he was despondent over the loss of my mother and the rest of the family and was reluctant to leave. After some more persuasion he agreed to run away, but as we were walking out of the building, he remembered that he had left his talis and tefilin (prayer shawl and phylacteries) behind. He went back to get them.

Suddenly, I heard the Germans near the building and it was too late to leave. We were trapped! I too retreated inside the building and looked for a place to hide. There were many bunks inside the building, and I quickly crawled in between them. In the spot where I found myself, I noticed another Jew, Yidel Beireshky, who was also hiding there. Within a short period of time we were discovered and dragged out by the Germans. They ordered us to join the other Jews sitting in the camp square, to undress to the waist and to turn in our belts.

The Germans walked around and ordered the people to surrender their rings, jewelry, .money, precious stones - anything of value. The baker, Hersz Katz, tore up his money because he didn't want the Germans to have it. For this action he was brutally beaten. Within half an hour my father was brought out from where he had hidden, and he too was stripped to the waist and joined the rest of us.

Shortly afterwards, some of the Jews were placed on trucks and then taken out of the camp to the prepared pits near the village of Nowosiolka, where they were shot. The trucks kept on returning for more Jews.

Suddenly a German by the name of Hoffman, who was in charge of the stone quarry near Nowosiolka, where I had worked, appeared on a motorcycle. Hoffman told the SS-man in charge of the **'action,'** that he needed twenty strong, able, young Jews to go with him. Among them Hoffman picked me. Not wishing to leave my father alone, I was reluctant to go. My father told me that by going, perhaps there will be a chance for me to survive and would be a trace left of our family. We said our farewells and I joined the twenty men.

After a while the SS-man returned to look over the twenty picked Jews and spotting my emaciated, weak body among them (I had just gotten over typhus), he ordered me with a few whips back to the group of the doomed. When Hoffman saw me for the second time among the doomed Jews, he took me by the hand and brought me over once more to the group of twenty. Then Hoffman walked away and the SS-man saw me again among the twenty Jews and once more whipping me and heaping insults, ordered me to go back to the group of the doomed.

The counting of twenty able Jews having been completed, Hoffman spotted that I was not among them. Hoffman then confronted the SS-man, told him that I was one of his best workers at the quarry and that he wanted me. Annoyed and impatient, the SS-man finally waved his hand and said that if he wanted such a sick. "Scheiss Jude" (shitty Jew), he could have me! Once more I joined the twenty men. We were now twenty-one "able-bodied" Jews, who were granted life.

We survived, but only after we had witnessed the executions and then covered the graves of our parents, brothers and neighbors.

[Page 120]

I survived this '**action**' because the SS-men knew that according to the official count of the Jews in the Skalat Camp, not enough Jews had been caught. "Let's leave these Jews working" they said, "we'll need them to bury the rest of them the next time." This was what I had heard on that day next to the just covered graves.

As told by Mordechai Weissman to Lusia Milch
Rechovot, Israel 1992

Page 121]

APPENDIX V

Commentary by Lusia Milch:
Two Visits to Skalat
Spring, 1970
Fall, 1995

[Page 122]

FIRST VISIT TO SKALAT
Spring, 1970

Outside of Skalat in the mass graves are the remains of my mother, Necha Rosenzweig-Goldberg (nee Rubin), and my sister, Ginia Goldberg. I saw the graves only once, in 1944, a few months after the liberation, when I, together with a group of Jews, went to say our farewells before leaving for the West.

Twenty five years later, during the height of the 'cold war,' my husband and I decided to visit our respective home towns once more. It was with great difficulty that we obtained permission to visit Skalat and my husband's town, Kozowa also located in the Tarnopol district.

When we finally arrived in Skalat accompanied by Russian intourist guides, who were also members of the police, the drastic change in the appearance of former Jewish sections of our town made it difficult to recognize what were once familiar houses and streets. I walked around the town with memories of the happiest and most painful years of my childhood.

An older peasant woman saw me and asked who I was. I told her my name and that my family owned a dry goods store before the war. She immediately told me that she knew my grandfather, Meyer Rosenzweig, quite well. She attached herself to us and accompanied us as we walked around the town. Along the way she also told me many other things.

After a while I started to walk up Panska Street towards the cemetery and mass graves. "Don't go there," the woman warned quietly. I told her that I had to go, since these sites were the main purpose of my trip. Again, she tried to stop me. "Why?" I asked. She told me that the Jewish cemetery had been made into a soccer field. I also found out from her, to my horror, that there were no more mass graves to be seen. They had been leveled and plowed under to make the site blend into the surrounding fields.

Who did such a thing?" I asked.

You know who," she answered cautiously. I knew that the local people had good reason to have the graves leveled. They were anxious to cover up their cooperation and culpability in the crimes which exterminated the Jews of Skalat.

And the authorities, didn't they do anything about it?" I asked.

No," she whispered, "no one cared! Besides, the soil there is good and they wanted it for planting."

The soil there is good!" I almost screamed. At that moment it was as if the Holocaust was still with me. I was grief stricken and stunned. There seemed to be no hope, no end to evil, and no bottom to human baseness.

My husband and I were so shaken, that we stood silently unable to shed tears. Then we turned around and walked back to the marketplace.

Lusia Milch nee' Rosenzweig
New York, 1970

[Page 123]

SECOND VISIT TO SKALAT

Fall, 1995

In September of 1995 I visited my native town for the second time in half a century. Unlike twenty five years earlier, when my husband and I first visited Skalat, now we were able to walk around unescorted and unrestricted by 'cold war' limitations.

As we approached the town, I recognized in the distance the familiar landmark of Skalat; its four cone-shaped, red-tiled roofs of the seventeenth century towers. They were the main site of the first pogrom massacre by the Germans and the Ukrainian collaborators, and brought back memories of the tragedy which took place there.

On first impression, the town seemed empty. The older generation, I was told, had passed on, the Poles had left for Poland and of those who had remained, only one third were natives. No one spoke about the conspicuous void left by the slaughtered Jews. No one missed or regretted the absence of those who had played such a pivotal role in the commerce, the cultural life, and the general development of the town. Skalat looked devastated; a town of ramshackle houses and dilapidated buildings. The deliberate destruction and fifty years of neglect had taken a heavy toll. Some quarters, especially the former Jewish areas, still lay in rubble. Dug-up streets, crumbling buildings and razed Jewish homes made it difficult for me to establish a landmark and to reconstruct the neighborhood of my childhood. Here and there a few meager looking vegetable gardens could be seen in place of the demolished homes. Otherwise, no vendors, no buyers, no tailors, no cobblers, no tinsmiths, and no glaziers. Since most of them were Jews, they had all been killed and no one had taken their place. I walked along a ruined, silent landscape which was both a reminder and a lament for the snuffed out lives, never to return again. The town was without a trace of its former vitality.

I wondered, "Did those who sowed the seeds of hate and those who committed the crimes, realize what future ruination they would bring to their native town? Was there some justice in what I was seeing?" The crimes perpetrated here were so outrageous and my pain was so great, that I could find no solace, even in thoughts of retribution.

I went back to Skalat to make a record in words and photographs of the remaining traces of Jewish life there because I knew that none of these would last another fifty years. I also came to remember, and to mourn. I tried to recall what our lives were like in this town before the war and sought tangible traces of that life. I remembered with great vividness the upheaval which destroyed our world, and I was looking for evidence of that destruction. When my family together with the entire Jewish community perished in Skalat, we did not have a chance to mourn because the killing went on unabated, and we expected our turn to come soon. At that time, even the opportunity to grieve was denied us. I, a survivor, came to this place of suffering, therefore, not only as a personal, but a communal mourner.

I started my day's pilgrimage in the Mantiawa outskirts, entering the town by the road leading from Tarnopol to Skalat. My first stop was the building where the Skalat Camp was located. Just as I had fifty years ago, I found myself in front of a fence with a locked gate. This time, I entered the enclosure by permission from the factory manager rather than having to crawl underneath the barbed wire of a side fence. The old building which stood in front of me, had the same flight of stairs leading to the door through which inmates entered the camp. To the side, I saw the open yard where daily, pre-dawn roll calls were conducted. I remembered the piles of furniture and household items that had been brought here from the ghetto after Skalat was declared Judenfrei. These furnishings were hiding a small group of desperate Jews who were still clinging to life, and I was among them. Within a few days they were all rounded up and shot at dawn. Fortunately, I had managed to escape the night before this slaughter. A narrow, little

[Page 124]

river still runs by the side of the former camp. Many of us had to jump across it both to enter and then to escape.

From here the road led to the area of the old fort, surrounded by the remnants of a stone wall and four tall towers. The grounds of the fort, once a place of green grass and tennis courts, the playground of the town's Polish "upper crust," were now littered with debris where chickens and ducks roamed freely. In the center, stood a newly erected, huge statue, honoring Hetman Bogdan Chmielnicki. Stern and erect this Ukrainian national hero had been responsible for pogroms on Jews during another era. I thought it an apt place for him to be, overlooking the spot where the slaughter of the Jews of Skalat began, ushering in the Holocaust in our town and the surrounding regions.

The road outside the fort running along the wall and the remnants of a moat led to the place where the Polish Catholic Church used to be. This site, the market square, and the areas below were changed beyond recognition. On reaching the market, I saw on one side of the square a row of old, boarded-up former Jewish stores. On another side stood a two storied building with a balcony. As a child, I used to play there. Above the front door, peering through a layer of peeling paint, I could clearly make out the black letters BERN.....the beginning of the name of the former store owner, my uncle, Moses Bernstein. I walked over to the spot where our house had stood and memory released echoes of long ago.

Once, Skalat was a lively and busy little town. That liveliness had been reflected in the crowded, narrow streets, the hustle-bustle of the marketplace, the sounds emanating from cheders*, prayer houses, merchants and hawkers, and from the laughter and cries of children. This affirmation of life had transcended the poverty and even the wretchedness of a sizable portion of the Jewish population. Here people had worked hard and long, and when work was done, they had observed the day of rest and prayers scrupulously and joyfully.

The rhythm of life and the appearance of our town would change with the seasons. White, long winters were cold and slow; warm springs and summers were busy with planting and harvesting; and falls alternated between golden, hazy Indian summer days and gray, rainy ones leaving the streets full of mud and puddles. Around the market square had been small stores and in the center, open stalls. Each day, but especially on Tuesdays (market day), the stalls were filled with fresh vegetables, fruits, eggs, chickens and geese; which the farmers would bring into town to sell. Once a year, when the feast of St. Ann was celebrated, our provincial town teamed with people. Worshipers and celebrants, farmers and tradesmen, cattle dealers and thieves would gather here from the surrounding towns and villages. The market square would turn into a place of magic for us, the children. While our parents looked forward to a busy day of commerce and trade, the children would delight in the carousel rides, the circus, and the small zoo which was always set up here.

As I looked at the empty scene in front of me, I recalled that one would also encounter here, Skalat's share of idlers, the chronically unemployed, the beggars and the town idiots. Of the latter, two came to mind: "Rosye myt di pek." Rose the bag lady, who always walked around with all her possessions tied around herself; and Ivan Bratrura, known in town as "Mykolcye myt di glek" (Nicholas with the bells). Nicholas, a truly mad, young fellow, bedecked in old medals, always rang pieces of tin and bells inviting the taunts of children and repelling them with a barrage of stones. Those that had been Jews, were killed No distinction was ever made between rich and poor, young and old, sane and mad.

I continued to walk around and found a cement rectangle in the middle of the market square. It was covering the former water pump, which I could see every day of my childhood from the front door of our house. Poor Jewish water carriers would eke out a living, carrying water from here to the neighborhood homes. Later, under this pump, Jews were tortured and drowned. From a hiding place in an attic near the market, I remembered hearing the screams of the first victims during the pogrom as well as the cries of the last victims, also gathered here during the final **'action'** in Skalat.

[Page 125]

From the market I walked to the big synagogue. When we were there twenty five years earlier the building had been used as a tractor repair station. Then, there were still some traces left of the building's former use. Now it had been converted into a factory .The main sanctuary with its high ceiling was divided into two stories. The beautiful wall frescos were gone as well as the stained glass windows and any other trace indicating that this was once the main synagogue of Skalat. Walking through the vestibule I remembered when this house of worship was regularly used for study and prayers, and on the Sabbath and holidays for solemn, religious services. Mostly, however, I retained in my memory the river of the doomed which flowed through these doors. Among them were my relatives, neighbors and townsmen. This sanctuary was their last shelter, their final gathering place, and for these victims, in the end, it proved no sanctuary. From here there was no way out, no hope, and no escape.

When we left the synagogue, we walked along the road leading to the railroad station. Along this route the victims of the "Wild Action" also walked, never to return again. On route we passed more destroyed former Jewish neighborhoods. Only a few of the better houses in town were still standing. On a side street and up a narrow alley, stood the building, barely recognizable, where before the war the Torah study house (Talmud Torah) was located. During the German occupation it was used as the seat of the Judenrat. I shivered, remembering stories of deeds which Jews were forced to commit vis-i-vis other Jews; deeds unimaginable and incomprehensible in ordinary times.

We stayed only briefly at the railroad station. The old station house, once neatly painted and adorned with planted flowers, was a shambles and closed. This had once been the point of departure, and often the beginning of adventure for the people of our town. Now there were no people, no signs of activity, and like the rest of the town it lay dormant and deserted. Only freight trains leave from this station occasionally, I was told. Across the railroad where the wetlands used to be, the land had been drained forming a small lake. Here, the largest number of victims taken from our town during the "Wild Action" were tortured and forced to spend a day and a night shivering in the cold, before being loaded into cattle cars for their fatal journey to the Belzec extermination camp.

Returning to town from the station we passed more former Jewish houses. Among them: the Friedman house, the Gelbtuch, the Rosenzweig, Dr. Kron's, Dr. Halpern's, and a few others. Down the road and close to the towers stood the Wagner house. Now dilapidated and boarded up, it had been one of the biggest and loveliest in our town and stood near the Milgrom house, where the revered Rabbi from Osiatyn used to stay during his Shavuot holiday visits to our town. We made a stop at the Gmina, where during the German occupation Meyer Grinfeld had climbed through a window in order to steal documents to be forged into "Aryan Papers." Another house, Dr. Kron's, was the seat of the *Schupo*, the headquarters of the feared German Security Police in our town.

The more prosperous people used to live along the main road known as Panska (Gentry) Street. Here were located some of the best homes and stores in town; among them the book, tobacco, candy and drug stores, as well as the homes and offices of a few of the town's lawyers, physicians and dentists. On Saturday afternoons, a segment of the Jewish population, bedecked in their finery, would promenade up and down this street and towards evening stop for candies or ice cream. Young couples and youth groups would pass along the street on their way to outings in the fields and meadows outside of town.

Further up Panska Street we passed landmarks familiar to us: the old schoolhouse, the Sokol - a sports and movie hall, the regional, administrative "Starosta" building and still further up, in opposite directions, the hospital and the former Jewish orphanage. Most of these places have associations for us, the survivors. Before the war, in one small house next to the hospital lived the Polish surgeon of our town, Dr. Strzalkowski. He often tended to the needs of the Jewish community. During the German occupation, for a fee, but nevertheless at a risk to himself, he performed forbidden surgery on Jews. This was often done on his kitchen table, under difficult conditions and with a minimum of medical equipment. One such victim who was treated by him was my cousin, Tynka Guss nee' Rosenzweig, for whom he removed the bullet after she was shot in the head during one of the village **'actions.'**

[Page 126]

At the Jewish cemetery the tombstones had been removed, the ground leveled and cemented, long ago. On our last trip, we had seen the sports field which was built there and, therefore, knew what to expect. Yet, when I approached the cemetery area and heard the cheerful shouts and peals of laughter coming from young athletes playing over the bones of my father and all those buried there, it was more than I could bear. I stopped for a few minutes, said a silent prayer, and left.

From here we went to Nowosiolka and the stone quarry where the Skalat Camp Jews, hungry, terrified and exhausted, had spent their waking hours cutting and breaking up stones. The quarry was now mechanized and the stones were being obtained from a new section. One could still make out, however, the old part of the hill and the road through which Jews, under guard, walked every day on their way to forced labor. I saw this scene when I was hiding in the nearby fields after Skalat was declared Judenfrei. One day, tired, hungry, and having no place to hide, I began to approach the Jews working there in hope of going back to camp with them. Suddenly my stepfather, who worked at the quarry with the other Jews, spotted me from a distance. Climbing to a higher level of the quarry, he started to sing loudly in Yiddish while continuing to break up stones. Through the words of his song he was telling me that I couldn't go back to camp, that it was dangerous there, and that all was lost. He warned me not to dare come any closer or I would be shot. He instructed me to run from this place and try to save myself. I listened for more advice, but his song stopped. Terrified and abandoned, I did as I was told. I turned around and ran as fast as I could.

From the quarry we got into a waiting taxi, hired for the day. With us, besides the driver, was a local man from Skalat. During the German occupation he had been a teenager. He told me how he and his friends had watched the Jews being driven through the streets and into the killing field. He saw them walking with bent heads, four or five abreast with locked arms and leaning against each other for support. I knew from my previous visit to Skalat that the mounds of the mass graves had long since been leveled and plowed under. As we approached the area, the local man pointed out the field and our car came to a stop along the road. Stepping out of the car I beheld a lush, green field planted with sugar beets as far as the eye could see. Familiar red poppies dotted the landscape and on the horizon a row of tall, poplar trees were towering upwards. It seemed unnatural that this pastoral scene should be hiding, deep within its soil, the remnants of such unspeakable violence and death. To camouflage their crimes, the killers picked the execution spots least visible from the road. We started to walk. silently, into the sloping fields. Then, my husband stopped, picked a red poppy, placed it into my hand, and watched me descend further into the field.

When I reached the lowest point, I stopped and sank to the ground. At that instant I sensed the mass graves underneath me, blanketed with fields of green. I imagined that day over fifty years ago when I came so close to sharing with the others my eternity underneath this field. Was the day then just as ordinary as this one? Were the tall, lovely poplars the same mute witnesses? And the sky above, was it as clear and blue? Was He there on that day and on thousands of such days watching just as silently?

I try to imagine what went through the minds of the doomed as I close my eyes. I feel myself among them, standing next to a heap of clothing, I huddle among the undressed men, women and children Suddenly, a real shiver of terror comes over me. In my ears I hear orders being barked. People in rows of five or six are forced to run towards the freshly dug pits. There is shooting and another row of Jews runs up and then another. Now it is our turn, I'm running along side of my mother and my sister. We reach the abyss...the mind goes blank.

After that I could imagine nothing!

[Page 127]

I am still clutching the red poppy in my hand, when I become aware of my surroundings again. I place the flower where I was sitting.

It is early evening as we leave. The taxi makes its way slowly along bumpy, old roads. Behind us we leave the dead, the unmarked graves, the pitiful remnants of what was once Jewish Skalat. I stare for the last time at the disappearing buildings. I seek words to give voice to my anguish, grope for expressions to convey the full measure of what befell us in this town. But I find none, and I leave as I came, in silence. The memories of those that I cannot take along and of what took place here, I take with me. I guard them carefully, to pass on to our children, grandchildren, and those who will come after them.

On the road outside of town I turn back deliberately to catch a final glimpse of the red tiled roofs of the old towers. Then, just as deliberately, I turn away and want to look back no more.

* cheders(s) -A Hebrew religious class for young boys.

Lusia Milch nee' Rosenzweig
New York 1995

[Page 128]

APPENDIX VI

Acknowledgments

I wish to express my gratitude to Abraham Weissbrod, who gave us this chronicle and told us what happened to the Jews of Skalat under the Nazi occupation. I also wish to thank my fellow survivors, an ever diminishing group of living witnesses, who contributed their testimonies in spite of the pain which these memories caused them. I'm especially glad that the voices of those who were children under the Nazi occupation of Skalat have now been heard. Their stories illustrate how deeply they had been seared by their childhood tragedies.

I am grateful to the following individuals for their help in editing the English text:

Adam Kanarek, a fellow survivor, for his sensitivity and ingenuity in helping to decipher unclear passages, abbreviations and foreign expressions, and for giving generously of his time;

Joseph Kofler, also a fellow survivor, for taping and reading the Yiddish text and for helping to compare it with the first version of the English translation;

Lewis Rosen. for making further valuable editorial suggestions; and

Lynda Pandolfo, for her patience and kindness in typing the English text.

I am indebted most of all to my husband, Bernard Milch. for his constant support. Having survived the Nazi occupation in Kozowa, Ukraine, only fifty miles from Skalat, he understood better than anyone and relived with me the stories told in this book. His love and that of our children, David Milch, Neal and Lesley Milch and our grandchildren. Cody and Julia, were the inspiration to undertake this effort and their encouragement helped to see it through to its completion.

Lusia Milch nee' Rosenzweig
1995

NAME INDEX

Milch, 238, 244, 257, 258, 274, 275, 295, 311,
    347, 351, 352, 362, 368, 370, 385, 390, 391,
    392, 398, 399

Milgrom, 49, 396

Molotov, 55, 66

Monias, 289, 348, 349

Moscicki, 374

Muller, 264, 267, 268, 269, 272, 273, 274, 276,
    279, 292, 301, 302, 361, 367

Müller, 201, 202, 203, 204, 207, 223, 224, 225,
    226, 227

Mussolini, 196, 320

Mykolcye myt di glek, 394

N

Nabodny, 288

Neiman, 260

Neimauer, 349

Neuman, 41

Niessenbaum, 352, 374, 376

Nirler, 71, 72, 259, 260, 261, 264, 268, 272,
    276, 277, 280, 282, 283, 303, 304, 308, 314,
    316, 319, 321, 322, 348, 371, 377

Nissenbaum, 379

Nowicki, 82, 85

O

Olejnik, 349

Olesker, 268

Onuferko, 254

Or, 151, 165, 172

Oren, 42

Orenstein, 133, 252

Orensztein, 260

P

Pandolfo, 399

Parnes, 259, 322, 352

Patti, 139, 140, 143, 144

Paul, 287, 302

Pavlovsky, 138, 144, 145, 150

Perl, 76, 81

Perlmuter, 259, 277, 326, 347, 349

Perlmutter, 5, 8, 9, 10, 11, 301

Pickholz, 49, 232

Picon, 374

Pikholc, 260

Pikholtz, 293, 336

Pikholz, 73, 76, 85, 95, 98, 105, 106, 320

Polak, 288

Polkovnik, 143

Poniatowski, 21

Porath, 203, 204

Pudles, 298, 299, 370

R

Rabbi Levi Yitzchak, 32

Rabbi of Kopyczince honored, 271

Rader, 107

Raiz, 73

Rathauser, 348

Ratzenshtein, 42

Ratzenstein, 352, 368, 386

Ratzinshtein, 41

Rebbe of Husiatyn, 34, 49, 50

Rebel, 283, 285, 286, 295, 303, 306, 314, 315,
    322, 335

Reinisch, 284

S

Skalat Memorial Scroll in the Hall of Names at Yad Vashem

Prepared by the Organization of the Former Residents of Skalat
and the Surroundings in Israel and the Diaspora
May 1961 (7 Sivan 5721)

**Our sincere appreciation to Yad Vashem
for the submission of this material for placement on the JewishGen web
site.**

———

This is from Skalat Memorial Scroll in the Hall of Names at Yad Vashem,
Prepared by the Organization of the Former Residents of Skalat
and the Surroundings in Israel and the Diaspora, 1961

Memorial Scroll in the Hall of Names at Yad Vashe

Translated by Jugend Gilberto

Family name(s)	Maiden name	First name(s)	Sex	Marital status	Father's names(s)	Mother's name(s)	Spouse's name(s)	Page in Original Document
ADLET		Moshe	M					9
ALENBERG		Dvora	F					10
ALESKER		Efraim	M					10
ALESKER		Shlomo	M					10
ALFEREN		Enzel	F					10
ALPEINBEIN		Israel Leib	M					10
ALPEINBEIN		Lucia	F					10
ALPEINBEIN		Sima	F					10
ALPENBEIN		Hermon	M					6
ALPENBEIN		Yakov	M					6
ALPENBEIN		Yehudit	F					6
ANGEL		Lea	F					6
ANGEL		Naftali	M					6
ANGEL		Niusia	F					6
ANGEL		Samuel	M					6
ASDERBEL	VILNER	Perl	F		Kopke			4/a
ASHKENAZI			M					10
ATOSDERBER		Levy	M					7
ATOSDERBER		Lipa	M					7
ATOSDERBER		Lucia	F					7
ATOSDERBER		Perl	F					7

Surname	Given name	Sex			No.
AUERBACH	Feige	F			6
AYSENSHTARK	Asher	M			6
AYSENSHTARK	David	M			6
AYSENSHTARK	Hana	F			6
AYSENSHTARK KLEINER	Lea	F			6
AYSENSHTARK	Reisel	F			6
AYSENSHTARK	Sonia	F			6
AYSENSHTARK	Tuvia	M			6
AYSENSHTARK	Yehuda	M			6
BALAVAT		F	Married	Leibish	7
BALAVAT	Bronka	F	Married		7
BALAVAT	Leibish	M			7
BALAVAT	Yosef	M			7
BAMBERG	Samuel	M			10
BAOR	David Yosef	M			7
BAOR	Fela	F			7
BAOR	Guitel	F			7
BAOR	Haim	M			7
BAOR	Hana	F			7
BAOR	Missia	F			7
BAOR	Mordechai	M			7
BAOR	Rachel	F			7
BAOR	Regina	F			7
BAOR	Yitzhak	M			7
BAOR	Yoel	M			7
BAOR	Yoshua	M			7
BAOR	Yoshua	M			7
BARZER	Shaike	M			10
BAUER	Moshe	F			10

Surname		Given name		Sex	No.
BAUM		Perl		F	6
BEIDER		Zeinvel		M	9
BEITEL		Shalom		F	10
BEITEL		Yitzhak		M	9
BEKMAN		Golda		M	7
BEKMAN		Libale		M	7
BEKMAN		Moshe		M	7
BEKMAN		Sara		F	7
BERENSHTEIN		Akiva		M	6
BERENSHTEIN		Avraham		M	7
BERENSHTEIN		Bat-Sheva		F	7
BERENSHTEIN		Bluma		F	7
BERENSHTEIN		Eliezer		M	6
BERENSHTEIN		Etka		F	6
BERENSHTEIN		Feige		F	6
BERENSHTEIN		Fishel		M	7
BERENSHTEIN		Ginia		F	6
BERENSHTEIN		Giza		F	6
BERENSHTEIN		Haya		F	6
BERENSHTEIN		Hika		F	6
BERENSHTEIN		Meir		M	6
BERENSHTEIN		Mordechai		M	6
BERENSHTEIN		Moshe		M	6
BERENSHTEIN		Moshe		M	10
BERENSHTEIN		Perl		F	6
BERENSHTEIN		Rachel		F	6
BERENSHTEIN		Sanie		F	10
BERENSHTEIN		Tova		F	6
BERENSHTIN		Sara	Eliezer	M	4/a
BERENSON	VA;TOK	Frida	Aba	F	4/a

Surname		First name	Sex	Status				Code
BERENSON		Mona	M		Tsvi			4/a
BERENSON		Nussia	F		Zeev			4/a
BERENZOHN		Israel	M					7
BERENZOHN		Pinchas	M					7
BERENZON								8
BERENZON	SHOIPTZ	Breina	F		Yitshak			3/a
BERGLER		Etel	F					4/a
BERGLER		Leib	M					4/a
BERGLER		Rosa	F					4/a
BERGLER		Sara	F					4/a
BERGLER		Yosef	M					4/a
BERLACH		Blanke	F	Married	Ysar			3/b
BERLACH		Ysar	M	Married		Ytke	Ytke	3/b
BERLACH	BERENSON	Ytka	F	Married		Breine	Ysar	3/b
BINSHTAK		Yeshihau Note	M					10
BIRENBAUM		Bela	F					7
BIRENBAUM		Yosef	M					7
BIRENBOIM		Alkena	M					7
BIRENBOIM		Bluma	F					7
BIRENBOIM		Dov	M					7
BIRENBOIM		Haim	M					7
BIRENBOIM		Israel Yitshak	M					7
BIRENBOIM		Lea	F					7
BIRENBOIM		Moshe	M					7
BIRENBOIM		Rivka	F					7
BIRENBOIM		Sara	F					7
BIRENBOIM		Sara Sima	M					7
BIRENBOIM		Shimon	F					7
BIRENBOIM		Simcha	M					7
BIRENBOIM		Sloiba	F					7

Surname	First Name	Father	Mother	Sex	No.
BIRENBOIM	Yehezkel			M	7
BLASHKE	Shlomo			M	10
BLOGTZ	Vita			F	2/b
BLUMENSHTEIN					9
BOMZA	Berna	Avigdor Natan		M	3/b
BOMZA	Haim	Tuvia		M	5/a
BOMZA	Matilda			F	5/a
BOMZA	Matilda			F	9
BOMZA	Nachman			M	1/b
BOMZA	Seche	Avigdor Natan		F	5/a
BOMZA	Shlomo	Nachman		M	5/a
BOMZA	Shlomo			M	9
BOMZA	Shlomo			M	10
BOMZA	Tsila	Avigdor Natan		F	5/a
BOMZA	Yakov			M	2/b
BOMZA	Yitzhak			M	2/b
BOMZA	Yitzhak			M	10
BOMZA	Yosef	Avigdor Natan		M	5/a
BOMZA	Zeev	Avigdor Natan		M	5/a
BOMZE	Yakov			M	9
BOMZE	Yosef			M	9
BOYER	David Yosef	Aharon Hacohen		M	5/a
BOYER	Guitel	Yitshak		F	5/a
BOYER	Mordechai	David Yosef		M	5/a
BRAS	Gusta			F	3/a
BRAS	Yakov	Haim Meir	Minia	M	3/a
BRIF	Yosef	Tsvi		M	8
BRIK	Biniamin	Israel		M	7
BRIK	Golda			F	7
BRIK	Hania			F	7

Surname		First Name	Sex	Status				No.
BRIK		Israel	M					7
BRIK		Miriam	F			Hania		7
BRITZ	HAVAN	Berta	F					2/a
BRITZ		Yosef	M					2/a
BROINSHTEIN		Feibish	M					5/a
BRONSHTIN		Bat-Sheva	F					7
BRONSHTIN		David	M					7
BRONSHTIN		Feibish	M					7
BRONSHTIN		Feige	F					7
BRONSHTIN		Hika	M					7
BUKSBOIM		Mordechai	M					10
DAGAN		Atia Rachel	F		Yehuda	Ester		2/a
DAGAN		Eliezer	M	Married	Yehezkel	Guissia	Feige	2/a
DAGAN		Feige	F	Married			Eliezer	2/a
DAGAN		Hania Perl	F		Yehuda	Ester		2/a
DAGAN		Haya	F		Yehuda	Ester		2/a
DAGAN		Haya	F	Married			Moshe	2/a
DAGAN		Israel	M	Married	Yehezkel	Guissia	Kuki	2/a
DAGAN		Kuki	F	Married			Israel	2/a
DAGAN		Moshe	M	Married	Yehezkel	Guissia	Haya	2/a
DAGAN		Neche	F		Yehuda	Ester		2/a
DAGAN		Yeheskel	M		Eliezer	Haya		2/a
DAGAN		Yehuda	M		Eliezer	Haya		2/a
DAGAN		Yosef	M		Yehuda	Ester		2/a
DALOGETZ		Ada	F					7
DALOGETZ		Beila	F		Eliezer			7
DALOGETZ		Hinde Feige	F					7
DALOGETZ		Vitia	F					7
DALOGETZ		Vitsa	F		David			4/a
DALOGETZ		Yitzhak	M					7

Surname	Alt. surname	First name	Sex	Relation	Name	Name	ID
DALOGETZ		Yosef Meir	M		Mordechai		7
DAYGEN	EPSTEIN	Ela	F		Moshe		1/b
DAYGEN		Zeilik	M		Yehezkel		1/a
DEUTSCHER		Haim Meir	M		Liv Arie	Feiga	3/a
DEUTSCHER		Liv Arie	M	Married	Yosef	Figa	3/a
DIKSHTIN		Hani	F				7
DRAT		Yona	M				10
DRYBLAT		Hinde	F				6
DRYBLAT		Yosef	M				6
DRYMER		Hana	F				9
EPSTEIN		Aharon David	M	Child	Kalman	Sara	1/a
EPSTEIN		Avraham	M		Kalman		1/a
EPSTEIN		Bat-Sheva	F				1/a
EPSTEIN		David	M				6
EPSTEIN		David	M		Moshe		5/a
EPSTEIN		David	M		Peltiel		5/b
EPSTEIN		David	M				6
EPSTEIN		David	M				10
EPSTEIN	KRAYNTSUA	Ester	F		Meir		1/a
EPSTEIN	BRYINTSA	Ester	F				6
EPSTEIN		Feige	F		Kone		3/a
EPSTEIN		Feige	F				8
EPSTEIN		Haim Munie	M				10
EPSTEIN		Hana	F		Samuel		5/a
EPSTEIN		Hova	F		Moshe		1/a
EPSTEIN		Leitsa	F				1/a
EPSTEIN		Malcha	F		Tsvi		3/a
EPSTEIN		Malcha	F				8
EPSTEIN		Mendel	M				1/b
EPSTEIN		Miral	F				10

Surname	Given name	Sex	Father	Code
EPSTEIN	Mirel	F	Peltiel	5/a
EPSTEIN	Miriam	F	Tsvi	3/a
EPSTEIN	Miriam	F		8
EPSTEIN	Moshe	M	Aharon David	1/a
EPSTEIN	Moshe	M	Shaul	5/a
EPSTEIN	Moshe	M		6
EPSTEIN	Moshe	M		9
EPSTEIN	Rachel	F	Moshe	1/a
EPSTEIN	Reiza	F		10
EPSTEIN	Reize	F	Peltiel	5/a
EPSTEIN	Samuel	M	Moshe	1/a
EPSTEIN	Sara	F		1/a
EPSTEIN	Sara Etel	F	Peltiel	5/a
EPSTEIN	Sara Etel	F		10
EPSTEIN	Sonia	F	Moshe	1/a
EPSTEIN	Tova	F		6
EPSTEIN	Yakov	M		6
EPSTEIN	Yakov Hersh	M	Kalman	1/a
EPSTEIN	Yeshihau	M	Aharon David	1/a
EPSTEIN	Yeshihau	M		6
EPSTEIN	Yitzhak	M	Tsvi	3/a
EPSTEIN	Yitzhak	M		8
EPSTEIN	Zissel	F	Peltiel	5/b
EPSTEIN	Zvi	M		8
EPSTEIN	Zvi	M	Peltiel	3/a
EXCEL	Avraham Yitshak	M		6
EXCEL	Rachel	F		6
EXCEL	Rivka	F		6
EXCEL	Russia	F		6
FARILES	David	M		10

Surname	Given name	Sex	Status	Father/Spouse	Other name	No.
FARILES	Yitzhak	M				10
FEINSHTEIN	Aharon	M				8
FEINSHTEIN	Basia	F				8
FEINSHTEIN	Beila	F				8
FEINSHTEIN	Ester	F				8
FEINSHTEIN	Shlomo	M				8
FEINSHTEIN	Velul	M				8
FEINSHTEIN	Yosef	M				8
FIK	Binhem	M				9
FINEK HASID		M			Scheindel	9
FINEK	Sheindel	F				9
FINEK	Shimon	M				9
FISHBACH YNBER	Moshe	M				9
FLASHNER	Clemens	F	Married	Mordechai	Zvi	4/a
FLASHNER	Hermon	M				8
FLASHNER	Menachem	M	Married	Moshe Aharon	Shoshana	4/a
FLASHNER	Monio	M				8
FLASHNER	Shoshana	F	Married		Menachem	4/a
FLASHNER	Vigdor	M				8
FLASHNER	Vilen	M				8
FLASHNER	Yakov	M	Married	Moshe Aharon	Yto	4/a
FLASHNER	Yakov	M	Married	Mordechai		4/a
FLASHNER	Yintsio	M				8
FLASHNER	Yto	F	Married	Moshe Aharon	Yakov	4/a
FLASHNER	Zeev	M	Married	Moshe Aharon		4/a
FLASHNER	Zvi	M	Married	Moshe Aharon		4/a
FLEISHFERV	Hana	F				9
FLEISHFERV	Hana	F				9
FLEISHFERV	Rivka Rachel	F				9

Surname		Given name	Sex		Father		Number
FLEISHFERV		Samuel	M				9
FLEISHFERV		Yitzhak Dov	M				9
FLEISHFERV		Yosef	M				9
FLEISHFERV		Zalman	M				9
FOGUEL		Dora	F				6
FOGUEL		Sabina	F				6
FOGUELMAN	EPSTEIN	Bela	F	Married	David		5/a
FOGUELMAN		David	M	Married	Bela		5/a
FOGUELMAN		David	M				9
FRANS		Samuel	M				8
FRANS		Samuel	M				8
FRANS		Yehiel	M				8
FRANS		Yehiel	M				8
FRANS		Yitzhak	M				10
FRANS		Zissel	F				8
FRANS		Zissel	F				8
FREMINGUER		Yitzhak	M			Shaul	10
FRIDMAN		Berl	M				4/a
FRIDMAN		David	M				9
FRIDMAN		Getsil	M				10
FRIDMAN		Hirsh	M				3/a
FRIDMAN		Israe Sherulka	M				7
FRIDMAN		Israel	M			Zisia	5/a
FRIDMAN		Kenia	F			Shaul	4/b
FRIDMAN		Munie	F				10
FRIDMAN		Pepe	F			Hirsh	3/a
FRIDMAN		Rachel	F			Hirsh	3/a
FRIDMAN		Rachel	F			Shaul	4/b
FRIDMAN		Ruben	M			Shaul	4/a
FRIDMAN		Shaul	M			Natan	4/a

Surname	First name	Father	Sex	Ref
FRIDMAN	Shimon	Shaul	M	4/a
FRIDMAN	Shoshana	Hirsh	F	3/a
FRIDMAN	Tova	Zeev	F	4/a
FRIDMAN	Yocheved	Yitshak	F	3/a
FRIDMAN	Yocheved		F	8
FRIDMAN	Yta	Shaul	F	4/b
FRIDMAN	Zushia		M	7
FRIDMAN	Yizik		M	9
FRIEND	Shalom		M	10
FUDHARDER	Aharon		M	2/a
FUDHORTSER	Aharon	Tsvi	M	8
FUDHORTSER	Fania		F	2/a
FUDHORTSER	Miriam		F	2/a
FUDHORTSER	Moshe		M	2/a
FUDHORTSER	Moshe		M	2/a
FUDHORTSER	Moshe		M	8
FUDHORTSER	Moshe		M	8
FUDHORTSER	Perl	Eliezer	F	8
FUDHORTSER	Pnina		F	2/a
FUDHORTSER	Shalom		M	2/a
FUDHORTSER	Shalom		M	8
FUDHORTSER	Yosef		M	2/a
FUDHORTSER	Yosef		M	8
FUDHORTSER	Yosef		M	8
FUHORILS	Feibish		M	8
FUHORILS	Malcha		F	8
FUHORILS	Moshe		M	8
FUHORILS	Pepe		M	8
GELBRAD	Guitel Feige	Betsalel	F	8
GERTEN	Frida		F	7

Surname	Alt. Surname	First Name	Sex	Status	Name	Name	Ref
GERTEN		Lion	M				7
GOLDBERG		Yakov	M				10
GOLDSHTEIN		David	M				10
GOLDSTIN		David	M	Married		Mina	4/a
GOLDSTIN		Getsel	M				7
GOLDSTIN		Hentse	F				7
GOLDSTIN	KATZ	Mina	F	Married	Aharon	David	4/a
GOLDSTIN		Rosa	F				7
GOTLIB		Yosef	M				10
GOTLIEB		Moshe	F				10
GRAS		Yoshua	M				10
GRINSHPUN		Israel	M				10
GROSSMAN		Hersh	M				8
GROSSMAN		Yosef	M				8
GUETER		Moshe	M				10
GURFINKEL		Sara	F				6
GUTERMAN		Baruch	M	Married		Golda	1/a
GUTERMAN	EPSTEIN	Golda	F	Married	Moshe		1/a
HALATE		Aharon	M				9
HALPERIN		Etel	F	Married	Aharon		4/a
HALPERIN		Shlomo	M				4/a
HALPERON		Andzel	F				7
HALPERON		Avraham	M				7
HALPERON		Helke	F				7
HALPERON		Misia	F				7
HALPERON		Nonio	F				7
HANIA		Perl	F				4/b
HARAK		Menachem Mend	F				10
HAREIN		Yakov	M				10
HECHT		Moshe Leib	M				10

Surname	Given name	Sex	Status			No.
HELDERN		F	Married		Avraham	2/a
HELDERN	Avraham	M	Married			2/a
HELDERN	Yoshua	M				2/a
HELSREN	Rina	F				7
HIRSBIN	Hava	F				2/a
HIRSBIN	Haya	F				2/a
HIRSBIN	Samuel	M				2/a
HIRSBIN	Shindela	F				2/a
HIRSHBEIN	Samuel	M				10
HOBEN	Berta	F		Eliezer		8
HOCHBOUM	Sara	F				6
HOFMAN	Hania	F				7
HOFMAN	Loritsye	F				7
HOFMAN	Yitzhak	M		Moshe		7
HOROWITZ PAPIR	Beula	F	Married	Shaul	Moshe	2/a
HOROWITZ	Moshe	M	Married	Arie	Beula	2/a
INBER	Nonie	M				9
KATSIUR	Fasia	F				9
KATSIUR	Hana	F				9
KATSIUR	Hersh	M				9
KATSIUR	Israel	M				9
KATSIUR	Leib	M				9
KATSIUR	Miriam	F				9
KATSIUR	Moshe	M				9
KATSIUR	Shimshon	M				9
KATSIUR	Yakov	M				9
KATSUR KATSELOV	Moshe	M			Tsvi	10
KATZ	Dina	F	Married			10
KATZ	Etka	F		Yakov		3/a
KATZ	Haya	F		Meir		3/a

Surname	First name	Sex				Code
KATZ	Haya	F		Samuel		4/a
KATZ	Meir	M		Yakov		3/b
KATZ	Moshe	M		Yakov		3/b
KATZ	Rachel	F		Yakov		3/a
KATZ	Rivka	F		Natan		4/a
KATZ	Samuel	M		Aharon		4/a
KATZ	Samuel	M				10
KATZ	Yakov	M		Aharon		3/a
KATZ	Yakov	M				10
KATZ	Yoshua	M				9
KATZ	Zvi	M	Married		Dina	10
KIBETZ	Tova	F				9
KIBETZ	Ytsio	M				9
KITSUR	Avraham	M				6
KITSUR	Betka	F				6
KITSUR	Mordechai	M				9
KITSUR	Tova	F				9
KITSUR	Yakov	M				6
KITSUR	Zissel	F				6
KLEINER		F	Married		Moshe	9
KLEINER	Babi	M				9
KLEINER	Haya	F				8
KLEINER	Hentzva	F		Natan		4/a
KLEINER	Hinde	F		Asher		4/a
KLEINER	Lea	F				9
KLEINER	Mania	F				10
KLEINER	Moshe	M				8
KLEINER	Moshe	M				9
KLEINER	Moshe	M	Married			9
KLEINER	Perl	F				8

Surname	Given name	Father	Sex	No.
KLEINER	Pinchas		M	9
KLEINER	Pinchas		M	9
KLEINER	Yehudit		F	9
KLEINER	Yehudit		F	9
KLENSON	Feige		F	9
KLENSON	Guitman		M	9
KLENSON	Moshe		M	9
KLENSON	Royija		F	9
KOPERSCHMID	Avraham Yitshak		M	9
KOPERSCHMID	Feivel		M	10
KOPERSCHMID	Israel		M	10
KOPERSCHMIDT			F	10
KOPERSCHMIDT	Ester		F	10
KORNVITZ		Zalmen	M	9
KORNVITZ		Zalmen	M	9
KORNVITZ		Zalmen	M	9
KORNVITZ		Zalmen	M	9
KORNVITZ		Zalmen	M	9
KORNVITZ	Bluma		F	9
KORNVITZ	Clara	Elihau	F	4/a
KORNVITZ	David		M	9
KORNVITZ	David		M	10
KORNVITZ	Fela	Elihau	F	4/a
KORNVITZ	Golda		F	9
KORNVITZ	Guitel		F	9
KORNVITZ	Haya		F	9
KORNVITZ	Lena		F	9
KORNVITZ	Matilda	Elihau	F	4/a
KORNVITZ	Pnina		F	9
KORNVITZ	Sima Lea		F	9

Surname	Given name	Sex	Father	Page
KORNVITZ	Zalman	M	Eliezer	9
KOVETZ	Arie	M	Mendel Tsvi	5/a
KOVETZ	Avraham	M	Samuel	5/a
KOVETZ	Avraham	M	Menachem	5/a
KOVETZ	Avraham David	M	Yosef	5/a
KOVETZ	Dov	M	Yakov Hacohen	5/a
KOVETZ	Dvora	F	Tsvi	5/a
KOVETZ	Eliezer	M	Moshe	5/a
KOVETZ	Etel	F	Tsvi	5/a
KOVETZ	Etil	F	Menachem	5/a
KOVETZ	Fania	F	Tsvi	5/a
KOVETZ	Guitel	F	Tsvi	5/a
KOVETZ	Haim	M	Eliezer	5/a
KOVETZ	Hana Haya	F	Mendel Abe	5/a
KOVETZ	Hana Haya	F	Menachem Mendel	5/a
KOVETZ	Hana Haya	F	Yosef	5/a
KOVETZ	Haya	F	Haim	5/a
KOVETZ	Haya	F	Yitshak	5/a
KOVETZ	Haya Tsirl	F	Yitshak	5/a
KOVETZ	Kopel Nachum	M	Yosef	5/a
KOVETZ	Lea Guitel	F	Menachem	5/a
KOVETZ	Mali	F	Yitshak	5/a
KOVETZ	Menachem	M	Israel	5/b
KOVETZ	Menachem Mend	M	Tsvi	5/a
KOVETZ	Mendel Abe	M	Yitshak	5/a
KOVETZ	Mordechai	M	Tsvi	5/a
KOVETZ	Mordechai	M	Tsvi	5/b
KOVETZ	Moshe	M	Eliezer	5/a
KOVETZ	Moshe	M	Tsvi	5/a
KOVETZ	Moshe	M	Menachem Mendel	5/b

Surname	Name	Sex	Name 2	Name 3	Name 4	Code
KOVETZ	Perl	F	Mendel Tsvi			5/a
KOVETZ	Pinchas Yakov	M	Yitshak			5/a
KOVETZ	Tame	F	Eliezer Halevi			5/a
KOVETZ	Tsirel	F	Yosef			5/a
KOVETZ	Yitzhak	M	Eliezer			5/a
KOVETZ	Yitzhak	M	Menachem			5/a
KOVETZ	Yitzhak	M	Menachem Mendel			5/b
KOVETZ	Yosef	M	Tsvi			5/a
KOVETZ	Zvi	M	Yitshak			5/a
KROIN		M				10
KUPERMAN	Ester	F				1/a
KUPERMAN	Haya	F				1/a
KUPERMAN	Meir	M				1/a
KUPERMAN	Simcha	M				1/a
KUPERSCHMID	Clara	F	Samuel			3/a
KUPERSCHMID	Moshe	M	Samuel			3/a
KUPERSCHMID	Perl	F	Samuel			3/a
KUPERSCHMID	Samuel	M	Arie			3/a
KUPERSCHMID	Tsila	F		Hana		3/a
KUPERSCHMID	Yoel	M	Samuel			3/a
KUPERWASSER	Miriam	F				4/a
KUPERWASSER	Shlomo	M	Natan			4/a
KUPERWASSER	Yitzhak	M	Natan			4/a
KUPERWASSER	Yosef	M	Natan			4/a
LANDESMAN	Batia	F				8
LANDESMAN	David	M				8
LANDESMAN	Meir	M	Haim	Hana Haya	Rachel	2/a
LANDESMAN	Mordechai	M				2/a
LANDESMAN	Moshe	M	Marcus			2/a
LANDESMAN	Moshe	M				8

Surname	Alt surname	Given name	Sex	Status	Name 1	Name 2	Name 3	Code
LANDESMAN		Perl	F		Marcus			2/a
LANDESMAN	SCHWARTZ	Rachel	F	Married	Peretz	Frida	Meir	2/a
LANDESMAN		Racheli	F					8
LANDESMAN		Rivka	F					2/a
LANDESMAN		Rivka	F					8
LANDESMAN		Rosa	F		Marcus			2/a
LANDESMAN		Shlima	F		Marcus			2/a
LANDESMAN		Tsipora	F		Marcus			2/a
LEMPERT		Yona	M					9
LERNER		Bela	F					8
LERNER		Moshe	M					8
LERNER		Yitzhak	M					8
LERNER		Zeev	M					8
LESHER		Dina	F					8
LESHER		Haya Sara	F					8
LESHER		Zelik	M					8
LIBERGAL		Bomo	M					5/a
LIBERGAL	WEHL	Haya Ester	F		Shlomo Zalman	Sara Reisel		3/a
LIBERGAL		Mendel	M					5/a
LIBERGAL		Moshe	M					5/a
LIBERGAL		Sara	M					10
LIBERGAL		Tsila	F					5/a
LIBERGAL		Yuliel	M		Michael	Haya Ester		3/a
LIBERGAL		Zmoire	M		Hersh			5/b
LIBERGAL		Zmoire Eliezer	M					5/a
LIBWEHL	VISTAUB	Guitel	F		Haim Meir	Pina		3/a
LINTSHITZ			F	Married			Eduard	10
LINTSHITZ			F	Married			Samuel	10
LINTSHITZ			F	Married			Shlomo	10
LINTSHITZ			M	Married			Regina	10

Surname		Given name	Sex	Status	Father	No.
LINTSHITZ		Betka	F			8
LINTSHITZ		Clara	F			10
LINTSHITZ		Dolek	M			10
LINTSHITZ		Eduard	M	Married		10
LINTSHITZ	KINKIS	Regina	F	Married		10
LINTSHITZ	KREMER	Rosia	F			10
LINTSHITZ		Samuel	M	Married		10
LINTSHITZ		Shlomo	M	Married		10
LUNTSHOTZ		Yakov	M			7
LUTER	VINRAUB	Hana	F		Yehiel	8
MAGAR		David	M		Yosef Halevi	1/a
MAGAR		Eliezer	M		Yosef Halevi	5/a
MAGAR		Etil	F			5/a
MAGAR		Fishel	M		Menachem Nachum	7
MAGAR		Haim	M			5/a
MAGAR		Haim	M			7
MAGAR		Menachem Nahum	M		Haim	5/a
MAGAR		Nussia	F			7
MAGAR		Nussia	F			7
MAGAR		Odel	F		Avraham	5/a
MAGAR		Pepe	F			7
MAGAR		Risel Zissel	F		Haim	5/a
MAGAR		Rivka	F			7
MAGAR		Toive	F		Yosef Halevi	5/a
MAGAR	EPSTEIN	Tova	F		Aharon David	1/a
MAGAR		Yehiel	M		Shaul	1/a
MAGAR		Yosef	M		Avraham	5/a
MAGDAN		Adelka	F			8
MAGDAN		Israel	M			8
MAGDAN		Sara	F			8

Surname	First name	Sex		No.
MAGDAN	Yehiel	M		8
MELAMED	Matie	M		9
MELAMED	Samuel	M		10
MENDEL	Perl	F		3/b
MENTSEL	Avraham	M		8
MENTSEL	Bracha	F		8
MENTSEL	Ester	F		8
MENTSEL	Miriam	F		8
MENTSEL	Pola	F		8
MENTSEL	Rachel	F		8
MENTSEL	Tuvia	M		8
MENTSEL	Yitzhak	M		8
MENTSEL	Yitzhak	M		8
MENTSEL	Yosef	M		8
MENTSEL	Zalman	M		8
MESING	Natan	M	Avraham	9
MESING	Nissan	M		5/b
MESING	Yakov	M		10
MILGRUM	Elta	F		10
MILGRUM	Lea	F		10
MILGRUM	Yakov	M		10
MILRAD	David	M		8
MILRAD	Dov	M		8
MILRAD	Eti	F		8
MILRAD	Shoshi	F		8
MILRAD	Tova	F		8
MINISTER	Henda	F		8
MINISTER	Mans Haim	M		8
MINISTER	Moshe	M		8
MINISTER	Prometsia	F		8

Surname	Alt. Surname	Given name		Father	Note	Sex	Age
MINISTER		Rosa				F	8
MITELMAN		Liva				F	7
MITELMAN		Rivka				F	10
MUSHLIN		Rivka				F	9
NAFT		Moshe				M	9
NAGAR	KATSOR	Hana				F	9
NISENBAUM		Avigdor				M	10
NISENBAUM		Rosia				F	10
NOIMAN		Israel				M	10
OKON return		David				M	8
OKON		Malcha				F	8
OKON		Rivka				F	8
OKON		Wolf David				M	8
ORHEN		Kopka				M	9
ORHEN		Tsipora				F	9
OSTERN		Charlote	Yehid	Mendel		F	3/a
OSTERN		Yehid	Feiga	Avraham		F	3/a
OYIERBACH	GELBERD	Feige		Mordechai		F	2/a
OYIERBACH		Haya		Simcha		F	2/a
OYIERBACH		Lea		Simcha		F	2/a
OYIERBACH		Simcha		Shlomo		M	2/a
PALBEL		David		Yitshak		M	4/a
PALBEL		Haya Dvora		Berl		F	4/a
PALBEL		Meir		Yitshak		M	4/a
PALBEL		Yitzhak		Aharon		M	4/a
PAPIR		Yitzhak		Yosef	Child	M	2/a
PAPIR		Alter				M	9
PAPIR		Clara		Zeilik		F	2/a
PAPIR		Fani		Yosef		F	2/a
PAPIR		Feige				F	8

PAPIR	Getsel		M	9
PAPIR	Guetsil		M	2/a
PAPIR	Hana		F	2/a
PAPIR	Hana		F	8
PAPIR	Matie		M	9
PAPIR	Shaul	Shaul	M	2/a
PAPIR	Shaul	Shaul	M	8
PAPIR	Shoshana		F	2/a
PAPIR	Tova	Mendel	F	2/a
PAPIR	Tova		F	8
PAPIR	Yehiel	Yakov	M	8
PAPIR	Yosef	Shaul	M	2/a
PAPIR	Yosef		M	8
PASTERNAK	Eli		M	8
PASTERNAK	Rachel		F	8
PASTERNAK	Zalman	Shaul	M	8
PASTERNAK	Zalman		F	10
PEREL	Netanel		M	10
PEREL	Yakov		M	10
PERL	Henie		F	10
PERLMUTTER	Baruch	Eliezer	M	4/a
PERLMUTTER	Batia		F	8
PERLMUTTER	Betka		F	8
PERLMUTTER	Gode		F	8
PERLMUTTER	Haim Mordechai		M	8
PERLMUTTER	Nachman Hersch		M	8
PERLMUTTER	Rissia		F	8
PERLMUTTER	Rosa		F	8
PERLMUTTER	Shlomo		M	8

Surname	Alt. Surname	Given Name	Sex	Status	Name 1	Name 2	Name 3	Ref.
PERLMUTTER		Yehiel	M					8
PERSER		David	M					9
PERSLER		David	M		Avraham			3/a
PETER		Aharan David	M	Married	Tsvi	Hinda Lea		3/a
PETER		Hermon Zvi	M	Married	Shlomo Zalman	Adela	Hinde	3/a
PETER	WEHL	Hinde Lea	F	Married		Sara Reisel	Zvi	3/a
PIKHALTZ		Tova	F	Child				10
PIKHOLTZ	MERDER	Beila	F	Married	Yakov		Moni	3/a
PIKHOLTZ		Betka	F		Yakov			7
PIKHOLTZ		Eliezer	M					9
PIKHOLTZ		Feige	F		Shimon			5/a
PIKHOLTZ		Feige	F					9
PIKHOLTZ		Haim	M		Moshe			5/b
PIKHOLTZ		Haim	M					9
PIKHOLTZ		Moni	M	Married	Moni		Beila	3/a
PIKHOLTZ		Monio	M					7
PIKHOLTZ		Regina	F		Tuvia			5/a
PIKHOLTZ		Regina	F					9
PIKHOLTZ		Rosia	F					10
PIKHOLTZ		Tuvia	M		Moshe			5/a
PIKHOLTZ		Tuvia	M					9
RATSENSTEIN		Bluma	F					9
RATSENSTEIN		Eli	M					9
RATSENSTEIN		Ester	F		Shlomo	Aidel		2/a
RATSENSTEIN		Ester	F					9
RATSENSTEIN	BRIKENSTEIN	Eydel	F	Married	Mordechai	Rivka	Shlomo	2/a
RATSENSTEIN		Eydel	M					9
RATSENSTEIN		Gershon	M					9
RATSENSTEIN		Kodel	F					9

Surname	First name	Sex					No.
RATSENSTEIN	Rachel	F		Shlomo	Aidel		2/a
RATSENSTEIN	Rachel	F					9
RATSENSTEIN	Rachel	F					9
RATSENSTEIN	Reisel	F					9
RATSENSTEIN	Sara	F					9
RATSENSTEIN	Shlomo	M	Married	Moshe Haim	Sara	Eidel	2/a
RATSENSTEIN	Shlomo	M					9
RATSENSTEIN	Tova	F					9
RATSHTEIN	Shimon	M					10
RECHEL	Israel	M					10
REISER	Natan	M					10
RIS	Moshe	M					10
RIS	Moshe	M					10
RITSENBEIN PETER	Sara Selke	F			Adela		3/a
ROSENBERG	Friederich	M					3/a
ROSENBERG VISTAUB	Zusha	M		Pauel	Rosa		3/a
ROSENBLAT	Beny	M					9
ROSENBLAT	Feige	F					6
ROSENBLAT	Feige	F					9
ROSENBLAT	Mali	F					6
ROSENBLAT	Moshe	M					9
ROSENBLAT	Pepe	M					9
ROSENBLAT	Yitzhak	M					6
ROSENBLAT	Yitzhak	M					9
ROSENBLAT	Zvi	M					6
ROSENSHTOK	Berta	F					9
ROSENSHTOK	Ruben	M					9
ROSENTSVEIG	Amalia	F			Malka		2/a
ROSENTSVEIG	Clara	F			Malka		2/a
ROSENTSVEIG	Clara	F					9

Surname	First name		Sex	No.
ROSENTSVEIG	Dadel		M	9
ROSENTSVEIG	David		M	10
ROSENTSVEIG	Emanuel	Salomon Leib	M	2/a
ROSENTSVEIG	Emanuel		M	9
ROSENTSVEIG GOLDENBERG	Neche		F	10
ROSENTSVEIG	Ochlia		F	9
ROSENTSVEIG	Salomon Leib	Meir	M	2/a
ROSENTSVEIG	Shlomo	Salomon Leib	M	2/b
ROSENTSVEIG	Shlomo		M	9
ROSENTSVEIG	Zalman Leib		M	9
ROSENTSVEIG	Zalman Leib		M	10
SAMET	Yosef		M	10
SAPIR	Yzia		M	10
SAS	Berl		M	10
SAS	David	Haim Yzik	M	3/a
SAS	David		M	8
SAS	Yakov	David	M	3/a
SAS	Yakov		M	8
SCHVALB				9
SCHWARTZ	Adela		F	8
SCHWARTZ	Frida		F	1/b
SCHWARTZ	Peretz		M	1/b
SCHWARTZ	Tunie		F	10
SCHWARTZ	Zola		F	8
SEGAL	Guitel	Elkana	F	5/a
SEGAL	Haim	Elkana	M	5/a
SEGAL	Haim		M	10
SEGAL	Haim		M	10
SEGAL	Peril	Elkana	F	5/a
SHABIFT	Golda		F	9

Surname		First name	Sex	Note	Age
SHABIFT		Haim	M		9
SHAFTSIRER		Welwill	M		10
SHAPIRA		Eli	M		9
SHAPIRA		Hersh	M		9
SHAPIRA		Lea	F		9
SHAPIRA		Miriam	F		9
SHAPIRA		Yakov	M		10
SHAPIRA		Yakov Leib	M		10
SHAPIRA		Yehiel	M		10
SHARF		Max	M		10
SHARF		Yosef	M		10
SHATSBERG		Abrametchi	M		9
SHECHTER	EPSTEIN	Fasia	F	Married	Shalom	5/a
SHECHTER		Shalom	M	Married	Pesia	5/a
SHECHTER		Yakov	M		9
SHECHTER		Zvi	M		10
SHEINBERG		Eliezer	M		9
SHEINBERG		Hana	F		9
SHEINBERG		Milo	M		9
SHEINBERG		Shevach	M		9
SHEINHAUT		Ashu	M		10
SHEINHAUT		Avraham	M		9
SHEINHAUT		Doni	M		10
SHEINHAUT		Eti	F		9
SHEINHAUT		Hershel	M		9
SHEINHAUT		Leitsha	F		10
SHEINHAUT		Moshe	M		10
SHEINHAUT		Munie	M		10
SHEINHAUT		Nechama	F		9
SHEINHAUT		Yosef	M		9

Surname	First Name	Gender					No.
SHEINHAUT	Yta	F					9
SHEINHAUT	Zelta	F					9
SHEINHOIT	Avraham	M					9
SHIFMAN	Reisel	M					10
SHIPIFETZ	Bat-Sheva	F		Aharon David			1/a
SHIPIFETZ	David	M		Haim			1/a
SHIPIFETZ	Haim	M		Moshe			1/a
SHIPIFETZ	Malcha	F		Haim			1/a
SHIPIFETZ	Moshe	M		Haim			1/a
SHIPIFETZ	Natan	M		Haim			1/a
SHISTER	Feivel	M					9
SHNEIER	Eliezer	M					9
SHNEIER	Haim	M					9
SHNEIER	Krantsia	F					9
SHNEIER	Sara	F					9
SHNEIER	Yakov	M					9
SHOIPTZ	Freidi	F	Married			Guetsil	3/a
SHOIPTZ	Guetsil	M	Married	Yitshak		Freidi	3/a
SHOIPTZ	Lola	F		Guetsil	Freidi		3/a
SHOIPTZ	Nahum	M		Guetsil	Freidi		3/a
SHOIPTZ	Shlomo	M		Guetsil	Freidi		3/a
SHOR	Moshe	M					10
SHRAGER	Yosef	M					9
SHRENDEL	Yosef	M					10
SHTEINBUCK	Shlomo Ozer	M					10
SHTERN	Michal	M					9
SHVALBNEST	Gedalia	M					10
TENENBAUM	Avraham David	M		Meir			8
TENENBAUM	Buzio	M					8
TENENBAUM	Dolek	M					8

Surname	Alt. surname	First name	Sex	Status	Relation	Father	No.
TENENBAUM		Elimelech	M				8
TENENBAUM		Gusta	F				8
TENENBAUM		Keyale	F				8
TENENBAUM	RINDER	Miriam	F				8
TENENBAUM		Rachel	F				8
TENENBOIM		Bruchia Keila	F			Yitshak	3/a
TENENBOIM		David	M			Elimelech	3/a
TENENBOIM		Elimelech	M			Tsvi	3/a
TENENBOIM		Rachel	F			Elimelech	3/a
TENENBOIM		Yitshak Zvi	M			Elimelech	3/a
TENENBOIM		Yosef	M				10
TEPPERBERG		Hana	F			Eliezer	4/a
TEPPERBERG		Yona	M				2/b
TREGUER		Berish	F				10
TSELERMAIER		Natan	M				10
TSELERMAIER		Pepi	F				10
TSHATSHEKE		Efraim	M	Married	Sara		10
TSHATSHEKE		Sara	F	Married	Efraim		10
TSIMERING		Haim	M				10
TUNIS		Aba Leib	M				8
TUNIS		Arie	M				8
TUNIS		Batia	F				8
TUNIS		David	M				10
TUNIS	VINRAUB	Etka	F				8
TUNIS		Lucia	F				8
TUNIS		Menachem Mend	M				10
TUNIS		Monio	F				8
TUNIS		Pepe	F				8
UNGUER		Dvora	F				6
UNGUER		Ester	F				6

UNGUER	Fania	F		6
UNGUER	Max	M		6
UNGUER	Michael	M		6
VAINSAFT	Yakov Israel	M		10
VALACH	Fradel	F	Tsvi	5/a
VALACH	Menachem	M		10
VALACH	Miriam	F	Yitshak Tsvi	5/a
VALACH	Moshe	M		9
VALACH	Yitzhak Zvi	M	Yosef Hacohen	5/a
VALTOCH	Avi	M		9
VALTOK	Aba	M		4/a
VALTOK	Dina	F	Aba	4/a
VALTOK	Haya	F		4/a
VALTOK	Nussia	F	Aba	4/a
VALTOK	Yitzhak	M	Aba	4/a
VASHITZ	Avraham	M		9
VASSERFIRER	Sender Meir	M		9
VEINBERG	Biniamin	M	Hilel	4/a
VEINBERG	Haya	F	Moshe	4/a
VEINBERG	Rivka	F	Biniamin	4/a
VEINBERG	Zelig	M	Biniamin	4/a
VEINZAFT	Moshe Yitshak	M		7
VEINZAFT	Sima	F		7
VEISMAN	Hana	F	Yehuda	5/a
VEISMAN	Hana Haya	F		7
VEISMAN	Hava	F	Yosef	5/a
VEISMAN	Hava	F		7
VEISMAN	Malcha	F	Yehuda	5/a
VEISMAN	Malcha	F		7
VEISMAN	Tsipora	F	Yehuda	5/a

Surname	Maiden name	Given name	Gender	Father's name	
VEISMAN		Tsipora	F		7
VEISMAN	FENTSIA	Yehuda	M	Eliezer Lipa	5/a
VEISMAN		Yehuda	M		7
VEISMAN		Yosef	M	Yehuda	5/b
VEISMAN		Yosef	M		7
VEISMAN		Zvi	M	Yehuda	5/a
VELECH		Shabtay	M		7
VEYSBRAT		Yona	M		10
VILNER		Aharon	M		10
VILNER		Ester	F	Tsvi	4/a
VILNER		Gina	F		7
VILNER		Ginia	F	Moshe	4/a
VILNER		Giza	F	Tsvi	4/a
VILNER		Kahat	M		10
VILNER		Koifka Shaya	M	Shlomo	7
VILNER		Kopka	F	Shlomo	4/a
VILNER		Levy	M	Lipa	4/a
VILNER		Lipa	M	Levi	4/b
VILNER		Lucia	F	Levi	4/b
VILNER		Moshe	M	Kopke	4/a
VILNER		Moshe	M		7
VILNER		Nussia	F	Tsvi	4/a
VILNER		Shlomo	M	Kubki	3/a
VILNER		Shlomo	M	Koipke Shyia	7
VILNER		Zvi	M	Kopke	4/a
VINBERG		Biniamin	M		7
VINBERG		Rivka	F		7
VINBERG		Zelig	M		7
VINRAUB		Fenka	F		8
VINRAUB	MEIMAN	Sara	F		8

Surname	First Name	Sex	Married	Father	Mother	Place	Page
VINTRAUB	David	M					7
VINTRAUB	Dina	F					7
VINTRAUB	Ester	F					7
VINTRAUB	Yitzhak	M					7
VISHNIAK	Avraham	M					7
VISHNIAK	Dvora	F					7
VISHNIAK	Lora	F					7
VISHNIAK	Perl	F					7
VISHNIAK	Pinchas	M					7
VISHNIAK	Zusia	M					7
VISTAUB DEUTSCHER	Figa	F		Haim Meir	Pina	Liv Arie	3/a
VOLECH	Freidel	F					7
VOLECH	Miriam	F					7
VOLECH	Yitzhak Zvi	M					7
VOLTOCH							8
VUDERHOREN	David	M					7
VUDERHOREN	Fania	F					7
VUDERHOREN	Haim	M					7
VUDERHOREN	Moshe	M					7
VUDERHOREN	Perl	F					7
VUDERHOREN	Shvil	M					7
VUDERHOREN	Tsila	F					7
VULOVITZ	Berl	M					6
VULOVITZ	Zvi	M					6
VULTO							7
WECHSLER	Betka	F					8
WECHSLER	Biniamin Samuel	M					8
WECHSLER	Perl	F					8
WEHL ANDA	Idel	F	Married	Biniamin	Mina		2/a
WISTAUB	Haim Meir	M		Arie	Hula	Pina	2/a

Surname	Alt Surname	Given Name	Sex	Status	Father	Mother		Ref
WISTAUB		Hona Yohanan	M		Haim Meir	Pina		2/a
WISTAUB		Pauel Philip	M		Haim Meir	Pina		2/a
WISTAUB		Roisa Lila	F		Yosef			2/a
WISTAUB	PAPIR	Rosa	F					2/a
WISTAUB		Yosef Yujo	M		Pauel	Rosa		2/a
WOHL		Avraham	M	Married	Shlomo Zalman	Sara Reisel	Guitel	3/a
WOHL		Biniamin	M	Married	Shlomo Zalman	Sara Reisel	Mina	2/a
WOHL	FELA	Feigue	F		Avraham	Guitel		3/a
WOHL	KARPAF	Guitel	F	Married	Avraham	Feiga	Avraham	3/a
WOHL	TSIREL	Tchecha	F		Biniamin	Mina		2/a
WOHL		Yulik Carol	M		Biniamin	Mina		2/b
WOHL		Zuzia Zicha	M		Avraham	Guitel		3/a
YAMPEL		Avraham	M					9
YARTSVUER		Shalom	M					10
YAVER		Leibale	F					10
YAVOR		Tsipora	F					7
YEVAR		Feige	F		David			5/a
YOR	DLOGETZ	Feige	F		David			4/a
ZEINDMAN		Avraham	M					10
ZEINDMAN		Entschel	M					10
ZEINDMAN		Moshe	M					10
ZEINDMAN		Rachel	F					10
ZEINDMAN		Ruchama	F					10
ZEINDMAN		Sara	F					10